Creative
Supervision

Creative
Supervision

KAREN R. GILLESPIE
New York University

HARCOURT BRACE JOVANOVICH, INC.

New York   San Diego   Chicago   San Francisco   Atlanta

London   Sydney   Toronto

ILLUSTRATION CREDITS

p. xvi, Courtesy Touche Ross & Co.
p. 74, Rogers from Monkmeyer
p. 128, Courtesy IBM
p. 314, Clara Spain
p. 362, Courtesy IBM

Requests for permission to make copies of any part
of this work should be mailed to:
Permissions, Harcourt Brace Jovanovich, Inc.,
757 Third Avenue, New York, N.Y. 10017.

ISBN: 0-15-515822-8

Library of Congress Catalog Card Number: 81-80299

Printed in the United States of America

preface

Supervision is a pervasive force in every type of enterprise. It exists in the home, in the school, in the workplace, in professional organizations, in churches, and even in informal groups. Everyone at some point has been supervised, and few people escape taking on the role of supervisor. Some have supervisory roles while in school (student government, for example) and later in their careers. Parents have supervisory roles, as do teachers, government officials, church leaders, and organizers of special events—social or professional. Every manager, every owner of an enterprise, has supervisory responsibilities.

Because supervision affects everyone's life, we must know what it is: its background and development, its requirements, its effective implementation, its limits, and its future. These are the central issues that are examined in this book, revealing creative and productive ways of supervising. Unlike most books on supervision, which largely pertain to blue-collar workers, *Creative Supervision* addresses white-collar workers, although the principles discussed are also applicable to blue-collar fields.

The text is divided into five parts:

o Part One is an overview of the supervisor's role and makes clear the difference between supervising and managing. Managing involves planning, organizing, directing, coordinating, controlling, and consolidating. Whenever a manager is given responsibility for the work of others, he or she is *supervising*. The supervisory functions of a manager's job are selecting, communicating, assigning, training, motivating, evaluating, counseling, rewarding, disciplining, and discharging. Part One also explains the historic emergence of both the workplace and education for management and supervision, as well as the organizational structure in which supervisors work.

o Part Two views the supervisor as both decision maker and communicator—roles that demand skill and tact. Here are delineated the steps in decision making and the factors that affect them, as well as the characteristics an effective decision-making supervisor must possess. As communicator, a supervisor must know the nature of communication and the different directions it takes, as well as the uses of internal and external, written and oral, and formal and informal communication. The importance of listening is stressed, as is the need for making dictation effective.

o Part Three shows how the supervisor interacts with employ-ees—selecting and training them; motivating, evaluating, and counseling them; rewarding and disciplining them. This part also covers the different types of meetings that take place and how to conduct them, and it concludes with a discussion of the procedures for handling employee grievances.

o Part Four considers the various restraints placed on supervi-sors by federal legislation and also by unions, civil service, and tenure measures that afford job protection to employees.

o Part Five looks toward the future. It reviews the trends that are changing the supervisor's environment and methods of working with people, and examines how these will change supervision.

Creative Supervision is student oriented. To help both students and instructors, each chapter presents behavioral goals, carefully developed text and illustrations, and a detailed summary. Review and discussion questions, assignments, a problem for resolution, a case study, and a list of suggested readings are appended to each chapter. An extensive glos-sary adds to the value of the text as a ready reference, and an Instructor's Manual is available.

For a one-semester course, instructors may assign approximately one chapter a week to cover the text. For a quarter-system course, about one and a half chapters per week will be necessary.

The conception and creation of a textbook is an enormous undertak-ing and responsibility. I am indebted to many people for the opportuni-ties they gave me to serve in various supervisory positions. I gratefully acknowledge Dr. Charles M. Edwards, Jr., Dean Emeritus of the New York University Institute of Retail Management, for giving me the re-sponsibility of running some college career-guidance functions and sem-inars; Isaac Liberman, former Chairman of the Board and Chief Executive Officer of the Arnold Constable Corporation, for affording me the oppor-tunity to serve on the board of directors; Dr. William R. Dill, former Dean of the Faculties of the Schools of Business, and Dr. Abraham L. Gitlow, Dean of the School of Business and Public Administration, both of New York University, for appointing me Director of the Institute of Retail Management; and Dr. Daniel E. Griffiths and Dr. John C. Payne, Dean and former Vice-Dean, respectively, of the School of Education, Health, Nursing, and Arts Professions (SEHNAP) of New York University, for appointing me Chairman of the Department of Business Education. These experiences, plus the opportunities to chair the Faculty Council of SEHNAP, to serve as an elected senator to the University Senate, to teach supervision for master's and doctoral students, and to work with employers and employees in many kinds of organizations, have all played a part in the background of this book.

Martin B. Seretean, a former student and presently Chairman of the Board of Coronet Industries in Dalton, Georgia, has shared his unique managerial knowledge with many of my students through the years since he graduated. Several of his experiences have inspired some of the examples in this book. I am grateful also to Dr. Herbert A. Tonne, former Chairman of the Business Education Department of SEHNAP, who gave me the initial opportunity to teach in that department, and to Dr. Martin Hamburger, Professor of Counselor Education and former Head, Division of Vocational Education and Applied Arts and Science, for his recommendation that I chair the Business Education Department after Dr. Tonne's retirement.

Two reviewers, Professor Jane M. Banks, of Brookdale Community College, and Dr. Marvin Karlins, of the University of South Florida at Tampa, were helpful in pointing out both weaknesses and strengths of the manuscript.

I am particularly appreciative of the roles played by the staff of Harcourt Brace Jovanovich. Alice Gallagher, Director of the Division of Business and Office Education, encouraged me to write the book. Laurel Miller, editor, scrutinized every word and made insightful contributions. Jeremiah Lighter, art director, skillfully designed the book. Nina Indig, production manager, saw the book through the various stages of production. Helen Faye, art director, researched and coordinated the photographs and figures.

I would like to dedicate *Creative Supervision* to my husband, Francis, for his patience and understanding of the enormous work needed and for sharing his own many experiences as a manager-supervisor, and to my son, Robert, for his equal patience and understanding.

KAREN R. GILLESPIE

contents

2
the skillful supervisor   75

3
the supervisor's interaction with employees   129

4

supervisory restraints   315

5

the supervisor in the future   363

Creative Supervision

an overview
of the
supervisor's role

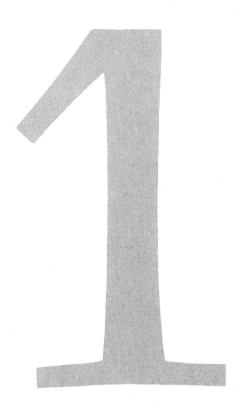

1

what
is the
supervisor's
role?

After studying and analyzing this chapter, you should be able to:

Define "managerial employee" and "nonmanagerial employee."

Name the two parts of the manager's job.

Define "management," and list and explain the functions of management.

Define "supervision," and list and explain the supervisory aspects of the manager's job.

Differentiate between the part of the manager's job that is related to supervision and the part that is related to managing.

Explain the other aspects supervisors need to understand about the world of work.

Describe the steps a person can take to become a supervisor and to advance to higher supervisory positions.

THIS BOOK IS ABOUT people who work with other people. More specifically, it is about people who supervise the work of others. To _supervise_ is to oversee for direction, to inspect with authority.

Have you ever attended a symphony concert? Members of the orchestra arrive, one by one. They find their assigned areas and set up their instruments. Then they tune the instruments, each playing different notes and segments of the score. The audience hears harsh and inharmonious sounds. These sounds swell as more musicians arrive, until the hall is filled with grating noises. Suddenly the conductor enters. A silence sweeps the orchestra members and the audience. Instruments are instantaneously poised, ready for playing. The conductor mounts the podium and raises the baton, while stillness pervades the hall. The baton descends, and pleasing sounds are heard. The melody swells and recedes at the direction of the maestro. The jarring notes have, under the skilled guidance of the conductor, disappeared. Only harmony issues from the assembled musicians.

The conductor is the supervisor of the orchestra, giving direction to the musicians. Similarly, the supervisor of a group in an office, bank, store, hospital, insurance firm, school, college, or other enterprise directs the activities of those people toward the overall goals of that enterprise.

As conductors of orchestras differ in their competency to draw forth the musical ability of groups of musicians, so supervisors in other organizations vary in their talent to direct the proficiencies of the people they oversee. Analyses of these varying abilities and of the results achieved will be of concern to the student of supervision as the examination of the supervisor's role proceeds.

The need for supervision

Whenever two people set out to accomplish a task, some form of authority must be established if the work is to be done effectively. Although neither may undertake to oversee the work of the other, both must understand the job to be accomplished and agree about the responsibility for various aspects of the task. All organizations, whether profit oriented or non–profit oriented, have found that assigning responsibility for units of work increases the production of the people involved. All enterprises having more than two employees, therefore, will have some form of supervisory activity.

In one way or another, everyone is supervised. In homes, children are supervised by parents, guardians, or older relatives. In businesses, employees are supervised by owners or designated bosses. In schools, students are supervised by teachers; teachers, in turn, are supervised by department chairpersons and/or principals or deans. In hospitals, nurses are supervised by more-senior nurses or hospital administrators. In offices, clerical workers are supervised by office managers.

Classifications of employees

All employees—whether they work in profit-oriented or non–profit-oriented organizations—are basically divided into two main categories: <u>nonmanagerial</u> and <u>managerial</u>. Nonmanagerial employees are known as workers, associates, or the rank and file. Those to whom they report, or managerial employees, may hold positions as supervisors, managers, administrators, chairpersons, bosses, executives, directors, inspectors, superintendents, vice-presidents, presidents, or owners.

Today, laws governing wages, overtime pay, and responsibilities officially separate nonmanagerial and managerial employees. Nonmanagerial employees are designated *nonexempt*. They are usually paid overtime or are given compensatory time off for working beyond forty hours a week. Managerial employees are classified *exempt*. They may work virtually unlimited hours without receiving overtime pay. According to the Fair Labor Standards Act of 1938, most exempt employees may spend no more than 20 percent of their time doing work performed by their subordinates. In the field of retailing, however, up to 40 percent is permitted.

Nonmanagerial employees

Nonmanagerial employees' responsibilities and salaries vary within organizations. Except for those who have minor supervisory responsibilities because they are more experienced in an organization, nonmanagerial employees are not looked on as "bosses." For example, in retail stores, one finds such nonmanagerial employees as salespeople, clerical employees, stock workers, office employees, comparison shoppers, truckers, receivers, wrappers, cashiers, and workroom employees. In offices, categories of nonmanagerial employees may include clericals, typists, bookkeepers, data processers, programmers, stenographers, secretaries, executive secretaries, administrative secretaries, and word processors. Each of these groups of workers has responsibilities that are related to those of other groups. However, no one group is considered to have authority over any other group.

Salaries may differ considerably among nonmanagerial employees because of seniority, skill requirements, scarcity of workers in a particular category, and competitors' payments for the same type of work. Some nonmanagerial employees are well paid because they perform specialized tasks or, as in the case of some retail salespeople, because they work on commissions that are quite profitable. Some nonmanagerial employees may even have higher take-home pay than the immediate supervisors who direct and evaluate them.

Managerial employees

Regardless of the number and categories of people who work in an enterprise, decisions must constantly be made about the manner of getting work done, the nature of the work to be done, the people who will do it, and the acceptable standards for work that is completed. Those decisions, in turn, generate other types of problems that need to be resolved. People must be assigned tasks, advised about those tasks, trained properly to accomplish those tasks, evaluated on how well those tasks are performed, and, sometimes, helped to solve personal problems, thereby allowing them to continue to perform their tasks competently. Managerial employees are responsible for all these activities.

In addition, managerial employees must understand the idiosyncracies, work habits, and abilities of nonmanagerial employees. They must also have knowledge of the specific technology used in the organization. In this way, maximum production may be attained through a combination of workers and machines.

Small firms may have just two levels of employees: managerial employees and nonmanagerial employees. As organizations grow, however, more managerial levels are added. In large organizations, managerial employees may be divided into at least three groups: top management, middle management, and first-level management (sometimes called "junior management"). As enterprises grow even larger, intermediate categories among these three levels may also be added.

Depending on the size of the organization and the work being done, salaries for managerial employees range widely. However, within each enterprise, first-level managerial employees earn less than higher-level managerial employees. In most firms, top executives make at least three to four times as much as people on the introductory managerial level. In very large organizations, this difference may be many times greater. High pay is one of the significant rewards for having top managerial responsibility and authority.

Managers and management

The terminology used to designate the various positions in organizations is not precise. Every enterprise chooses its own titles for the people whom it hires and promotes. The general terms "managerial" and "nonmanagerial" are used in all firms and apply to their respective levels of employees. But such specific titles as "manager," "supervisor," "director," "executive," "vice-president," and "administrator" may have different meanings in different organizations.

As used in this book, a _manager_ is an owner or an employee whose job is to carry out two major activities: (1) to perform the functions of management (as outlined in the next section) in the area of work to which he or she has been assigned and (2) to oversee, or supervise, the people within that area of responsibility.

The process of management

All organizations must have management. The term _management_ has been variously defined as "the process of organizing and employing resources to accomplish a predetermined objective with and through people"[1] or "a process of getting things done by people who operate in organized groups."[2]

Most of the writers who analyze management as a process agree that five functions are performed to a greater or lesser degree by all managers: planning, organizing, directing, coordinating, and controlling. One additional function, not usually included in discussions of management, is also performed in most organizations: consolidating.

Planning.   The first function of management, _planning_, is the process of setting overall goals for the organization or part of the organization and then developing ways—objectives and plans—to reach those goals. _Goals_ are the long-range targets toward which an enterprise aims. For example, a goal for a profit-making organization, such as a firm in the computer industry, may be to develop products that will make the firm the primary source for its particular market. A nonprofit service organization, such as a hospital, may set a goal of serving the community better by expanding its facilities to allow it to treat a larger segment of the population.

Objectives are the short-range targets aimed for in order to achieve the long-range goals. For instance, the computer firm may set an objective of developing a home computer capable of gathering and displaying information that will plug into both a television set and a telephone. Accomplishment of this objective will contribute to the firm's long-range goal of becoming the primary source for the computer market. The hospital may set a short-range objective of adding one hundred beds to enable it to increase its in-patient capacity. Achieving this objective will allow the hospital to serve the community better and thereby contribute to the attainment of its overall goal.

Plans are the outlines or schedules that detail the specific actions needed to reach the goals and objectives. For example, if a firm's objective is to market a new computer, the plans would include the amount to be spent on advertising, the kinds of advertising and the media to be

FIGURE 1–1
LONG- AND SHORT-RANGE PLANS:
From Top Managers' Plans Grow Those
for Middle and First-Line Managers

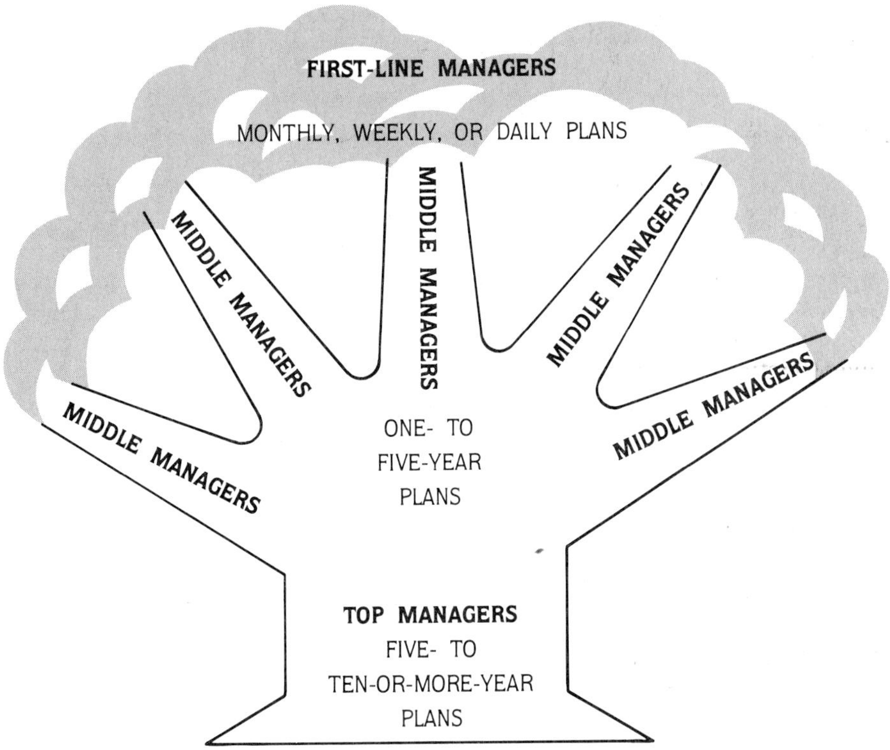

FIRST-LINE MANAGERS

MONTHLY, WEEKLY, OR DAILY PLANS

MIDDLE MANAGERS

MIDDLE MANAGERS

MIDDLE MANAGERS

MIDDLE MANAGERS

MIDDLE MANAGERS

ONE- TO
FIVE-YEAR
PLANS

TOP MANAGERS
FIVE- TO
TEN-OR-MORE-YEAR
PLANS

used, the approaches to be used by salespersonnel, the public-relations events to be developed, the publicity desirable to launch the product, and the designation of the people who would have the responsibility to carry out the plan. Similarly, the hospital might plan community events and newsletters to carry its message. Employees would be designated to perform these assignments.

With the goals and objectives of the organization in mind, top managers plan for five to ten or more years in advance. Middle managers usually plan for one to five years, while first-level managers plan on monthly, weekly, and daily bases (see Figure 1–1).

For any planning, alternatives must be considered. The most successful managers are those who are able to select the course of action that is most likely to succeed.

Once goals, objectives, and plans are made, they must be communicated to those who are responsible for carrying them out.

Organizing. The second function of management, *organizing*, involves analyzing and classifying each goal, objective, and plan. Then each classification is further subdivided—first into activities and then into specific tasks that will enable the organization to use its personnel most effectively.

Once tasks have been classified, specific individuals are assigned to perform each one. Through these assignments, people often become specialists in certain duties. When work is organized and competent people are assigned to do it, increased quality and quantity of production should be attained.

For example, if a conference has been planned as an activity, organizing would then entail dividing the work to be done into separate tasks and finally assigning those various tasks to the people best able to complete them. One person might be assigned to set the date and to obtain the main speaker and group leaders. Another person might be asked to rent the hall needed and to arrange for audiovisual aids. Another person might be charged with writing and placing the publicity in the appropriate media to attract the audience for the event. A fourth person might be in charge of financial matters.

Directing. The third function of management, *directing*, involves integrating all the various tasks within the firm. Given the plans to be achieved and the organization of the work and the work force, the manager now marshals the talents of the people who will carry out those plans. Directing is the ultimate job of managers such as the conductor of the orchestra that will produce melodious music, the boss of the office staff that will turn out a given number of letters and reports, the head of the bank tellers who will handle money and keep records of accounts accurately, the manager of a sales staff that will successfully sell the products of the firm, and the head of a conference.

Directing involves selecting; communicating, including holding meetings; training; and motivating. Employees who are told why certain work needs to be done, assured of the importance of that work to the overall goals of the department or organization, trained properly, and stimulated to do their jobs effectively will contribute to the productivity of the entire firm.

Coordinating. The fourth function of management, *coordinating*, is the meshing of all tasks so that a smooth flow of work results. It involves *synchronizing* the work, or bringing all the parts together so that activities are completed on time and as planned. If work done by certain employees must wait until other jobs are done, coordination becomes of the utmost importance. Through coordination, all tasks are unified into one finished whole.

For example, in planning a conference, the audience, speakers, and

necessary equipment must all arrive on the date and at the time scheduled. If the hall is available and the audience is present but the speakers
do not come, the conference will be a failure. Bringing all the activities
together so that the audience and speakers arrive at the specified time in
a convenient space that provides adequate comfort results from proper
coordination.

Controlling. The fifth function of management, *controlling*, involves
measuring or evaluating the performance of each employee and analyzing each job to ensure that plans are being carried out effectively. Performance is compared against the initial goals or against standards. A
standard is a model level of performance. Standards must be communicated to employees so that they will know exactly what is expected of
them. If employees perform well, they may be rewarded. If they perform
poorly, they may be disciplined, or even discharged. Employee grievances may result from actions taken and these will need resolution.
Counseling may also be needed as a result of some aspect of controlling.

For example, if the notices for the conference to be given were
poorly typed or illegible, if the visual aids for the speakers were not
correctly set up, or if the speakers had not been carefully briefed on the
knowledge level of their audience, even though the planning, organizing, and directing had been well done, the conference would still be
ineffective.

Consolidating. As mentioned, consolidating is not usually included in
the functions of management. Some people may question this function,
but virtually every manager performs it.

Consolidating is strengthening and holding the position of a given
section in relation to other sections within an enterprise. Every firm or
part of it is subject to a "takeover" by other like groups. In some instances, such takeovers may strengthen the particular unit, eliminate du-
plication of work, reduce costs, and improve production. When such
improvements have been shown, the manager has little recourse but to
permit the uniting of the two groups. However, every manager has the
responsibility to strengthen the unit of which he or she is in charge so
that if combining two units is desirable, his or her unit will be the one
that survives. The employees in a unit support a manager who has the
strength to withstand the onslaught of other units and to emerge the
victor in any such attack.

In schools, departments are always juggling for position against
other departments—foreign languages against vocational subjects, mathematics against applied arithmetic, home economics against consumer
education, for example. Similarly, managers jockey to absorb other units
to give themselves a larger power base. Employment managers have
been known to attempt to absorb training departments, merchandising

managers to enlarge their units' scope by absorbing other merchandising units, and word-processing managers to extend their units' services to others that have not sought those services. Thus, managers attempt to improve the strength of their units to avoid incorporation by other managers unless the action will benefit the overall goals of the organization.

Supervisors and supervision

As noted, the meanings of the various names given to managerial employees vary from firm to firm. For example, the term "supervisor" is used in two distinct ways. In some organizations, "supervisor" is used for the first-level overseer, who has direct responsibility for the workers in that area. Thus the term is a *specific* title used to identify a certain level of managerial employee.

In other enterprises, "supervisor" is used to designate any person who is responsible for the work of others, regardless of his or her level or position. Used in this way, "supervisor" is a *general* term. Therefore, in these organizations, whatever their size, the owner, president, vice-presidents, administrators, superintendents, managers, principals, chairpersons, directors, and department heads are all supervisors of the employees who report to them. This book uses the word "supervisor" in this general sense.

A *supervisor*, as defined by the National Labor-Management Relations (Taft-Hartley) Act of 1947, is "any individual having authority, in the interest of the employer, to hire, transfer, suspend, lay off, recall, promote, discharge, assign, reward, or discipline other employees, or responsibility to direct them, or to adjust their grievances, or effectively to recommend such action, if in connection with the foregoing the exercise of such authority is not of a merely routine or clerical nature, but requires the use of independent judgment."

The nature of supervision

Good *supervision*, as defined by the National Research Council's Committee on Work in Industry, means that "the supervisor gets the people in his department to do *what* he wants done, *when* it should be done, and the *way* he wants it done, because they want to do it."

Many other explanations of supervision exist. Figure 1–2 shows a composite definition of supervision. Thus, one definition may read, "Supervision is a process of selecting employees fairly to help them to do their assigned tasks skillfully." Any other combination among the various columns in Figure 1–2 may be used to define "supervision." Note that the supervisor's job also includes discharging those employees who cannot do the assigned work to meet the standards set by the firm.

FIGURE 1-2
WHAT IS SUPERVISION?

SUPERVISION
IS

a process	a program
an activity	a service
a synthesis	an effort

OF

selecting	communicating with
attracting	rewarding
training	harmonizing
measuring	motivating
rating	directing
assigning	coordinating
correcting	counseling

commending

EMPLOYEES

fairly	patiently

tactfully

TO HELP THEM
DO THEIR TASKS

skillfully	completely
accurately	satisfactorily
intelligently	efficiently

enthusiastically

OR

discharging those who cannot meet those standards

The relationship between managing and supervising

Who is a supervisor? Who is a manager? Is the manager also a supervisor? Is the supervisor also a manager?

The work of managing encompasses the work of supervising. The manager is the overseer of the people assigned to a given unit. Any time a manager has responsibility for the work of others, regardless of the manager's position or level, the manager is also a supervisor. The references to people in the definitions of "management" on page 6 refer to the supervisory aspects of managing. Any tasks that a manager performs that do not involve the activities of other employees in that unit are not classified supervisory. Thus, if a manager draws up a budget, sells a product or a service, creates a product or an advertisement, or develops a report or a new way of handling a service without the help of other employees in the unit, the work is not of a supervisory nature.

Most work that a manager does involves supervising people. Each of the functions a manager performs—planning, organizing, directing, coordinating, controlling, consolidating—includes work with, for, or about people. Those functions, therefore, involve the supervisory part of the manager's job in selecting, assigning, communicating and meeting with, training, motivating, evaluating, counseling, rewarding or disciplining, and discharging people.

Supervisory aspects of the manager's job

The specific supervisory work that each manager performs is incorporated into all of the six functions of management discussed earlier. No order of importance or sequence can be assigned to these supervisory aspects of the job, since several may take place at the same time and with every task performed.

Selecting and assigning.   An important part of the supervisor's job, selecting includes both hiring employees, transferring them, promoting them, and assigning specific tasks for them to do (see Chapter 6). Selecting the right people to perform the necessary tasks greatly improves the overall productivity and the quality of job performance.

Growing out of the need to accomplish work, assigning involves the distribution of tasks. The supervisor must assess the employees' abilities, aptitudes, usual roles, willingness to work, availability, and, on occasion, seniority to determine which person or persons should perform certain tasks. Assigning and communicating, discussed below, are interrelated. The supervisor explains all details of the task to both the assigned employee and those with whom he or she will work.

Communicating.   Oral or written discussion about tasks or about the organization with an employee or a group of employees is communicating (see Chapter 5). Communicating is pervasive throughout any enterprise. The supervisor who explains the what, why, when, where, who, and how regarding every job will find that cooperation increases, resentment decreases, and the need for gossip disappears. One of the frequent means of communication, either with one's staff, one's peers, or one's superiors in an organization, is the meeting (see Chapter 9).

Training. Preparing a person through explanation, demonstration, and/or practice to perform a job properly is *training* (see Chapter 7). Training is one of the most helpful tools a supervisor has for ensuring that workers perform tasks efficiently and productively. As technology has increased, more and more training has become necessary for initial employment, for advancement, and for maintaining a competitive advantage.

Motivating. The source of *motivation*, or the desire to do a job well, is disputed. Some analysts believe that motivation comes from within the person performing the job and cannot be generated by supervisors. Others believe that one of the important roles of a supervisor is *motivating* employees, that is, moving them to want to do a good job. Many methods, ranging from rewards to punishment, have been suggested for motivating employees (see Chapter 8).

Evaluating. Assessing the general attitude of an employee and the quality and quantity of work produced is *evaluating*. The supervisor's job requires constant evaluation of employees (see Chapter 10). Part of this evaluation is formal and takes place at assigned intervals, while the other part is informal and takes place in every contact the supervisor has with an employee. The combination of these formal and informal judgments forms the total evaluation of the employee.

Counseling. Advising or deliberating with an employee about a problem is *counseling* (see Chapter 11). Counseling is usually a formal part of the supervisor's job only in relation to an employee's performance on the job. For example, the supervisor may counsel an employee who is performing below-standard work, receiving evaluations that are not as good as they should be, not living up to the rules and regulations of the organization, or having difficulty with other employees. However, counseling may also be an informal part of the supervisor's job. Often, if an employee just needs someone to turn to when problems occur, the supervisor can help the employee to solve those problems. A good supervisor is available for counseling whenever a need for such help occurs.

Rewarding and disciplining. The most desirable aspect of the supervisor's job is rewarding and the least desirable aspect is disciplining (see Chapter 12). Commending or granting some advantage to a person for a well-done job is *rewarding*. Withholding rewards, threatening punishment, or actually penalizing an employee for low productivity, faulty work, or antisocial behavior is *disciplining*.

Terminating a person's employment is *discharging*, also known as *outplacement*. While discharging is viewed as the final disciplinary action for employees who cannot or will not do a job satisfactorily, many other reasons exist for discharge.

Employees who are disciplined, discharged, or treated in a manner they deem unfair may file grievances. Supervisors need to know how to handle grievances (see Chapter 13).

Knowledge aspects of the supervisor's job

Most supervisors were initially hired or promoted because of their specialized knowledge, such as law, medicine, accounting, computer analysis, editing, marketing, merchandising, or public relations, which was needed within the firm. Discussion of such background knowledge is not included in this text.

Knowledge about other aspects of the supervisor's job, which helps a supervisor understand the role and serve both bosses and employees more effectively, needs also to be known. The history of the world of work and of education for managing and supervising (see Chapter 2) gives supervisors a broad overview of their jobs.

Understanding how organizations develop (see Chapter 3) and acquiring decision-making ability and other skills (see Chapter 4) are also integral parts of the supervisor's job.

Government regulations (see Chapter 14), which are growing in number and complexity, restrict many things that supervisors may say and do. Working with union, civil-service, or tenured employees, who are job-protected (see Chapter 15), demands another facet of knowledge for supervisors. Finally, knowledge of what supervisors can anticipate in the future (see Chapter 16) will help direct them toward changes that will occur in the world of work.

Career ladders to management-supervisory positions

When people first enter an enterprise, they have many decisions to make about their future. They must determine the kind of work they wish and are able to do, their salary aspirations, and their desire to be promoted.

Some people who have skills may not wish to supervise others in the use of those skills. They, like the members of an orchestra, may be good performers. They may consider their talents wasted if they have to take time from the performance of certain tasks to oversee, give directions to, and evaluate others. Such people are usually happiest in their jobs if they can concentrate on perfecting their abilities. By not performing supervisory activities, they are able to get the highest payment possible for the work they do and have no responsibility for overseeing others. These people are happy "doing their own thing."

Other equally talented people, entering that same organization, may want the challenge of a management-supervisory position. They may join the organization in an entry-level position and, if successful, they are then promoted.

Entry-level positions

Most inexperienced people who aspire to managerial positions begin by taking an *entry-level position*, either in a nonmanagerial job or in a management-training program.

Nonmanagerial jobs. People who enter a firm through a nonmanagerial position may begin work while they are still in school by taking a part-time or summer position. If a person shows initiative, enterprise, willingness to work hard, and interest in the organization, he or she may find that a full-time job is available upon graduation.

Other inexperienced people—those who have not worked during school years, are returning to work after a long absence, or are changing firms—will find that the nonmanagerial position is usually the most easily acquired. Whether part-time or full-time, the entry-level, nonmanagerial position usually involves some routine work.

Management-training programs. People about to receive college degrees are often interviewed on their campuses by representatives of firms seeking applicants for *management-training programs*. These entry-level positions are reserved for those whom the interviewers believe have managerial potential. Successful applicants spend from a few weeks to a year or more in the program. Those who successfully conclude the program are assigned to a beginning managerial job.

Management-training programs vary in content, form, and length with every firm. All of them, however, have two roles: to prepare novices to do the managerial work necessary in a given area and to provide the skills and abilities to enable trainees to work successfully with subordinates when they become supervisors.

Promotions and transfers

Success on a job on one level makes the person eligible to be considered for another position on another level. A person who has entered an organization through a nonmanagerial job and has performed a job well and enthusiastically may be moved into a management-training program or promoted to a beginning managerial position. A person who has gone through a management-training program and has effectively performed the duties of the beginning managerial job to which he or she was assigned may be promoted to a higher-level managerial position.

In some organizations promotion is rapid. These organizations may have a high turnover of personnel, be expanding rapidly, or have difficulty in finding qualified people for the positions. In other organizations, promotion may be slower. These organizations may have a lower turnover of personnel, be expanding more slowly, or have a larger staff of well-qualified employees. Employees who wish more rapid promotion than their organization provides usually transfer to other firms doing similar work. They enter the new organization on the same or a higher level and then continue to march up to executive-level positions.

Fairness to people seeking promotion requires that organizations announce openings when they occur and that all people who wish be allowed to apply for those openings. These procedures are also required by law. Thus any person with the proper work background, the desirable personality characteristics, and the potential for success that the selectors seek may be promoted.

Promotions go not only to people who have demonstrated ability in the area in which the job opening occurs. Sometimes people in nonrelated work areas are able to show the necessary qualities and abilities, enabling them to be promoted to that position.

Effective managers are generalists rather than specialists. That is, they need not have a detailed understanding of all the work the people they manage do. The qualities that make good managers are transferable. Thus, lawyers have become bank executives, hospital managers, retail merchandisers, or managers in insurance firms; accountants have headed nonaccounting businesses; and people with nonbusiness backgrounds have become successful business executives. Once an individual discovers his or her ability to deal successfully with people and to get production from a work force, there are many directions in which he or she may move to reach the upper levels of management.

SUMMARY

o The supervisor is the overseer or director of the people assigned to a given area of work.

o All organizations basically have two types of employees: nonmanagerial and managerial. Nonmanagerial, or nonexempt, employees are limited in the hours they work without receiving either overtime pay or compensatory time off. Managerial, or exempt, employees may work virtually unlimited hours with no overtime pay. As organizations grow, various levels of managerial jobs are created. These range from first-level, or junior, management through middle management to top, or senior, management.

o Management is the process of getting the long-term goals of the organization accomplished by planning, organizing, directing, coordinating, controlling, and consolidating the work to be done.

o Whenever managers have responsibility for the work of others, they are supervising. The supervisory aspects of the manager's job involve selecting; assigning; communicating with individuals or through meetings; training; motivating; evaluating; counseling; rewarding and disciplining; on occasion, discharging; and handling grievances.

o Workers may advance to management-supervisory positions in several ways. They may begin in an entry-level position, either in a nonmanagerial job or a management-training program, to gain experience and knowledge. If they are successful, they may be promoted or transfer to a higher-level position.

REFERENCES

[1] James E. Morgan, Jr., *Principles of Administrative and Supervisory Management* (Englewood Cliffs, N.J.: Prentice-Hall, 1973), p. 4.

[2] Harold Koontz, "Making Sense of Management Theory," in *Toward a Unified Theory of Management*, ed. Harold Koontz (New York: McGraw-Hill, 1964), p. 3.

REVIEW AND DISCUSSION QUESTIONS

1. Why do work assignments need to be made when two or more people are working on a job?
2. Why is a supervisor needed on a job if the two or more persons working in that field are familiar with the work they each do?
3. How does the federal government differentiate between exempt and nonexempt employees?
4. Why are the salaries of nonmanagerial employees occasionally higher than those of their immediate supervisors?
5. What factors affect the salaries of managers?
6. What are the six functions commonly associated with management? Explain each one.
7. How does the supervisory part of a manager's job differ from the managerial work of that same manager?
8. What are the supervisory aspects of the manager's job? Explain each one.
9. Why are some people uninterested in managerial jobs?
10. How can people reach the managerial level in an organization?

ASSIGNMENTS

1. If you are presently working or have previously worked, draw a diagram showing the various levels of managers within the organization.

    If you have never worked, draw such a diagram for the school or college you are now attending. How many layers of managerial employees did you find? Chart the progress one person might make in going from a nonmanagerial position through the organization to the top position.

2. If you have ever worked, analyze the work of the supervisor in your area. What did he or she do to spur you to work harder? to check that your work was done properly? to check that your work was done on time? to counsel you? to discipline you? to communicate with you?

    If you have never worked, select a teacher in one of your courses. How does he or she get students to perform the work satisfactorily? How are students evaluated? How are they counseled? How are they disciplined? How are assignments made?

PROBLEM FOR RESOLUTION

What requirements would you establish for people applying for an entry-level managerial job? Would you establish different criteria for employees applying to be promoted to such a job?

CASE STUDY

Gerald Washer was elated when he was told by the personnel director that he was being made chief of the mail room in which he had worked for the past three years. The personnel director told Mr. Washer that he would manage the six other people who had worked in the mail room for from one to three years and that he could hire, assign, discipline, and, if need be, fire them. For this new responsibility, he would receive a $10 per week raise.

    As the weeks rolled by, Mr. Washer noticed that he was no longer paid overtime for the extra hours of work he put in. Weekly, he was working anywhere from five to ten hours of overtime, as were other members of his staff. The others, however, were paid overtime, and in most weeks, their pay exceeded his. He further found that except for preparing some minor paperwork (regarding the hours worked by employees and absenteeism) and assigning vacation periods, lunch periods, and other routine matters, he was performing the same chores of mail sorting and distribution that he had before the promotion.

Finally, Mr. Washer complained to the personnel officer that he was not truly a manager and asked to have his status as worker with over-time-pay privileges restored.

Free From Obligation

Did the duties performed by Mr. Washer qualify him as an exempt employee?

What changes would have to be made in the job to have it appeal to a person seeking to be promoted to manager?

FURTHER READING

Barnard, Chester I. "The Functions of Organizations in Cooperative Systems." In *The Functions of the Executive.* Cambridge, Mass.: Harvard University Press, 1938, pp. 214–96.

Cites maintaining communication, securing essential efforts by employees, and formulating and defining purpose as the essential executive functions.

Cammann, Cortlandt, and David A. Nadler. "Fit Control Systems to Your Managerial Style." *Harvard Business Review,* January–February 1976, pp. 65–72.

Shows control to be a central dimension of the manager's job.

Coventry, W. F., and Irving Burstiner. "A Practical Approach to Management." In *Management: A Basic Handbook.* Englewood Cliffs, N.J.: Prentice-Hall, 1977, pp. 1–17.

Defines management and divides its traditional functions into the "mechanics" and the "dynamics."

———. "Objectives and Long-Range Planning." In *Management: A Basic Handbook.* Englewood Cliffs, N.J.: Prentice-Hall, 1977, pp. 128–43.

Discusses the importance of objectives and the role of planning to achieve objectives.

Drucker, Peter F. "Management's New Goal." In *Skills That Build Executive Success.* Cambridge, Mass.: Harvard College, 1970, pp. 11–16.

Explains that managers must be innovative and more knowledgeable and must be concerned with basic beliefs and values as well as with accomplishment and measurable results.

———. "The Dimensions of Management." In *Management: Tasks, Responsibilities, Practices.* New York: Harper & Row, 1974, pp. 39–48.

Explains that the purpose of a firm, the production of work, the social responsibilities, the dimension of time, and the administration of resources and personnel are all part of the functions of management.

19

ıry. "The Manager's Job: Folklore and Fact." *Harvard
view*, July–August 1975, pp. 49–61.

     ıns that managers play a complex, intertwined combina-
ıon of interpersonal, informational, and decision-making roles.

Morgan, James E. "Introduction to Management." In *Principles of Administrative and Supervisory Management*. Englewood Cliffs, N.J.: Prentice-Hall, 1973, pp. 3–19.

    Defines management, explains the various management levels, and outlines the functions of administrative management and supervisory management.

Randolph, Robert M. *Planagement®—Moving Concept into Reality*. New York: AMACOM, 1975.

    Discusses how old and new ideas can be integrated to combine the concepts of management with the realities of the operation of an organization.

2
historic view of work and education for management and supervision

After studying and analyzing this chapter, you should be able to:

Differentiate among slaves, indentured servants, and apprentices.

Trace briefly the development of education for management and supervision.

Explain the events that helped to make women important as office workers.

Trace the evolution of the supervisory treatment of people.

Compare Henri Fayol's concepts of the functions of management to the functions of management studied in Chapter 1.

Explain the roles played by Frederick W. Taylor and the Gilbreths in the scientific-management movement.

Explain the role of the Hawthorne experiments in the human-relations movement.

Describe how technology has affected work in white-collar jobs today.

T O UNDERSTAND OUR concepts of work and education for management and supervision in today's world, one needs to look backward to see how those ideas evolved. Change occurs in everything. The values that people hold, the technology that is available, and the skills and knowledge that people have attained have all changed the manner of working with and supervising others.

Modern technology has released people from many of the routine, repetitive, and laborious jobs of the Industrial Revolution era. It has allowed them more time to analyze events that occur in the workplace. Furthermore, the move from the production-oriented economy of earlier times toward the service-oriented economy of the present has also changed the nature of supervision. Working with unskilled or slightly skilled laborers is different from working with highly skilled workers or well-educated technicians.

The entry of large numbers of women into the world of work has also caused some supervisors to change their manner of supervising. The first women to enter the work force were more sheltered than their male counterparts and often reacted more emotionally to reprimands. The rough character of many workplaces changed as supervisors sought to avoid offending women working in offices, stores, and other enterprises.

Analysts of the supervisor's job, observers of supervisors, and researchers of human resources have all contributed to the changes in the attitudes about supervision that have occurred. Education has also changed supervision. When relatively few people were able to read and write, those who could often became the bosses over the illiterate masses. Now, however, with education an almost universal commodity, the selection of supervisors depends on merit rather than literacy. In addition, the way in which supervisors use responsibility has altered somewhat as principles and concepts of supervision have changed and as the psychological and sociological reactions of people to each other and to the workplace have been understood.

The historical eras into which this chapter is broken appear to be sharply divided time periods. However, no such sharp separations actually exist. Ideas and thoughts evolve. Discoveries and concepts born in one era come to be accepted at a later time and weave themselves into the fabric of business and organizational life continuously thereafter.

Ancient times to 1699: the age of the apprentice

Throughout this period in history, people lived mostly by tradition. Sons followed in their fathers' footsteps, and daughters led the sheltered lives of their mothers. For most people, *barter*, or the exchange of one item for another, was the method of acquiring material things. Money either did not exist or was in short supply.

The world of work

The people in these early societies had to provide their own food. Therefore, most of them were tillers of the soil. Slaves, indentured servants, and apprentices made up a large part of the work force.

Slaves were the property of and entirely subject to the wishes of their masters, or supervisors. They were often abused and beaten, and they had no hope of future freedom. *Indentured servants* were bound by contracts, or *indentures*, to work for others for a certain period of time, often in return for their maintenance. Their masters assigned them whatever work needed to be done. At the end of the period the contract specified, indentured servants were freed.

The accepted way for young people of modest means to enter a business or other enterprise was to become an *apprentice*. An apprentice was also bound by contract to work for a person for a certain period of time. The difference between an indentured servant and an apprentice was that the apprentice was bound to a master in order to learn a specific craft, trade, or profession, including law, medicine, teaching, and ministry. Children born into poverty often became apprentices to ensure that they would not remain poor as they grew up.

The apprenticeship system began as early as 2285 B.C. "There is evidence in the Code of Hammurabi [a collection of ancient laws] that the [apprenticeship] practice was so firmly established in ancient Babylonia as to warrant state supervision." [1] The apprenticeship system that the code described flourished and achieved its greatest popularity in Europe during the Middle Ages, with the rise of the guild system.

Guilds were medieval associations of men who practiced the same craft, trade, or profession. They were formed to pursue the common objectives of their members: to maintain standards of workmanship and to defend the members' interests. Guilds were the forerunners of unions.

Under the apprenticeship system, both boys and girls, usually ten to twelve years old, were bound to the guild masters as their legal wards. Boys stayed with their masters until they were twenty-one and girls until they were eighteen. During this time they perfected their skill in the craft, trade, or profession they were learning.

The master, or supervisor, was the model for the apprentice, who closely followed every part of the job as the master performed it. Some masters were kindly, and apprentices who were willing to work hard had a relatively pleasant period of learning. Other masters used harsh measures to force obedience. Masters had total power over apprentices. Laws favored owners and overseers. No studies of human behavior had been made. Therefore, masters based their attitudes toward and their handling of apprentices on what they observed and on their own ideas of reward and punishment. They rarely cared about the likes and dislikes of workers.

In America, in the early seventeenth century, poor children were required to become apprentices under the English Poor Law (1601). By 1642, in Massachusetts, parents and masters were ordered to see to the education of their children and apprentices. Under Virginia law in 1642, reading and writing were required to be taught to apprenticed children.

The contracts for apprentices in America were often filed in an official place of records. The records show how widespread the practice of apprentice training was during this period. It continued to be used into the nineteenth century.

Education for management and supervision

Formal education about managing enterprises, other than through apprenticeship, emerged gradually and would drastically alter such work in the future. It began with the study of bookkeeping (the process of recording all the financial records of an enterprise). Bookkeeping was studied as early as the thirteenth century. By 1358, a more sophisticated method of handling and interpreting financial information, known as *accounting*, was well developed. A textbook on accounting was written by the latter part of the fifteenth century. By 1581, a college of accountants had been established in Venice.

1700–1799: the age of emerging managerial standards and practices

During this period, many people left the farms and moved to the cities. Businesses and professional enterprises in law, medicine, and social service grew, and the need for more and better records and for stricter codes of conduct increased.

The world of work

Throughout this period, emphasis in business was on the process of keeping records. People were viewed as having value to a firm only for the work they could produce. A strict code of conduct was recommended for workers.

With the Industrial Revolution (approximately 1750–1850) in both Europe and the United States, machines replaced hand tools and industry became concentrated in large establishments. Vast job changes,

APPRENTICE : one bound by legal agreement to work for another for a specific amount of time in return for instruction in a trade, art, or business.

1700–1799   **25**

which speeded production, took place as people moved into large, mechanized factories.

Most firms were run by their owners or by relatives of the owners. As supervisors, these people made employees work very long hours. Training was usually given through the apprenticeship system or by observation of others. For those who did not learn or work fast enough, harsh, uncompromising discipline was the accepted method of "motivation."

Penalties for infractions of any rules were severe. People could be hired or fired on the whim of the boss. Workers in factories were fined for any articles that were damaged during manufacture, and retail clerks had their wages docked to cover shortages in their cash boxes. These practices further reduced the paltry wages that were paid.

Few people voiced concern over the manner in which an overseer controlled workers. Eventually, however, during this period, some craft unions began to be organized. They tried to ease the poor pay, long hours, strict rules, and brutal punishment inflicted on workers. In 1786, the printers' union held the first recorded strike for higher wages.

In the United States, slaves were an important part of the work force. Slaves were categorized as agricultural (field) workers, domestics (houseworkers), artisans (skilled workers), or workpeople (general workers). When, as part of the Industrial Revolution, the cotton gin was introduced in 1793, slaves became even more important to cotton farmers in the United States than they had been before.

During this period, some services were performed by indentured servants. For example, two-thirds of the schoolmasters employed in Maryland just prior to the American Revolution were indentured servants or convicts.

Education for management and supervision

In the study of running an enterprise, bookkeeping and accounting continued to be important. In London, Thomas Watts established the first school of commerce. Watts stressed four basic elements for quantitative studies: accounting, arithmetic, mathematics, and measurement theory.

In the United States, Benjamin Franklin published his *Proposals Relating to the Education of Youth in Pensilvania* (1749). He suggested that the following topics be emphasized in education: English language; English classics; pronouncing through speeches and orations; writing letters and stories; grammar, rhetoric, and logic; elementary art work; arithmetic, geometry, astronomy, and especially accounting; and history and geography. He urged that Latin and Greek be offered but not required of everyone; that French be offered for those preparing to be medical doctors; and that French, German, and Spanish be offered for merchants and mechanics. He also stressed the need for good breeding, manners, and morals. Although Franklin's ideas were not immediately accepted, they did lay the foundation for curriculum changes to come in the nineteenth century.

1800–1899: the industrial age

During this period, great wealth was amassed by a few/entrepreneurs/ who had the ingenuity to develop new ideas and the courage to put them into effect. Seeking a better life, thousands of immigrants from Europe sought refuge in the United States and became low-paid factory workers. The great open spaces and the lure of gold and silver drew many people westward to settle in California and the surrounding states.

The world of work

The Industrial Revolution had changed many people's way of living and working. More and more people began to work in factories and to leave the country for the cities. Business offices grew in number, and the techniques and tools used in them changed.

The typewriter made increasingly important inroads into offices. The first typewriter had been patented in 1714. This model was modified and subsequently patented in 1829. Both these machines were cumbersome to use and produced embossed (raised) letters on paper.

The typewriter that was to revolutionize the office was a practical modification of the earlier models, and manufacture of it was begun in 1874 by the firm of E. Remington. Constant improvements and increasing production made the typewriter a principal tool in offices.

Until this period, the shorthand of Tiro, a secretary in ancient Rome, had been used for centuries, as long as Latin was important. In 1837, a new shorthand system, developed by Sir Isaac Pitman in England, emerged. Pitman shorthand was based on phonetic principles of the English language. In 1852, this system was brought to the United States. In 1888, John Robert Gregg created another system of shorthand that subsequently became popular in the United States.

During the early years of shorthand development, men were the specialists in the field. In 1870, Eliza Boardman Burnz, a well-known teacher of shorthand, noted that very few women—less than half a dozen—were working as stenographers in New York City. She began to recruit women to learn shorthand. Because they were traditionally paid less than men, women were added to offices in increasing numbers. The character of the office began to change radically.

Until the nineteenth century, only primitive calculating machines had been available. These ranged from the ancient abacus (still used in many Asiatic countries such as Russia and China) through the slide rule, a simple adding machine, and a machine that could multiply. In 1820, a primitive machine that could add, subtract, multiply, and divide was first produced on a commercial scale.

These machines were all rather awkward to use and slow to process the numbers after the keys had been depressed. Often, wheels had to be turned in one direction for addition and in the opposite direction for subtraction. Multiplication and division involved several turnings of wheels. Speedier machines were patented in 1850. In 1887, the *comptometer*, which could add, subtract, multiply, and divide quickly, was patented.

In 1864, for the first time in the United States, an income tax was imposed on businesses and wage earners to raise money to finance the Civil War. This tax was discontinued in 1872.

In addition to the increase in the number of working women, another vital change in the work force took place after the Civil War. In the United States, slavery was abolished. However, even in places of business that had had no slaves, the nature of supervision changed little from previous eras. The idea persisted that workers were commodities and could be abused. Those who were privileged to be hired had little or no protection from the wrath of a boss who was displeased by one of their actions. Job training, except for skills and knowledge acquired in school, was still largely a matter of learning from those who were already experienced in the work.

In 1886, the American Federation of Labor, which combined many craft unions of printers, carpenters, tailors, and weavers (known as *blue-collar workers*), was formed. *White-collar workers* (people who worked in offices, banks, and stores), however, were rarely attracted to unions during the nineteenth century.

Education for management and supervision

In the early nineteenth century, education for management and supervision became more theoretical. The practical studies of accounting and bookkeeping lost their preeminent positions. *Economics*, the study of how goods and services are provided for the well-being of society, became the major subject in the study of business.

Economics had first been popularized by Adam Smith (1723–1790) in his famous book *The Wealth of Nations* (1776). In this book, Smith proclaimed that the total sales of all goods and services bought and sold constituted the economic wealth of a country. He explained that the method of buying and selling was a "market system." Through this system, he showed how demand and supply made prices rise or fall.

Other economists also shaped people's thoughts. Reverend Thomas Robert Malthus (1766–1834) explained that population tended to grow faster than the amount of food that could be provided. David Ricardo (1772–1823) exposed the contests between the newly rich people, who had made their money by manufacturing goods, and the great landowners, who had inherited their wealth. The latter were accused of keeping food prices exorbitantly high. Karl Marx (1818–1883) coauthored with Friedrich Engels the *Communist Manifesto* (1848). This book claimed that a communist revolution was both desirable and inevitable. John Stuart Mill (1806–1873) pointed out that producing goods was more important than distributing them, since once goods have been created, people can dispose of them according to the laws and customs of society, which determines how wealth is distributed.

Although accounting lost its top position in the study of business, it continued to expand in use and importance. Following the Civil War, and with the rise in the number of offices, training in various practical aspects of office work—office machines, accounting, bookkeeping, and secretarial duties—became increasingly popular. This training was first offered through private business schools and then through public schools. People began to be specialists in the use of business techniques and machines even before they were employed. In 1881, the Wharton School of Business, the first college to have a complete business program, was founded in Philadelphia.

1900–1928: the age of business pragmatists

The people who were in charge of organizations during this period believed that practical outcomes should result from every action. They planned very carefully, analyzed each movement made by employees to ensure that waste was at a minimum, and rewarded employees for unusually high productivity.

The world of work

This period saw the continued growth of American cities, resulting from the great influx of immigrants from Europe and the continuing influx of farmers from the country.

In 1913, for the first time since 1872, both corporate and individual income taxes were assessed. This action increased the need for clerical workers in all organizations, including the government.

A great deal of activity surrounded the massing of men and machinery for World War I. To fill the void left when men were drafted for military service, women in large numbers entered the factories, stores, and offices as workers.

Both vocational psychology and psychological testing were introduced into American business and industry following World War I, during which both had been extensively developed.

Salaries at this period were low, the usual work week was six days long, and the hours of work were also long. Workers continued to be looked on as commodities.

Education for management and supervision

Books that analyzed business and laid down principles for organizations to follow began to appear early in the twentieth century. Through these books the authors proposed many theories that were to shape business and management.

Thorstein Veblen (1857–1929), an American economist and sociologist, proclaimed human nature to be savage in his *Theory of the Leisure Class* (1899). In his second book, *The Theory of Business Enterprise* (1904), Veblen portrayed business owners as vultures devoted only to making profits.

Alfred Marshall, the great English economist, wrote *Study of Industrial Technique and Business Organization and of Their Influences on the Conditions of Various Classes and Nations* (1919). In this book, Marshall introduced organization (management) to land, labor, and capital, which were the three elements considered basic to all organizations at that time.

Henri Fayol, a French management theorist, wrote *General and Industrial Administration* (1916). Fayol also believed that management was a separate entity from finance, production, sales, and other business activities. Fayol taught that management consisted of five specific functions: planning, organizing, commanding, coordinating, and controlling. Some of Fayol's ideas concerned the supervisory role of the manager:[2]

- o Employees, intentionally or unintentionally, put something of themselves into the transmission and execution of orders; they do not operate merely as cogs in a machine.

- o Managers must be able to sacrifice some personal vanity in order to grant satisfaction to their subordinates.

- o To be a good manager requires more than specialized skill or technical ability.

- o No scientific rules apply to management, so the application of principles of management requires intelligence, experience, decision, and a sense of proportion.

During this period, the concept of scientific management was introduced. *Scientific management* is a systematic approach to managing that emphasizes productivity. Through scientific management, output is analyzed in terms of units and costs. Work tasks are simplified, fragmented, and compartmentalized. Under continuous supervision, workers are required to do efficiently and effectively what the manager demands. Three people who contributed immeasurably to scientific-management theory were Frederick W. Taylor, Frank B. Gilbreth, and Lillian Gilbreth.

Known as the "father of scientific management," Frederick W. Taylor (1865–1915) was noted for conducting time and motion studies. These studies analyzed the motions involved in individual tasks in order to determine which ones were useless or time wasting. Taylor believed that by eliminating the useless motions and by making the time-wasting ones more efficient, tasks could be performed more rapidly. With time and motion studies Taylor proved that high productivity could be attained through a systematic approach.

Taylor urged supervisors to treat workers with respect and consideration. He advocated that supervisors find out what their workers wanted most and then attempt to provide it. By doing so, Taylor believed, supervisors could obtain work that was done well and quickly and therefore cheaply. The first hints of the changes that would come in business practice and theory were contained in Taylor's emphasis on consideration and respect for the worker.

Frank B. Gilbreth (1868–1924), a mechanical engineer, and Lillian M. Gilbreth (1878–1972), a psychologist, performed many experiments as both researchers and consultants to industry. Through their books and experiments, they advanced the concept of scientific management. Their time and motion studies continued to emphasize the "commodity feature of labor."

In 1911, Frank authored *Motion Study.* In 1914, Lillian wrote *The Psychology of Management,* which showed the importance of a person's mind in determining, teaching, and installing the methods of least waste in industrial production. As coauthors they wrote *Applied Motion Study* (1917) and *Fatigue Study* (1919). These books explained that unnecessary motions in doing a job and unnecessary fatigue caused by incorrect or wasted motions were humanity's greatest waste.

The years from 1908 to 1916 were a period of considerable business expansion. This growth also set the stage for the expansion of education for management and supervision. Courses and programs in advertising, banking and finance, marketing, research, retailing, wholesaling, sales management, and personal selling were developed. Those in economics, accounting, and secretarial studies were already commonplace. By the end of 1928, forty-seven schools of business had been founded.

Shortly after World War I, schools of business and education organized departments to teach prospective high-school business teachers the fundamentals of such subjects as bookkeeping, general business, shorthand, typewriting, office practice, business law, and retailing.

1929–1950: the age of human relations

From the end of World War I until 1928, people had witnessed rapid technological development. Mass production on assembly lines brought new affluence to the owners and new problems for the workers of the next generation.

The world of work

The Great Depression that followed the booming stock market of the late 1920s caused many displacements in the work force. Engineers, lawyers, and other highly trained specialists often could not find jobs in their specialities. As a result, many of them took jobs in business and other organizations and brought their unique knowledge to these enterprises. In turn, they displaced less able workers, who were then often unable to find other jobs. These displaced workers became part of the long lines for food handouts. Some people who were unable to find jobs returned to school to upgrade their skills and knowledge.

The beginning of the United States' involvement in World War II created many new demands for workers. The need for men for the armed forces left vacancies in the work force that were filled by women.

With the end of World War II, veterans, aided by government appropriations, entered college in record numbers. Many of the women who had taken jobs during the war found they preferred working outside the home. Aided by many gadgets that simplified and shortened the hours needed for housework, they were able to continue in ther jobs.

In the office, hints of electrified mechanization began to emerge. The electric typewriter was first patented in 1935. However, it did not become a force in the business office until after World War II, when mass production made it readily available. In addition, electric calculators, developed in the years 1944–1947, changed the speed with which numerical operations could be performed.

Business grew in size, numbers, and complexity. Government imposed many laws and added taxes on business operations. The growth of business and the regulation by government required that managers use more judgment and have more technical knowledge. To maintain good labor relations, supervisors had to have an entirely new body of information on the psychology and sociology of work, labor laws, and unionization.

Education for management and supervision

The Depression caused people to be shaken in their beliefs about the science of economics. This new skepticism helped them to accept the ideas being proposed by the behavioral scientists who were beginning to analyze the marketplace. The study of business emphasized the study of people. Thus was ushered in the age of human relations.

Mary Parker Follett (1868–1933), a social researcher, concentrated her attention on the causes of human behavior. In her book *Creative Experience* (1930), she explained that compromise was not a satisfactory way to solve difficulties. She urged that people "integrate" experiences. This, she said, necessitated seeking alternatives that would not cause either party to lose ground but would offer a satisfactory solution to both. She further noted that no person should have power "over" any other. Power should come from the situation and should always be "with" people in relation to the action that needs to be taken.

Elton Mayo (1880–1949), of Harvard University, was a prime champion of the working person. He believed that employers still thought of workers as just another production cost rather than as people fulfilling a social function. He was also concerned that too much stress was placed on time and motion studies and wages. Mayo believed that human nature made workers respond to the supervisor's concern for their welfare, much as a child likes to please a parent.

Mayo, together with Frederick J. Roethlisberger and W. J. Dickson, performed the now-famous Hawthorne Studies at the Western Electric plant near Chicago in the 1920s. These controlled experiments initially sought to determine how a selected group of workers would respond to altered amounts of light at their work station. They were broadened to include the effects of rest periods, hot lunches, later starting times, and earlier leaving times. The researchers concluded that varying the work hours and the amount of light had little effect on production. The most important finding was that work is a group activity and that the social world of adults is patterned around this activity. They found that the need for recognition, security, and a sense of belonging were more important in increasing workers' production than the physical conditions of the workplace. Finally, these researchers found that workers who worked together daily exerted strong social controls over the work habits and attitudes of one another.

Once all these ideas became known, classes on human relations began to be offered in colleges and universities. Enterprises gave human-relations training to supervisors, and employees began to be included in discussions about their jobs and other concerns.

1951 to the present: the age of management strategy and technological communication

Increases in the world's population; industrialization of previously underdeveloped countries; hordes of people fleeing from despotic dictators; and growing shortages of oil, metals, and foodstuffs caused displacements of people around the world. Wars further added to the upheavals that were occurring. Young people, incensed over some of the attitudes of their elders, government officials, business executives, and school administrators toward social change and abuse of natural resources, rebelled and held demonstrations on campuses across the United States.

Blacks, long discontented with their status, staged sit-ins and marches as they sought equal treatment under the law. Similarly, women, classified as a minority group, sought liberation from restrictive practices. Subsequent laws issued by Congress and decisions handed down by the Supreme Court increasingly attempted to ensure equality for all people throughout the United States.

Vast developments in atomic power; in the capacity of computers to store, calculate, and dispense data at lightning-fast speeds; and in space and communications technology added to the knowledge explosion. The growth of *multinational corporations* (companies established in more than one country) also brought the need for added knowledge and ability.

The world of work

Following World War II, analytical tools and methods for using them were increasingly emphasized. Mathematics and research began to have a very strong impact on organization planning and decision making. Statistical and calculating machines were improved, enabling managers to use them more effectively.

Computers, initially brought into all types of enterprises in the 1950s, were constantly improved, made smaller, and made more accessible. Today they provide vast amounts of data at the touch of a button. Thus information gathering and dissemination have been simplified. Furthermore, computers have eliminated many tedious, routine, clerical-type positions.

The technological revolution in offices has also affected methods of communication. In large offices, the traditional secretary who takes dictation manually or by machine is rapidly being replaced by operators of word-processing machines. These machines enable the word originator (dictator) to dictate into a telephone-recording device or other machine, have dictation transcribed by secretaries, and, after errors have been corrected, have one or more perfect copies produced by the mere pushing of a button. This technology is rapidly being improved and expanded. Many technical experts foresee that in a few years voice-manipulated machines will speed communication even more. Already, telegrams automatically transmitted from firm to firm, pictures and copy flashed throughout the country, and communication by satellite are realities. All these technological advances are causing as great a change in the office of today as the Industrial Revolution caused in the factories of the eighteenth and nineteenth centuries.

During this period, psychological tests began to be used extensively to select supervisors and managers. The human relations approach continued as a basic management philosophy. As part of this approach, supervisors:[3]

o Take a personal interest in the workers assigned to them

o Provide workers with information about the job and the company

o Make workers feel important

o Listen to what workers have to say

o Give workers a chance to participate in activities and decisions of the firm

In the 1960s, laws began to change the composition of the work force. The Civil Rights Act of 1964 opened the way to fair employment practices. Large numbers of women, blacks, Puerto Ricans, and other minority groups moved into jobs not readily available to them previously. The Age Discrimination in Employment Act of 1967 expanded the role of older people in the economic life of the country. Handicapped persons were also ensured equal opportunity for jobs they could perform.

Other changes occurred in the work force during this period. Many young people who participated in the college riots of the late 1960s were antibusiness. However, by the following decade, these same young people had become even more business oriented than earlier students. In fact, the first large numbers of women to get M.B.A. degrees came from this group. Educated to use electronic calculators and computers as management tools, these young people demanded high competence from their supervisors, systematic processes for making decisions, and regular and thorough performance reviews when they entered the work force.[4]

New ideas about people and their interactions were introduced in the 1960s. Businesses began to use these ideas to develop their personnel. One technique, known as the *T-group* or *sensitivity training*, gained particular popularity. With this technique, people met together in groups without an assigned leader, decided the agenda for the meeting, and attempted to arrive at a consensus about an emotionally charged issue, such as discrimination. The group's dialogue was tape recorded and then played back and analyzed. Feelings, attitudes, and personality conflicts were all exposed through the dialogue.

This interchange, which allowed workers and supervisors to expose their feelings openly, helped workers to accept the authority of supervisors and supervisors to understand the frustrations of workers. Thus, both groups had an opportunity to improve their relations with each other. Some business people believed in this method of changing both people and their methods of working together, while others condemned it.

Other research changed attitudes toward supervision. The concepts, developed mainly by psychologists and industrial managers, have provided supervisors with information on how to select people, how to understand people's reactions to job assignments, what motivates people, how to increase productivity, and how workers can become more involved in and enthusiastic about their employment. These sophisticated methods of working with people and meeting organizations' goals will be discussed later in this book. They, coupled with huge leaps in the technology of the workplace, have brought great changes in the nature of supervision.

Laws and presidential orders that were favorable to unionization were enacted during the period from the 1940s to the 1960s. These enabled unions to be more aggressive in soliciting members. Government workers were allowed to join unions. For the first time, white-collar workers were brought together in large numbers into unions. Unionization of substantial numbers of workers in offices, stores, and schools has changed the relationship of those employees to their supervisors by giving employees a union representative to turn to when something about the job displeases them.

Education for management and supervision

By the 1950s, there were over 163 schools of business in addition to over 400 departments of business or business administration in nonbusiness colleges and universities. Business courses increasingly became "how to do it" courses, and business students often had as little as 20 percent of their four-year college programs devoted to the liberal arts.

In the late 1950s, two studies were made that were to have considerable influence on curriculums in business schools in the ensuing decades. Professors Robert Aaron Gordon and James Edwin Howell wrote *Higher Education for Business* (1959), and Professor Frank C. Pierson wrote *The Education of American Businessmen: A Study of University College Programs in Business Administration* (1959).

Although the studies had been commissioned independently, the three professors' findings were remarkably similar. Both reports stressed that young people were not being given adequate training for business. Business schools as a whole, the authors claimed, were adhering to outworn ideas and were placing an overemphasis on training for specific jobs. This, the authors believed, would block a person's maximum intellectual growth, thus preventing the achievement of the highest career goals possible.

Both studies complained about the low standards of most business schools, the low calibre of students, the poor quality of teaching and teachers, and the lack of research on business management.

To offset these problems in the business courses, the reports urged that:

o Academic standards be raised

o Admission requirements be increased

o Courses that were overspecialized be reduced or eliminated completely

o At least half of the undergraduate programs in business consist of liberal arts courses

o Business courses include business policy, business development, and organizational theory, in addition to the standard courses in accounting, marketing, management, and business law

o Business studies focus on managerial decision making

o Graduate programs in business be two-year programs and cover quantitative methods, economics, psychology-sociology, law, management, policy making, plus free electives

Many schools and colleges either strengthened their business programs in line with the recommendations or eliminated them. Some highly vocational schools, such as schools of retailing, were closed. Some colleges dropped courses such as secretarial studies.

As computers were increasingly used, the study of computer science was added to most business curriculums. This further necessitated the requirement of more advanced mathematical courses in the liberal arts segment of the program. International management courses were also developed.

With the changes in the four-year college business programs, *community colleges*, two-year colleges that serve the needs of the populace in a local area, began to be established in large numbers across the country. The "how to do it" courses dropped by the four-year colleges were, in many cases, adopted by the community colleges. Programs to prepare people for entry-level skill or managerial jobs were especially popular.

These two-year colleges are less costly to attend than most four-year colleges and do not necessitate added charges for room and board. These advantages, combined with lower admission standards and programs in English, reading, and math remediation, made it possible for many people who would not have had the opportunity otherwise to attend college. Completion of the two-year college program also gives ambitious students an opportunity to transfer to and complete a four-year college course at another college.

The changes that have occurred over the ages in the world of work and in education for management and supervision are vast. Table 2–1 briefly summarizes them.

TABLE 2–1
THE EVOLUTION OF WORK AND OF EDUCATION FOR MANAGEMENT AND SUPERVISION

Period	World of Work	Education for Management and Supervision
Ancient Times to 1699: The Age of the Apprentice	Most workers were employed in agriculture. Slaves, indentured servants, and apprentices were the main sources of labor for other occupations.	Bookkeeping and accounting were developed, and books about them were published.
1700–1799: The Age of Emerging Managerial Standards and Practices	The Industrial Revolution introduced tools that replaced handwork. Workers from home and shop industries moved into factories. Discipline at work was usually harsh, hours were long, and pay was low.	The first school of commerce was established in England. In America, Benjamin Franklin set down standards for the education of young people.
1800–1899: The Industrial Age	The Industrial Revolution continued to change rural workers into city workers, and machines for office use were developed. Unionization began to be important as a protection for workers.	To accounting and bookkeeping studies was added economics, a new social science. In America, following the Civil War, private business schools mushroomed to prepare people for office occupations.

(Continued)

(Table 2–1 continued)

Period	World of Work	Education for Management and Supervision
1900–1928: The Age of Business Pragmatists	World War I, imposition of income taxes, women in the work force in large numbers, and testing for employment all contributed to changes in the world of work.	Economic theorists presented new concepts. The idea of management as a separate business activity from finance, production, and sales was introduced. Scientific management, with its time and motion studies, was begun. Education for the teaching of business was introduced.
1929–1950: The Age of Human Relations	Mass production flourished in factories. Electric machines became available in offices. World War II brought many more women into the labor market.	World War II veterans returned to classrooms in large numbers to increase their skills and knowledge. Human-relations training became important both in enterprises and in colleges.
1951 to the Present: The Age of Management Strategy and Technological Communication	Technology revolutionized both the factory and the office. Workers, freed from performing tedious chores, needed technical skills to obtain jobs. Displacements resulted as jobs for unskilled persons became scarcer. Laws opened jobs hitherto in scarce supply for minorities, including women, older people, and the handicapped. Unionization of white-collar workers increased noticeably. Large corporations moved toward multinational status.	Education for business, management, and supervision expanded. More women began studies in these fields. Community colleges increased opportunities for those who had not earlier been admissible to college. Vocational subjects became increasingly popular in the 1970s.

*I dun i half t
to print chapter*

SUMMARY

A historical review of the world of work reveals:

o Workers originally worked primarily on farms.

o Even until the middle of the nineteenth century in the United States, slaves, indentured servants, and apprentices were subject to the whims of owners and employers and were often treated cruelly.

o Crafts people banded together into guilds, which both established standards for their members and defended their interests.

o The Industrial Revolution changed the nature of work for many people who left the farms to take factory jobs in the growing urban centers.

o The development of office machines made them available after the Civil War. Office work attracted women into the work force, and World War I speeded their entry into all types of jobs.

o In the early twentieth century, scientific management became the popular method of supervising. Work was broken down into units, and studies were made to eliminate wasted motions and thereby speed production.

o Imposition of income taxes and other changes requiring record keeping increased the need for white-collar employees.

o The Hawthorne experiments were an important contribution to the human relations concepts about supervision, which became accepted during and after the 1930s.

o Management turned to the use of computers in the 1950s as the need for more detailed planning and analysis of all aspects of organizations grew.

o Technology expanded and speeded the ability to communicate from both long and short distances.

o Minorities, including women, have increasingly entered the work force. Equal opportunity laws opened more jobs to them and increased their representation at all levels of paid employment.

Education for business has shown constant growth and improvement:

o Bookkeeping and accounting were the first subjects added to the curriculum for people interested in the world of work.

o In the early nineteenth century, economics became an important subject of study for business and management.

o After the Civil War, education for business expanded to include courses in office machines and secretarial subjects.

o In the early twentieth century, education for business included advertising, banking and finance, marketing, research, retailing, wholesaling, sales management, and personal selling.

o In the 1920s, many courses were added in colleges of education to prepare high-school teachers of business.

o In the 1930s and 1940s, human relations became a popular course for most people planning to enter the world of work.

o In the late 1950s, examination of business courses revealed that improvements were needed in course content, calibre of students, and preparation of business teachers.

o Developing technology necessitated the addition of courses in computer science and data and word processing so that young people would be properly prepared to enter the world of work.

REFERENCES

[1] Charles R. DeCarlo and Ormsbee W. Robinson, *Education in Business and Industry* (New York: Center for Applied Research in Education, 1966), p. 2.

[2] See "Famous Firsts: Discoveries from Looking Inward," *Business Week*, June 6, 1964, p. 152.

[3] William F. Whyte, "The Manipulation Problem," in *Individualism and Big Business*, ed. Leonard Sayles (New York: McGraw-Hill, 1963), pp. 49–50.

[4] Peter F. Drucker, "Report on the Class of '68," *Wall Street Journal*, February 3, 1978, p. 22.

REVIEW AND DISCUSSION QUESTIONS

1. Why has a function as basic as supervision changed over the ages?
2. What is meant by the statement "People do things in the traditional way?" What are the advantages and disadvantages of following tradition?
3. What were the differences among slaves, indentured servants, and apprentices?
4. What role did guilds play in medieval times?
5. What subjects were the first to be studied as specific preparation for business? Why were those subjects considered so important?
6. What contributions did Frederick W. Taylor make to the study of scientific management?
7. What events were notable in inducing women in rather large numbers to enter the work force?

8. What impact did the imposition of the income tax law in 1913 have on business?
9. What effect did the studies done in the 1950s have on college education for business?
10. How has education for business changed over the ages?

ASSIGNMENTS

1. Visit a bank in your community. As you look around at the employees, is it easy to tell the supervisors from the subordinates? Are some of the employees easily identifiable as subordinates? Why? Do any of the employees wear uniforms? Are they supervisors or subordinates? What are some of the other differences you notice that tell you which persons are supervisors? Do the supervisors appear to be doing work similar to that of the subordinates? Explain your answers.
2. Analyze your own experiences as a subordinate either in a school or a job. If in a school, consider these questions: What person or persons made the decisions? What person or persons delegated the work? Who checked on the performance of tasks? How efficient were the workers? How were the officers of the organization chosen? Write a short report of your analysis of the work done.

   If a job, consider these questions: What position did the person to whom you reported hold? How many others reported to that person? How often did you see that supervisor? Did one or more persons assign work for you to do? How was the quality and quantity of your work checked? Write a short account of your experiences in reporting to a supervisor on the job.

PROBLEM FOR RESOLUTION

Analyze the business program(s) at your school. How many different majors in business are available? What courses are devoted to the use of the new technology that has developed in the last twenty years? Are all business students required to take any courses that involve technology? Are any courses on behavioral sciences offered through the business department? Write a report of your findings.

CASE STUDY

Sondra d'Angelo has become the supervisor in an office that has four full-time employees. The previous supervisor had wanted each employee to know about all the work in the department. Therefore, although each handled certain tasks individually, all shared in answering telephones, doing computations, and typing letters from dictation tapes, handwritten copy, bulletin and manual copy, reports, and mailing lists. In addition, they all were responsible for filing and for acting as receptionists when visitors came to see the executives in the firm.

Just after Ms. d'Angelo was appointed supervisor, a word-processing machine and an electronic calculator were brought into the office. Their purpose was to speed typing and computational chores. Typing involving identical copy, which, except for minor updating, had previously had to be entirely retyped for use, would be routinized. The equipment was not meant to replace any worker, but rather to increase the output of the group. Each employee, in keeping with the previous work assignments, was asked to become an expert in using the word-processing machine and the calculator. Representatives from the companies that had sold the machines came to the office to train the workers.

Two of the employees were fascinated with the word-processing machine and took every chance possible to use it. The other two employees were almost afraid to touch the machine, saying they preferred their usual way of handling the chores. One of these women, however, was delighted with the electronic calculator and used it whenever a list of figures needed to be compiled.

Ms. d'Angelo began to notice other abilities and reluctances of the employees. They reacted in different ways to telephone answering, greeting visitors, filing, and handling arithmetic chores. Ms. d'Angelo decided to make a chart of each employee's special abilities for these shared tasks. Analyze her chart, on page 43, and answer the questions.

FURTHER READING

The American Association (Assembly) of Collegiate Schools of Business, 1916–1966. Homewood, Ill.: Richard D. Irwin, 1966.
> Explains the founding and development of the accrediting association for collegiate schools of business and the standards they have set for their membership.

Berczi, Andrew, and J. M. Ventura. "The Evolution of Education for Business and Its Effect on the Accounting Profession." *Collegiate News and Views,* December 1969, pp. 11–14.
> Explains the emergence of accounting as a profession from the early studies of bookkeeping and the first attempts to chronicle the work of accountants.

Chandler, Alfred D., Jr. *The Visible Hand: The Managerial Revolution in American Business.* Cambridge, Mass.: Harvard University Press, 1977.

CHART OF INTERESTS AND APTITUDES OF FOUR EMPLOYEES

Tasks	Ms. A.	Ms. B.	Ms. C.	Ms. D.
Use of word-processing machine (primarily for typing of bulletins, reports, and mailing lists)	Enjoys and is good at handling machine	Fascinated by and handles routine typing of bulletins and reports well	Not enthusiastic but can handle	Avoids
Transcription from machine dictation	Accurate but not enthusiastic	Willing to do but makes many grammatical and spelling errors	Enjoys and does quite well	Refuses to do except under duress = _Constraint by_ _threat_
Telephone answering	Does it mechanically	Gracious but rarely knows answers to questions	Does it mechanically	Enjoys and is gracious and very knowledgeable
Reception of visitors	Does it mechanically	Gracious but not always tactful	Can do but dislikes leaving desk	Acts as superb hostess and is tactful and knowledgeable
Filing	Willing to do only under duress	Willing to do but requires careful supervision	Does well but puts off until reminded	Enjoys neatness and files promptly
Use of electronic calculator	Dislikes anything related to math	Unable to do except for routine addition	Enjoys and handles all computations well	Careful and meticulous in use as needed _extremely careful_

On the basis of this chart, would you make any changes in the way these tasks are currently handled? Explain the reasons for your answers.

Discusses how the increasing specialization in trade and finance arose from the expansion of world markets in cotton and textiles and allowed the growth of big business; how railroads slashed the cost of freight transport and made it possible for single plants to serve large markets; and how subsequent mergers made organizations complex and spurred the development of modern management.

De Carlo, Charles R., and Ormsbee W. Robinson. *Education in Business and Industry.* New York: Center for Applied Research in Education, 1966.

Describes concisely the development of education for business and industry in the United States.

Follett, Mary Parker. *Creative Experience.* New York: Longmans, Green, & Co., 1930.

Is an analytic, objective study of human relations and of how to develop coactive power within organizations, which enriches and advances human beings.

Gilbreth, Frank B. *Motion Study.* New York: D. Van Nostrand, 1911.

Explains how waste motions may be eliminated by workers to provide improved productivity on the job.

Heilbroner, Robert L. *The Worldly Philosophers.* 3rd ed. New York: Clarion Books, 1967.

Describes the great economists and their impact on the thinking of people during and after their eras.

Jernegan, Marcus W. *Laboring and Dependent Classes in Colonial America, 1607–1783.* Chicago: University of Chicago Press, 1931.

Gives a history of workers from the time America was settled until the American Revolution ended.

Marshall, Alfred. *Study of Industrial Technique and Business Organization and of Their Influences on the Conditions of Various Classes and Nations.* London: Macmillan & Co., 1919.

Explains that the experience of the past sheds light on the present; that the similarity of management functions are observable at different times and in different institutions; and that good management is essential for the prosperity of any organization.

Mayo, Elton. *The Social Problems of an Industrial Civilization.* Boston: Harvard Graduate School of Business Administration, 1945.

Explains that the time and motion studies put too much stress on wages and not enough on concern for the welfare of the workers. Predicts that with the fast changes in business, rapid reorganization and expansion and the need to view workers as part of the team of interested participants will occur.

Silk, Leonard S. *The Education of Businessmen.* Supplementary Paper No. 11. New York: Committee for Economic Development, 1960.

Succinctly analyzes the Ford Foundation (Gordon-Howell) and

Carnegie Foundation (Pierson) studies of the late 1950s that condemned collegiate education for business and suggested improved
curriculums, student admission standards, and teaching.

*Work in America: Report of a Special Task Force to the Secretary of
Health, Education and Welfare.* Cambridge, Mass.: MIT Press, 1973.
Describes the importance, meaning, and extent of work and the
relation of work to the health, education, and welfare of people.

3

the organizational structure

After studying and analyzing this chapter, you should be able to:

Explain the role that policies play in furthering the goals and objectives of the enterprise.

Describe how procedures help ensure that policies are carried out, and explain how rules and regulations grow from procedures.

Explain what is meant by the chain of command.

Define "authority" and "responsibility," and explain why the supervisor must have both.

Describe the concept of unity of command.

Define "span of control," and list the factors that determine how wide the span will be.

Describe an organization chart and the various methods of organizing work.

Differentiate between line and staff functions, and explain nonfunctional and functional authority of staff members.

Differentiate between the formal and the informal organization, and explain why the supervisor must be aware of the informal organization.

T HE SUPERVISOR WORKS WITHIN the framework of the goals and objectives of the organization. These in turn are interpreted by the policies that are established. Procedures grow from the policies and determine the rules and regulations needed to govern the actions of employees.

The supervisor also works within the boundaries of the formal organization of the enterprise—the way in which work is allocated and authority and responsibility for work are designated. This chapter covers these important topics.

Policy development

Every enterprise, regardless of size, must develop policies. *Policies* are statements of principles and standards that will help the enterprise achieve its goals and objectives.

Policies affect every person in and every activity performed by a firm: Hiring, training, paying wages, promoting, giving fringe benefits, counseling, retiring and discharging, providing products and/or services, maintaining the building, servicing clients, accounting, observing legislation, financing, and marketing are covered.

The flexibility of policies

Policies, although meant to give stability to an enterprise, its clients, and its employees, must be flexible. Many reasons exist for having to retract or change policies: changes in customers' demands, development of new products, need for new services, expansion of the enterprise, extension of the community served, new laws, new or changing competition, union rules and contracts, need for added sources of income, new directions being taken by the enterprise, new ownership, and a change in top executives.

Although policies must be flexible in all enterprises, they are easier to change in small firms. Consider the need for a change in policy and the ease with which it was effected in the following example.

The Quick-Copy Company opened for business across the street from a large university. The long-range goal of the owner, Gregory Sharp, was to capture the copy business of the students and faculty. His immediate objective was to make a certain amount of money weekly for the first six months.

To do this, Sharp made several plans and carried them through. He arranged the shop attractively for customers. He installed a long counter on which the work to be copied could be spread out. He ordered three large new copy machines that did work quickly and without smudging. He hired two young male employees to help him.

Sharp's initial pricing policy was meant to attract students and faculty to his facility instead of the university library. At the library, people could do their own copy work for 10 cents per page. To undersell the library, Sharp charged 7 cents per page, with a minimum of 25 cents for any one job. A large sign on the side of his shop announced these prices.

From the day the shop opened, it attracted a large volume of business, as Sharp had anticipated. Approximately two months after Sharp started his shop, another copy firm opened about three blocks further from the university. Its charge was a flat 5 cents per page, with no minimum.

When customers began to point out this discrepancy in pricing, the Quick-Copy Company announced that the charge for overnight work would be 6 cents per copy, with the same 25-cent minimum charge. However, students and faculty who had many pages of copying to be done still found it advantageous to walk the additional three blocks to the competitor to save several dollars.

Continued customer resistance and complaints to the Quick-Copy Company about its higher rates again caused a change in Sharp's policy. He put another sign on the wall, which stated WE WILL MEET ANY OVERNIGHT PRICE THAT IS LESS THAN OURS. He did not change the 7-cent price for copies made while a customer waited. He believed that his location would continue to draw customers who sought immediate service, and that those with large jobs would normally be willing to use the overnight service at the lower rate. This change in policy allowed him to retain his business without experiencing further pricing problems.

As this example shows, policies can easily be amended as needed in small firms. Sharp did not need to consult anyone else in order to change his pricing policy. He could, of course, have consulted his employees, but even doing that would have taken only a few minutes.

Larger firms, or those with complicated advisory panels, cannot move so quickly to change policy. Consider the following example. A professional journal had an executive board of seven people, who came from widely different geographical areas. They met once a year at the journal's headquarters to discuss policy matters.

In recent years, the financial condition of the journal had put business in jeopardy. Added charges for paper, ink, printing, distribution, and salaries of employees made the cost of running the journal greater than income. The circulation manager, Roy Schrag, and the head of the executive board, Beth Palmer, discussed the financial problems of the journal. They reasoned that it would soon be impossible to continue publishing unless subscription prices were substantially raised or money was obtained from journal advertising. They noted, however, that the journal's board had established a policy against accepting advertising.

Raising money by increasing subscription prices also involved problems. They agreed, after examining the records of past increases, that the number of subscriptions always went down for one or two years after rates were raised. Therefore, just raising the subscription price would not offset the losses being incurred.

Finally, they drew up a proposal for the executive board to consider at its next meeting. They suggested that the subscription price be raised modestly and that the policy about accepting advertising be modified to allow appropriate types of ads to be included. Their arguments were accepted, and the new policy permitted certain types of advertising to be accepted. The entire process, from the time the problem was first discussed until the proposal had been presented and accepted, took over six months. Contrast this with the immediate policy changes made by the Quick-Copy Company.

Major and minor policies

In large enterprises, there are two kinds of policies. *Major policies* are general statements of principles and standards formulated by the top executives of the enterprise that apply to the firm as a whole. *Minor policies* are specific statements derived from major policies for use in the various departments. Both kinds of policies must support the enterprise's goals and objectives.

For example, one multiunit firm's goal is to increase profits. One of the objectives set to achieve this goal is to increase the number of clients served. The major policy set to achieve the objective is to be accessible to clients. The managers of the various branches of the firm may have to tailor the minor policy—the hours that their buildings are open—to fit customers' life-styles. In a rural area, hours of 9:00 A.M. to 5:00 P.M. Monday through Friday and 9:00 A.M. to 1:00 P.M. on Saturday might prove convenient. In an urban area, hours of 10:00 A.M. to 6:00 P.M. four days a week, 10:00 A.M. to 8:00 P.M. one day a week, and no Saturday hours may be better. Thus, each branch would observe the major policy by tailoring the minor policy to its community.

Oral versus written policies

The managers of small single-unit enterprises, such as the Quick-Copy Company, often do not take the time to write out their policies. Because they have few employees, these managers can easily communicate their policies, and any necessary changes, orally.

Large enterprises, however, need to write policies down and to distribute them in printed form to their employees. For flexibility, policy manuals usually take the form of loose-leaf binders. This allows pages to be replaced as policy changes are made. In many large enterprises, new employees are given a booklet that covers those policies that apply directly to them. Supervisors need a copy of all the policies relevant to their areas of work. Increasingly, the government views written policies as contracts with employees.

Procedures, rules, and regulations

Procedures are the guides to actions that must be taken to observe the firm's policies. Procedures tell employees what path to follow to get the job done correctly. For example, in the Quick-Copy Company, the policy was to give speedy, efficient attention to each customer who entered the firm. If an employee was in the middle of preparing a large amount of material for a customer who would be in for it the following day, the employee was to stop that job and take care of the just-entered customer. In addition, certain procedures were to be observed. Each customer was to receive a receipt detailing the number of copies made. Because the policy of the firm was not to accept checks for payment, employees could receive only cash for the jobs done. If a customer was not prepared to pay, no work could be delivered to him or her. These procedures were necessary to carry out the policies of the firm. Each was explained to the employees, who were cautioned to observe them exactly. Having set procedures permits employees to conduct transactions efficiently.

Rules and regulations are controls over employees that state exactly what may and what may not be done within the enterprise. They govern the behavior of employees without prejudice. Rules need to be established to cover the time designated for lunch periods, breaks, and arrival and departure. Rules and regulations also inform employees where to put coats, handbags, and briefcases during working hours. They may also explain to the employee what door to use, how to sign in for the workday, where to smoke, and other specific details about conduct during working hours.

The chain of command

The *chain of command* refers to the directives for getting work done that come from the top person (or persons) in the organization and filter down to those on lower levels. Organizations are by nature *hierarchical.* That means that the person who holds the top position passes orders, assignments, and information down to those who hold lesser positions, until the level at which they are carried out or needed is reached. Similarly, responses, suggestions, and reports move up the hierarchy from the least important workers through the various levels of supervisors, until they reach the point at which they are resolved or acknowledged.

In small firms, like the Quick-Copy Company, only one level of su-

FIGURE 3–1
ONE-LEVEL CHAIN OF COMMAND

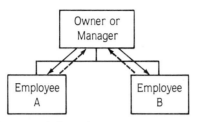

Solid arrow—Orders, assignments, information
Dotted arrow—Responses, reports, suggestions

pervisory control exists in the chain of command (see Figure 3–1). As a firm grows, however, additional levels of supervisory control may be added.

As Gregory Sharp reviewed his business after it had been open for one week, he became aware that the students and faculty used the copy service before 9:00 A.M. classes, but that only a few people came in after 6:00 P.M., when late classes began. He therefore scheduled his firm's hours from 8:30 A.M. to 6:30 P.M. on Monday through Friday and from 8:30 A.M. to 12:30 P.M. on Saturday, when a few morning classes were in session. The firm was open a total of fifty-four hours per week.

Each of his two employees worked a forty-hour, five-day week. Sharp was willing to work all fifty-four hours, but he soon found that he was tired from such constant work and had no energy to do other things that he enjoyed. In addition, his employees had lunch periods and coffee breaks, during which customers still came in. One employee was absent for a few days, and that caused additional problems. Sharp soon realized that he needed at least three more employees and that one of his two existing employees should be assigned as an assistant to cover those hours when Sharp himself was not on the premises and to help Sharp in other ways. Therefore, the chain of command grew to two levels (see Figure 3–2).

The number of different levels of supervisory control needed in a firm varies with the size and complexity of the enterprise. As the number of people employed grows, the chain of command is inevitably lengthened. Intermediate levels of management are formed. In general, however, the most efficient communication and functioning are achieved with the fewest layers of management between the workers and the top executives of the enterprise. The typical number of levels of

FIGURE 3-2
TWO-LEVEL CHAIN OF COMMAND

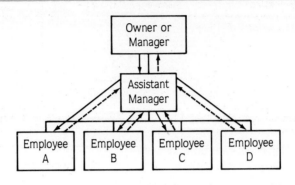

management in the chain of command for organizations of various sizes is shown in Table 3–1.

Authority and responsibility

Authority is the right of a supervisor to give job-related orders to a subordinate, to make decisions, and to take actions that will help achieve the goals and objectives of the enterprise. The authority of the supervisor is achieved in two ways: It must be *delegated* (granted) by the executive to whom the supervisor reports, and it must be *accepted* by the employees whom the supervisor guides and directs.

Delegating authority

Authority flows from the top to the bottom of the enterprise through the chain of command. Top management delegates authority to those lower on the scale, and they in turn delegate it, until it reaches the supervisor whose employees are to perform the tasks. Each person who has been delegated authority by someone above his or her level may delegate it to a subordinate employee as needed.

Responsibility for achieving the desired results should accompany the granting of authority. *Responsibility* is the obligation to do the assigned tasks in order to achieve results as determined by the goals of the enterprise.

In a small organization, the manager may not want to delegate authority, since in doing so, some degree of control is lost. He or she, then,

TABLE 3–1

LEVELS OF MANAGEMENT IN THE CHAIN OF COMMAND

Size of the Organization	Number of Employees	Number of Levels
Small	150	3
Medium	1,000	4
Large	7,500	5
Very large	30,000	6
Largest	200,000	7

Source: R. B. Kemball-Cook, *The Organization Gap* (London: George Allen & Unwin, 1972), p. 92. Reprinted by permission.

will have to be present at all times, since no one else will have the authority to make a decision. His or her absence, for any reason, will cause problems for employees and customers. The supervisor who does not delegate is bogged down in detail and must be present to make every decision and answer every query that is not routine.

For example, the day that the Quick-Copy Company's competitor opened with its lower price, Mr. Torres, a customer, stopped in to see Mr. Sharp about a large copy job he needed for the next day—seven copies each of 250 pages were to be made. Mr. Sharp was out of the office, and so Mr. Torres asked an employee if the 5-cent-per-page price of the competitor would be met. However, no employee had as yet been empowered to change any prices. Mr. Torres said, "The three-block walk will save me $35 on this job. Therefore, I shall take my business there." The Quick-Copy Company lost an $87.50 order because no one but Mr. Sharp was authorized to meet competitors' prices.

Initially, Mr. Sharp had *centralized* authority by resolving all the problems himself. The realization that he must have a second person to help make decisions when he was not around meant that some authority had to be delegated to that assistant. Thus, he began to take steps toward decentralization. *Decentralization* means granting authority to make decisions to subordinates.

Small organizations usually have only limited decentralization because the manager is physically present and available for consultation to resolve most problems. As organizations grow, however, decentralization of authority becomes increasingly necessary. A boss in a large organization who attempts to keep control of most authority would soon be unable to run the enterprise efficiently. Both employees and customers would be served poorly in such a setting.

Authority, once granted, may be taken back or extended further depending on the results that have been achieved.

Accepting authority

Authority, to be effective, must not only be granted by superordinates but also must be accepted by subordinates. If the supervisor in a book-keeping department asks an employee to figure the costs of a shipment of goods, the employee should not refuse because the request fits under the function of the position and is reasonable to further the goals of the firm. If, on the other hand, the supervisor asks the employee to use his or her lunch hour to run a personal errand for the supervisor, the employee can refuse to perform the task. The authority of the supervisor can be rejected by the subordinate because the request was not made within the framework of the authority granted to the supervisor nor did the task contribute to the overall goals of the enterprise.

Coexisting authority and responsibility

When responsibility does not reside with authority, or vice versa, conflicts and confusion usually result. The following situation illustrates such a difficulty.

Ms. Carron had just been promoted director of a unit of a large firm. There were three departments in her unit: a seminar department, a career-counseling department, and a publications department. The heads of the seminar and career-counseling departments reported directly to her, but the head of the publications department reported to the previous director, Ms. Cole, who had moved to another unit within the company. Ms. Carron, however, had the budgetary responsibility for the publications department in addition to total responsibility for the other two departments. Thus, even though she had no authority over the publications department, she was responsible for its financial performance.

The employees within the publications department were confused by the divided responsibility and authority. They soon found that for budgetary matters they had to see Ms. Carron, but their orders and assignments continued to come from their previous boss, Ms. Cole. When Ms. Cole issued orders that involved expenditure of funds, they had to have the expenditure approved by Ms. Carron. This situation led to frustrating delays, annoyance, and some friction. The publications department's employees were upset by the dual "bossing" to which they were subjected.

Ms. Carron repeatedly discussed the problem with her boss, who, at first, was unwilling to listen. However, as she detailed the problems, the split in authority became obvious, and she was finally given both the authority and the responsibility for that unit of her work.

In large enterprises, authority and responsibility are found at every level. Only by delegating authority and responsibility can a large company function expeditiously. However, delegation does not mean the loss of authority and responsibility by those higher in the chain of command.

Unity of command

The chain of command should lead to *unity of command*, meaning that each employee reports to only one supervisor. The problem in the office headed by Ms. Carron and Ms. Cole illustrated a lack of unity of command. When one boss gives orders to an employee, the boss knows how much has been assigned, and the worker usually has little problem in getting the work done. However, when two supervisors delegate work, conflicts usually arise. The subordinate is then torn between deciding which authority to obey.

For example, Mr. Lawford was employed to work as a secretary in a new law office. Two lawyers, Mr. Birdwell and Ms. Carson, were to give him work. Each one asked that work be done promptly, but neither considered the work given by the other. As a result, Mr. Lawford was constantly torn between the two of them. As soon as he had some work in the typewriter for Mr. Birdwell, Ms. Carson would come along and demand that he attend to her work first. Similarly, when he was doing her work, Mr. Birdwell would say, "Well, I thought you knew how important my work was." Finally, in desperation, Mr. Lawford tried dividing his day. He informed his bosses that morning hours would belong to Mr. Birdwell and afternoon hours to Ms. Carson. Even then, demands arose for him to rush some job through for one lawyer during the other's time.

Divided responsibility between two bosses rarely works satisfactorily. Most enterprises attempt to follow the concept of unity of command.

Span of control

The number of employees who can be supervised effectively by one person is the *span of control*. Spans of control may range from a few persons to many. In Figure 3–3, the owner or general manager has three persons reporting to him or her. The general manager's span of control is three managers to supervise. Manager A has ten employees to supervise, Manager B has six, and Manager C has twelve. When many employees report to one supervisor, the span is *wide*; when few employees report to one supervisor, the span is *narrow*. In Figure 3–3, Manager C's span is wider than Manager A's or B's.

Factors that determine the span of control

How many people should one person supervise? No exact answer can be given to that question because many factors determine the answer. Even

FIGURE 3-3
SPAN OF CONTROL

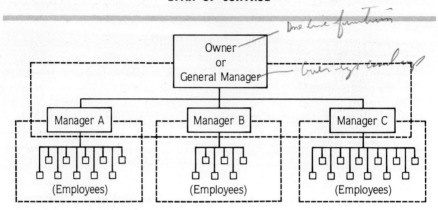

Broken lines—Span of control
Solid lines—Authority and responsibility

within one firm, the span of control may differ widely from one area of work to another. The following considerations affect the span of control:

o *Number of employees in the firm*—Small firms have a limited number of employees to be supervised.

o *Simplicity of the operation*—The simpler the work to be done, the more people the supervisor can effectively manage. More complex operations require a narrower span.

o *Character of decision making*—If the same or similar problems recur frequently, policies that permit the supervisor to respond routinely to dilemmas may be established, and the span can be wider.

o *Related character of the problems*—If the problems that occur are related so that the solution of one suggests appropriate solutions to others, one supervisor can handle more subordinates.

o *Ease of communication*—If the physical location of the employees and their hours of work are arranged so that communication may be conducted with all of them at one time, more workers may be supervised by one person.

o *Ability of the supervisor*—The more knowledge the supervisor has about the firm and about the problems that arise, the wider the span can be.

o *Ability of the individual employees*—If workers are very skilled or knowledgeable about the tasks they perform, the supervisor will be able to work with more of them.

o *Uniqueness of problems raised*—If the operation requires research to solve problems, extensive interaction with other agencies, or other time-consuming activities, fewer workers can successfully be supervised by one person.

o *Complexity of the technology used*—Very complex technology requires more specialists, and this, in turn, requires supervisors who have special expertise to oversee the equipment and personnel. Usually, this narrows the span of control.

o *Geographic location of the units of the enterprise*—If units are located in one community, the span of control may be wider than if those units are in different cities, states, or nations.

Advantages of a wide span

Where possible, the span of control should be wide, for several reasons. First, the fewer the supervisors who need to be employed, the greater the economies that can be achieved in supervisory ranks.

Second, if one supervisor can work with many people, the number of layers of supervision are reduced, and the chain of command from the top executives to the workers is therefore shortened. Communication thereby becomes more effective because the amount of time needed for orders to pass down from the top and for responses to move up from the bottom in the chain of command is reduced.

Basic forms of organization

As the supervisor's role is examined in more detail, the word "organization" needs to be clarified. This word has two meanings. First, as used previously, it refers to the enterprise, business, firm, library, school, doctor's office, law office, or other entity discussed.

Second, it describes the method of arranging the work people do to achieve the goals and objectives of the enterprise. Whenever work involves two or more tasks, they must be put into a state of order. If two or more people are involved in performing those tasks, some agreement must be reached about the portion of the work to be done by each and about how those portions will be integrated. *Organization*, therefore, refers to the division of the work to be done into parts and the integration of those parts into the whole. Organization occurs when duties are divided and related in a coordinated scheme.

The organization chart

As firms grow in size and complexity, the assignment of specific tasks becomes cumbersome unless some plan is made that can be followed for day-to-day activities. This plan expands in time into an organization chart. An *organization chart* is a map that shows the divisions of work, the lines of authority, and the relationships among the various jobs to be performed.

Each part of the work of a firm should be manageable by one or more people or teams of people. All these people or teams should then be coordinated so that each relates to the others. In turn, as already discussed, responsibility for an activity that involves two or more people must then be assigned to or assumed by one person. Organization provides not only for the division of work but also for the role of the person who will oversee the work of others.

There are many ways of organizing work. These are discussed in the following sections.

Organization by function

With *functional organization*, work is divided along the lines of the main activities (*functions*) of the company. Even the smallest firm has different functions, although they may all be performed by just one person. For example, Gregory Sharp of the Quick-Copy Company was asked by his nephew when Sharp first opened his shop what he did in his company.

Mr. Sharp replied, "I wear five imaginary hats called place, personnel, purchase, promotion, and profit. In the morning, I put on my *place (operations)* hat to open the doors of the firm, sweep the sidewalk, and get the store ready for employees and customers. Then I put on my *personnel (people)* hat, and I greet the employees I previously hired as they enter, remind them how to work the machines, answer their questions, and assign them to their stations for the day.

"I then put on my *purchase (purchasing)* hat and go to my desk to check orders and merchandise needed. When that is done, I put on my *promotion (marketing)* hat and decide what change, if any, I want in the messages that customers read, or meet with the sign painter if I want to order new signs for my windows. When that task is completed, I put on my *profit (finance)* hat and check the records of cash receipts from the previous day and note any money that I owe for taxes or other bills. If I have any extra money, I take it to the bank to deposit so that it will be there to pay the salaries of my employees. When I return to the shop, I put on my place hat again and help wait on customers. Throughout the day, I continue to change hats as my various tasks dictate."

The functional organization of the Quick-Copy Company is shown

FIGURE 3–4
FUNCTIONS IN THE QUICK-COPY COMPANY

Place	Personnel	Owner Purchase	Promotion	Profit
Operates physical space and oversees services for customers	Hires, trains, assigns, and keeps records of employees	Buys supplies and equipment	Displays and advertises firm's services	Keeps money records and pays bills
(OPERATIONS)	(PEOPLE)	(PURCHASING)	(MARKETING)	(FINANCE)

Employee A   Employee B

Provide copy
service for
customers

in Figure 3–4. Small enterprises of any kind have owners (or managers) who perform a variety of functions. As these enterprises grow, the work load becomes too great for a few people to handle, and so others are employed to share the load. Thus the functional organization as divided by people assigned to do each major task begins to take shape.

The functions performed by the owner of the Quick-Copy Company could become departments headed by managers if the company grew large enough to need another twenty or thirty employees (see Figure 3–5).

As enterprises grow, arranging work by tasks results in having several people perform related jobs. To give coherence to these groupings, they are formalized and named for the primary work, or functions, they do. Functions of all enterprises are determined by their primary needs.

For instance, insurance companies have specialized departments for underwriting, sales agencies, claims, control, and information-processing, in addition to departments for place, personnel, purchase, promotion, and profit. Public utilities have specialized departments for electric operations, gas operations, and engineering and construction, plus the regular functions. Express companies that haul freight have specialized departments for traffic, safety and insurance, special-freight handling, terminals and transportation, equipment, and labor relations.

FIGURE 3-5

FUNCTIONAL ORGANIZATION CHART FOR QUICK-COPY COMPANY AFTER DEPARTMENTALIZATION

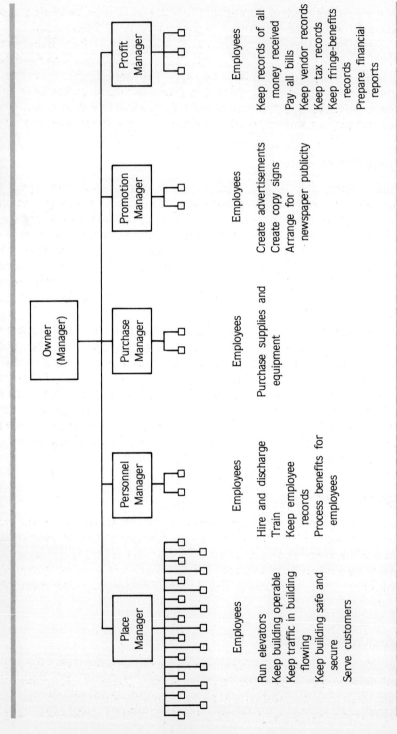

Large stores have departments for buying and merchandising, operations, selling, marketing, financial management, and personnel.

Sometimes these units are called by names other than "department," such as *group, division, area, branch,* or *bureau.* The head of the department, or other unit, then becomes the department supervisor, the division head, the bureau chief, the group director, or the head of the branch. How those individual departments relate to one another to comprise the entire company further defines the type of organization used.

Organization by territory

When enterprises expand the territory they serve and open new branches, the organizational needs of the company change. In many cases, the functional organization of the main branch is duplicated in each new addition. Thus, *chain organizations (multiunit firms)* may have the same functional jobs in as many different locations as they have branches. Many enterprises have branches, such as banks, insurance companies, stores, barbershops, typing-service firms, answering services, restaurants, newspaper stands, gas stations, beauty parlors, and manufacturers' sales offices.

As these geographical units grow in number, they, in turn, are usually grouped by area and organized by their proximity to one another. Groups may be organized by cities, states, or regions, such as an East Coast group, a Southern group, a North Central group, and a West Coast group. In turn, these divisions may be subdivided by the functions each performs. Some enterprises are international in scope (called *multinationals*). They have divisions classified by the nations or areas in which they operate, such as a French division, a European division, or a Far Eastern division.

Organization by client

Another method of organizing work is by the kinds of clients served. Banks, for example, have departments for corporate customers and individual customers, since the kind of work done and the size of the accounts for those two groups differ widely. Still other firms divide customers by age, income, or life-style to develop the work of the enterprise.

Organization by product

Manufacturing firms may have widely varied products that they market in different ways to their various customers. Therefore, they may divide their work by products. For example, a manufacturer of costume jewelry may divide work by metal jewelry, stone-set jewelry, pearls, and novelties.

Organization by specialization

Another method of dividing work is by the technology required to do it. Information processing, for example, requires specially trained, knowledgeable persons. Whether information is being processed by data processing, word processing, or an integrated system of data and word processing, the equipment and the skilled workers required set the work apart from that performed in other units of the enterprise. Separate organizational structures are sometimes developed for such specialized work.

Organization by time shift

Some firms are open for selling or service to customers much more than the forty hours that most employees work. For example, telephone companies, transportation systems, telegraph services, taxi companies, supermarkets, drug stores, department and specialty stores, hospitals, and fire and police departments are typical enterprises that run on shifts. Each time shift of workers needs at least part of the entire work force. Therefore, dividing work by time shifts helps to organize the work and to ensure continuation of service regardless of the hour at which it is needed.

Matrix organization

The normal flow of assignments and authority is from the top to the bottom of the enterprise through the chain of command. As technology has increased, as firms have become more complex, and as knowledge has increased, decision making has come to require the abilities of specialists from different parts of the enterprise. Therefore, enterprises have begun to use a type of organization known as *matrix organization* (see Figure 3–6).

The purpose of this type of organization is to work on special projects or solve special problems, such as those involved in producing a new product or developing a new service. Specialists from various parts of the enterprise are brought together to share their expertise and solve the problems. Depending on the time needed for resolution of the problems, team members are either released from their regular jobs and assigned to the new team for a given period of time, or they devote just part of their work week to the new assignment and the remainder of their time to their regular job. A team leader is appointed to supervise the group. This person has temporary authority for the group's activities.

These teams are task oriented; that is, the members are assigned for special work and they remain together until that particular assignment

FIGURE 3-6
MATRIX ORGANIZATION

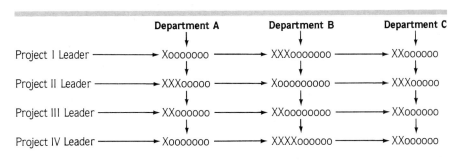

X—Employees assigned to the special project
o—Employees remaining in the original department
↓—Regular authority
→—Temporary authority

is finished. They then either return to their original department full time or move on to other team assignments or departments.

For example, if a magazine publisher is arranging for a special issue, a team consisting of members of the editorial, design, marketing, and sales departments may be brought together to work out the problems associated with this particular issue. When their work on this issue is finished, the team is disbanded.

Matrix organization has several advantages:

o People with specialized expertise are brought together to solve specific problems or develop specific projects.

o The team leader is appointed for the special expertise that he or she has.

o The team leader's role is to see that the objectives of the organization are being met by the employees assigned to the team. However, this leader does not have the routine supervisory duties of the ordinary department head.

o The people chosen for the teams consider the assignment to be a reward for their previous contributions to the achievement of the goals of the firm.

o Novelty or change is introduced into the workplace.

However, matrix organization also has several disadvantages:

o The people who left their original departments may feel out of tune when they return after a period of working with the other team members.

o Team members may have been overlooked when promotions and raises were given out in their regular departments.

o New work and different procedures may have been instituted during the team members' absence, and they may feel like strangers in their own departments.

o The team project may have been more exciting than the regular work assignments, so the team members may become bored when they return to their regular tasks.

o Regular departments are disrupted by losing key members to special assignments.

Combinations of organizational groupings

Most of the organizational plans discussed involve dividing work by more than one consideration. For example, if a bank needs various shifts to cover its customer-service hours, a representative number of tellers, bank vault personnel, guards, new-account advisers, and special-services personnel, as well as a bank manager or assistant manager, need to be available for each shift. Thus, the bank is organized by both time shifts and functions.

If a public-relations firm assigns its personnel by type of client, each client has to have assigned people who can develop reports, write speeches, do graphics, write press releases, develop brochures, and give advice on image creation. Therefore, organization is by client and function.

An enterprise organized by territory similarly must have in each branch a number of people for finance, production, marketing, personnel, purchasing, and any other function the firm requires. Thus, territory and function are the bases of organization.

Organization by line and by staff functions

The main tasks done to achieve the goals of an enterprise are the *line functions*. Activities that assist line workers to do a better job are *staff functions*.

The line organization

In small, uncomplicated firms, such as the Quick-Copy Company, a line organization exists. In a line organization, each person knows to whom to report and from whom to take orders. Each works on the primary function of the enterprise, which, in this company, is to produce copies of prepared materials for customers speedily, and at low cost. The owner of the firm, however, has many additional tasks to perform that are staff duties. Mr. Sharp has to keep records of sales, prepare checks weekly for payment of his employees, keep tax records, and send necessary payments to the government. He also has to make deposits of receipts of money to the firm's bank account. In addition to these record-keeping tasks, he has to purchase and pay for supplies, arrange for machines to be kept in good condition, see that windows are washed at intervals, and keep the area clean for customers and workers. As needed, he must arrange with a sign painter for additional signs for his shop. On occasion, as business increases, he must hire additional employees.

After Mr. Sharp decided to promote an employee to be his assistant, he also allocated some of his extra duties to this young man, thus reducing the number of tasks he performed, but still retaining his line organization. If, on the other hand, he had hired an outside bookkeeper one day a week to aid in keeping the books, that person would perform a staff function.

The staff organization

The organization of the Quick-Copy Company is simpler than that of most enterprises. Most modern business is quite complex. Thus, in a large firm, specialists need to be employed to solve problems that line personnel do not have the expertise to work out. These specialists perform *staff functions.* Examples of staff personnel include researchers, tax experts, systems analysts, data and word processors, expediters, psychologists, employment people, and trainers. Many times, the specialists become a permanent part of the enterprise. When they do, the structure of the enterprise changes from line organization to *line and staff organization.*

Because some of the work different departments do helps other departments, some departments serve as staff to others. For example, the personnel department may in itself be a line department, keeping records of employment, salaries, raises, absences, fringe benefits, promotions, and length of service. But since it aids other departments to screen potential employees, it also serves as staff to them. The operations department performs line functions when maintaining the building, the flow of traffic in the building, and the smooth functioning of the elevators and escalators. But when it moves the goods ordered by the purchasing department to the designated areas, it serves as staff. Similarly, when the purchasing department buys goods and supplies for all the departments, it performs a staff function. Staff, then, means not only specialists from outside the firm but also specialists within the firm whose expertise aids other departments to perform their work.

Nonfunctional and functional authority

Within a firm, staff personnel may be given one of two kinds of authority: nonfunctional and functional. *Nonfunctional authority* is the right of staff personnel *only* to advise, assist, and provide service to line personnel. In this case, only line personnel have the authority and responsibility to perform the functions, or major work, of the enterprise. Staff personnel may not decide, order, or control in matters pertaining to line.

Nonfunctional authority is illustrated by the Ready-Riter Company, which has several branches headed by branch managers. The company provides temporary office help for any kind of office. Recently, some of the branch managers had complaints that their temporary helpers were not producing as effectively as they had in previous years. The main office of the firm decided to employ a specialist to analyze their testing process to see if it was properly screening and evaluating employees. Mr. Kramer, an expert on testing, was hired. After analyzing the old program and developing a new one, he was sure that the new one was an improvement. However, as he made his rounds to the branch offices, he was careful merely to suggest that the managers adopt the new program. If a manager objected to the additional expenditure of time and money needed to institute the new program, Mr. Kramer merely reiterated its advantages and left a copy of the new tests and procedures for the manager to examine. He carefully observed the role of a staff specialist having nonfunctional authority.

In other cases, staff personnel are given the power to make decisions and issue orders in a department other than their own; that is, they are given *functional authority*. This authority is granted by the higher management of the enterprise. For example, if Mr. Kramer had been given functional authority to implement his testing program, he would have had an entirely different relationship with the branch managers. Since he believed that he had an improved program, he would have been able to order its adoption by each branch.

When staff personnel have functional authority, the position of the line manager is weakened and the unity of command is violated. On the other hand, when staff personnel have nonfunctional authority and can only suggest what needs to be done and must depend on others to do it, they may become frustrated. In addition, when a staff specialist is in the position of adviser, he or she may see only the specific problem being wrestled with and not all the problems that line personnel may have to handle by putting his or her advice into effect.

The staff specialist may also have a feeling of superiority to the line personnel with whom he or she must work. Therefore, friction may develop between those who must carry out the work and those who are seen as advisers. Unless the conflicts between what the specialist recommends and what the line personnel must do are resolved, the flow of work and the effectiveness of a department or a firm may be seriously impaired.

Concern for the efficient functioning of the entire enterprise should ultimately take precedence in resolving problems of conflicting authority. One group should not gain control over another unless the efficiency and productivity of the firm are improved.

The formal and informal organization

All the structures discussed previously comprise the *formal organization* of an enterprise. The people in authority decide the type of structure and delegate the authority and responsibility for tasks in an orderly fashion. However, within each enterprise there also exists another kind of organization.

Employees of a firm or department informally meet and talk with one another in cafeterias, elevators, hallways, at their work stations and a variety of other places. These casual contacts and conversations form the basis of the *informal organization*.

Whereas the formal organization is created by management, the informal organization is created by its own members. Just as the formal organization has leaders (managers), the informal organization also has people who take charge. These informal leaders are chosen by their own peers and have no authority vested in them by the firm. Although they lack formal authority, informal leaders can often affect the production and the attitudes toward work of the other employees. Most informal leaders help managers in a positive way and keep the work force operating efficiently. Occasionally, though, informal leaders may deter other workers from doing their jobs. They may ask peers to slow their performance or make other discouraging comments. When workers are dissatisfied with some aspect of their employment, their informal leader usually becomes their spokesperson and is the one who initiates slowdowns, work stoppages, or, in rare cases, sabotage on behalf of the group.

Supervisors who are alert to relationships within their departments know about the informal organization and its activities. If the activities are making the workers more efficient, the supervisor usually encourages them. If, however, the activities are slowing work or hampering communication, the supervisor must take the necessary steps to offset the informal organization and to reestablish the channels of authority that will expedite work.

SUMMARY

o Policies are statements of principles and standards that help an enterprise achieve its goals. Major policies are general guides formulated by the top executives of the firm. Minor policies are derived from the major policies for use by specific departments. In large enterprises, policies should be written to ensure that all employees receive the same information about the firm's standards.

o Procedures are the guides to actions that must be taken to observe the firm's policies. Rules and regulations are controls over employees that state exactly what may and what may not be done.

o Enterprises are hierarchical. Orders and directives pass from the top-level managers to those lower on the scale. The path that they take is the chain of command. Each different level of management separates workers from the top executives and complicates communication.

o Authority is the right of a supervisor to give job-related orders to a subordinate, to make decisions, and to take actions that will help achieve the goals of the enterprise. Responsibility is the obligation to perform assignments as needed to obtain the goals of the enterprise. Both are essential at every level of the hierarchy.

o Unity of command means that each employee should be responsible to just one boss.

o Span of control is the number of subordinates one person can successfully supervise. It may vary from a few people to many, depending on a variety of factors. No optimal span of control exists.

o Organization is the division of the work to be done into parts and the integration of those parts into the whole.

o Enterprises can be organized in a variety of ways: by function, by territory, by clients, by products, by specialization, or by time shifts. In addition, firms may use matrix organization or a combination of organizational groupings.

o Line functions are the main tasks done to achieve goals. Staff functions are those activities that help line workers perform their jobs more effectively. With nonfunctional authority, staff specialists may merely advise line personnel. With functional authority, staff members may require that their recommendations be carried out by line personnel.

o The formal organization is established by management and has assigned lines of authority and responsibility. The informal organization is developed by the workers, who choose leaders to set their
standards and to decide their work loads and general responses to
management. The supervisor should try to use the informal organization to further the goals of the enterprise and keep it from hampering
the effectiveness of the workers.

REVIEW AND DISCUSSION QUESTIONS

1. What is a policy? Why must policies be flexible even though objectives have not changed?
2. What is the chain of command? How do orders pass through an
   enterprise? How do complaints from employees pass through an enterprise? What is unity of command? Why is reporting to just one
   boss desirable?
3. Differentiate between authority and responsibility. Why must both
   be delegated to a supervisor?
4. What is the span of control? List and explain five factors that affect
   the span of control.
5. Why is work organized? What is meant by an organization chart?
6. How might firms be organized by territory? By product? By specialization? By time shifts?
7. What is matrix organization? What advantages does it offer? What
   are its disadvantages?
8. What is a line organization? A staff organization? Why do most
   large firms have both line and staff organizations?
9. How does functional authority of staff personnel weaken the line
   manager's authority?
10. Discuss the role of the informal organization in a firm. What is the
    supervisor's responsibility in relation to the informal organization?

ASSIGNMENTS

1. Analyze a student organization, fraternity or sorority, or any other
   group of which you have been a member. Who led the group? How
   was that person chosen as leader? Did other people have assignments, such as collecting money, planning programs or activities,
   keeping minutes, or sending out notices of the meetings, to perform
   for the group? Draw up an organization chart for the group. Is it
   organized by function? Is your group a branch or division of a larger
   group (such as a national fraternity)? If so, show the relationship to
   the parent organization. How many levels of authority are there in

the group? What is the span of control for the leader of the group? Does the group have written rules? If not, how are the members informed about the rules and regulations? Write a report of your findings.

2. If you have ever worked, answer the following questions by using your work experience. If not, use your position as a student to respond. From whom do you take orders and directives? Who checks your work to be sure it is done according to certain standards? Do you have more than one person giving you assignments? If so, what difficulties, if any, does this cause? Is the person to whom you report in a line or a staff position? Draw a chart to show the chain of command from you upward to the top of the hierarchy.

PROBLEM FOR RESOLUTION

Gregory Sharp, the owner of the Quick-Copy Company, decided to expand his firm to offer a typing service for students to use for reports, master's theses, and doctoral dissertations. To do this, he rented another office adjoining the present shop, bought three electric typewriters and one word-processing machine, and installed shelves to hold supplies and file cabinets to protect work in process. He hired three good typists and one word-processing specialist, whom he asked to supervise the typists' work in addition to doing some work on the word-processing machine. He now had five employees including an assistant in his copy area, and four employees including an assistant in his typing division.

Draw up an organization chart for his enlarged operation.

CASE STUDY

Ms. Belding, a young woman who has just entered her only child in the first grade, secured a temporary position with a government agency in her home town. She wanted to work long enough to buy the refrigerator that she needed. The job for which she was hired was a routine, rather uninteresting clerical position, but Ms. Belding thought she would like to do the job well in case she wanted to be rehired later. After she was shown how to do the work by the supervisor, Ms. Falcon, she was given a pile of materials to sort. She began to work. Ms. Falcon watched for a short time to see if she had any questions. When Ms. Belding appeared to grasp what she had to do, Ms. Falcon walked to her office and closed her door.

Ms. Belding found the work to be quite easy, and she began to speed her production. She noticed that about ten other people around her were doing similar tasks.

After about an hour, a Ms. Girard, another worker in that section, tapped her on the shoulder and asked, "Where's the fire?" Ms. Belding answered superficially and continued to work. After a few minutes, Ms. Girard asked, "Are you trying to show the rest of us up?"

Ms. Belding was surprised at that question. She paused long enough to reply, "No. I just wanted to get this pile of work done quickly."

"Well," Ms. Girard explained, "you are just here on a temporary assignment. The rest of us work here the year 'round. If we worked at your speed, we would all be worn out and there would not be enough work for all of us. So, just cool it. Don't try to break any speed records. Remember, all of us are watching you."

Ms. Belding glanced around and she noticed ten pairs of eyes directed at her. Reluctantly, she slowed her production to match that of the workers around her.

Analyze this situation. Was the formal supervisor doing her job correctly? *no* *No quality control*

What role did Ms. Girard play? Who was actually controlling production? *informal group leader, Girard & other members* *created by members*

What should Ms. Belding do in a situation such as this? What should Ms. Falcon, the supervisor, do about it? *Go to Supervisor, Observe more*

Would you have slowed your production as Ms. Belding did? Explain. *No*

FURTHER READING

Famularo, Joseph J. *Organization Planning Manual.* New York: American Management Association, 1971.

  Provides organization charts of various types of companies, and includes information on how the organizations developed and the jobs within them.

George, Claude S., Jr. "How Your Company Is Organized." In *Supervision in Action: The Art of Managing Others.* Reston, Va.: Reston Publishing Company, 1979, pp. 240–70.

  Shows the organizational structure of a typical company and how organization charts are made and used.

Hampton, David R. "Organizing." In *Contemporary Management.* New York: McGraw-Hill, 1977, pp. 199–245.

  Explains alternative ways of dividing an organization into departments, need for coordination, centralization and decentralization, and how work is divided into jobs for groups and individuals.

Kemball-Cook, R. B. *The Organization Gap.* London: George Allen & Unwin, 1972.

Discusses the study and design of organizational structures, and methods of understanding and solving organizational information.

Matteis, Richard J. "The New Back Office Focuses on Customer Service." *Harvard Business Review,* March–April 1979, pp. 146–59.

Explains how Citibank redesigned the jobs in its services-management group for greater efficiency.

Schwartz, David. Chapters 8–10. In *Introduction to Management: Principles, Practices, and Processes.* New York: Harcourt Brace Jovanovich, 1980, pp. 206–90.

Covers the organizing process, basic organizing principles, departmentalization, span of control, and line and staff authority.

Slocum, John W., Jr., and Don Hellriegel. "Using Organizational Designs to Cope with Change." *Business Horizons,* December 1979, pp. 65–76.

Explains how, in order to operate efficiently in the face of uncertainty and rapid change, managers must employ organizational principles appropriate to the demands of each firm's business environment.

the skillful supervisor

4

the supervisor as a decision maker

After studying and analyzing this chapter, you should be able to:

Explain the decision-making process through the stages of recognizing the problem, determining the information needed, analyzing the information, considering alternative choices, making the decision, communicating the decision, and evaluating the decision.

Explain the factors that affect supervisory decision making.

Discuss how supervisors vary as decision makers.

Identify the skills and abilities that able supervisors possess.

Explain how appearance, attitude, and many other abilities affect the work the supervisor does.

Differentiate between leadership and supervision.

Describe a workable time-management system for an efficient supervisor.

Discuss how self-evaluation can aid a supervisor.

THE TWO MOST IMPORTANT tasks that a supervisor performs are decision making and communicating. Many skills and abilities contribute to the success of the supervisor in carrying out those two tasks. In Chapter 4, the skills the supervisor needs that are related to decision making are discussed. In Chapter 5, the many ways the supervisor communicates decisions and other pertinent information are analyzed.

Decision making

Decision making, an inherent part of the supervisor's job, pervades every function performed and every problem faced. It involves developing a conscious choice by selecting among alternatives. Decisions may be made about both familiar and unfamiliar tasks and problems: Who shall do it or resolve it? What would be the best way to do it? Where would it best fit into the smooth functioning of the organization? When should it be undertaken? How should it be done? Why should it be done that way?

Steps in decision making

Because decisions are made constantly both on important and unimportant matters, the steps taken to resolve problems may not be evident. However, the following steps are present in all decision making.

Recognize the problem. Problems that need resolution abound in any enterprise. They may concern such factors as people (employees, customers, vendors, competitors), government rulings or laws, industry agreements, physical accommodations, ways of conducting the enterprise, productivity, and introduction of new projects or products. The supervisor must be alert to factors that need alleviation, that might disrupt the work force, or that might lead to more serious problems unless they are resolved.

For example, if a usually industrious employee suddenly becomes lax and disinterested in the job, the supervisor should be alert to these changes. If a productive department suddenly becomes unproductive, the supervisor should recognize the reduction in output.

Recognizing the problem as soon as it occurs is an important challenge for the supervisor. Once the supervisor recognizes the problem, it should be verbalized: Ms. Avery has changed from an interested to a disinterested employee, or production has dropped. The accurate statement of the problem enables the supervisor to move to the next steps that will help in its resolution.

<u>Determine what information is needed to solve the problem</u>.   Once the problem has been recognized, the supervisor must determine what information, if any, is needed to solve it. In the case of Ms. Avery, the supervisor may want to discuss the evidence with her to find out what, if anything can be pinpointed, has caused the change. The supervisor may also want to review her work-history record in the personnel office. If production has slumped, the supervisor may want to watch the employees to see where the slow-ups have occurred and question them about the reasons for the delays.

After the supervisor uncovers some of the facts, a decision may be possible. If more facts are needed, the supervisor may go to other sources for more information. For example, he or she may find that production has lowered because equipment is getting old and, therefore, functioning less effectively. The supervisor is not likely to be able to gather all the necessary facts, but informed judgments in addition to the available facts will help the decision maker.

<u>Analyze the available information</u>.   After assembling the information that is available, the supervisor should analyze it. The supervisor may need to determine how much is wrong with the new equipment. After talking with Ms. Avery, the supervisor may find that she is having home problems.

<u>Consider alternative choices</u>.   The supervisor next considers the alternatives available to solve the problem. Is it better to repair or to replace the faulty equipment? How much would each solution cost, and which would fit into the budget?

Is any employee personally close enough to Ms. Avery to help her with her home problem, or should she be urged to consult a counselor? Could other actions, such as giving her a few days off or placing her in a less demanding job temporarily, be taken? Which solutions would be most likely to help her?

<u>Make the decision</u>.   Once all the alternatives have been examined, the supervisor is ready to choose the action to take. If repairing the equipment would not be too costly, or if the budget could not accommodate the cost of new equipment, the supervisor might have to opt for repair.

If, after talking with Ms. Avery, the supervisor believes that putting her temporarily into another job may relieve tension, that might be the decision.

<u>Communicate the decision</u>.   Once a decision has been made, everyone who might be affected by it must be informed. For example, Ms. Avery had been working on mailing lists, a job that involved not only careful checking, but also removing incorrect names and addresses from the list,

inserting others in alphabetical order, and then keyboarding them into the memory bank of the computer. When pressure was on for the lists to be finished, she had to work at top speed. Many people tended to hover over her to see that she was getting the work done.

When the supervisor decided to move her into another area of work that would relieve the pressure and remove the tension of the job, the need arose to discuss this move with her co-workers and with the other supervisors who relied on the mailing lists for their work. If the supervisor had neglected to inform them, many problems might have arisen for the person who was taking Ms. Avery's place. Also, many people might speculate about Ms. Avery's job change and end up gossiping about those speculations.

Evaluate the success of the decision.   After making the decision and communicating it to all relevant people, the supervisor must analyze how effective that choice was in resolving the problem. If the repaired equipment allows the employees to regain their earlier production record, the solution may be considered to be satisfactory for the time being. If the equipment continues to break down, however, the decision would need to be reevaluated. An appeal for a budgetary supplement to buy new equipment may need to be made. The supervisor also may have the option of buying slightly used equipment at a lower cost than that of new equipment, again necessitating a decision among alternatives.

If Ms. Avery appears to be able to function effectively in her new position, she may be left there until she requests a return to her former job. If she does not function well, another alternative might be chosen to try to restore her usefulness to the enterprise.

The various steps in decision making are illustrated in Figure 4–1.

Factors that affect supervisory decisions

Decisions may be major or minor; based on constraints or "free-floating"; concerned with the entire group or just one person; and made by just the supervisor or the supervisor and others.

Major versus minor decisions.   In general, the higher supervisors are in the hierarchy of the firm, the more important the decisions that they make. Conversely, the lower the level of supervisors, the less sweeping the decisions that they make. However, regardless of whether a decision is major or minor, each one can affect to some degree the attainment of the goals of the organization. Therefore, all decisions have some measure of importance.

The more effort and the more employees needed to carry out a decision, the more it is considered to be major. For example, deciding which products to develop during the next year is far more important

FIGURE 4–1
STEPS IN DECISION MAKING

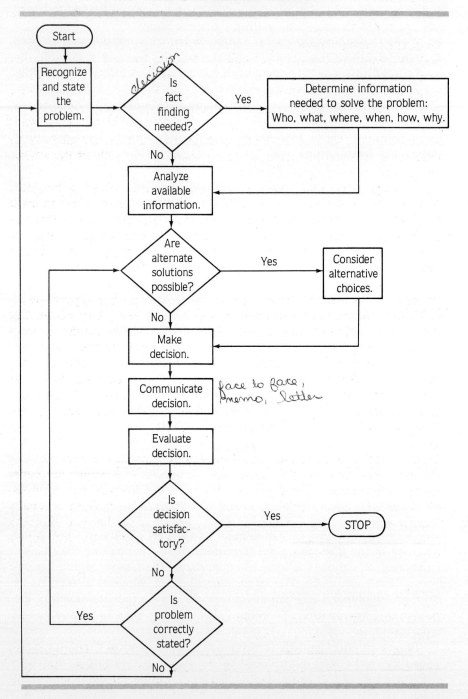

than deciding what the color of the office walls should be. Or, deciding the payment policy for all employees is far more important than deciding if one employee's pay should be docked for unauthorized time off.

Constrained versus free-floating decisions. *Constraints*, or limits placed on actions, often affect decisions. Policies, laws, rules, and agreements are constraints that may dictate the decision of the supervisor. For example, suppose the company policy is to pay employees for holidays if they work both the day before and the day after the holiday. If an employee has met those conditions, the decision must be to pay him or her. Or if an enterprise has an agreement to provide a certain quality goods to its customers, it may not decide to change those goods without the written consent of the customers affected.

  If no policies, laws, rules, or agreements are involved in the problem, the decision is *free-floating*. That is, the supervisor is free to make the best decision possible. For instance, if a supervisor notices that employees enjoy bringing their lunch to the work space and eating together, and there are no rules against this, he or she may set aside one office for the lunch-hour period as a meeting and eating place.

Decisions for the individual versus decisions for the group. If a supervisor decides that one employee deserves to have his or her salary raised, that decision is vastly different in scope from one to raise the minimum wage for all the employees in the department. The former decision may cost the firm a few hundred dollars a year, while the latter may cost many thousands of dollars. Making decisions on an individual basis may cause some employees to accuse the supervisor of favoritism. Making decisions for the entire group may disgruntle some employees who believe they deserve to be singled out for special merit.

Decisions made by a group versus those made by an individual. Although many decisions are made by the supervisor alone, some decisions are better made by the supervisor together with the employees or the other supervisors who have similar problems. Group decision making is usually more satisfactory than individual decision making for the same problem, since groups offer more alternatives, foresee more pitfalls, and supply expertise from several areas. *the more people involved, the more time it takes for a decision*

Decision-making supervisors

Supervisors differ in their desire to make decisions and in the speed with which they make decisions.

  Some supervisors dislike having to make decisions. They seek advice from their employees, peers, and superordinates before coming to any decision. Only when they have a consensus from their various sources are they willing to make a final choice. Other supervisors see decision making as a challenging part of their job. They enjoy both gathering the information necessary and later observing the results of their final judgment.

The speed of decision making may be related to the enjoyment of decision making. Those who dislike making decisions almost always take longer to come to a conclusion than those who enjoy decision making. Some supervisors delay decisions so long that they forego the advantages to be gained from any decision. When this affects productivity, they are either demoted or discharged. On the other hand, supervisors can make decisions too speedily, without taking enough time to consider alternatives properly. The result may be a new problem for the supervisor or the department.

Supervisors must make decisions that will further the overall goals of the enterprise. The more their decisions move the department ahead and meet the goals of the organization, the better the job they do.

Characteristics needed by decision-making supervisors

Ability refers to the capacity to perform given tasks or duties. If a supervisor has been promoted through the ranks, he or she may be able to perform any job in the department as competently as any other person currently holding the job. The ability to perform each job that one supervises is often important to have. However, in itself it does not necessarily make a person a good supervisor. Getting a job done through people requires a many-faceted individual. Thus, to be a successful supervisor, one needs to possess or develop a number of abilities and talents. These are discussed in the following sections.

Positive attitudes

Attitudes are shaped throughout a person's life. Research has indicated that successful supervisors have the following attitudes: singleness of purpose; anticipation of success in all activities; willingness to devote much time and energy to the job; commitment to, enjoyment of, and enthusiasm about the job; interest in subordinates' welfare; and willingness to accept new ideas and innovations.[1] These attitudes, in general, reflect a positive view of activities and people.

Some other positive attitudes and their negative counterparts that supervisors exhibit in the workplace include: pleasant or unpleasant, friendly or unfriendly, accepting or rejecting, helpful or frustrating, enthusiastic or unenthusiastic, relaxed or tense, close or distant, warm or cold, cooperative or uncooperative, supportive or hostile, harmonious or quarrelsome, self-assured or hesitant, cheerful or gloomy, and open or guarded.[2]

The results of a positive attitude.   Supervisors who have positive attitudes usually generate positive responses from their subordinates. More harmony, greater productivity, more willingness to cooperate, and a more pleasant atmosphere thereby result.

Contrast these two departments in the same company: Office A is headed by Phil Jones. He is an amiable man who daily greets his employees with a jolly, "Hi, how are you doing? Isn't this a fine day to be coming to work?" or similar remark. As each person goes to his or her station, Mr. Jones walks around to see if he can be of any help. When he later goes into his office, he leaves the door open. Employees know they are welcome to stop by to ask questions or to make comments about their work. When they leave in the evening, he sees them out with a smile. He calls each person by name and makes some comment such as, "Good evening. Enjoy yourself tonight. See you tomorrow—bright and early."

Office B is headed by Burton Delbert. He arrives each morning and goes directly to his office. Promptly at 9:00 A.M., he goes to his door to check that each employee is at his or her station. He neither smiles at nor greets anyone. He then closes his door. Employees who need to ask a question knock on the door and wait until he says, "Come in." He looks up from his work and grumbles, "What can I do for you?" Any question is answered brusquely. If Mr. Delbert thinks that the employee should have known the answer to the question, he reprimands him or her for wasting his time. During the day, Mr. Delbert walks around observing the workers. He never commends anyone, but he often condemns them for some action he dislikes. Shortly before quitting time, he silently stands at his door to be sure that no one leaves early.

Office A employees generally like their jobs and enjoy coming to work. Their productivity is high, and turnover is low. Conversely, Office B employees are usually resentful and somber. They have a moderate to low productivity, high absenteeism, and high turnover.

Conveying positive attitudes.   Supervisors must not only have positive attitudes, but they must convey them to subordinates. Attitudes are conveyed by a combination of what is said, what is done, and the manner in which action is taken. If what is said is positive, what is done supports what has been said, and enthusiasm is shown in doing it, a positive attitude is expressed to others.

If, on the other hand, what is said differs from the action that is taken, and if only halfhearted support is given to what is said, the attitude becomes diffused and contradictory. For example, Mercedes Froeling was told when she was employed that rules about time off were strict, but if a person had a good record, was loyal, and worked hard, an occasional short time-off period would be allowed. During the rush season, Ms. Froeling came in every morning fifteen or twenty minutes early and took only part of her lunch period. She put in the extra time not for overtime credit but because she wanted to do an outstanding job.

One day, she asked if she could leave work one hour early for an important appointment with her doctor. Her request was graciously approved by the supervisor, who said, "Certainly. You've shown yourself to be a very interested, capable worker." When Ms. Froeling received her pay, she was astounded to find that she had been docked for the time off. She realized that the supervisor's positive attitude was not reflected in her actions, so she started coming in just on time and relaxing during her full lunch period.

In conveying attitudes to subordinates, supervisors often influence subordinates' reactions. If a supervisor shows a positive attitude about an issue, a subordinate who is slightly in favor of it or neutral about it may be swayed to positive action. However, a subordinate who has strong feelings against the matter may be made more antagonistic than ever by the positive feelings expressed by the supervisor.

Studies of attitude change reveal that people who have firmly held positions on a given issue reject ideas that do not support their position. People who have taken no position or who see advantages on both sides of an issue, however, can be swayed to change their attitudes. Unless the supervisor can determine the cause of a firmly held attitude, no amount of persuasion is likely to alter it.

Knowledge of the supervisor's job

Knowledge of the supervisor's job is threefold. To a certain degree, supervisors must know how to do the jobs for which they are responsible. They must know how to manage and supervise, and they must know task abilities. A supervisor's knowledge of the job and ability to perform it is revealed by the productivity of the department.

Knowledge of subordinates' tasks. The degree to which a supervisor must be able to perform the tasks that he or she oversees depends on two factors. The first is whether or not the supervisor needs to teach subordinates how to perform those tasks. For example, the supervisor of a typing pool need not know how to type to be able to point out the errors in a letter. On the other hand, if this supervisor needs to teach subordinates how to check material, he or she must know the proper way of doing it.

The second factor is the level of supervision. The supervisor of introductory-level workers usually has to know how each job is done in order to oversee the tasks performed. But most supervisors of higher-echelon workers find their managerial and supervisory knowledge to be more important than their need for special skills because their employees are more experienced and knowledgeable. A top executive who supervises an executive secretary and several vice-presidents has little need to worry about their skills. The supervisor of a word-processing center, on the other hand, may need to be particularly proficient in arranging material on a page, spacing, spelling, and proofreading.

Knowledge of management and supervision.   All supervisors must also be able to manage. That is, they must know how to plan, organize, direct, coordinate, control, and consolidate. In addition, they must have knowledge of all the supervisory aspects of the manager's job.

Knowledge of task abilities.   *Task abilities* are skills that allow supervisors to function on the job. Depending on their job requirements, supervisors may need to be able to buy goods, sell products, promote products or services, keep accounts or records, operate special machines, proofread, or check materials. These tasks are needed in addition to those necessary to supervise employees.

Leadership ability

The word *leadership* has been defined in various ways. Figure 4–2 shows a composite definition. Note that in order to lead a person must have one or more followers.

Leaders can evolve in a number of ways. They may be *chosen* by the group, as informal leaders are (many believe that this method is a true test of leadership); *appointed* by someone in authority, as supervisors and managers are; *born* to the role, as kings and queens are; *elected*, as some government officials are; or *self-appointed* and even perpetuated in office by force, if necessary, as some dictators are.

Supervisors as leaders.   As noted in Chapter 3, within an enterprise there are two kinds of leaders. *Informal leaders* are chosen by their peers and are not designated as leaders by the formal organization. *Formal leaders* are appointed by the formal organization. The ability to lead is generally assumed to be one of the prerequisites for the position of supervisor. Why?

Supervisors are responsible for the accomplishment of certain work. Supervisors, in turn, assign subordinates to do certain parts of the jobs. To get subordinates to do their tasks most effectively, supervisors must guide, control, direct, and stimulate them and their actions. That is, su-

›

FIGURE 4–2
WHAT IS LEADERSHIP?

LEADERSHIP
IS

task	function
process	requisite
power	

OF

influencing	stimulating
releasing	controlling
making	directing
guiding	coordinating
facilitating	

EMPLOYEES'

actions	attitudes
capacities	energies
decisions	activities

TOWARD

goal setting	a desired situation
goal achievement	getting work done
goal changing	a common cause
action	desired accomplishment

pervisors must lead subordinates. If supervisors were unable to get proper responses from workers, they would not retain their positions very long.

The ability to lead is based on a number of factors. Personality, knowledge, and understanding of good personnel practice used in working with subordinates and peers are some. In addition, supervisors must be able to get along with people, present information about the job to be done, energize the group, follow up, and sense the reaction of the group in order to fulfill the leadership requirement of their job. Effective leadership is shown primarily by the high productivity of the group that is headed by the supervisor.

Leadership styles. There are several styles of leading: autocratic, democratic, laissez-faire, and a combination of these.

Supervisors who are *autocratic leaders* usually like to make decisions on their own. They assume full responsibility for the work of their departments and ask only that employees be completely obedient. They usually check frequently to see that orders are being carried out. Employees who work for autocratic bosses know what is expected of them and what standards of work are acceptable, and are usually able to function effectively under such supervisors. Autocratic bosses rarely seek advice or accept suggestions from their employees. *1. low morale 2. low productivity*

Supervisors who are *democratic leaders* seek opinions from their followers, ask that employees help to set the department's goals, and ask employees to help make decisions about their work. They believe that workers who have a role in decision making will enjoy their work more and contribute enthusiastically to increasing production. Decision making under a democratic supervisor usually takes more time than that under an autocratic boss. *1. high morale 2. high productivity*

Supervisors who are *laissez-faire*, or *free-rein*, leaders allow employees to take full responsibility for decisions and control of their own work. They answer questions and help employees when asked, but they take no role in directing or coordinating the work of the department. *everybody lacks direction* This type of leadership has both serious disadvantages and important advantages. New or inexperienced employees rarely prosper under it because chaos often results. Conversely, highly skilled specialists may be more successful in achieving high productivity than they would be under either of the other types because they are left to work on their own.

Combinations of two or three methods may be used by some supervisors. They may, on occasion, be autocratic. For other tasks, they may be democratic, and on some occasions they may give their employees free rein. The main disadvantage of this mixed method is that the employees never know which approach the supervisor will use. Most employees function better if the supervisory style is consistent.

Creativity

Creativity is the ability to get something done through original thinking or actions. Creativity means freeing oneself from doing things as they are normally done, seeing unique ways of accomplishing tasks, and daring to try the unusual. Supervisors need to be creative in order to perform tasks in innovative ways and to develop new tasks and different

good communication of goals

ways to raise productivity. A supervisor's creativity helps an enterprise to realize goals, raise productivity, and increase services.

An example of a creative solution to a minor problem is illustrated by the following situation. Mary, Jack, Annabel, and Fred were assigned to work in a small office adjacent to a corner meeting room that was rarely used. The door to the meeting room was always closed. The office had an air conditioner, but the four had agreed to use it only on hot, sticky days to save energy. On other days, all the employees except Annabel liked to open the windows to have a breeze. Annabel objected. She said that she could not stand the air that blew on her back and that it gave her a stiff neck. As soon as someone opened a window, Annabel shut it. The supervisor noticed that tension was building over this seemingly unimportant matter.

One day, the supervisor opened the windows in the meeting room and the door to the office. The breeze that came from that source satisfied Mary, Jack, and Fred, and Annabel said it did not bother her. Everyone relaxed, tension diminished, and the workers proceeded to get jobs done efficiently. By this simple action, the supervisor had creatively solved the situation.

Ability to manage time

The ability to manage time is particularly important for supervisors to have, since they have many things to do. Supervisors must complete assignments on schedule and, at the same time, think about ways to improve the productivity of their areas. In addition, they usually must deal with many unanticipated interruptions. Telephone calls, visits by clients, emergency problems with employees, and additional assignments are examples of *contingencies,* or unplanned events, that use up supervisors' time. Such a hectic working situation requires that time be managed efficiently.

A carefully developed time-management program can help supervisors get important work accomplished. In developing such a program, they find the following four steps helpful.

Make a list of tasks to be done.   In today's fast-moving business and industrial world, any list of tasks to be done is only partial. During any one day, additional tasks will almost always have to be added to the list. To solve this problem, one executive keeps a pad by his desk, and as each job arises following a discussion, telephone call, or other event, he notes what must be accomplished. Whenever he leaves the office on business, he takes the pad so he can amend the list as new tasks develop.

Making a list of tasks to be performed has several advantages. First, the list is a reminder of what needs to be done. Second, it shows definitively how much must be accomplished. Third, it allows time limits to be set for each task. Finally, it provides an opportunity to check that all facets of each task—the boss's needs and expectations, the area's needs and expectations, the subordinates' needs and expectations, and the relationship of the task to the overall work of the firm—are being considered.

Set priorities. When the list is complete, urgent, less urgent, and delayable tasks (if any) must be differentiated. The executive referred to previously marks urgent tasks with two stars and less urgent tasks with one star, leaving delayable tasks unstarred. The tasks may also be marked A, B, or C, for urgent, less urgent, or delayable, respectively.

Schedule sufficient time for each task. A monthly or weekly calendar can be used to schedule time for the tasks. For each urgent task, the deadline should be filled in and time allotted by working backward from it. Holidays and previously scheduled meetings and appointments must be taken into account. Extra time needs to be allowed for emergencies. Inclement weather that prevents employees from getting to work, illness, and added work assignments are among the contingencies that supervisors must consider in planning the time each task will take.

A good idea is to leave a buffer time before a deadline, that is, to schedule no appointments for a period of one-half hour or more prior to any important meeting, deadline, or speech. This may accommodate any unusual delay in completing a task. Finally, time should be left free for daily needs that are likely to occur. Most supervisors find that at least one hour needs to be allotted for unexpected interruptions.

After the urgent tasks have been scheduled, the operation should be repeated for the less urgent tasks. In the time left, all the delayable tasks possible should be placed.

The daily schedule should be checked to see how it fits with the long-term planning. Each morning, priorities for the day should be checked. A balance must be kept between things that must be accomplished that day and the long-term projects.

As each task is completed, it should be crossed off the list. Doing so will keep the list up to date and give a sense of accomplishment, since the number of tasks to be done will decrease.

Depending on the frequency with which additional tasks must be added to the list, a new one may be made daily, weekly, or monthly. Tasks not crossed off the previous list must be added to the new list, given a priority rating, and scheduled.

Make adjustments as needed. Even though the supervisor has scheduled carefully and left buffer times, additional adjustments usually have to be made. Any decisions about how to accomplish the work must be made with higher productivity in mind.

If work is not being done efficiently, the work of the department should be analyzed. The supervisor should make a list of all the tasks that are normally assigned to him or her, plus the telephone calls, mail, messages, and other routines that are handled. Each task should be done by the person who can do it most efficiently. The way in which common tasks are handled should be preplanned so that no one wastes time doing them. Using form letters, responding by telephone rather than mail, and delegating any work possible will free the supervisor for more important matters.

Whenever possible, all materials should be handled only once. Mail should be answered promptly so that it is no longer around to clutter the desk and be rehandled. Efficient, immediate filing of material further speeds work. Everyone concerned should know the filing system. Things removed should be put back promptly and in the right place. Searching for unfiled or misfiled materials is a needless waste of time and prevents more important things from getting done on schedule.

Sometimes, to meet deadlines for urgent tasks, supervisors *block interruptions* (are unavailable for telephone calls, unexpected visitors, or other unanticipated events) by secluding themselves and/or the subordinates involved. If the supervisor or any subordinates are working at unpleasant or tedious tasks, and productivity therefore decreases, those tasks should be interspersed with more pleasant work.

All of these methods will improve efficiency. And effective time management will better the productivity of both the supervisor and the subordinates.

Ability to take appropriate actions

How supervisors perform their jobs constitutes their *actions* and becomes the way in which they are judged. Employees tend to observe supervisors' actions and to determine the standards for the job more from the things supervisors do than from the things supervisors say. Employees often copy their supervisors. For example, a supervisor who is rude to people over the telephone may find the employees being similarly rude to callers.

There is no universal pattern by which employees react to supervisors. However, in general, the more dedicated, prompt, reliable, courteous, and able supervisors are, the more their subordinates will reflect those characteristics. Supervisors must be able to hold an imaginary mirror up to observe their actions if their effectiveness is to be analyzed.

Through their actions, supervisors demonstrate their abilities. If a supervisor knows how to be efficient but handles certain tasks inefficiently, his or her actions belie the ability. If a supervisor knows the steps to take to complete a job but skips some, causing a faulty end product, his or her actions supersede the ability. Thus, supervisors must demonstrate their abilities by their actions if they are to be successful.

Routine jobs allow supervisors to plan many of their day-to-day actions. However, in most jobs, unusual situations arise at unexpected times. Supervisors must be particularly alert to sense these events and be ready to take action on emergencies as efficiently as they handle routine work. Emergencies test the action-taking ability of supervisors more than routine tasks do.

Ability to work with superiors, peers, and subordinates

The position that supervisors hold involves simultaneously reporting to a superior, working with peers, and overseeing subordinates. At all three levels, supervisors must be equally effective.

Supervisors as subordinates. As subordinates, supervisors are delegated certain segments of their superiors' jobs. Supervisors can prove that they can handle those delegated tasks as well as their superiors by following this advice:[3]

- o Examine the assigned tasks from the superior's point of view.
- o Be informed about the job, careful, and accurate.
- o Know every facet of the job thoroughly.
- o Anticipate what the boss might want to know.
- o Do the job as fast as possible?
- o Communicate accurately and to the point at an appropriate time.
- o Assess one's own actions critically. Self-evaluate
- o Recommend improved ways of doing things, or present new ideas only after careful analysis of the past history of such matters.
- o Avoid complaints, excuses, buck-passing, personality conflicts, or going to the boss with minor problems.
- o Develop one's own subordinates so one does not become indispensable at the present level of assignment.

In addition, supervisors must have order-taking ability. Not only must they be leaders, they must also be good followers. To accomplish this, supervisors should accept orders graciously, follow them through expertly, and report back promptly on the outcome of each assignment.

Supervisors as peers. In large firms, supervisors usually have responsibilities on a par with other supervisors, their peers. Interaction within this group is usually necessary for work to be productively accomplished.

Working with peers requires that supervisors be cooperative, able to communicate effectively, and willing to assume an equal share of team responsibility.

Supervisors as superiors. The role of supervisors as superiors is the primary focus of this book. All supervisors hope that their subordinates will serve effectively as detailed previously. The goal of each supervisor when acting the role of superior is to communicate, hire, train, motivate, evaluate, counsel, reward, and discipline subordinates effectively, so that they will be productive and dedicated to the good of the enterprise.

Personal stability

Dependable, even-tempered, understanding, willing-to-work-hard, and emotionally mature people are those that exhibit *personal stability.* By contrast, undependable, ill-tempered, self-centered, lazy, and childish people lack personal stability. When the latter people become supervisors, they usually are unable to hold the position because they are rarely able to get employees to produce even moderately well.

Personally stable supervisors are levelheaded, know that crises will occur, but keep calm in the face of even multifaceted problems. They put the welfare of the employees and the goals of the organization first in making decisions and in taking action on those decisions.

Good appearance

Anyone meeting a person for the first time immediately sees his or her overall *appearance,* or way that person looks. What impression do you make on the casual observer? You may believe that "clothes do not make the person," but your clothes do affect the first impressions that people get of you.

In general, people dress the way their peers do. The college man or woman who has lived in jeans for four years suddenly emerges in an appropriate suit or other tailored clothing when he or she gets a job. The success-oriented person plays the role that has been assigned on the job. Any young person who has promotional aspirations will be particularly careful to be dressed appropriately at all times on the job. One never knows when the bosses will be making a tour of the place, or when one will accidentally meet a superior. Being dressed correctly always helps a person to feel at ease with others and frees him or her to concentrate on the issues at hand. Proper dress does not ensure supervisory success, but the successful supervisor is usually attired in a suitable manner. In addition to the right clothing, appropriate hairstyle, proper accessories, and absolute cleanliness should all be part of the total businesslike appearance of the concerned supervisor or supervisor-to-be.

A well-groomed, appropriate job appearance also shows that you respect the people with whom you work. A person who does not observe the amenities of proper dress and grooming implies that fellow workers are not worthy of the best efforts possible. *business - like dress*

Ability to evaluate oneself

Most firms spend considerable effort at specified times of the year on formal evaluations of employees. Informal evaluations, however, occur constantly. Every time an employee meets a superior, a peer, or a subordinate, informal evaluations take place. Supervisors, though, should also be able to evaluate themselves.

Supervisors can begin the self-evaluation process by asking themselves some general questions. For example:

o How well do I know my firm, my department, my work?

o How enthusiastic am I about my firm, my department, my work?

o How much reading and analysis do I do about the ongoing developments in my field?

o Do I organize and plan my work and the work of my department?

o Am I interested in my subordinates, and am I helping them to do a better job?

o How willing am I to listen to my subordinates and to concern myself with their problems?

o Do I believe others have ideas worth listening to?

o Do I have the ability to sell my ideas to my bosses? To my subordinates?

o Do I report promptly on the accomplishment of any task assigned by my superordinate?

Supervisors should evaluate themselves at the end of each day. By taking a few moments to review each of the activities of the day, each of the decisions made, and the results of their actions, supervisors can constantly improve their performance. More extensive evaluations should be made every six months. By comparing and analyzing them, supervisors will be able to improve abilities, modify actions, change attitudes, and spruce up appearance. Table 4–1 presents a form for self-evaluation. However, supervisors may wish to prepare one that more specifically fits their job.

TABLE 4–1
SUGGESTED FORM FOR SUPERVISOR'S SELF-EVALUATION

	Excellent	Very Good	Good	Fair	Poor	Not Applicable
Appearance						
Well-groomed						
Clean						
Business attire appropriate						
Attitudes						
Positive						
Cooperative						
Enthusiastic						
Friendly						
Interested in doing a good job						
Interested in and able to work with peers						
Interested in and able to work with subordinates						
Interested in and able to work with superordinates						
Optimistic						
Personal stability						
Supportive of firm's activities						
Willing to accept others' ideas						
Abilities						
Planning						
Organizing						
Directing						

(Continued)

(Table 4–1 continued)

	Excellent	Very Good	Good	Fair	Poor	Not Applicable
Coordinating						
Controlling						
Consolidating						
Leading						
Writing						
Speaking						
Listening						
Disciplining						
Decision making						
Technical aspects of job						
Quantity of output						
Quality of output						
Time management						
Creativity						
Actions Attendance						
Carry out orders						
Develop new procedures						
Maintain open door to employees						
Promptness						
Share knowledge						
Show no favoritism						

SUMMARY

o Decision making is an important aspect of the supervisor's job. The steps in decision making are to recognize the problem, determine what information is needed to solve it, analyze the available information, consider alternative choices, make the decision, communicate the decision, and evaluate the success of the decision, if necessary, considering other alternatives.

o Decisions may be major or minor, based on constraints or free-floating, concerned with the entire group or just one person, and made by just the supervisor or by the supervisor and others.

o Supervisors differ in their desire to make decisions and the speed with which they make decisions.

o To be effective, supervisors need to have positive attitudes toward their work and their employees and to be consistent in those attitudes.

o Knowledge of the job, including subordinates' tasks, management and supervision, and task abilities, is essential for the supervisor.

o Supervisors need leadership abilities to perform their job well. Leaders may use autocratic, democratic, laissez-faire, or a combination of styles in supervising.

o Supervisors often need to be creative in their solutions to department problems.

o Managing time successfully is one of the important skills the supervisor needs.

o The standards the supervisor sets must be followed by actions that conform to those standards.

o Able supervisors work effectively with their superiors, peers, and subordinates.

o Effective supervisors exhibit personal stability in working on the job and with people.

o Neatness, good grooming, and proper attire are attributes of effective supervisors.

o To be sure they are maximizing their potential in their jobs, supervisors should do an informal self-evaluation frequently and a more formal one at least every six months.

REFERENCES

[1]Herbert T. Mines, "Characteristics and Skills of Top Managers," *Personnel News and Views*, Winter 1977, pp. 7–12; and J. Kenneth Matejka, J. Donald Weinrauch, and Michael K. McCuddy, "The Relationship Between Perceptions of Success and Subordinate Ratings of Management," *Akron Business and Economic Review*, Spring 1977, pp. 50–52.

[2]Fred E. Fiedler, *A Theory of Leadership Effectiveness* (New York: McGraw-Hill, 1967), p. 41.

[3]Roy C. Smith, "How to Be a Good Subordinate," *New York Times*, November 25, 1979, Section 3, p. 16.

REVIEW AND DISCUSSION QUESTIONS

1. List and explain briefly the steps in the decision-making process.
2. Why are decisions that are made by knowledgeable groups usually better than decisions made by just one person?
3. Why are positive attitudes toward the job, workers on the job, and the work to be done important to the success of supervisors?
4. Why is leadership ability needed by a supervisor?
5. Differentiate among autocratic, democratic, and laissez-faire leadership styles. Under which type of leadership would you prefer to work? Give reasons for your answer.
6. What importance does creativity have in a supervisor's role?
7. Explain the rules for effective time management.
8. Why are the actions of the supervisor important?
9. Why must a supervisor be able to be a good subordinate?
10. Why is an appropriate businesslike appearance important for supervisors to have?

ASSIGNMENTS

1. If you have ever worked on a job, select your most recent supervisor to rate on the evaluation chart presented in Table 4–1. Use 5 for excellent, 4 for very good, 3 for good, 2 for fair, and 1 for poor. What is the overall rating of the supervisor? Explain the ratings given.

   If you have never worked, select a recent teacher as your model for the evaluation.
2. Think about some kind of supervisory experience you have had in sports, school organizations, or social groups. Using that experience, rate yourself on the evaluation chart. Does your rating exceed that of your supervisor or teacher, or does it fall short in some respects? Explain.

PROBLEM FOR RESOLUTION

The Supervisor's Weekly Calendar

	MONDAY	TUESDAY	WEDNESDAY	THURSDAY	FRIDAY
9–10 A.M.					
10–11 A.M.					
11–12 A.M.					
12–1 P.M.					
1–2 P.M.					
2–3 P.M.					
3–4 P.M.					
4–5 P.M.					

It is Monday morning, and a supervisor faces filling in the calendar for the week's activities. This supervisor and one secretary have the following tasks to accomplish by 5:00 P.M. on Friday, within the limits specified:

o Both the supervisor and the secretary go to lunch from 12:00–1:00 daily.

o Meetings with other divisions are scheduled on Tuesday from 10:00–12:00 and on Thursday from 3:00–5:00. The secretary will not attend these meetings.

o An interview with a young assistant to be considered for the department is scheduled for Tuesday at 1:00.

o The secretary must leave on Friday at 12.

o A ten-page report for a conference must be composed and typed. Writing the report will take five hours and will have to be done over a three-day period. Typing and proofreading will take a minimum of three hours for the secretary. Corrections and retyping will take another hour.

o A proposal for the introduction of a new product must be finished. The proposal has been written, but another hour is needed to revise and edit it before it can be typed. Typing and proofreading will take from three to four hours.

o Routine correspondence must be answered. This usually occupies the first two hours of each morning or the hours following a morning meeting. The typist fits this correspondence in whenever possible.

o Telephone queries from customers must be answered. These queries are sporadic, but often as many as ten occur in a day. Each requires five to ten minutes. These calls are usually answered by the supervisor.

Fill out the time allotments you would suggest for this supervisor so that all the work will be accomplished on time.

CASE STUDY

A supervisor of a large office force decided to phase out, as quickly as the budget would permit, the older typewriters in the department. These all used a carbon ribbon encased in a special type of cartridge, which did not fit other machines. Because the typists working on those machines wanted to be sure they had sufficient ribbons to last until they received new machines, they ordered large supplies of that special ribbon from the stockroom. As a result of these large orders, the stockroom head, in turn, increased his orders from the manufacturer for these ribbons.

At the end of the year, when inventory was taken, the stockroom head found he had several hundred dollars' worth of these typewriter ribbons in stock. He further noticed that for the past six months no one had ordered any. When he talked with the supervisor of the office force, he was told that the old-model typewriter was no longer in use in the firm and that those ribbons would not be ordered in the future.

Analyze this situation. Who was at fault for the excessive orders of the special typewriter ribbons? Could the situation have been avoided? *Supervisor, you by informing the stock room head* What action should have been taken? When? By whom? *Supervisor*

FURTHER READING

George, Claude S., Jr. "You and Your Job." In *Supervision in Action: The Art of Managing Others.* Reston, Va.: Reston Publishing Company, 1979, pp. 1–108.

Explains the role of the supervisor, the skills and qualities needed, the importance of leadership, how human relations affect supervision, and how to identify and solve problems.

Hackman, J. Richard, and J. Lloyd Suttle. *Improving Life at Work: Behavioral Science Approaches to Organizational Change.* Santa Monica, Calif.: Goodyear Publishing Company, 1977.

Attempts to lay the groundwork for improving the quality of the work experience of people in organizations. Demonstrates ways of increasing the productivity of those people. Explores changes in the design of work, in reward systems, in group and intergroup relations, and in supervisory roles, and relates those to the ways in which improvement might be obtained.

Hill, Napoleon, and W. Clement Stone. *Success Through a Positive Mental Attitude.* New York: Pocket Books, 1977.

Discusses principles that have worked for many people who have sought success through positive thinking and positive actions. Uses many examples to illustrate how people have changed from negative to positive thinking and how successful they have become.

Lorsch, Jay W. "Making Behavioral Science More Useful." *Harvard Business Review,* March–April 1979, pp. 171–80.

Explains that universal theories often do not fit the specific situation for which they are intended, and that supervisors must reject theories that are not relevant, diagnose situations, and use reason in determining changes that need to be made.

Nielsen, Eric H., and Jan Gypen. "The Subordinate's Predicaments." *Harvard Business Review,* September–October 1979, pp. 133–43.

Discusses dilemmas that commonly confront subordinates in their relationships with their supervisors. Explains how to become aware of these dilemmas and how to handle situations in order to reduce friction and make solutions to problems possible.

Work in America: Report of a Special Task Force to the Secretary of Health, Education, and Welfare. Cambridge, Mass.: The MIT Press, 1973.

Explores why people work, attitudes toward work, functions of work, changing attitudes toward work, sources of satisfaction and dissatisfaction, the decreasing role of the entrepreneur, the increasing role of large organizations as places to work, and the responsibilities of corporations.

Care study
By Wednesday
or
This thursday

5

the
supervisor
as a
communicator

After studying and analyzing this chapter, you should be able to:

Define "communication," and explain how noise and feedback play a part in it.

Differentiate between and explain one-directional, two-directional, and multidirectional communication.

Explain the four communications channels in an enterprise: downward, upward, horizontal, and diagonal.

Discuss the grapevine and huddling as forms of informal communication.

Explain how a firm communicates with outsiders.

Describe the advantages and disadvantages of both written and oral communication.

List the rules for sending messages effectively.

Explain how to issue instructions, assignments, and orders effectively.

Describe how one can become a good listener.

Explain the rules for effective dictation.

I N CHAPTER 4, VARIOUS factors that determine a supervisor's success were discussed. In addition to these is the ability to communicate effectively. The functions of management—planning, organizing, directing, coordinating, controlling, and consolidating—all involve working with others. _Communication is the means of getting and receiving ideas; giving directions; and explaining the what, why, where, when, and how of things that need to be done_. Without adequate communication, no firm can reach its peak of efficiency and productivity. Therefore, the ability to communicate effectively is the essential ingredient in a person's supervisory success.

There are several reasons why communicating with employees is more important today than at any previous point in the history of business and industry: [1]

o The higher educational background of employees in today's work force enables them to question and to understand better than employees could in previous decades.

o The people entering the work force now have been raised on television and nurtured on the "right to know."

o Today, people are mobile in their jobs and rarely remain permanently with a company unless it provides more satisfaction than might be obtained in another firm.

o Employees may now use the law to gain fair treatment in the workplace.

Because the supervisor is the direct link between employees and upper management, the supervisor's ability to communicate effectively is the essential ingredient in supervisory success. Supervisors agree that both good oral and written communication are necessary to be successful. In a study of 223 middle and top managers in twenty industrial firms in Tennessee, they rated oral and written communication as the most important abilities for managers. For oral communication, 92.82 percent, and for written communication, 73.09 percent checked "very important." For both types of communication, 100 percent rated them as very or moderately important—a rating given no other factor. [2]

What is communication?

Communication is the process of exchanging information, ideas, or opinions between a sender and a receiver. Communication may occur through speech, writing, symbols, or _body language_ (facial expressions or movements of the arms, legs, or torso).

Note that communication always involves at least two people—a sender and a receiver. Effective communication occurs only when the receiver understands the meaning that the sender intended. If the message is not understood as it was meant to be, satisfactory communication has not taken place. Ineffective communication on the part of the supervisor results in confusion, waste, inefficiency, poor morale, and lost profits.

Two factors enter into the communication process: noise and feedback.

Noise in communication

Any factor that prevents a receiver from understanding a message as the sender intended or that complicates the receipt of the message is called noise. One cause of noise is omission.[3] An omission is left-out information or a gap in information. Omissions occur through oral, written, or mechanical errors.

For example, a supervisor may say, "We need information on Representative Fred Eberle. Look up his bio in *Who's Who.*" Because the supervisor did not state that only his date and place of birth were needed, an employee may needlessly take time to gather other data also. Because the supervisor did not state that Fred Eberle was in office in the 1940s, the employee might spend needless time searching more recent editions of *Who's Who.*

Noise may also be caused by distortions.[4] A distortion is an alteration of what is correct or normal. Distortions also occur through oral, written, or mechanical errors. Examples of distortions are mispronounced words, misspelled words, static in radio transmission or on telephone lines, errors in typewriting or keyboarding, mistakes in printing, imprecise use of language, or a combination of two or more of these irregularities.

Both distortions and omissions occur in the sending of a message. In addition, interference may be present at the receiving end, which further complicates the problem of understanding the message as intended. The receiver may not be able to comprehend the message for several reasons. He or she may have hearing or vision problems, may not listen intently to a verbal message, may read only part of a written message, or may have a limited span of attention and miss part of the message.

Finally, either the sender or the receiver may have biases that twist the message intended. Thus, the greatest care must be taken on the part of both the sender and the receiver to ensure that the message intended to be conveyed is the one that is received and understood.

Feedback in communication

In communication, *feedback* is the reinforcement the sender receives that indicates that the message was received and properly understood or not understood. Feedback may be expressed in different ways and at various levels, ranging from simple to complex.

On the first level, only simple acknowledgment that the message has or has not been received and understood is necessary. If the sender and receiver are visible to each other, simply a nod of the head or a wave of the hand may be sufficient feedback. If the reply is written, a simple statement such as "Message received" would suffice. If the message was not received or understood by the receiver, a request might be made that the message be repeated. First-level feedback does not require further proof of understanding by the sender. For example, the directive "Please read this and pass it on" requires only first-level feedback, such as merely initialing the document.

The second level of feedback requires proof that the message was received as sent. The receiver may be asked to repeat the message word for word. For example, a supervisor who is out of the building on an assignment may call an employee to ask that an important package be brought to an address. The supervisor may ask the employee to repeat the address and directives for bringing the package to ensure that it arrives at the correct destination. If the receiver omits some part of the message, the sender can resend that part until the receiver is able to repeat all of the message accurately.

The third level of feedback involves the demonstration that the message has or has not been understood. The judgment used in handling the reply shows whether or not the receiver understood the message. For example, a supervisor who has ordered a complicated new machine for the office may ask a trainer from the manufacturing company to come to instruct the office force on the use of the machine. Before leaving the office, the trainer would want each employee to demonstrate the correct use of the machine to ensure the message about its use was completely and accurately understood.

In complicated directives, sending, receiving, and feedback may take place repeatedly until the sender is satisfied that the receiver understands the message as intended.

Directions of communication

Communication may be one-directional, two-directional, or multidirectional.

One-directional communication

Some communication is one-directional only (see Figure 5–1). One-directional communication involves a sender and a receiver, but the receiver does not have to reply. For example, a manager may send the

FIGURE 5-1
SIMPLE ONE-DIRECTIONAL COMMUNICATION

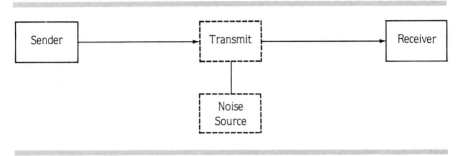

following notice of the closing hours for a unit of the company: "This department will close at 4:30 P.M. on Friday, December 23." No immediate feedback is necessary, since the information is clear, correct, complete, and concise.

Delayed feedback occurs in one-directional communication, however, if action is needed to carry out the message. For example, if an announcement of a meeting is sent out with an incorrect date, the sender may only get the feedback that will reveal the error when people arrive on the wrong date. Asking for immediate feedback, such as filling out a reply card, helps to ensure that such errors can be rectified, but converts this to two-directional communication, discussed later.

Even in one-directional communication, the message is rarely as simple as that discussed previously. Most messages have to be encoded, or converted into a set of signals such as verbal or written words, holes in a punch card, typed or printed words, or codes. The message is then transmitted by air, wire, cable, telephone, paper, television or other medium, using appropriate signals, to the receiver, where it is decoded for arrival at its intended destination. Noise may hamper the transmission of the message (see Figure 5-2).

Two-directional communication

Little communication is as simple or readily accepted as one-directional communication. Because feedback is required in virtually all communication, two-directional is the most used method. *Two-directional communication* resembles a tennis game with two players, who keep hitting the tennis ball as it comes into their court. Each person serves and receives the ball intermittently during the game. Most messages involve give-and-take between sender and receiver. Thus, the sender and re-

FIGURE 5–2
COMPLICATED ONE-DIRECTIONAL COMMUNICATION

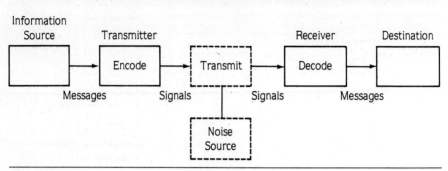

Source: Louis W. Stern, *Distribution Channels: Behavioral Dimensions* (Boston: Houghton Mifflin, 1969), p. 229. Reprinted by permission. Adapted from Claude Shannon and Warren Weaver, *The Mathematical Theory of Communication* (Urbana, Ill.: University of Illinois Press, 1949), p. 5. Copyright 1949 by the University of Illinois Press. Renewed 1977. Reprinted with permission of the publisher.

ceiver continue to change roles until both are assured that the message is understood by each (see Figure 5–3).

Multidirectional communication

Multidirectional communication involves both sending and receiving messages among three or more people. On many occasions, one sender transmits a message for several receivers. For example, one supervisor

FIGURE 5–3
TWO-DIRECTIONAL COMMUNICATION

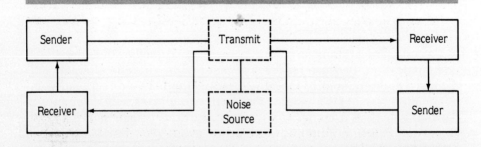

FIGURE 5-4
MULTIDIRECTIONAL COMMUNICATION

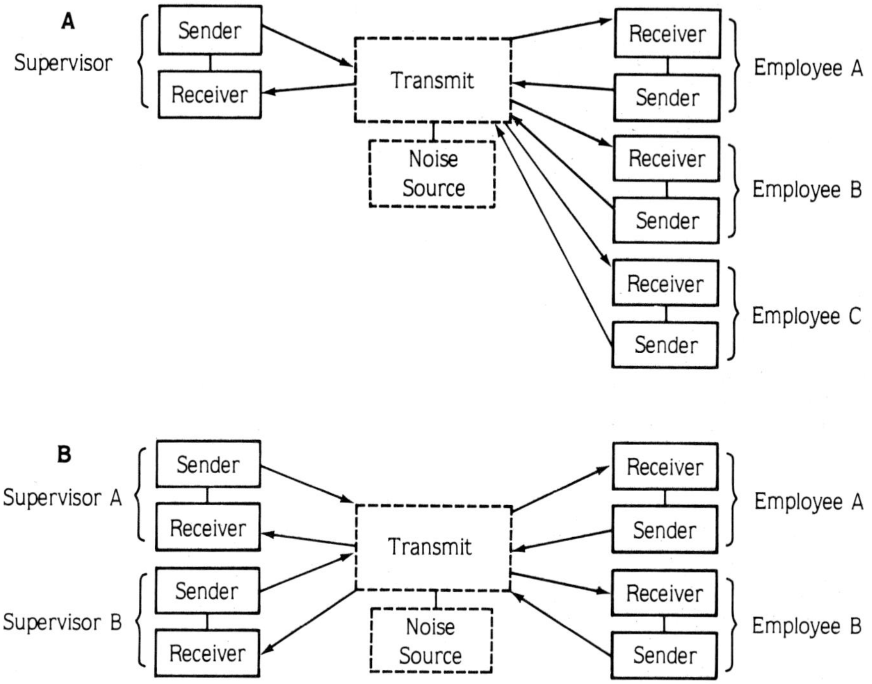

may inform all of the subordinates about some desired action or some new directive requiring feedback, or several subordinates may communicate with one supervisor (see Figure 5-4A). Sometimes several supervisors may communicate with several other supervisors, or several employees may communicate with several supervisors (see Figure 5-4B).

Multidirectional communication is far more complicated than either one- or two-directional communication. The noise that would normally be present in communication is multiplied by the many senders and receivers involved.

Communication within a firm

Communication follows pathways, or *channels*, between people (or machines) in firms. Within any enterprise, communication is generated within both the formal and the informal organization.

FIGURE 5–5
FORMAL COMMUNICATION DIRECTIONS

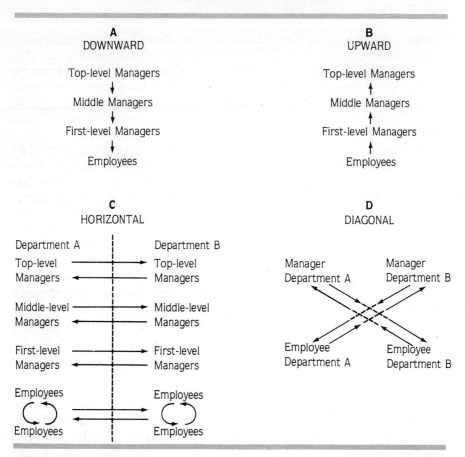

Formal communication

Formal communication is the interchange between people who are involved in conducting the affairs of the enterprise. It occurs in order to further the goals of the enterprise and within the framework of the authority and responsibility assigned to each person. Formal communication flows in four channels.

Downward communication. Communication that flows from supervisors to employees through the usual lines of authority is *downward communication* (see Figure 5–5A). Supervisors at any level of the hierarchy make a decision and pass the information down to the subordinates. This type

of communication is the most frequently used. It is the approved channel for superiors to communicate information, instructions, assignments,
and orders to subordinates.

Upward communication.   Communication that flows from subordinates to
superiors along the line of authority is *upward communication* (see Figure 5–5B). For example, if an employee wishes to make suggestions for
improving some activity, he or she would communicate with the immediate superior, who, in turn, would communicate with the boss next in
line. The message would move up the chain of command until it was
received at the level at which action on it takes place.

Upward communication is more difficult to set in motion than
downward communication, since subordinates are often hesitant to express their ideas to supervisors. To overcome this problem, one firm
publishes key questions and answers in a widely read company newspaper to get employees to express opinions.[5] Or hesitant subordinates
may wish to go to the personnel department or a counselor to discuss a
problem. This practice is encouraged by most personnel-minded firms.

Horizontal communication.   Communication that flows between employees
on the same level, either in one department or in different departments,
is *horizontal communication* (see Figure 5–5C). For example, within one
department, peers working on the same project or on similar projects
may discuss various problems in order to solve difficulties without involving superiors. Or, the supervisor of one division may talk directly to
the supervisor of another division to discuss the resolution of a mutual
problem.

Horizontal communication has several advantages. It speeds change,
avoids involving people who might impede the change, and usually results in the correction of a problem with a minimum of delay. However,
some firms discourage it because they believe supervisors lose control
when workers can confer and handle problems by themselves.

Diagonal communication.   Communication that flows between employees
on different levels in different departments is *diagonal communication*
(see Figure 5–5D). Diagonal communication may be downward or upward. For example, the supervisor of one department may directly contact a receptionist in a different department (downward), or, conversely,
this receptionist may contact this supervisor (upward). Diagonal communication usually occurs only with the consent of the supervisors
concerned.

Diagonal communication also speeds change, since the people involved communicate directly with each other rather than through inter-
mediaries.

Informal communication

Communication that does not come through the formal organization, is unrecorded, and is unofficial is called *informal communication*. There are several kinds of informal communication.

The grapevine. The unstructured communications network of the informal organization is the *grapevine*. Much of the information that filters through the grapevine is based on rumor, gossip, or innuendo. The grapevine exists in all enterprises. However, the more open and forthright a company is in keeping its employees informed, the less need there will be for gossip to spread through the grapevine.

Grapevines cannot be stopped, but in some instances they may have positive effects. For example, John Inchon arrived at work one day with a wise look on his face. When he was queried by his co-workers, he said, "Well, I've just heard the best news! Old John Bart, who has given us such problems with his snooping and snitching and bad disposition, is about to reach mandatory retirement age, and he'll be gone before summer. I know, because my friend in the personnel department told me he had just processed Bart's retirement papers."

"Gee," exclaimed Mary Salmon, "I was thinking of getting another job, but if he's leaving, I won't have to."

Others agreed that they, too, had thought of leaving, but this news would change their plans. Through the grapevine, the employees had obtained information even before the supervisor was told about the planned retirement. The grapevine's report worked to stop resignations of valued employees.

Grapevines may also have negative effects. In one office, employees had heard rumors about the planned phasing out of that office. Only a few employees would be kept, and they would be transferred to another branch. Work slowed and production dropped as employees gathered to voice their fears. The supervisor, Frances Brown, had noticed the grapevine at work. Finally, she called Debra Grant, the senior employee in the office, and asked her what was happening. Under direct questioning, Ms. Grant explained the rumors. She further remarked that morale was low, production was off, and several people were already job hunting.

Ms. Brown immediately called all the employees into her office. She explained that she was indeed sorry about the rumors. She admitted that the executives had discussed merging the two offices, but, she said, after analyzing the functions of each, the space available, and the needs of the firm, the bosses had determined the plan was shortsighted and had decided not to go ahead with it. Ms. Brown's action stopped the rumors and restored the productivity of the work force.

Huddling. Some types of informal communication may be especially beneficial to a firm. One writer on management explained that the tangled, ineffective disorder that afflicts most businesses is greatly overcome by workers who have task-oriented, informal communication, called *huddling*, with one another.[6] "Huddlers accomplish the most critical, sensitive work of organizations and are the most respectable, productive workers."[7]

Two or more people's huddling over an idea before it goes into the formal communications channels of the organization has several advantages. A message can be carried to many people, who are then ready to react when a formal meeting is held. Red tape is reduced, consensus is reached, and excessive reporting is drastically curtailed. Huddling speeds the understanding of people who have discussed the problem and, thereby, speeds decision making. Moreover, employees react more positively to an idea when they have had a chance to mull it over with friends earlier.

Dangers also lurk in huddling because it usually takes place among people who are friendly with one another, are willing to make things happen (often without getting credit for results), and may leave out of the discussion those who are not intimate friends. One of the main dangers is the jealousy that may result on the part of those who were not included in the huddling sessions. They may suspect that the huddlers are seeking advantages for themselves or that they are deliberately trying to gain favor with the bosses at the expense of the other employees.

Huddling is likely to occur in every firm. It is practically impossible to control, and therefore supervisors should recognize it for the positive force that it can be.

Communication between a firm and outsiders

To project an image to the public, to advise the community about a firm, and to tell those with whom a firm does business about its progress, publicity and advertising are used.

Publicity is any nonpaid-for written or oral report about an enterprise that informs customers about its products, activities, or services, or that keeps the name of the enterprise in the public mind. Publicity may appear in any kind of media, such as newspapers, magazines, radio, and television. *Advertising* is any paid-for report that informs customers of the enterprise's products, services, or background. It, too, may appear in any media.

These types of communication are handled by people specially employed for their talent in interpreting an enterprise's activities to its many publics. Most firms have policies that restrict regular employees from giving speeches, appearing on panels, or writing articles about the firms without prior clearance from those people in charge of the firms' public image.

Oral versus written communication

All enterprises use both oral and written communication. Each has advantages and disadvantages.

Oral communication

Oral communication is speedy, allows for immediate feedback, and permits an instant interchange of ideas. It is the least expensive method of communicating unless a machine, such as a telephone, is involved. Even with a machine, oral communication is often less costly than written communication. However, oral communication does have some drawbacks. Usually, no record or proof is available. Since memory is sometimes faulty, a commonly heard statement after oral communication is, "Oh, I thought you said . . ." Misquotes frequently result from oral statements. Even when oral communication is tape-recorded, some words may be inaudible.

For oral communication to occur, the channels between people must be open. For example, if a television or radio is not turned on, no communication is taking place at that location even though the station is sending out messages. Only when the machine is turned on is the channel open. Similarly, a telephone only becomes a channel of communication when a sender and receiver are both using it. Even when communicators are face to face, a sender may find a closed channel because the receiver is not listening to what is said.

Written communication

Written communication eliminates some of the drawbacks of oral communication. Written communication provides a permanent record of a message's being sent and of the exact statements made. Unless a tape recorder is used to record an oral message, no exact record of what was said exists. Secretarial notes of oral communication, if available, do give some assurance of what was said, but such recordings are written records. Written communication may be checked over and over to make sure of the accuracy of the message. Oral communication, unless tape-recorded, may not be so checked.

Written communication also has some drawbacks. It is, by its very nature, more costly to develop. Such tools as pen, ink, pencil, typewriter, or other mechanical devices may be needed. Many of the expensive tools used in written communication need skilled operators. These people further increase the cost of written communication.

For the same material, written communication takes longer to develop than oral communication because more care is usually taken in producing a written document. In addition, feedback to a written communication usually takes longer to create than feedback to oral communication does.

Innovators interested in efficiency have devised various means for reducing the time used in written communication and feedback. For example, stationery and business forms that have spaces for replies simplify feedback. Written communication is speeded by typewriters with memory devices that can type a label or an envelope once an address has been placed on a letter, and by word-processing machines that allow the typist to make corrections on the original document and produce perfect copy without retyping the entire document. Other machines can send copies of prepared materials over airwaves to faraway places almost instantaneously. In addition, printed forms that have spaces left for the insertion of words or numbers are used in business whenever practicable. When used, these speedier methods may add somewhat to the costs of written communication.

Sending messages effectively

In sending messages, certain rules should be followed if communication is to be effective:

o _State the reason for the communication_—People want to determine the importance of communications quickly. Business letters, memorandums, and reports to supervisors should state near the top or in the title the major concern. Oral communications should come to the point quickly. Employees, similarly, should be advised by an agenda, a memorandum, or an announcement of the main focus of an upcoming meeting.

o _Consider the attitudes and the interests of the receiver_—For example, if an executive is to receive a message, he or she may be too busy to read details but may be interested in the overall project on which you are reporting. If a union employee is to receive a directive, he or she may not be interested in management's position but may want to know if the directive meets the provisions of the union contract.

o _Check to see that the message includes "what, who, why, where, when, and how"_—Omission of important details often causes faulty or incomplete communication with the receiver. Time may be lost or errors may occur if some facts are not given as intended.

o _Be clear_—For example, if you say, "This will be followed by a later memorandum," the receiver does not know whether "later" means an hour, a week, a month, or more. Be specific by saying, "This will be followed by another memorandum next Tuesday," or by citing the exact date, "January 10."

o *Use language appropriate to the receiver*—One supervisor asked a subordinate to figure the remuneration for part-time employees. Later, when the job was not done, the subordinate was rebuked. Her reply was, "I didn't know what you meant by 'remuneration.' " If the supervisor had considered the receiver, she would have seen the body language of the subordinate—the look of perplexity—and restated the request using the term "wages" or "the amount of money earned."

o *Specify clearly what action needs to be taken as a result of the communication and when that action is needed*—For example, if a report is to be completed, specify what form it should take, who will work on it, when it is needed, and what information it should contain. Being definitive about the assignment will help to speed the completion of the report.

o *Act consistently with words*—One supervisor stressed courtesy in handling outsiders who came to the office. The supervisor, however, showed by body language that he was visibly annoyed whenever he was stopped in his routine activities by having to greet a visitor. Often, when people stopped into the office, he would turn his back and continue to work on the folders on his desk. Subordinates listened to his words that spoke "courtesy" and watched his actions that spoke "discourtesy." Because actions tend to speak more loudly than words, the subordinates soon ignored the order to display courtesy to outsiders and began to copy the supervisor by ignoring people who came to the office. Complaints to the executives in the firm subsequently forced a change in personnel.

o *Keep communication channels open*—Open communication channels allow messages to get through promptly. Communication with supervisors is often made possible by maintaining an *open-door policy,* which means that subordinates have access to the boss within a reasonable period of time. Open-door policy is an important means of discouraging gossip or rumor that can serve as noise in communication.

Telephone lines also need to be kept open so that important business communication can get through to employees. Many enterprises allow only official calls on business phones. Personal calls are allowed only for emergencies. In this way, telephones are open for use as needed.

o *Minimize noise in communication*—Noise can distort the message and cause the feedback to be faulty. To minimize noise, its cause must be identified. Noise may be caused by omissions or distortions on the sending end or by problems in the span of attention or listening at the receiving end. If faulty machines cause the noise, they should be promptly repaired. If operators cause the noise, they should be retrained or, if necessary, replaced. Careful proofreading may also eliminate noise. People with hearing loss may be aided with special equipment designed to overcome that problem.

Noise caused by machine or operator errors is less difficult to eliminate than noise caused by defects in speaking, writing, span of attention, and listening. By paying special attention to these more difficult types of noise, supervisors can help remove them.

Issuing instructions, assignments, and orders effectively

Because supervisors have authority and responsibility for the work of their areas, they have the power to direct employees to do the work required. Regardless of the level of the supervisor, he or she is responsible for seeing that the goals of the organization are met.

The supervisor, therefore, must issue instructions about how work is to be done, make assignments of tasks to be accomplished, and give orders, when necessary, about important and relevant tasks to be accomplished. The manner of giving instructions, assignments, and orders often determines the success with which they are carried out, and is an important consideration in making communication productive.

Several factors, in addition to the rules for sending messages listed previously, make directives effective:

o *Issue orders directly*—People are usually flattered when important people ask them to perform a task. If the supervisor gives an order, most people will comply. However, if the supervisor asks another person to give the order, workers may not take it seriously or may ignore it altogether. Therefore, the more directly the order comes from the supervisor, the greater the chance that it will be acted upon.

o *Give reasons for orders*—If the supervisor explains why an order is to be carried out, employees are more likely to perform properly than if the supervisor simply says, "Do this," and gives no reason. If employees understand that carrying out an order will further the goals of the organization, they will be more willing to act on that request.

On occasion, after directives have been given, new orders must be issued. A new problem may have arisen, or more urgent work may need to be completed. The supervisor should explain the reason for this change so that employees are not resentful about being taken from one already-started job to another job that takes priority.

o *Be consistent and courteous*—How an order is given depends to some extent on the supervisor's style. The autocratic supervisor usually says, "Do this." The democratic supervisor will often say, "Let's discuss how this should be accomplished." The laissez-faire supervisor might just say that certain goals are sought and leave each employee to select his or her task.

Order giving should be consistent. Employees get used to their supervisors' styles. If a supervisor suddenly changes style, employees become confused.

Supervisors also need to know how individual employees respond to directives. Some may like each detail—who, how, when, where, why, and what—explained specifically. Others may prefer merely to be told the outline of the job and be allowed to determine for themselves the way in which the order will be carried out.

All employees appreciate being approached courteously when they are given directives.

o *Select an appropriate time*—Timing directives is also important. If an employee has just been given an order for a lengthy, difficult task, and the supervisor returns shortly to add other demands, the employee may become resentful and feel overworked.

Employees usually dislike having directives given late in the day when they are rushing to complete work prior to leaving. Whenever possible, directives should be given early or in the middle of the work period. Only in cases of considerable urgency should late-day, last-minute directives be given.

After directives have been given, many employees resent being constantly reminded about the time limit for a job's completion. Occasional checking to determine if help is needed to get the job done on time may, however, be welcomed.

Listening

In oral communication, the sender is the speaker and the receiver is the listener. Few abilities are more important in communication than the ability to listen effectively. Yet not many people have ever been taught or have ever learned how to do so. "We confuse hearing with listening, believing that, because hearing is a natural function, then listening must be effortless."[8] One speech communications expert, Dr. Harrel T. Allen, has stated, "Listening is hard work and requires increased energy—your heart speeds up, your blood circulates faster, your temperature goes up."[9]

One of the deterrents to listening is that our minds work much faster than most people speak. We can listen at a rate of 300 to 500 or more words per minute, but few people talk faster than 125 to 200 words per minute.[10] This gap allows time for the mind of the listener to wander, thereby causing listening to be difficult for many people. Moreover, a possible lack of interest in what the sender is saying further confuses the problem of listening.

To combat the difference between speaking and listening ability, new machines called *speech compressors* are being used. Without distorting sound, these machines can speed talk by 25 to 50 percent.[11] They are currently used in the fields of radio and television, and may also be used in training sessions.

"What makes a good listener? It all begins with concentration. We listen to other people through a thick screen of physical and psychological distractions."[12] To improve listening ability, several steps can be taken:[13]

- o *Train yourself to listen for facts*—This is known as *selective listening*. Ask yourself, "What is the point being made?"

- o *Be aware of feelings expressed by the speaker*—For example, a person asking the time of day really may be wondering if it is near quitting time, may be concerned about an appointment, or may be wondering if sufficient time is left to complete a job that is overdue.

- o *Observe, if possible, the body language of the sender*—Determine the sincerity, urgency, annoyance, or other emotion the person exhibits.

A good listener is appreciated by the sender of a message. One way to increase one's popularity is to become a good listener. Nothing is more flattering to a communicator than to have a message retained accurately by a receiver.

Making dictation effective

Because so much of the communication in business must be written, most supervisors have secretarial help to prepare memorandums, letters, and other written documents. For such written communication, supervisors may start the process by either handwriting or dictating the message. Since handwriting is laborious, dictation has become the accepted mode of getting communications onto paper. However, the ability to dictate effectively is a skill that few supervisors have developed sufficiently to use with confidence.

Handwriting versus dictating communication

Even in this day of advanced communications techniques, some supervisors still handwrite reports, memos, and letters in preparation for having them typed. By handwriting material, supervisors can ensure that the message says what it was intended to say, that the choice of words is appropriate, that the progression of ideas is correct, and that all essential information is included. Changes, such as deletions, insertions, or different words, can be made in the handwritten copy before it is typed. The typist can determine the approximate length of the material without difficulty and arrange the material neatly on the typewritten page.

Handwriting communications, however, takes a considerable amount of a supervisor's time. Moreover, unless the handwritten copy has been carefully proofread, it may contain some errors. Since handwriting is not always easy for a typist to decipher, the material must be carefully proofread after it is typed. Therefore, both speed in getting the message out and economical use of the supervisor's time are lost when communications are handwritten.

Dictating communications to a secretary

Secretaries have usually been schooled in a particular method of taking dictation by shorthand, either manual or machine. *Manual shorthand methods* include such well-known symbol systems as Gregg and Pitman, and such *abc systems* as Speedwriting, Stenoscript, and Forkner. Symbol systems use lines, curves, circles, and dashes to represent letters of the alphabet, words, and phrases. In abc systems, letters of the alphabet are used instead of symbols as abbreviations for words and phrases. In addition, some secretaries have devised their own systems of writing shorthand.

Machine shorthand systems, such as Stenograph and Stenotype, require that a special machine be used. Machine shorthand is used today for court reporting, where consistently high speeds of oral communication must be recorded word for word. Manual systems are more famil-iarly used in offices.

Both kinds of systems have advantages and disadvantages. The slower pace and the informality of taking manual shorthand permit more interchange between the dictator and the recorder. Manual short-hand also allows a secretary to prop the paper used for recording in a convenient location. The small, portable shorthand machine takes time to set up, and machine systems are not quite as flexible to use or as readily available as manual systems.

Both machine and manual systems involve face-to-face contact be-tween the dictator and the recorder. Thus, if one is delayed, the other is kept waiting. Delays may be caused by needed rest periods or by other duties, such as welcoming callers or answering telephones. For example, a supervisor may have important work to send out immediately but the secretary may be interrupted by a phone call. The work is therefore slowed down.

When the dictator and the recorder work together for a certain pe-riod of time, they form a communications interchange that speeds and improves the dictation process. The secretary becomes familiar with the vocabulary of the supervisor, can note repetitions in the dictation, and aid in the selection of the exact word to achieve the meaning intended. The supervisor relies upon the secretary to fill in certain facts that are not readily at hand, such as addresses or titles, or other important details that must be included in correspondence. The supervisor can also ex-plain certain facets of the business to the secretary as the dictation pro-ceeds. This knowledge helps the secretary to understand better the purpose behind the memo, report, or letter and makes the secretary feel more a part of the management team.

The speed of the dictation can be controlled by both the secretary and the supervisor. The secretary can ask for material to be repeated or for the spellings of certain words that are difficult to understand. Simi-larly, the supervisor may need extra time to decide exactly how the next phrase or sentence should be stated. The supervisor may also ask that certain sections be read back to check their accuracy or to amend the word choice. The time of both the supervisor and the secretary, of course, is taken while the dictating process continues.

Following typing of the work by the secretary, proofreading by the supervisor is essential in most offices and businesses.

Dictating communications to a machine

Many types of machines are available for recording dictation by the mes-sage sender. These may be individual machines, hand-held or desk-top models, that record dictation on tape. Some machines can be attached to a telephone or other long- or short-distance transmitter and connected to the office of a typing pool or a word-processing center.

To transcribe a tape, the typist or secretary places the tape on a listening device. The spoken word of the dictator is then transcribed onto paper or forms.

There are a few disadvantages to dictating to a machine. First, the supervisor must supply all the needed data and should also indicate spacing, punctuation, approximate length, and other details that will help the typist to arrange the material attractively and effectively. Markers on the machine also help the typist to know the length of the communication. Second, the face-to-face assistance that a secretary can provide during dictation and the explanations and feedback that a supervisor can give are missing. The supervisor may find that some words or ideas have been repeated; that collecting certain data, such as exact names, spellings, and addresses, has taken considerable time; and that at-hand files have to be established to supply those facts. The secretary, in turn, is less involved and learns less about the enterprise.

There are, however, advantages to dictating to a machine. Because the supervisor does not need to wait for a secretary, and the secretary does not need to be present while the dictation occurs, this is a time-saving method. Many types of machines may be hand held, and so the supervisor may carry one and dictate whenever the need arises. Many supervisors use dictating machines when traveling, and the tapes can be mailed to the firm and transcribed before the supervisor gets back.

Developing dictating-for-transcription ability

Schools, in general, do not teach potential supervisors how to dictate for transcription. Most people have to learn this skill on the job. Since most people are used to thinking with pencil in hand or in front of a typewriter, thinking and organizing thoughts in the presence of a secretary or a dictating machine present a new challenge.

To build dictation skill, one should begin first with short notes or responses. The length of messages should be increased over a period of time, until one is able to dictate multipage reports or letters with little difficulty. One learns to dictate effectively by dictating and then analyzing that dictation for necessary improvements. Certain practices are particularly helpful in learning to dictate precisely and without necessitating many later corrections:

- o Gather all the material that will be needed for the message: names, addresses, dates, times, meeting places, technical terms, reference materials.

- o Make a short outline of the major points to be stressed. Include the "who, what, where, when, why, and how."

o Organize the material so that it moves logically from one idea to another.

o Decide what you are going to say before you record.

o Speak distinctly so that each word is clearly understood. Pronounce word endings, such as "ed's," clearly and distinctly.

o Spell unusual or hard-to-understand words.

o If an accent or regional inflection makes your words hard to understand, speak slowly.

o Ask the secretary to read back the material or play back the record of your dictation so you can make sure you have developed your thoughts in an organized fashion before the message is typed.

SUMMARY

o Effective communication is an important asset for supervisory success. Supervisors communicate with others orally, in writing, and through body language.

o Communication involves both a sender and a receiver. To be satisfactory, the receiver must understand the meaning as the sender intended it.

o Noise in communication, which prevents understanding, may be caused by omissions, errors, distortions, lack of comprehension, receiver's physical limitations, or a too-short span of attention.

o Feedback, the reinforcement given the sender by the receiver, may be first-level, acknowledging that the message was sent; second-level, restating the message accurately; or third-level, demonstrating the ability to perform what the communication requested.

o Communication may be one-directional, requiring no response; two-directional, in which the sender and the receiver reverse roles as the communication continues; or multidirectional, in which three or more people both send and receive messages.

o Formal communications within a firm may flow downward, from supervisors to employees; upward, from employees to supervisors; horizontally, between peers on any level; or diagonally, between supervisors and employees in different departments.

o Communication within a firm may also be informal. The grapevine, which may be either harmful or helpful, and huddling, which is usually beneficial, are two kinds of informal communication.

o An enterprise may extend its communication to persons outside the organization through publicity and advertising.

o Communication may be either oral or written. Oral communication is speedier and less costly, but it is also less reliable and provides few, if any, records. Written communication takes longer, and is costlier, but it provides permanency in the form of records, which may be checked for accuracy.

o Rules for transmitting effective messages are to state the reason for the communication; consider the attitudes and the interests of receivers; check to see the message includes "what, who, why, where, when, and how"; be clear; use language appropriate to the receiver; specify clearly what action needs to be taken; act consistently with words; keep communication channels open; and minimize noise.

o When giving instructions, assignments, and orders, in addition to observing the rules for transmitting effective messages, supervisors should also issue orders directly, give reasons for orders, be consistent and courteous, and select an appropriate time.

o Effective listening ability is an important asset for the receiver of oral communication. To improve listening, train yourself to listen for facts, be aware of the feelings expressed by the speaker, and observe the body language of the sender.

o Effective dictation of written communication speeds the output of work. Dictation may be taken by a secretary or recorded on a machine for later transcription. Rules for effective dictation are to gather all the material needed for the message; make a short outline of the major points to be stressed; organize the material so that it moves logically; decide what you are going to say before you record; speak distinctly; spell difficult words; speak slowly to ensure comprehension; have material read back or played back before it is typed.

REFERENCES

[1] "Employee Communications—Neglected Need," New York Times, December 28, 1975, p. 10.

[2] Harriet McQueen, "Pre-Employment Training Needed for Middle Management Positions in Selected Tennessee Industrial Firms," Delta Pi Epsilon Journal, July 1980, pp. 28–38.

[3] Harold Guetzkow, "Communications in Organizations," in Handbook of Organizations, ed. James G. March (Chicago: Rand McNally, 1965), p. 551.

[4] Guetzkow, "Communications in Organizations," p. 551.

[5] Bruce Harriman, "Up and Down the Communications Ladder," Harvard Business Review, September–October 1974, pp. 143–51.

[6]V. Dallas Merrell, *Huddling: The Informal Way to Management Success* (New York: American Management Associations, 1979).

[7]V. Dallas Merrell, "What Makes Companies Work? Huddling?" *New York Times*, March 11, 1979, p. 14F.

[8]"The Act of Listening," *Royal Bank of Canada Monthly Letter*, Janury 1979, p. 2.

[9]"The Act of Listening," p. 2.

[10]Ron Zemke, "Learning to Listen to Your Trainees," *Training*, July 1977, p. 20.

[11]*Training*, January 1978, p. 25.

[12]"The Act of Listening," p. 2.

[13]Zemke, "Learning to Listen to Your Trainees," pp. 20–21.

REVIEW AND DISCUSSION QUESTIONS

1. Why is communication an important part of all businesses today?
2. Explain what effective communication achieves in a firm.
3. What is meant by "noise" in communication? What are its causes? Give some examples.
4. Why is feedback in communication important?
5. Communication flows in four different directions in the formal channels of a firm. What is the most usual direction of flow? Why is that direction more commonly used than other directions for communication?
6. How can informal communication that filters through the grapevine be reduced or made less harmful?
7. What are the advantages of oral communication?
8. What are the advantages of written communication?
9. What are the rules for sending messages effectively? For dictating effectively?
10. How can one develop good listening habits?

ASSIGNMENTS

1. Assume that you are the supervisor in an office with ten employees who work staggered hours. You have an important notice about a change in salary structure that has to be discussed with them. The issue is a touchy one and may cause some hard feelings, especially among the more senior members of the staff. How would you plan to communicate management's message to these employees to ensure that the grapevine does not contaminate the information before you can tell each of them about it?
2. Rewrite the following memorandum according to the rules for sending messages effectively:

> Sometime early next week we think a meeting of the staff would be desirable. We have set the date for Tuesday, in the conference room. This is October the 18th, and we

know that everyone will want to be there on that date.
Come early, as the meeting will start immediately. We will
be discussing a number of things that you may find important, such as the new minimum wage and its effect on salaries and the new hours that have been suggested for our
department. We will meet around 10:00 A.M. The conference room is on the eighteenth floor. We will want your
comments, so keep in mind the meeting for next week.

PROBLEM FOR RESOLUTION ✓

Your boss has asked you to devise a form that can be used for memorandums to employees. What format would you suggest? Be sure to consider all types of information that may be communicated to employees.

CASE STUDY

In one office in a large organization, seven people, including the supervisor, Mr. Zamore, who had just been appointed to that job, were employed. Mr. Zamore inherited three employees—a budget officer, an
administrative aide, and a clerk-typist—from previous department heads
who had held his job over the past fifteen years. In addition, he had
hired three new people: an assistant administrator, a project head, and
an executive secretary. The last three with Mr. Zamore became the "in"
group, while the other three were looked upon as the "out" group.

Mr. Zamore chose to confer in his office frequently with his three
appointees and to ignore the other three employees. In fact, he only
bothered greeting them when they came face to face in the hallway or
elevator.

The three holdover employees ate lunch together. As Mr. Zamore
bypassed them increasingly, they stepped up their grapevine activity,
even enlisting friends in adjacent offices who were able to get bits of
information of interest to them from time to time.

Bitterness grew between the "in" group and the "out" group. The
"out" group began withholding minor bits of information, stalling, and
purposely slowing work. The office became a hotbed of friction, slowed
production, and stalled projects.

Following meetings in Mr. Zamore's office, the executive secretary
would mete out orders to the other three "out"-group employees. Because they did not know the overall plans, they frequently made mistakes in their work. Once the executive secretary asked that a report be
redone because it was not "what Mr. Zamore wanted." The adminis-

trative aide said, "If Mr. Zamore wants that redone, let him tell me himself."

On another occasion, the budget officer ignored the executive secretary's directive, replying, "I am the budget officer. I work on the financial records of the department. This is not part of my job."

Frustration and anger resulted from the various directives given and the work the "out" group had to perform without knowing how particular jobs fitted into the overall plans of the department. Feeling they were second-class workers in the department did not add to their desire to work more efficiently either.

Explain what steps Mr. Zamore could take to improve communications within the department.

What steps would help to lessen friction?

How could the production of the department be improved?

Was Mr. Zamore right in delegating his order-giving authority to his executive secretary? Give reasons for your answer.

♪♩

FURTHER READING

"The Act of Listening." In *The Royal Bank of Canada Monthly Letter,* January 1979.

    Explains that listening is an important human activity, and discusses how it may be improved.

Archer, Dane, and Robin M. Akert. "How Well Do You Read Body Language?" *Psychology Today,* October 1977, pp. 68–72.

    Presents a test using real-life situations to show how individuals react to nonverbal cues.

Baird, John E., Jr., and Gretchen K. Wilting. "Nonverbal Communication Can Be a Motivational Tool." *Personnel Journal,* September 1979, pp. 607–61.

    Notes that motivation is a product of the communication between staff and supervisor. Observes that masking negative nonverbal cues aids supervisors to get work done effectively.

Clinksdale, Bella C. "Thirteen Strategies to Improve Oral Communication Skills." *American Business Communications Association Bulletin,* September 1979, pp. 11–14.

    Explains how practice using cases, debate, brainstorming, panel discussions, forums, and symposiums improves oral communication skills.

Drucker, Peter F. "Managerial Communications." In *Management: Tasks, Responsibilities, Practices.* New York: Harper & Row, 1973, pp. 481–93.

Discusses how people are talking more, but noise and nonlistening result in less communication; how communication and information are different, yet interdependent; how communication makes demands on people; and how downward communication is doomed to failure because it concentrates on what the speaker wants to say—not what the listener wants to hear.

Harriman, Bruce. "Up and Down the Communications Ladder." *Harvard Business Review,* September–October 1974, pp. 143–51.

Explains the steps one company took to improve its upward communications problem.

Siegel, Alan. "Fighting Business Gobbledygook: How to Say It in Plain English." *Management Review,* November 1979, pp. 14–19.

Uses samples of documents to illustrate the legal nature of the language that laypersons cannot understand and the need to simplify language.

Swift, Marvin H. "Clear Writing Means Clear Thinking." *Harvard Business Review,* January–February 1973, pp. 59–62.

Discusses how saying what we mean and meaning what we say must be in harmony for good communication. Shows how a supervisor revises a memorandum to make it short and succinct.

the supervisor's interaction with employees

6
selecting
employees

After studying and analyzing this chapter, you should be able to:

Explain the conditions under which new employees are sought for a firm.

Differentiate among job analyses, job descriptions, and job specifications.

Describe how recruitment takes place inside the organization, outside the organization, and among minorities.

Explain how application blanks, résumés, references, and initial interviews are used in selection.

Discuss the various kinds of tests that may be used to select employees.

Describe how preliminary evaluations are conducted.

Explain the various kinds of second-stage interviews, how they should be conducted, and how they are evaluated.

Discuss how assessment centers are used in the selection process.

Explain the importance of matching the applicant to the job and the supervisor's role in selecting employees.

MANAGER ONCE STATED, "If you want to have motivated people in your organization, you must hire motivated people." One of the key responsibilities of the supervisor is to serve as the employer in selecting the people who will contribute to the success of the department and who will advance the progress the organization is making in the community it serves.

A person's attitudes, abilities, actions, and appearance have usually been fairly well established by the time he or she is to be hired. Therefore, the selection of a person who will bring positive characteristics is important to avoid or reduce subsequent employee friction and discontent. The process of building the work force involves analyzing the need for employment, analyzing the job to be filled, recruitment, and selection.

Analyzing the need for employment

Any number of events may take place before a new person must be added to a work area:

o Someone may be promoted, transferred, fired, or retired or leave for a variety of other reasons. A subsequent vacancy needs to be filled to keep the work area at its traditional labor strength.

o The work load may increase because more customers are demanding the products or services of the enterprise, additional steps are needed to complete the work, or personnel are given extra work assignments. Thus an additional person may be needed to handle the overload.

o The range of activities the organization performs may be expanded, and new personnel are needed to help introduce the new functions.

o Specialized machines may be introduced into the organization, and personnel familiar with them may be needed.

o The workday may be expanded, and additional personnel are needed to cover the added hours.

Employee requisition

When a position needs to be filled or added, most supervisors use an *employee requisition form* to make the request (see Figure 6–1). This form details the work area, the job title, the employee grade (if a grading plan is used), the suggested pay rate, the classification of the job

FIGURE 6–1
SAMPLE REQUISITION FORM

Department making request_____

Job title_____

Grade_____

Pay rate: Minimum_____   Maximum_____

_____Full-time

_____Part-time

_____Permanent

_____Temporary (Indicate approximate length of employment: _____)

Hours daily_____   Hours weekly_____

Reason for request:
_____Replacement (Give name of person replaced: _____)
_____Addition to staff (Rationale:_____

_____)

Requested by_____   Approved by _____

Title_____   Title_____
     (Supervisor)   (Supervisor's Superior)

Date _____   Date _____

(temporary or permanent, full-time or part-time), the hours to be worked, the reason for the replacement or addition, and the person who is being replaced (if appropriate). The signatures of the supervisors involved and the dates are required. In a large firm, the requisition is sent to the employment office. In a smaller firm, the form is sent to the person responsible for employing personnel. The process of selecting the appropriate person for the job then begins.

Analyzing the job to be filled

To determine the job needs in a particular area of work and to aid supervisors in assigning the most able people to those tasks, each job must be examined. This examination requires the use of job analyses, job descriptions, and job specifications.

Job analyses

The study of all the basic factors involved in a job is known as *job analysis*. This analysis may be based on several sources, including observation of the person on the job and the conditions under which he or she works, an interview with the person doing the job, an interview with the supervisor of that worker, a written list of job activities prepared by the worker, a written list of job activities prepared by the supervisor, and a review and critique of these lists by both the worker and the supervisor. If several people perform the same job, observation of, an interview with, and a written list from each worker may be used as a basis for analyzing the job.

In a small organization, the supervisor is responsible for the job analysis. In larger organizations that have a personnel manager or a personnel department, the analysis will be done by that person or department in cooperation with each supervisor.

Job descriptions

After the analysis of the job has been made, a job description can be formulated from it by the supervisor and the personnel office. A *job description* is a written statement explaining the specific tasks involved in a job, the reporting relationships of the job holder, and the results expected. It explains the details of the job in relation to both the amount of time spent on each task and the importance of that task.

Thus, for example, a job description may reveal that although a given office worker spends more time answering the telephone than doing anything else, answering the telephone may rank only fifth or sixth in importance on that specific job. For another job, say a receptionist or a telephone operator, answering the telephone may rank first.

A job description should include the following details:

o Title of person holding the job

o Date of the development of the description

o Number of employees with whom the job holder works

o Location of the job

o Hours worked

o Work performed (by percentage of time and by importance)

o Minimum skills needed

o Background education needed

o Relation of the job to other jobs and of the job holder to other people o Salary range

o Performance requirements (responsibilities, job knowledge, speed of activities, mental requirements, dexterity, accuracy, machines or equipment to be used)

o Working conditions (alone or with other people, inside or outside, any variations in temperature, condition of atmosphere [humid, dry, dusty, odored], noise levels, lighting, hazards, toxic conditions)

o Physical activities to be performed by the individual (sitting, standing, walking, crouching, kneeling, climbing; balancing, lifting, carrying, pushing, pulling, handling; hearing; listening; seeing [including color vision needed]; conversing; filing; organizing materials; weighing; wrapping, packing, mailing; cutting, pasting, stamping)

Job specifications

Using the information from the job analysis, and after developing that information into a job description, the supervisor together with personnel representatives now creates a job specification. A *job specification* is a concise statement for use by the supervisor or other person or agency empowered to refer employees or to select employees. The statement should give sufficient detail about a particular job to enable an applicant's characteristics and abilities to be matched to a specific job. A job specification should include the following details:

o Name, address, and telephone number of the employer

o Date to apply for the job and way to reach the firm

o Number of openings, number of applicants to refer to the employer, and time limit for filling the job(s)

o Occupational title for the job, rate of pay, and hours of work

o Summary of the job (work to be done, equipment to be operated, basic working conditions)

o Special skills, knowledge, and abilities required and special physical requirements, if any

o Experience requirements, if any

o Education and training requirements, if any

o Miscellaneous requirements, if any

FIGURE 6–2
SAMPLE JOB SPECIFICATION

```
Job Title:  Bookkeeper/Accountant

Salary:  $10,000-$12,000 depending upon experience and qualifications.

Hours of Work:  40 hours per week (8:30 A.M.-5:30 P.M., Monday through Friday).

Job Begins:  September 1, 1981.

Qualifications:  Two-year college degree in accounting.

Experience:  Prefer person with one or two years of successful experience with a
             small firm.

Personal:  Must enjoy working with people, meeting customers, and keeping accurate
           records.  Reliability and dependability essential.

Job Duties:  Keep all financial accounts, accounts payable, accounts receivable,
             payroll, tax reports, fringe benefits reports, financial reports for
             government.  In addition, should be able to run desk-top computer.
             Person should be willing to service customers when needed.

Opportunity for Growth:  Person has unlimited opportunity to progress as firm
                         grows.  Since it opened in 1980, the firm has quadrupled
                         its volume.  Further impressive growth is anticipated.
                         After one year of employment, employees may join profit-
                         sharing plan.

Schedule for Interviews:  Gregory Sharp, owner
                          Monday through Thursday
                          10:00 A.M.-1:00 P.M.
                          Beginning August 10

THE QUICK-COPY COMPANY
151 Main Street
Falls River, New Jersey  07418
(201) 555-3323
```

o Date and time of interview, interviewer's name, reference number, and telephone number for the interviewee to use (see Figure 6–2)

Using job analyses, descriptions, and specifications

Detailed breakdowns of jobs through job analyses, descriptions, and specifications help both the supervisor and the applicant to know the characteristics of the job, the kinds of work required, and the abilities and knowledge needed to do that work satisfactorily. These statements are not only helpful but are sometimes mandated: Organizations that are unionized are usually required to have them for every category of work.

Once job analyses, descriptions, and specifications have been developed, they must be updated periodically. A careful reevaluation should take place at least once every five years. In addition, a reevaluation should be conducted by an enterprise that is modernizing its equipment or changing its routines.

Recruitment

Through *recruitment*, people are sought to fill jobs in an organization. Applicants may be found both within the organization and outside of it.

Inside the organization

Large organizations, to comply with equal opportunity laws, maintain a policy of listing all job openings. These lists are publicized to all employees through bulletin boards, company newsletters, or memorandums. This publicity enables people who seek advancement or change within the enterprise to apply for the jobs.

Both transfers and promotions may occur through this practice. If the new position pays the same and requires about the same amount of ability as the old position, the move is a *transfer*, or a lateral move. If the new position carries more pay and responsibility, the change is a *promotion*, or a vertical move. Some positions, especially in government offices, carry grade-level numbers. If a person moves to a higher grade level in a job, the move is a promotion. A transferee would move but remain at the same grade level.

Listings of job openings may be used to recruit not only present employees but also former employees who are seeking to reenter the job market or to come back to a particular firm. Some organizations have a policy against rehiring former employees unless their reason for leaving earlier was unrelated to their job evaluation. For example, a person who left to care for a child, return to school, or move to another area of the country may be welcomed back. But a person who left because of friction within the department or poor performance would probably not be rehired.

Insiders also include relatives or friends of present employees. An enterprise's policy about *nepotism* (the hiring of relatives) determines whether or not relatives are employed. Friends may be especially sought if a valued employee highly recommends them.

Outside the organization

Many avenues may bring people from outside an organization to apply for a job. They may hear or read about the firm and want to join it; they may read or hear an advertisement specifying a particular job; they may be recruited through a school employment office, a government employment office, a private employment firm, or a community agency; or they may just contact the organization on the chance that an opening exists.

Recruiting people from outside is usually more costly than recruiting them from within or through other employees. If the enterprise has good public relations with the community, articles about it in the local newspaper or advertisements about its own goods or services may bring it to the public's attention enough to attract job applicants. In this case recruitment is not very costly. However, many organizations recruit by advertising in the classified section of newspapers or magazines or on radio or television—all costly methods. The Bureau of National Affairs has reported that of the 188 companies it surveyed about methods of recruitment, more than 80 percent used classified advertisements for professional and managerial employees, 75 percent for salespersonnel, and 70 percent for office workers.[1]

Two types of classified advertisements exist: open and blind. *Open advertisements* use the name of the organization and urge people to come in person to fill out application blanks. If the response is large, many employees will be involved in screening and interviewing the applicants. This procedure can be both time-consuming and costly for the organization, and it can also generate ill will among applicants, since those turned away may be resentful about not getting the job.

Blind advertisements do not name the organization or ask the applicants to apply in person but, rather, ask for a written résumé to be sent to a box number. Doing so allows the organization to screen the résumés at its leisure and to inform only the most likely candidates of an interview appointment.

School employment offices are another way to recruit new employees. High schools and colleges are particularly good sources for new, entry-level employees. Some high schools have vocational counseling services that match job requests with capable graduates. Most colleges have placement divisions that arrange for employers to visit the campus, interview students, and invite those students who they believe may be potential job candidates to visit the organization for additional interviews. Personnel officials in some firms make direct contact with instructors, who then recommend students with the particular skills and abilities sought whenever such students are available.

Costs for recruiting from school employment offices may be low if local schools are used. If the schools are located at some distance from the organization, thus necessitating travel expenses for personnel to visit the schools and for prospective employees to visit the organization, the costs may be quite high.

Government employment offices are also good sources of personnel. Recruitment through these is inexpensive, and often the people recruited are not available through schools or private employment firms.

Private employment firms, sometimes called "headhunters," charge a fee for their services. For entry-level positions, the employee often pays the fee, which is usually equivalent to one or more week's salary. For more advanced positions, the employer pays the fee, which depends on the salary of the person and is based on a sliding scale. Most private employment firms specialize both in level of employee with whom they work and in type of industry. Thus, employment firms that supply entry-level employees would not place managers.

Both public employment offices and private employment firms pre-screen potential applicants. They do not recommend anyone for a position unless that person is at least minimally qualified. Thus, their fees are offset by the reduced amount of work the employer needs to do to find the best employee for the job.

Community agencies, such as church groups, social agencies, or local clubs, may also serve as sources of job applicants.

"Drop-in" job seekers, or "walk-ins," are usually looking for entry-level or part-time jobs. They may visit, telephone, or send a letter to the supervisor or personnel office requesting an interview. The organization's location, public relations, or general image may have attracted them to seek a job. This kind of recruitment is usually inexpensive. The Bureau of National Affairs found that in spite of the wide use of classified ads, more firms hired walk-ins than responders to formal ads for clerical and service-worker jobs.[2]

Recruiting minorities

Minority employees may be recruited from any of the sources discussed. However, one-third of the organizations surveyed by the Bureau of National Affairs found the best source to be community agencies, closely followed by employee referrals. One-fifth recruited minority employees through employment agencies.[3]

Many large enterprises have actively sought to add women and members of minority groups to their employee lists. Equal opportunity laws for employment mandate that firms keep records of their recruitment and selection efforts to ensure that equal opportunities are provided. Finding qualified minority employees for jobs in highly specialized areas has often proven difficult. Appeals have been made by firms to colleges to urge minority students to enroll in specialized programs. For example, the shortage of qualified minority-group members for marketing positions in businesses caused a group of top personnel officers in large firms to meet with college educators in New York City in 1978 to determine ways to increase the applicant pool of minority men and women capable of performing these jobs.[*]

---

[*] The author was a member of this group and helped to organize a summer work internship for minority students in marketing departments of large firms with offices in New York City.

Selection

Even when many qualified applicants are available, selection is a difficult and very important step. If recruitment has been careful, the selection of the person capable of doing the job will be simplified. The selection, however, can be made only from among those who apply for the job.

The selection process usually includes several procedures and involves many busy people. First, the completed application blank and résumé must be looked over, and the work background must be investigated. Then initial interviewing occurs. This is often followed by job-related testing, which is also time-consuming. These tests must all then be evaluated before the second-stage interviews with various executives can take place. References are usually checked after second-stage interviews. Sometimes people are employed before all their references have been checked. All these procedures, coupled with the need to be especially cautious because of government and union rules that make the firing of unfit employees more difficult and costly, have increased the attention and time given the selection process.

Application blanks

Organizations carefully develop the application blank they use so that it will both conform to government rulings and ask for all the information needed to assess the applicant. Most applications request information about name and aliases (if any), address, schooling, age as being between eighteen and seventy years (specific age cannot be asked), references, ability to meet specified work schedules, physical well-being if related to the job, position being sought, skills or unique abilities, and previous work record. Because discrimination on the basis of race, color, religion, age, sex, or national origin is forbidden by law, questions about those matters may not be asked. Questions on credit rating, savings accounts, insurance, investments, or alcohol or other drug habits may also not be asked. Questions about convictions for crimes may be asked if the crimes are related to the job being sought (see Figure 6–3).

Résumés

Most applicants for jobs that require special skills, knowledge, educational background, or work experience prepare a résumé to present when applying for a job. *Résumés* are brief (rarely more than one page) explanations that give an applicant's name, address, age, education, work experience, special honors or achievements (if any), and specific job interests or aspirations. If one is available, it supplements the application blank, but it is purely optional on the part of the applicant.

FIGURE 6–3
EMPLOYMENT APPLICATION RECORD

QUICK-COPY COMPANY*
PERSONAL DATA

Date _____

Social Security
Number _____

Last Name _____ First Name _____ Middle Initial _____

Present Address—Street and Number ____ City ____ State ____ Zip Code ____ Telephone Number, including area code

U.S. Citizen? ☐ Yes
               ☐ No   If no, give Alien Registration or Visa Classification Number _____

Have you applied ☐ Yes (If yes, state when _____)   Are you under 18 years of age? ☐ Yes ☐ No
here before?   ☐ No   Are you over 70 years of age?   ☐ Yes ☐ No

Work Preference (check one) ☐ Full-time ☐ Part-time ☐ Temporary

Job Category (check one or more): ☐ Clerical   ☐ Keyboarding
                                   ☐ Bookkeeping   ☐ Mechanic
                                   ☐ Customer service ☐ Other _____

Are you available for work: Days   ☐ Yes ☐ No
                             Evenings ☐ Yes ☐ No
                             Saturdays ☐ Yes ☐ No

What brought you to this company: ☐ Advertisement
                                   ☐ School
                                   ☐ Agency
                                   ☐ Friend
                                   ☐ Other _____

Have you worked under any name other than the one on this application? ☐ Yes ☐ No   If yes, give other name or names used:
_____

Do you consider yourself to be handicapped? ☐ Yes ☐ No   If yes, what is the nature of your handicap? _____
_____ (Note: Qualified applicants are eligible to be hired if their handicap will not restrict their ability to do the job.)

Have you ever been convicted for a violation of the law or a felony involving dishonesty or breach of trust, or one closely related to your future work here?
☐ Yes ☐ No

EDUCATION AND TRAINING

	Name of School	City and State	Date Began	Date Left	Graduated? Yes No	Major Course
High School						
College						
Other						

Extracurricular Activities and Special Honors:

EMPLOYMENT BACKGROUND

Previous Employment (List most recent job first)

Dates Employed	Company Name and Address	Position Held	Final Salary	Reason for Leaving
From: To:				
From: To:				
From: To:				

If you are currently employed, may we contact your employer for a reference? ☐ Yes ☐ No

*The Quick-Copy Company is an Equal Opportunity Employer. Federal laws prohibit discrimination because of sex, race, color, religion, age between 18 and 70, handicap, and national origin.

Please Read the Following Statement Carefully Before You Sign This Application Blank:

By signing this application blank, I authorize the Quick-Copy Company to conduct investigations, including verification of prior employment history and education. I also have been informed that false statements or failures to disclose information may be sufficient to disqualify me for employment or, if employed, to dismiss me.

Signature of Applicant _____   Date _____

References

As noted, the application blank may ask for *references*, or people whom the employer may contact about the applicant. Former teachers, church officials, professional associates, or former employers may be references. For sensitive or important positions, references may be thoroughly checked. For less sensitive or less important positions, a quick check may be all that is required. Because applicants rarely name as references people who have not shown a liking for them, references are often questionable sources of definitive information. In analyzing the personalities and backgrounds of applicants for sensitive government posts, investigators, such as those in the FBI, call on neighbors, co-workers, and former teachers and employers.

An organization's files about a person are open to perusal by that person. This is a further reason why references usually send only positive information about an applicant. If an interviewer is in doubt about an applicant, the interviewer may prefer to telephone a reference to obtain any negative information that person may have about the applicant.

Initial interviews

An *initial interview* is a screening to determine whether or not the applicant should be asked to take a battery of tests and be invited to go through additional interviews. If this interview indicates that the applicant does not have the background or ability to do the job, the applicant is not subjected to additional time-consuming activities but is told that the organization's representatives will contact him or her if additional interviews are to take place. Because the law requires proof that no prejudice exists in hiring, careful records must be kept about people who have not been employed.

Interviewers with somewhat limited experience and authority are usually assigned to do the initial interview. Although they are prohibited from asking certain questions, they may obtain information in other ways. For example, an application blank can reveal a great deal about an applicant. The person's high-school graduation date can be used to get a rough calculation of age. A person who has held jobs for considerable periods of time is probably reliable. A person who filled out the application blank neatly and completely will undoubtedly be precise and careful on the job. A person who has shown leadership in school will undoubtedly show some leadership on the job. A person who has won scholastic honors will probably work hard. A person who has advanced quickly in another organization will undoubtedly advance rather quickly in this one.

The general appearance of the applicant is also considered. Most applicants look neat and clean. The appearance at the interview may have little relationship to the way a person looks later on the job, however.

During the interview, the interviewer will notice the person's characteristics, such as nervousness, desire to smoke, mannerisms, speech patterns, vocabulary, body language, and ability to look directly at the interviewer. All these factors will become part of the total impression that will help the interviewer to judge the applicant in relationship to the job's requirements.

Testing

If the applicant passes the initial interview, the supervisor or other interviewer may next ask him or her to take one or more tests. Any test given must relate specifically to the job for which the person is applying. Many kinds of tests may be used.

Proficiency tests. To measure an applicant's degree of adeptness in an acquired skill, an enterprise would give a *proficiency test*. Arithmetic, typing, shorthand, spelling, transcription, word-processing, data-processing, programming, or other skills may be tested. In some cases, certification or a degree may substitute for tests. For example, a certified professional secretary (CPS) may not have to take shorthand and typing tests, since the certification ensures the employer that the applicant has proven skills. Similarly, a certified public accountant (CPA) does not need to take an accounting test to prove his or her ability to handle financial accounts. Nurses, lawyers, teachers, and dental and medical technicians likewise have degrees that attest to their abilities.

Aptitude tests. To determine whether or not an applicant has the ability to learn a particular skill or concept, an *aptitude test* may be administered. Aptitude tests are available for clerical work, mechanical work, and other skills and abilities that the applicant may not already possess but will need on the job after being trained. However, most organizations prefer to hire people who possess entry-level skills rather than provide training for those skills. Hiring a trained typist (keyboarder), for example, is much less costly than training one on the job.

Intelligence (I.Q.) tests. A test that attempts to measure a person's ability to use acquired knowledge in novel ways is an *intelligence test*. Intelligence tests have been challenged by many people who believe they are culturally biased and discriminate against minority groups. Therefore they have fallen into disfavor for general use. As noted, a test can only be used if it relates to abilities needed on the job. Therefore, intelligence tests are still administered, but only in situations in which their need can be demonstrated.

Personality tests. A test that is designed to measure a person's distinguishing characteristics, attitudes, interests, and habits is a *personality test*. Personality tests are used in those organizations that believe that people with certain interests or attitudes perform certain types of jobs better than other people with different interests or attitudes. To ascertain whether the applicant possesses the needed characteristics for a specific job, a personality test may be administered and the results compared with a profile of the successful people within the organization who hold that same position. For example, salespersons may have been found to be more successful if they are extroverts as opposed to introverts. Thus a firm seeking a new salesperson would look for someone whose interests are directed outwardly rather than inwardly.

Polygraph tests. Sometimes administered by firms whose employees handle money or valuable products, *polygraph*, or *lie-detector*, tests attempt to measure honesty. The polygraph machine measures galvanic skin response, breathing, and blood pressure to indicate if stress is shown in answering a question. These tests have been accurate over 86 percent of the time.[4]

Polygraph tests are prohibited in some states. Where they are used, they have been found to be more accurate than recommendations and less costly to administer than traditional security checks are to obtain.[5]

Physical tests. *Physical tests* reveal the fitness of a person to perform a job. The minimum health checks made during physical tests are height, weight, blood pressure, urinalysis, and heart and lung conditions. The history of the person's health from infancy through adolescence is also noted. Small firms usually send applicants to a local doctor for these examinations. Large firms may have doctors and nurses available to administer them.

If certain physical specifications, such as height, strength, or requirement to stand continuously for long periods, are needed for a job, the capacity to fulfill these demands is carefully checked during the physical examination.

Not all jobs are so physically demanding. Therefore, some people who are disabled have opportunities to work. Many large firms have installed ramps, special elevators, and other conveniences to permit people in wheelchairs or those who use crutches or canes to have access to work areas. Jobs that do not require hearing skills or excellent vision may be offered to people with hearing or vision impairments.

Using tests. Most organizations that must assess specific knowledge or skills before hiring personnel will either develop their own tests or purchase tests. Tests are of little value unless they are both reliable and

valid. If a test is *reliable,* it will yield the same results when administered to different, similar populations or twice to one group after about
a one-week interval. If a test is *valid,* it will accurately assess the specific
skills or abilities being tested.

Validation of tests rests on three kinds of measurements:[6]

o *Criterion measures*—What is required on the job, such as specific aptitudes, intelligence, and skills

o *Construct measures*—What the test is supposed to measure

o *Content measures*—How performances on sample tasks included in the job will be judged

The federal departments of Justice, Labor, and Civil Service and the
Equal Employment Opportunity Commission have agreed on new guidelines for testing the validity of applicant and employment questionnaires
and tests, which were effective in September 1978. Testing, when it does
not discriminate against groups because of some bias in the tests or because it is not job related, is authorized by a statute in the Civil Rights
Act. Tests today need not be validated unless they have an adverse impact on a specific group.

Developing tests, assessing them for validity and reliability, and ad-
ministering and evaluating them can cost a large organization $25,000
or more for a total battery of tests.[7] However, job-related tests are considered to be the best scientific basis available on which to select the right
person for a job. But although tests are used extensively, they are only
part of the criteria employed in the selection of personnel.

Preliminary evaluations

After the initial interview and necessary tests have been completed, one
or more people from the employment office and the supervisor will review the results. If the applicant has successfully passed all parts of the
initial interview and the tests, recommendations will be made for additional interviews and/or activities. Because all these procedures add further to the cost of hiring personnel, they are usually performed only for
positions that lead to further promotion or that are not easily filled.

The supervisor examines the available information to note especially the strengths and weaknesses revealed that relate to this specific
job opening. For example, a candidate for a research assistantship had
no research work listed on her résumé or application form. In her covering letter, however, she claimed that she was thoroughly qualified for
the job. The supervisor would plan to question her in detail about her
experience in doing research.

Second-stage interviews

Second-stage interviews are held for applicants who have successfully passed the preliminary evaluation. For these, the interviewer has the application blank, references (if available), résumé (if one has been submitted), initial interviewer's record, and test results as background information. The supervisor or personnel officer now involved is intent on searching more deeply into the background of the applicant to ascertain more precisely his or her abilities and interests. Any one of several kinds of second-stage interviews may be used. The interviewer must conduct the interview and evaluate it when it is over.

Conducting the interview.   Interviewees are understandably nervous when anticipating and undergoing an interview. The supervisor, therefore, should select a place for the interview that will permit as much privacy as possible with few or no interruptions. When a supervisor conducts business by giving directions to employees, answering telephones, and chatting with other people during the interview, the applicant feels like an intruder and believes that the company is not seriously considering him or her for the job. Interruptions also distract both the supervisor and the applicant because they must remember at what point they were in the discussion when it resumes.

The interviewer-interviewee relationship is also affected by the seating arrangement. Talking across a desk puts a barrier between the two and makes it difficult for the supervisor to establish an aura of relaxed informality, which may help to put the applicant at ease.

Kinds of second-stage interviews.   For a *patterned interview*, the interviewer preplans the questions, which are typed or printed on a form, and asks the same ones of all applicants. The questionnaire has spaces to record answers, and the interviewer is then able to compare the answers and select the best applicant for the job. Questions such as the following may be asked:

o What courses did you take in school that might help you in the job for which you are applying?

o Which of your courses did you enjoy the most?

o Which of your courses did you find least interesting?

o Did your schooling prepare you adequately for the previous job(s) you have held? If not, explain why.

o What previous jobs have you held? Were they part-time or full-time?

o Why did you leave your most recent job?

o What was your position in that job?

o How long did you remain on that job?

o How would you rate yourself in your performance on that job in comparison to others doing the same or similar work?

o How well did you get along with your immediate supervisor?

o How well did you get along with your peers on the job?

o What did you particularly like about the job?

o What did you particularly dislike about that job?

o What are your career goals five years from now? Ten years from now?

In a *direct interview*, the supervisor may ask the interviewee questions about his or her goals, aspirations, hobbies, vacation interests, travel, reading, leisure-time activities, previous jobs, or schooling. Questions about the topics are usually easily answered and not threatening in any way to the applicant. The questions may be adapted for each applicant, and they may be asked in the order in which the topics arise. The interviewer may wish to make some notes about the interviewee's responses.

In a *nondirect interview*, the supervisor gives little or no guidance to the interviewee. This type of interview allows the applicant to talk about anything that interests him or her. After introductory remarks, the supervisor might begin by leaning back in the chair and simply saying, "Tell me something about yourself." The interviewer may reinforce the applicant's remarks from time to time by saying, "That is interesting" or "Tell me more about that particular topic."

A *stress interview* involves minor to considerable harassment of the applicant. The supervisor may ask rapid-fire questions without giving the interviewee time to respond, ask questions requiring spur-of-the-moment judgments on difficult issues, or appear to be bored or annoyed as the interviewee answers. This type of interview is used when the interviewers need to know how a person will respond to job pressure.

Evaluating second-stage interviews.   The interviewer finds the patterned interview the easiest to evaluate. The answers of different applicants may be compared, and the applicant who most nearly meets the standards set by the organization may be chosen.

Direct interviews offer the next easiest method of evaluating applicants. Even though different questions may have been asked of different applicants, the questions were specific and the quality of the answers can be compared.

Nondirect interviews are less easy to compare. The applicant can choose the material covered, and the interviewer has no control over the information obtained. However, the material the applicant chose to discuss as well as the manner of explaining it provide the supervisor with an opportunity to evaluate the interviewee.

For the stress interview, the interviewee who is able to remain calm, handle the situation well, show good judgment, and not become flustered or irritated will undoubtedly be the one chosen.

If interviews are conducted by two or more people, the interviewers' ratings are compared before the final selection is made. The supervisor's rating must be positive for a person to be assigned to the supervisor's area. However, other departments may be able to use an applicant who is rejected by one supervisor.

Assessment centers

In some enterprises, after the applicant has been through the second-stage interview, still another screening device, the assessment center, may be used. An *assessment center* is a place where, during a day-long interview, managerial/supervisory applicants are evaluated in terms of oral and written communications skill, leadership ability, organization and planning ability, decision-making skill, delegating skill, flexibility, and resistance to stress. Several people (usually from six to twelve) applying at the same time for similar jobs are placed in a room and then given various tasks to perform. Three or four members of management are present to observe and assess. Following are some typical tasks and situations used to evaluate candidates:

o Applicants are asked to write out solutions to several key management problems, such as how to reduce the work force by closing down one phase of an operation. Responses are checked for their appropriateness and clarity.

o Exercises are given to test the ability of the applicants to establish priorities in handling day-to-day problems. For example, an applicant, playacting a given role, may have several essential duties to perform by a given time and then would be told to choose which of two meetings he or she would attend—one on union activities involving that particular supervisor or one on cost control for that particular department. The applicant has to give a rationale for the decision. *Explanation*

o Interviewees and assessors attend a luncheon together. During the luncheon that has no scheduled purpose other than social, the assessors evaluate the topics discussed, the leadership shown, and the general sociability of the participants.

o Members of the group are assigned to teams. A film is then shown that presents a supervisory problem. Each team discusses the situation shown in the film. Participants then rate themselves and the other team members on their effectiveness.

o Applicants are given a list of hypothetical candidates for a proposed job. Each applicant selects the person he or she considers best for the job and then campaigns to persuade *authoritarian* the others to switch their vote. The objectivity, dogmatism, or indifference that the applicant shows in this campaigning is then analyzed by the assessment team.

o A management-decision game is assigned to teams of three people. The game may entail such problems as deciding how to price products in a competitive market, restructure an office that is to get word-processing equipment, increase profits, or improve a product. No leaders are assigned to the groups, but the assessors determine how well the groups function, what the strengths and weaknesses of individuals are, and what initiative, flexibility, creativity, communication ability, leadership, and decision-making expertise have been evident.

Following participation in assessment-center activity, each applicant is evaluated by the assessors. Decisions about hiring are made on the basis of these evaluations. In some enterprises, applicants are counseled on their weaknesses and strengths after the assessment.

The use of assessment centers has been so effective in selecting capable people that some organizations have also adopted it for promoting within the firm and determining the training needs of supervisors. Not only are those who go through the assessment center benefited, but those supervisors who do the assessments find that their skills and abilities are improved.

Importance of matching the applicant to the job

The more difficult the job is to perform, the longer the search for an appropriate person usually takes. Positions that require lesser skills and abilities are usually easier to fill. Even for entry-level, easy-to-fill jobs, several careful screening practices may be used to ensure employers that the most able person has been added to the work force.

The more careful an enterprise is in matching qualified applicants to jobs, the more satisfied both the employee and the employer will be. People like to be employed where their skills and abilities can be properly demonstrated and where they enjoy working. Similarly, organizations seek dedicated, eager-to-work, able people to further their goals.

Job seeking is a time-consuming, costly activity for both the applicant and the employer. Careful screening and selection reduce the need to repeat the process for both.

The supervisor's role in selecting employees

Only if an organization has loyal, dedicated, creative, and able employees can it hope to achieve its goals. Selection, therefore, is one of the most important tasks in an organization. The supervisor is involved in all stages. His or her role, however, varies depending on the size and complexity of the organization.

In small firms, the person who supervises employees is usually also the employer who performs all the hiring steps. Also, in a small unit of a large multiunit firm, such as a chain organization, the supervisor may be the sole person in charge of hiring for that unit. In larger organizations, a personnel officer usually performs the recruiting part of the task and the initial screening of applicants, but the supervisor makes the final decision to hire a particular applicant.

In some organizations, the supervisor may wish to delegate the selection of entry-level persons to the personnel department. In this case, entry-level office workers, part-time salespeople, clerical workers, and receptionists may be employed without the advice and consent of the supervisor.

In organizations in which management trainees are employed, supervisors from several different sections may join together in assessing and choosing new recruits.

In all organizations, if job analyses, descriptions, and specifications are developed, supervisors are involved in every step of the process both in overseeing the activity for their departments and in using the final documents produced.

SUMMARY

o Because employees determine the ability of an enterprise to meet its goals, selection of them is one of the most important tasks to be performed.

SELECTING EMPLOYEES

o Reasons for employing additional people include transfers, promotions, retirements, discharges, increased work loads, expansion, broader scope, new machines, and expanded workdays or workweeks.

o The employment process begins with an employee requisition, the official request to employ one or more people.

o Job analyses detail information about each task performed on a job; job descriptions organize this information; and job specifications summarize the information to explain the job to recruiters.

o Inside a firm, present employees, former employees, and friends and relatives of employees may be recruited. Outside the firm, the firm's reputation, advertisements, community agencies, local school counselors, and private and public employment offices may attract applicants.

o A variety of sources on which to base the selection decision exist. Depending on the job to be filled, application blanks, résumés, references, initial interviews, tests, second-stage interviews, and/or assessment-center activities may be evaluated.

o Testing may include proficiency tests, aptitude tests, intelligence tests, personality tests, polygraph tests, and/or physical tests.

o The four kinds of second-stage interviews are patterned, direct, nondirect, and stress.

o Assessment centers evaluate applicants in terms of their ability to perform job-related tasks in the presence of management representatives.

o Both the firm and the employee benefit when the right person is matched to the job.

o The supervisor plays the major role in hiring new people for a small organization. In a larger enterprise, the supervisor plays a key role in hiring those employed in his or her department.

REFERENCES

[1] Urban C. Lehner, "Labor Letter," *Wall Street Journal*, September 11, 1979, p. 1.
[2] Lehner, "Labor Letter," p. 1.
[3] Lehner, "Labor Letter," p. 1.
[4] "Test Measure: Polygraph Accuracy," *Retail Operations News Bulletin*, Vol. 6, No. 3, 1977, p. 11.
[5] Anna Quindlen, "Polygraph Tests for Jobs: Truth and Consequences," *New York Times*, August 19, 1977, p. B1.
[6] "Making Your Tests Effective—and Legal," *Training*, April 1979, pp. 80–82.
[7] Peter Koenig, "Testing: The Industrial Psychologist's Headache," *Management Review*, October 1974, p. 41.

REVIEW AND DISCUSSION QUESTIONS

1. Discuss at least three reasons for adding personnel to a firm.
2. What steps does an organization take to develop a job analysis? What are some advantages of job analyses?
3. What value does a job description have? How might it be used?
4. What are the factors that may make recruitment costly?
5. What is the role of the initial interviewer in the selection process?
6. Explain the statement "Employment tests must be job related."
7. What are the various kinds of tests that might be used in selection, and what is the purpose of each?
8. What is an assessment center? For what types of positions are assessment-center evaluations used?
9. Why is matching an applicant to a job very important?
10. What role does the supervisor play in the selection process in a small firm? In a large firm?

ASSIGNMENTS

1. Draw up a job analysis for a job that you currently hold. If you are not employed, do a job analysis on your activities as a student. How much time did it take to do this analysis? What benefits, if any, resulted from your doing this assignment?
2. Examine the help-wanted columns in a daily newspaper. Do any blind ads appear? If so, how did you identify them? What was the proportion of them to open ads? To which would you prefer to respond? Give reasons for your answer.

PROBLEM FOR RESOLUTION

A supervisor of the office staff in a law firm received the following two résumés on page 152 from applicants for an entry-level position. The job specification for this position stated:

JOB SPECIFICATION: Entry-level position with potential for promotion. Duties include typing, clerical work, answering the telephone, filing and retrieving documents, and providing messenger service for other employees.

Which applicant appears, on the basis of the résumés, to be more suited for the position?

Would you be satisfied to hire a person based on a résumé only? Give reasons for your response.

If you were to interview these two people, what other information would you seek?

Mattie B. Harland
602 Sutter Avenue
Falls River, New Jersey 07419
Telephone: (201) 555-1579

EDUCATION:

1978 - present   Falls River Community
                        College
                 Major - Liberal Arts
                 Graduation - June 1981
                 Overall average - 2.8

WORK EXPERIENCE:

1979 - present   Student assistant,
                 Falls Counseling
                 Center, Main Street,
                 Falls River, N. J.
                 Duties: General rec-
                 eptionist; answer
                 the telephone; dis-
                 tribute mail; make
                 appointments for
                 people to see coun-
                 selors; direct people
                 to appropriate depart-
                 ment for assistance.

MEMBERSHIPS: Student Council of
                 community college.

HOBBIES: Joggering, tennis,
                 baseball, basketball

REFERENCES: Supplied on request.

Dorrette M. Dale
813 Crown Street #B4
Falls River, New Jersey 07419
Telephone: (201) 555-2367

Occupational Goal: To find a position
   in the area of legal stenography

Education: Falls River Community
                    College
            A.A.S., June 1981
            Major: Legal Secretarial
            Science
            Overall average - 2.5

Experience: Falls River C. C. Admis-
            sions Office.
            Student Aide: Typing, fil-
            ing, and answering tele-
            phone, etc.

Special   Typing 45 - 50 words per
   Skills: minute, IBM Selectric,
            Smith Corona, some knowledge
            of Dictaphone. Steno 80 -
            100 words per minute.

Membership:Phi Beta Lambda Club,
            Falls River C. C. Coal-
            ition for Special Pro-
            grams, and in process of
            forming an organization
            for students of Special
            Programs at Falls River
            C. C.

Hobbies: Sewing, crocheting, reading,
            outdoor sports.

References: Will be furnished upon
               request.

CASE STUDY

You are a supervisor of a group of people who sell computer systems. The employees' work requires a knowledge of both the hardware and its components and the manner in which these may be linked to other hardware the buyer already owns.

Two months ago, after an equally long search, you hired an experienced, particularly able man, Anthony Jared. His record in this first period of work, following a few days of training, has been quite remarkable. Just as you are beginning to pride yourself on your skill in

selecting this newest recruit, you receive a call from the personnel office. They advise you that they have uncovered a case of grand larceny
in Mr. Jared's previous work record some seventeen years ago and that
according to the written policy of your company, he is to be fired immediately.

You know that getting a satisfactory replacement for Mr. Jared is
almost impossible. His showing to date is so good that you envision his
becoming a leading salesperson within a year. You discuss this dilemma
with your boss, who agrees that a valuable addition to the staff should
be salvaged, if possible.

Considering your problems, your boss's reactions, the policy of the
company, and the demand from the personnel office, what recommendation would you make? Give reasons for your decision.

FURTHER READING

Bruno, Jim. "Search for Weaknesses with Psychological Tests." *Administrative Management*, May 1979, pp. 28–31.
    Presents an in-depth interview with Dr. Arthur A. Witkin, chief
psychologist for the Personnel Sciences Center of New York.
Einstein, Kurt. "Job Interviewing: The Art of Hearing What the Candidate Would Rather Not Say." *Association Management*, Vol. 30, No.
11, pp. 32–37.
    Describes three main areas of the selection process: develop-
ment of job specifications, setting criteria against which to measure
the candidate, and techniques to use in gathering the necessary information. Explains that interviewers need a well-developed intui-
tive sense.
Herman, Robin. "Lie Detector Use on Jobs Growing." *New York Times*,
August 7, 1980, pp. B1 & B5.
    Explains that the New York Civil Liberties Union has opposed
the use of polygraphs but increased theft has forced their use, and
that a typical polygraph test takes between sixty to ninety minutes
and currently costs from $50 to $200 per subject to administer.
"How One Company's 'Assessment Center' Paid Off on the Bottom
Line." *Training*, April 1976, pp. 24–25.
    Reports one company's attempt to obtain and keep skilled and
dedicated people.
Rout, Lawrence. "Going for Broker: Our Man Takes Part in Stock Selling
Test." *Wall Street Journal*, April 4, 1979, pp. 1 & 31.
    Explains the use of assessment-center techniques in selecting
people.
Swain, Robert. "Job Interviews: Questions of Style." *New York Times*,
June 22, 1980, p. F16.

Explains that unexpected, apparently unrelated questions are sometimes asked by interviewers in the middle of a job interview. If an applicant's confidence is lost, or if unintended biases are revealed by the answers, the job may also be lost.

Thompson, Donald B. " 'Headhunters': Can You Trust Their Aim?" *Industry Week*, December 11, 1978, p. 66.

Discusses how long it usually takes to place people and the advantages and disadvantages of using headhunters.

Whitehead, Ross. "Interviewing—The Test Most Managers Flunk." *Industry Week*, September 18, 1978, pp. 85–89.

Reports how organizations need to spend more time training their managers to interview properly.

7
training
employees

After studying and analyzing this chapter, you should be able to:

Differentiate between training and education, formal and informal training, centralized and decentralized training, planned and unplanned training, and group and individual training.

Explain how training can be given outside a firm.

Discuss why and how initial training, retraining, continuation training, and promotion training are given.

Describe the uses of job analyses, behavioral objectives, and evaluation in establishing a formal training program.

Explain the use of the various methods of formal training.

Describe how audiovisual aids are used in training.

Discuss the problems in determining the costs and rewards of training.

THE APPLICANT WHO WAS carefully selected has now become an employee of the firm. From the moment an employee enters a firm, training begins. Even in firms that have no formal training programs, training exists. Just by observing experienced employees and supervisors, a new employee learns many of the ways used to accomplish the work of the firm. The company that does not want this informal and uncontrolled method of training to be the guide for new employees will establish a more formal program to impart needed and desirable information. Employees are important assets, and training upgrades their abilities and further increases their value to a firm.

Most large enterprises not only maintain staffs of in-house trainers but also refund some or all tuition for college and other outside courses that are designed to improve employees' job knowledge or skills.

What is training?

Training is the process of continuously developing people to enable them to perform specific tasks adequately and to form the kinds of attitudes necessary to accomplish those tasks, work with others, and obey rules. Whereas *education* is primarily aimed at a general broadening of a person's knowledge, training is directed at specific behaviors.

According to a survey of over one thousand firms, the American Society for Personnel Administration concluded that first-line supervisors are trained by more firms than any other single group of employees. Of those firms, 86 percent trained first-line supervisors.[1]

Training programs are developed taking many factors into consideration (see Figure 7–1):

o *The needs of employees* to learn specific skills and information

o *The policies* that determine how organizational goals will be attained

o *The wants and needs of the customers* who use the organizations' products and services

o *The supervisors' perceptions* of departmental goals

o *The new concepts and theories,* that, if used, may help employees increase productivity

o *The constraints* on the organization, such as laws; rulings; union contracts; competition, which forces changes to be adopted more quickly than was originally planned; and costs, which may be too high to permit the optimum program to be developed

FIGURE 7–1
FACTORS INVOLVED IN THE DEVELOPMENT
OF A TRAINING PROGRAM

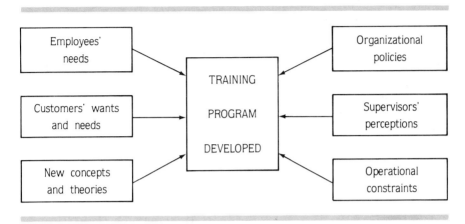

Training combines many types of activities and is performed for many different levels of employees. It can take place either within or outside a firm. The goal of training is to produce a capable and efficient group of employees, each member of which is knowledgeable about the job he or she is performing or will do at some future time.

The supervisor's role in training

Who trains employees is determined by many factors. Both the amount of training and the kind of training vary. In small firms, the supervisor either does all the training or delegates that task to one or more of the experienced employees. As enterprises grow in size, they consolidate certain parts of training so that each supervisor does not have to repeat instructions to each new employee. Thus, the personnel officer or department usually takes charge of the organized parts of the training process. The training staff of the personnel department confers with individual supervisors in developing a training program. Thereafter, training that pertains to everyone or to sizeable groups of employees is done by the personnel department. However, specific training that applies only to certain areas or to certain individuals is still handled by the supervisor.

The supervisor's role in training is important regardless of who does the actual training because the trained employee returns to the department to perform work according to the standards set for that particular area. The supervisor must evaluate the results of the training and supplement the training as needed.

Training within a firm

Training within a firm varies from that given for new entry-level employees to that provided for manager-training groups to that offered for executives to improve their job performance or to ready them for promotion. Such training may be formal or informal, centralized or decentralized, planned or unplanned.

Formal training. Activities that have been established as part of the training plan of the firm comprise *formal training*. If, for example, an introduction to the firm has been developed and time is set aside for it to be presented by one or more designated persons to new employees, then it becomes a part of the formal program of training.

Informal training. Training that is left to each individual supervisor to handle in any manner deemed desirable is *informal training*. For instance, if the introduction is performed by individual supervisors as they notice a need for it, the training is informal.

Centralized training. Formal training that takes place under the direct jurisdiction of the training staff is *centralized training*. It is usually given to people from different departments, and it occurs in training classrooms or other places assigned for the training staff's use. *Vestibule training* is a form of centralized training. Equipment identical or similar to that used on the job is placed in a convenient isolated area away from the center of work. Employees practice on this equipment until their proficiency reaches the level that makes them productive enough to join their department.

Decentralized training. Formal or informal training done by individual supervisors within their own departments for members of their own staffs is *decentralized training*.

Planned training. Formal training for which a need has been noted and a program established is *planned training*. Centralized training is almost always carefully planned. Decentralized training may also have been carefully planned before it occurs.

Unplanned training. Informal training that takes place constantly as employees observe one another and their supervisors during working hours is *unplanned training*. Unplanned training may also occur during spur-of-the-moment meetings to handle some crisis that has arisen and needs immediate attention.

Training outside a firm

Many enterprises believe in helping employees to upgrade their background knowledge by paying all or part of the cost of specially created training programs, conferences, and formal schooling. Various tuition-reimbursement plans are available, mainly for job-related education. These plans not only help employees to expand their knowledge but also add to their fringe benefits.

Sometimes employees assume personal responsibility for training outside a firm. For example, supervisors who are in line for top executive positions may seek training to help them speak and write more effectively, dress more appropriately, and project a more executive manner.

When is formal training given?

Informal training occurs constantly throughout a person's tenure on a job. Formal training, on the other hand, is given at one or more career points and takes several forms.

Initial training

Any activities that are needed to prepare a new employee to handle his or her first job assignment are called *initial training*. The purpose of initial training is to make the new worker productive as quickly as possible. Uusually, initial training includes orientation training and an explanation of the specific job to which the person has been assigned.

Orientation training is the process of giving a new employee an overview of the firm. It may incorporate information about the firm's history, founders and their successors, present executives and their major areas of responsibility, and organization chart. Orientation training also usually includes explanations of the policies of the firm, the responsibility of each employee for carrying out those policies, and the rules that govern behavior within the firm. The latter usually cover days and hours of work; doors by which to enter and leave; space in which to store coats and other belongings during the workday; use of employee lounges, lunchrooms, and restrooms; medical services available; emergencies; and other important general directives.

Orientation is usually the same for all new employees. The balance of initial training differs depending on the area in which the new employee will work. In this second part of initial training, the new employee is given a detailed explanation of the specific job he or she will perform. For example, the forms to be used, the method of handling money, the way to record the receipt of money, the flow of work, and the expected productivity may all be carefully demonstrated.

Retraining

If a person makes many mistakes on the job or does not know the routines of the position, retraining may be necessary. *Retraining* is the process of reinstructing an employee in the skills he or she should have learned in initial training. Retraining may be centralized if the skills are general and were initially taught by the training staff. For example, the correct operation of word-processing or data-processing equipment may be effectively redemonstrated by central trainers. For more unique skills, such as the handling of special forms or machines, which are performed in only a few locations, decentralized training within the department may be better.

Retraining is often more difficult to accomplish than initial training. The employee not only must unlearn an incorrect way of doing the job but also must learn the correct procedure. If the employee did not understand the directions during initial training, he or she may be even slower in understanding the directions during retraining, since the knowledge of having failed once makes him or her apprehensive about a second failure.

Continuation training

Continuation training goes beyond initial training in giving employees desirable and necessary information. Its purpose is to keep employees up to date about any changes in the work environment, to extend their training to incorporate more advanced job information, or to improve their attitudes toward fellow employees, supervisors, and customers.

The increase in the number of government laws, rulings, and standards has made continuation training essential for all employees who deal with other people. Equal-opportunity laws and corresponding company policies, for example, must be explained in continuation-training sessions.

Promotion training

When an employee is ready to progress from one job to another, he or she may need to acquire skills and/or knowledge to perform the new job. These are developed through *promotion training*.

The specific instruction given in promotion training depends on the job to which the employee is being promoted. For instance, promotion training for an employee being readied for a junior executive position often includes an explanation of the tasks of the job, drill on the forms that are used, some type of supervisory training, and talks by and discussions with major executives in the firm. For higher-level managerial promotions, promotion training may be less formal and may be given by the person's new supervisor on a one-to-one basis. Usually the supervisor develops a training program that is tailored to the needs of the person being promoted.

Establishing a formal training program

The results of training are difficult to measure. One reason is that trainers often fail to set specific goals. This problem can be overcome by using a *systems approach* to training, that is, by carefully planning every step. The systems approach helps to make goals more definite and results more measurable.[2] It is based on the use of job analyses, behavioral objectives, and evaluation.

Use of job analyses

The first step in the systems approach to training is to determine what training is needed for a certain job. To do this, the trainer must first know the characteristics and requirements of that job. The job analysis (discussed in Chapter 6) can give the trainer this information and therefore becomes the basis for determining the training needs.

Use of behavioral objectives

The systems approach requires that the tasks to be learned specify the behaviors that should result. To do this, the trainer must first make certain that any training goal is measurable, that the behavior to be expected is specified, and that the standards for acceptable performance are stated. In a training session, behavioral objectives are put into practice as follows:

- o A statement of the desired behavior is made. This tells the learner what he or she will be able to do if the training is successfully completed.

- o An explanation of the circumstances under which the desired behavior is expected to occur is given.

- o A standard of the quantity and quality of the desired behavior that the trainer will accept as evidence that the learner has acquired the behavior is set.

For example, for word processing, the desired behavior, circumstances, and standard may be stated as follows:

o The trainee using a mag-card typewriter will be able to transcribe from a dictation tape four ten-line business letters with no errors in fifteen minutes.

or

o The trainee using a mag-card typewriter will be able to type from rough copy a ten-page report with insertions and footnotes in two hours. The finished copy should have no errors.

For telephoning:

o The trainee will be able to answer the telephone according to the telephone-usage standards of the company, direct calls to the people requested, and handle calls efficiently and courteously. If a callback is requested, the trainee will be able to take the message details courteously and to transfer them immediately and correctly to the department or person concerned.

To determine desired behaviors, a great deal of preparatory work must be accomplished by the supervisor, training staff, or others who work on such training:

o From the task descriptions prepared for each job for which training is to be done, the skills, knowledge, and attitudes that must be developed are determined.

o The training objectives are then derived from a careful analysis of the skills, knowledge, and attitudes.

o These training objectives are then put in order, and the teaching techniques that are to be used to achieve them are determined.

o Depending on the amount and time needed, the learning is divided into segments, called *units*. The training program for each unit is designed.

o The training program is then used as the basis for the pretest and the posttest of the unit. A *pretest* is a written, oral, or performance check given before any training occurs on a particular subject matter in the organization. It determines what level of knowledge or skill the trainee has at that point in time. A *posttest* is a written, oral, or performance check given after the training occurs on the particular subject matter in the organization. It determines if the trainee has reached a satisfactory level of performance. The pretest and posttest should cover the same material for a specific unit. If the trainee passes the pretest, he or she skips that unit and progresses to the next. The trainee who does not pass the pretest studies the material for the unit and takes the posttest. This process is repeated until the posttest, which certifies the trainee's knowledge of that unit, has been passed. A successfully passed posttest assures the trainer that the trainee is ready for the next unit of study.

Evaluating the program

Even though trainees may pass the posttests for various units, the final determination of the success of training is their performance on the job. Therefore, constant feedback from supervisors is needed to ensure that the training is properly preparing workers. Frequently, units of study have to be revised in order to keep the information in them current and to improve their power to instruct. In addition, changes in training programs have to be made because jobs themselves are always being altered. Only by evaluating the performance of people on the job can the worth of a training program be determined.

One large computer firm evaluated its training program in an interesting way. The company first designed, with the help of professional educators, a training program for its experienced salespersonnel. Prior to the administration of the program, a group of salespersons, called Group A, was chosen and matched for performance against another group, called Group B, in the same geographical area. The three-week training program was then given only to the members of Group A.

During the following six-month period, records of performance of all the salespersonnel in both groups were carefully kept. At the end of that time, Group A's record was 40 percent better than Group B's. The only difference had been the training that Group A members had received. The company concluded that the training program was effective and began to train other units within the company in the same way.* This type of evaluation assured management that the training program did increase productivity of workers and simultaneously decreased overall costs to the firm. Figure 7–2 summarizes the development and evaluation of a training program.

* The author was involved as an adviser on this series of programs.

FIGURE 7–2
MODEL FOR DEVELOPING AND EVALUATING TRAINING

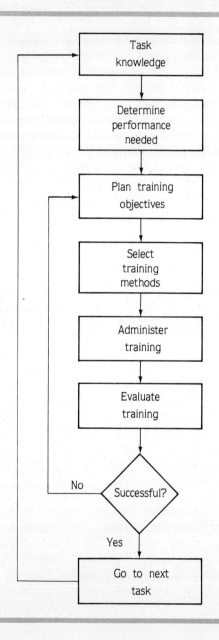

Methods of formal training

Depending on the number of people needing training, formal training takes place either in groups or individually. For both kinds of training, trainers may prepare visual aids and written material as supplements.

Group training

Training people in groups is familiar to all. It is the way training is done in schools and colleges throughout the country. People who have similar training needs are assembled and taught the necessary information. At the conclusion, testing may or may not be performed, depending on the nature of the training materials and the need to determine whether the trainee has properly learned the information.

Contingent upon the size of the group and the information to be imparted, group training may be given through various methods.

Lectures. A common method of presenting material, lectures are especially useful when the lecturer has essential knowledge that must be imparted to the group in a minimum amount of time. Often, this information could also be supplied through brochures or other written material. However, a forceful presenter can not only package the information more interestingly but also interpret and expand on it as needed.

Lectures are often used to present the history of an enterprise, introduce new ideas or concepts, advise a group about the firm's rules, or inspire employees to be more productive or dedicated.

A lecture allows the trainer to select the material to be presented, the form of presentation, and the length of time to be given to each item. The number of people who can attend a lecture is virtually unlimited, and therefore many people may be trained simultaneously.

The lecturer should be aware that people who are just sitting and listening are prone to think about other things unless the trainer is unusually effective in holding their attention. Therefore, a lecturer should carefully prepare and persuasively deliver the address if trainees are to benefit optimally.

Visual aids are often used by lecturers to hold the attention of the audience and to dramatize and emphasize certain points further. (Types of visual aids will be discussed later.) The use of visual aids may be accompanied by the distribution of handouts (also visual aids) that duplicate the charts, graphs, or other materials used in the illustrations. Trainees can later refer to these handouts to reinforce their learning.

Question-and-answer sessions, or learner-controlled instruction (LCI). These sessions are used when trainees need a further explanation of information.

They may be held following a lecture or may be instigated by the training department, the supervisor, or the trainees themselves.

Question-and-answer sessions have several advantages. They usually command the attention of trainees somewhat better than lectures. A person who asks a question has shown interest, has been thinking, and will usually listen intently to the answer. Control of the learning is put into the hands of the trainees instead of the trainers. Co-workers are often interested in what their peers ask, and they may find the answers pertinent to their job problems. Such sessions are usually devoted to questions for which specific answers exist, and they permit trainees to ask about those phases of the work they least understand. However, because question-and-answer sessions are not controlled by the trainers, trainers may find some questions difficult or impossible to answer without further investigation.

The group for a question-and-answer session may be large or small. The smaller the group, the greater the chance for everyone to ask questions. Groups of ten to twenty people are most effective when using this technique.

Discussions. These differ from question-and-answer sessions in several ways. A discussion may be held following a lecture, and if so, the audience is usually divided into smaller groups of five to fifteen persons each. These groups may or may not include the lecturer. Other persons knowledgeable about the lecturer's topic may substitute. A discussion is not used to supply specific information but rather to get opinions about certain issues. Various points of view are usually expressed, and an agreement may be sought. The leader of the discussion may take little or no part other than to introduce the topic and to moderate. A discussion is ordinarily used only after people have had orientation and other initial training and have been with the firm long enough to have opinions about matters of mutual concern.

Discussions are usually more successful than lectures in bringing about change. When people take part in discussions, they become involved, and the topics being considered become more meaningful. This is a slightly modified form of learner-controlled instruction.

For example, following a lecture on the policies of the company that suggest courtesy be shown to the customer regardless of his or her display of bad temper or unreasonableness, the employees may discuss experiences they have had and the results. Ms. Bryant, a beauty parlor customer, complained after receiving a shampoo and set that her hair looked too flat. She was berating the operator, Paul, about how awful she looked with a "flat top." Without argument, Paul reached for a current fashion magazine and flipped pages until he found a picture of a leading socialite. As he handed the magazine to Ms. Bryant, he noted the similarity of her hairstyle to that of the socialite and commented that Ms. Bryant looked even more attractive. Ms. Bryant looked at the picture and then examined her own image in the mirror. She smiled, tipped Paul, and left. In a discussion training session, Paul explained he never argues—he uses gentle persuasion with demanding customers.

Demonstrations. These are used when trainees must be taught specifically how to do something. The trainer shows the way a task is done and then asks the trainee to perform that task. For example, the correct way to fill out forms may be demonstrated by the trainer and then practiced by the trainee. Similarly, the correct use of a dictating machine, typewriter, word processor, copy machine, calculator, computer terminal, or telephone might be demonstrated and then practiced.

The number of people who can be present when a trainer demonstrates a task varies depending on how well the demonstration can be seen and the amount of supervision needed during the practice session. If many people need to be trained for a specific task, the group may be divided, and several or as few as one may be trained at a time. Or a record of a demonstration may be made on videotape or film to use later as needed. When the tape or film is used, a trainer is usually present to ensure that trainees have learned to perform the task correctly.

Trainees may fear or resent using new machines, forms, or techniques. Therefore, trainers need to be patient with and considerate of trainees when teaching by demonstration.

Role playing. This is used to prepare trainees to meet situations that are either unfamiliar or have been improperly handled previously. Through role playing, trainees learn under circumstances that are not as threatening as they may be on the job.

In role playing, a situation that may occur on the job is described by the trainer or supervisor. The trainee is asked to play his or her role in the firm or the role of another, such as receptionist, secretary, salesperson, customer, or supervisor. Other trainees play other roles and act out the situation described. Still other trainees, who are not role playing during this session, observe the action. Following the role playing, everyone involved critiques what took place. The trainees who played roles are asked to comment on how their performance might have been improved. By playing different roles, trainees can empathize with those with whom they will be dealing and can analyze their jobs from a more objective point of view.

Role playing is usually done with a few people at a time. However, as noted, a larger audience of trainees may be present to observe and critique the experience.

Behavior modeling. Similar to role playing, behavior modeling requires that trainees imitate a particularly skillful person demonstrating the ideal way to handle a particular situation. It is used to teach employees how to deal with unfamiliar or previously improperly handled situations.

Trainees first observe a film or videotape of a person (preferably someone they all know and respect) handling a situation in the desired way. Any one of a number of situations may be shown: for example, orienting new employees, disciplining an employee who is chronically late, presenting a new form, or answering the telephone.

Following the viewing, the trainees discuss what they have seen. Each trainee then practices the behaviors that were demonstrated. Increasingly more difficult situations are introduced as the trainees become proficient in the new techniques. The trainer gives positive feedback by encouraging the trainees as they practice their new behavior.

After several trial runs, the exercises are videotaped so that trainees can see themselves and analyze their actions. Trainees are then asked to try out the new technique on the job and to report back at a given time about their progress.

Sensitivity training. Also called *T-group training* or *encounter training*, sensitivity training was first used in England in the early 1940s and became common in the United States during the 1960s and 1970s. This method is used to develop managerial skills by increasing a trainee's self-awareness both in relation to others and in the group's relation to the trainee. If a manager can get along well with other people, spark their interests, and inspire their self-confidence, he or she can usually succeed in getting subordinates to be productive on the job.

The goals of a person in sensitivity training are to understand and accept oneself by viewing one's personality as others see it, to try to understand other people, and to comprehend how behavior like one's own either keeps groups functioning smoothly or causes friction.[3]

Encounter sessions focus on the present. Group members are encouraged to express thoughts, feelings, and impressions. They are further urged to rely on one another. For example, half the group may be blindfolded and led by other members down corridors, steps, and even outdoors. Having to trust another person completely to be sure of not taking a misstep is an important part of sensitivity training.

Sensitivity training is particularly used to reveal frustrations, fears, jealousy, bigotry, and resentments. Therefore, the training group should consist of people from different socioeconomic, ethnic, and religious backgrounds so that members will understand better one another's repressed feelings and attitudes, which they are encouraged to express.

Several sensitivity-training sessions are usually scheduled for a group. They may take place either all day during a weekend retreat or over a period of several days during regular workweeks. The group should have an outside adviser, who serves primarily as an observer to see that the purposes of the group are constantly pursued. The adviser also notices the behavior of the various people present.

Sessions are sometimes videotaped for later playback and analysis. Even if they are not, the manner in which group members respond to and solve problems is evaluated by the trainer and discussed with each group participant. This evaluation and discussion make participants aware of their behavior patterns, their ability to relate to others and their environment, and the way in which others relate to them.

Assertiveness training. Also called *assertion training*, assertiveness training is a method of balancing employee behavior between passivity and aggressiveness and emphasizing self-responsibility. For interpersonal relations, this training has been especially popular since women began to seek equal salaries, promotions, and status with men. Men as well as women benefit from this training.

Behavior runs on a continuum from passive through assertive to aggressive. *Passive behavior* is demonstrated by those who seek to win the approval of others and to avoid upsetting or hurting anyone. Such people tend to hold back their opinions and do not attempt to change the status quo. They allow others to push ahead of them in lines or for jobs and to take credit for their ideas. They resent these actions, but they are too timid to assert their resentment.

Aggressive behavior is demonstrated by those who have little or no concern for the opinions of others. They often belittle others' opinions, are obsessed with a desire to win, tend to boast of their achievements and activities, and are determined to change anything they do not like. They take ideas wherever they can get them and push ahead of others without a qualm.

Assertive behavior, between these two extremes, is shown by people who respect others' opinions and positions, but believe their opinions are also worth stating. Assertive people are self-confident, are able to win or lose gracefully, and stand up for their rights without violating others'.

All three behaviors involve two or more people. Three main areas of concern are requests, refusals, and expressions. Assertive people are able to ask for what they want and to receive requests graciously. Similarly, they can refuse what they do not want and accept others' refusals. They express both positive and negative messages and receive these messages from others (see Figure 7–3).

In assertiveness training, trainees are urged to take neither the passive "flight" reaction to situations nor the aggressive "fight" attitudes. Instead, they are urged to seek problem solving as the solution. If an issue can be resolved in a way that helps everyone concerned, a middle ground has been found between passivity and aggression.

FIGURE 7–3
MODEL OF PASSIVE, ASSERTIVE, AND AGGRESSIVE BEHAVIOR

REQUESTS	Passive	Assertive	Aggressive
	Person ↑ from Other(s)	Person ↓ ↑ to from Other(s)	Person ↓ to Other(s)
REFUSALS	Self ↑ from Other(s)	Self ↓ ↑ to from Other(s)	Self ↓ to Other(s)
POSITIVE AND NEGATIVE MESSAGES	Self ↑ from Other(s)	Self ↓ ↑ to from Other(s)	Self ↓ to Other(s)

For example, Ms. Birch, a new supervisor, was faced with a domi-
nating older employee who was chronically late and Ms. Birch feared
reprimanding her. At the urging of the other employees, she realized
that she had to confront the problem. With determination, Ms. Birch
invited the older employee to discuss her tardiness and the resulting
damage to the work of the other employees and to their morale.

This problem-solving approach shows respect for others but allows
one to express feelings, opinions, and needs openly and forthrightly.

Several steps are taken in group sessions to help people become
assertive:

o Each person is asked to determine his or her own place on
  the behavior continuum.

o Assertiveness is practiced, beginning with simple statements
  and progressing to more difficult ones.

o After watching tapes of peers and films of model situations,
  behavior modeling is practiced.

o Reinforcement from the trainer, one's peers, and oneself aids in making the training appear desirable.

o The trainee is urged to use assertive behavior in job situations.

o The trainee reports these job situations to the group for analysis and discussion.

Constant use of this behavior, evaluation of the results, and discussion with one's peers is needed to have assertive behavior become a natural reaction in situations.

Seminars. These resemble discussions except for the basic procedure. Seminars consist of a series of meetings about a specific topic. The same group of trainees continually interacts for the duration of the training period. For each session, one or more trainees prepare and give a presentation about some aspect of the topic under study. The other trainees then analyze and discuss the ideas. At each meeting, a different concept is presented, analyzed, and discussed. The trainer or supervisor may be involved as only the initial arranger of the meetings or as an onlooker as the various meetings are held.

The total involvement of all the trainees makes seminars a unique and important way of developing people. They are particularly useful for supervisory personnel and may also be used for any persons who have decision-making responsibilities and opportunities to interact with others in their daily routines. However, they are not useful for teaching basic skills or knowledge.

Case studies. These are used by both colleges and firms as part of management or supervisory training. Case studies present unsolved situations that have no single right answer but may be handled in a variety of ways, and ask trainees to suggest ways to deal with the situations. For example, a case may supply information about a department, list the number of employees and their work assignments, and ask how production could be increased. Based on the information supplied, trainees make suggestions. These are evaluated by other trainees or by teams that have been assigned within the group. Training through case studies develops decision-making ability and judgment. Individuals as well as groups may be taught by this method.

Computer game analyses. This technique is used for case studies that contain numerical data concerning costs and expenditures. Teams of trainees are chosen, and each is assigned the same case. The team members first analyze the problem and consider several solutions. Then they agree on decisions about the data and program them into a computer, which has been instructed previously about producing results from the data fed to it. The results that each team receives are used for succeeding phases of the game. The winner is the team whose profits, or cash on hand, are the most satisfactory at the end of a given number of cycles according to the computer report.

In one game, trainees were supposed to be part of a management team of a firm that was in financial difficulty but had a new product to market. Facts about the amount of profit in the previous year, the money available for publicity and advertising, the costs of personnel, and the costs to purchase the item were all supplied to each team. The teams worked on monthly statements for a six-month period. Each month's solution, when fed into the computer, brought forth the results upon which the decisions for the following month had to be based. The team that had the highest net profit according to the computer at the end of the six-month period was declared the winner. Because the computer could calculate a large number of figures in a few seconds, the entire six-month operation could be observed in one four-hour training session.

Computer games require high motivation and intensive concentration from all team members. Since the results change for each period and depend on decisions made in earlier periods, as really happens in business, the games more nearly resemble actual decision making than other methods of training. However, the costs to develop the games and the equipment needed to play them make their use possible only in large firms or schools that have computer equipment.

Individual training

Although individual training is more costly than group training, it is given at least sporadically in all firms. At the conclusion, testing may or may not be done, depending on the nature of the training materials and the need to determine whether the trainees have properly learned the information. Many methods, in addition to those already mentioned, may be used to train people individually.

Counseling. Counseling is a deliberate effort to help an employee by holding private discussions. It is considered an ideal method of individual training when someone has made an error or when things are not being handled as efficiently as they might be. Everyone makes mistakes on occasion. However, no one likes to be told, especially in front of others, about the mistake. The counselor usually chooses to discuss the problem in a place that is neither public nor frightening to the trainee. When the counselor meets with the person, he or she usually says something positive before voicing any condemnation. The counselor may use the session for retraining or for discussing the reason that the error or poor performance occurred. The counselor takes a particular interest in the employee. If the counseling is well done, it may improve not only the employee's performance but also his or her attitude toward the firm and the particular job.

Programmed learning. This technique is used extensively for individual training. One method of programmed learning is *linear programming*, developed by B. F. Skinner in the mid 1950s.[4] In linear programming, the material to be taught is broken down into small segments, each segment is placed into a *frame*, and the frames are put in order. Each frame presents information about the fact or idea to be learned and then asks a question. After responding, the learner checks his or her answer with the correct answer, which appears in a convenient place on the page. This immediate feedback either supplies reinforcement or advises the learner that the frame should be restudied. In this way, each segment of learning is taught and reinforced before the learner moves on to the next frame (see Figure 7–4).

A second method of programmed learning, *multiple-choice programming* or *intrinsic programming*, was introduced by Norman A. Crowder.[5] As with linear programming, the material is divided into small segments, and a question is asked after each segment is taught. However, three or four possible answers follow each question, and the trainee must choose one. Then the trainee is directed to a page within the program that discusses that response. If the answer is correct, the trainee is rewarded with a compliment and directed to move to the next frame. If the response is incorrect, the trainee is either given further explanation or directed back to the same frame to restudy the material and answer the question again. In most cases, after a second trial, the trainee gets the response correct and is able to move ahead to the following frame.

Programmed learning has both disadvantages and advantages. Both kinds of programs require a great deal of time to create. They must be carefully developed and tested many times before they can be used for trainees. Once developed, however, they may be used over and over as long as the material remains current. In addition, because the material is reduced to small bits, each segment is explained clearly and succinctly.

Programs may be self-administered, so the time of the trainer is saved while the trainee learns on his or her own, and the trainee can proceed at his or her own optimum speed. Most firms that have created and used these programs have found that they speed learning and retention. The trainees must read and understand the material before a correct response can be made, and the immediate reinforcement encourages retention. However, even with these advantages, the time involved and the resulting costs have made this method less popular than its results would indicate.

FIGURE 7–4
LINEAR PROGRAMMED INSTRUCTION EXAMPLE

ALPHABETIC FILING	**Answer Key** (Cover this column and slide cover down to reveal answers after you finish each frame.)
1. Filing names accurately so they may be found quickly requires that certain rules be learned. The first rule is, Always list names by the last name. Which name, among the following, would be listed first in an alphabetical system? Marilyn E. Davis Arthur M. Bailey Phyllis B. Grant _____	
2. When arranging names alphabetically, single- or multiple-initial names precede all other names beginning with that same letter. Using this principle, place the following names in correct order. Annabel Ivarry _____ A. L. Iasco _____ I.B.M. Corporation _____	1. Bailey, Arthur M.
3. Abbreviations and numbers used as names are filed as if they were written in full. How should the names below be arranged so they will be in correct order? Martin Suber _____ 16th Avenue Bazaar _____ Sixth St. Café _____	2. I.B.M. Corporation Iasco, A. L. Ivarry, Annabel
4. Arrange the following list of names in their correct alphabetical order. Please apply the rules you have learned thus far. Fred C. Rawley _____ F. L. Rawley _____ 7th Avenue Card Shop _____ RCA Television Corporation _____ St. John's Church _____	3. 16th (Sixteenth) Avenue Bazaar Sixth St. (Street) Café Suber, Martin
	4. RCA Television Corporation Rawley, F. L. Rawley, Fred C. St. (Saint) John's Church 7th (Seventh) Avenue Card Shop

Computer-assisted instruction (CAI). A form of programmed learning, CAI presents lessons on a computer instead of on a series of printed frames. The computer is accessed through a typewriterlike terminal, which prints answers on a typewriter console or displays answers on a panel. The computer provides directions and grades the responses immediately. As more firms increase their use of computers, this type of training will become more readily available.

In-basket exercises. This method gets its name from the "in" and "out" baskets on the desks of employees. In this technique, communications that might arrive at an employee's desk are presented to the trainee. For example, the trainee might be given several forms to fill out, a list of phone messages to take care of, and the information for letters that must be written. He or she must then decide in what order to respond to those communications, determine what needs to be done to accomplish each task, perform the tasks, and ready them for the out basket. A time limit is usually specified so that the trainer can ascertain how efficiently the trainee would handle situations that are bound to occur in a normal working day.

In-basket exercises may be used from the clerical level to the top-executive level to develop judgment, tact, and efficiency. They help trainees to assess their own ability to react to demanding situations and allow the firm's management to assess that ability under controlled conditions.

Projects. These also develop a trainee's judgment and decision-making ability. The trainee is presented with an imaginary or real situation that has to be resolved. The trainee may discuss the problem with others, test ideas on others, and submit several proposals as solutions. Each proposal, however, has to be defended. The trainee's responsibility is to sell the proposal to the supervisor.

This method is called *action learning* when the person is drawn from his or her own department and given a real problem to resolve alone, with members of other departments within the firm, or with employees of other firms with which business is conducted. Action learning helps develop the abilities to interact with other employees, to communicate, and to sell an idea.

The various methods of individual and group training are summarized in Table 7–1.

Audiovisual training aids

The training room that once contained only a chalkboard and chalk eraser may today be a well-equipped training laboratory with inexpen-

TABLE 7-1
METHODS OF TRAINING

Type	Optimum Number of Trainees	Purpose of Training	Presenter of Material	Frequency of Training	Results Expected
Lecture	10 to 100 (or more)	To impart general information or to inspire during initial, continuation, or promotion training.	Member of training staff, supervisor from any level, or outside consultant.	Two or three times a year.	Employees will broaden scope of knowledge and information about organization or about expectations on the job.
Question-and-Answer	10 to 20	To answer employees' specific questions about their jobs.	Member of training staff, any level supervisor, or, if needed, outside consultant.	Following informational sessions or as needed.	Employees will be reassured that they understand material about their jobs or the organization.
Discussion	5 to 15	To allow employees to express opinions and ideas on specific topics.	Member of training staff or any level supervisor.	Following informational sessions.	Employees' morale will improve as a result of participation in idea-expressing sessions.
Demonstration	1 to 15	To teach steps in performing a specific task.	Member of training staff or supervisor.	Whenever systems are changed, new machines, new forms added, or new forms developed.	Employees will be able to handle new machines, forms, or routines with no errors.
Role Playing	2 to 20	To offer a chance to experience job situation vicariously.	Member of training staff or supervisor. Employees play all roles.	Whenever complaints or problems arise within department.	Employees will improve performance on the job.

Behavior Modeling	3 to 15	To have employees learn desired behavior by watching ideal manner of doing job and then practicing.	Supervisor or consultant. Videotapes or films of model performance may be used.	As needed to correct behavior or teach new behavior.	Employees will perform correctly when faced with a similar situation.
Sensitivity Training	3 to 15	To help employees learn to appreciate people who have different ethnic or cultural backgrounds and to learn to trust others.	Psychologist or consultant. Videotapes or films may be used, plus analysis and discussion.	Meetings over a period of several weeks, until group agrees attitudes have changed.	Employees will be more tolerant and trusting of others.
Assertiveness Training	3 to 15	To help employees who are too shy, passive, bold, or aggressive to take a middle ground—assertive.	Psychologist or consultant. Videotapes or films may be used, plus analysis and discussion.	Meetings over a period of several weeks, plus practice sessions and application on the job.	Employees will learn to state their beliefs and ideas and to reveal their problems forthrightly but without violating the rights of others.
Seminar	6 to 20	To allow employees who are knowledgeable about certain job-related tasks to participate on a rotating basis in presenting material to their peers for subsequent discussion.	Supervisor or trainer attends only as an observer. Employees present material.	As needed to have employees learn new material and discuss that material with their peers.	Employees' knowledge about work other employees do will improve, and employees will have a chance to exhibit their knowledge.

(Continued)

(Table 7-1 continued)

Type	Optimum Number of Trainees	Purpose of Training	Presenter of Material	Frequency of Training	Results Expected
Case Study	1 to 30	To have employees study written material, analyze it, and come to decisions that will later be discussed with the trainer, supervisor, and peers.	Trainer or supervisor may prepare material or use published cases.	As needed to develop decision-making skills and judgment.	Employees will learn that all aspects of a problem must be considered and that many solutions are possible.
Computer Game Analysis	3 to 15	To have employees analyze fictitious numerical data about costs of operations for several periods, with each period reflecting previous decisions.	Trainers, supervisors, or computer specialists oversee games that are specially prepared or purchased from publishers.	As needed for supervisory-level training to learn the importance of decisions on simulated departmental costs and charges.	Employees will learn to consider all aspects of the costs of taking certain actions.
Counseling	1 only	To help a troubled employee make useful decisions.	Supervisor or counselor.	Continues until problem is resolved.	Employees will achieve desired productive level.
Programmed Learning	Each person works individually.	To help employees learn factual information or skill-building at their own fastest pace.	Programmed materials used as self-teaching devices provide immediate feedback on correct responses. Trainer or supervisor usually prepares.	As needed for parts of initial training, new knowledge, or new skills.	Employees will perform tasks or skills accurately.

Computer-Assisted Instruction (CAI)	Each person works individually.	To help employees learn factual information or skill-building at their own fastest pace.	Programmed materials used as self-teaching devices provide immediate feedback on correct responses. Usually packaged program for use with computer is purchased.	Used as needed or when available.	Employees will perform tasks or skills accurately.
In-Basket Exercise	Each person works individually.	To help employees learn decision making when several tasks must be performed.	Trainer or supervisor prepares lists of activities that employees typically handle. After employee makes decisions, trainer or supervisor checks and discusses.	As needed for decision-making knowledge and for promotion training.	Employees will show adequate ability to select the most important tasks and do them properly and promptly.
Project	1 to 4 on a team	To assign employees a complicated series of tasks that needs to be developed and analyzed with suggested solutions.	Supervisor selects situation(s) and evaluates proposals.	Usually for those being considered for promotion or for positions with more responsibility.	Employees will be able to take an assignment, analyze what needs to be done, and complete it effectively.

sive to costly audiovisual aids. *Audiovisual aids* are any viewing and/or hearing supplementary *hardware* (equipment) and *software* (materials) used to reinforce or illustrate information or to provide specific training or practice facilities.

This equipment may include, in addition to any machines that are used on the job, overhead transparency machines; easels; videotape recording and playback machines; sound filmstrip machines; sound-slide machines; film projectors; wireless microphones; carrels with individualized materials in manual, film, and tape forms; and a plethora of color and black-and-white transparencies, posters, and other software for all these devices.

Some training departments also have computer terminals and computers with display panels. In some large firms that give continuous training, entire training classrooms are wired to a machine that records trainees' responses and at the end of the session gives summaries of trainee's responses to a variety of subjects. This allows the trainer to have immediate feedback on the effectiveness of the learning.

Recently, an electronic blackboard that allows visual information to be transmitted to several sites simultaneously for *teleconferencing* (conducting conferences by telephone) was developed. A pressure-sensitive surface transmits chalk impressions to other blackboards on the circuit.

Simulators are another type of very sophisticated and costly equipment. *Simulators* are devices that permit a person to practice use of a machine under conditions that imitate real-life situations. For example, a data-processing simulator allows a person to practice entering data without actually being linked to a computer. Simulators save time in training, reduce hazards, allow the trainee to learn at his or her own pace, and provide hands-on experience without endangering the real equipment or the user.

Because audiovisual equipment can be quite expensive and because new, improved models are offered almost yearly, the trainer should choose carefully those aids that will be used frequently. Highly technical equipment may require special operators, and this should be a consideration in its purchase. Moreover, once obtained, equipment should be used in the most effective manner possible. For example, visual aids should be used when:

o The idea can be more effectively presented or reinforced through their use.

o Identical material has to be taught over and over again.

o Material can be individualized for self-teaching.

o Different people need more or less time to learn a routine.

o Skill in using certain equipment must be attained before a person can begin a job.

Costs and rewards of training

Two kinds of costs are involved in training: direct and indirect. *Direct costs* are those that can be easily identified, such as salaries of trainers, salaries of trainees when all their time is spent in training, cost of space allocated for training activities, and tuition reimbursements for courses taken by employees at other locations. *Indirect costs* are those that are more difficult to identify. The costs of employees who spend only part of their time in training, supervisors who devote some time to training, space used for training but not assigned for that use, and supervisors who consult with staff about training are costs of training that are not charged to that function but that need to be considered if the true cost of training is to be determined.

Another hidden cost of training is the ineffectiveness of new employees until their training is complete. Most enterprises estimate that new employees take from three to six months to become productive enough to earn the salary and fringe benefits they are being paid. Some formal, centralized training may continue throughout that period. However, informal, decentralized training is continuously given to bring employees to a point of reasonable productivity.

The rewards that training provides are also difficult to assess. Although firms know that a well-trained work force increases productivity, reduces costs, and expands profits, measuring those changes that are due specifically to training is virtually impossible. Some managements, therefore, do not impute to training the true value that it represents within a firm. Nevertheless, training is essential in every firm and for every individual. Effective training eliminates or reduces trial-and-error learning; speeds the learning process; helps to improve the employee's productivity, morale, efficiency, effectiveness, and confidence; and reduces the need for constant supervision.

SUMMARY

o Training is a continuous program of improving employees' performance. It is developed in response to employees' needs, organizational policies, customers' wants and needs, supervisors' ideas, new concepts, and operational constraints.

o In small organizations, supervisors are responsible for all training. In larger enterprises, training staffs may give some training, but the supervisor is still responsible to see that employees are adequately trained.

o Training may be formal or informal, centralized or decentralized, or planned or unplanned.

o Formal training may consist of initial training, retraining, continuation training, or promotion training.

o Formal training programs are based on job analyses and developed with behavioral objectives to measure learning. They must be evaluated to ensure that they are effective and accurate.

o Types of group training include lectures with or without visual aids, question-and-answer sessions, discussions, demonstrations, role playing, behavior modeling, sensitivity training, assertiveness training, seminars, case studies, and computer game analyses.

o Types of individual training include some group methods, especially demonstration and behavior modeling. In addition, individuals may be trained by counseling, programmed learning, computer-assisted instruction, in-basket exercises, and projects.

o Audiovisual aids are supplementary viewing and/or hearing materials, including both hardware (equipment) and software (materials to be used with hardware).

o Training is expensive and because many of the charges are hidden, the costs are difficult to assess. Training results are also difficult to assess because few supervisors can determine exactly what productivity increases are due to specific training efforts. In spite of the difficulties in evaluating training, training is valuable for both the organization and the employees.

REFERENCES

[1]Urban C. Lehner, "Labor Letter," *Wall Street Journal*, September 11, 1979, p. 1.
[2]"AT&T Systems Approach for Love and Money," *Training in Business and Industry*, May 1968, p. 45.
[3]Marylin Bender, "Sensitivity Training: A Workout for the Psyche and Emotions," *New York Times*, July 7, 1969, p. 36.

[4]B. F. Skinner, *Science and Human Behavior* (New York: Macmillan, 1953).
[5]Norman A. Crowder, "Automatic Tutoring by Means of Intrinsic Programming," in *Automatic Teaching: The State of the Art*, ed. E. H. Galanter (New York: John Wiley, 1959), pp. 109–16.

REVIEW AND DISCUSSION QUESTIONS

1. How are both centralized and decentralized training used in most firms?
2. If the training program in a firm is well developed and conducted, would any need exist for unplanned training? Why or why not?
3. Explain the role of job analyses in establishing a formal training program.
4. Of the following methods of training, which are trainer controlled and which are trainee controlled? Which might be classified under

both categories: lectures, question-and-answer sessions, discussions, demonstrations, role playing, behavior modeling, sensitivity training, assertiveness training, seminars, case studies, computer game analyses, counseling, programmed learning, computer-assisted instruction, in-basket exercises, and projects?

5. Which training methods mentioned in question 4 would you suggest be used to teach the following: history of the firm, rules and regulations, use of forms, use of machines, management of people, understanding employees, retraining of employees who make excessive errors, and development of creative attitudes among supervisory employees?
6. How are visual aids used in training?
7. Under what conditions are visual aids desirable as a supplement to training?
8. Why are the costs of training not easily computed?
9. How can the value of a training program be assessed? What are the difficulties that face the trainer in such an assessment?
10. What are the advantages to the supervisor of a well-conducted training program?

ASSIGNMENTS

1. For a survey of training types and benefits, draw up an evaluation chart including types of training (formal or informal, group or individual, centralized or decentralized, planned or unplanned), methods of training, visual aids, and length of time spent in training for a specific job. Using this survey chart, record the answers to questions from this survey asked of three of your classmates who have held jobs. Ask them also how necessary the training given was for their specific job and how effective the training was on an A, B, C, D, F scale (for excellent to failure). Write a report that summarizes your findings. What did you learn about training from this exercise?
2. Analyze the methods of teaching used in the courses you have taken in college. What methods are most commonly used? How does the subject matter affect the method of teaching? How do teachers measure the "productivity" of their teaching? Is that a useful method to determine their effectiveness? Give reasons for your answers.

PROBLEM FOR RESOLUTION

You are an employee in the Kay-Zee book firm. You arrive at work a few minutes before 9:00 A.M. and find several items in your in-basket. Your boss is out of town on business, and you cannot contact her. Before she left, you had promised to get two hundred announcements ready for mail pickup before 11:00 A.M. today. All that remains to be done on that job is to fold the announcements, insert them in envelopes that are due from the stockroom this morning, and place address labels on the envelopes. A box of envelopes has already arrived. When you open it, you find that the stockroom employees have sent the wrong size envelopes, and the announcements will not fit into them.

In your in-basket are the following urgent matters:

o A telephone message from the vice-president of the firm asking you to call as soon as you arrive

o A telephone message from your mother about a problem at home

o A telephone message from a customer complaining about a recent book shipment

o Three letters that were typed by an employee in the typing pool: These must be carefully proofread, and from previous experience, you know they will undoubtedly need some correction. They must also make the 11:00 A.M. mail pickup.

o Four book orders that need to be distributed to the correct departments so that they can be filled by the 11:00 A.M. mail pickup

In what order would you handle each of these situations. State your reasons for taking them in that particular order.

CASE STUDY

The firm for which you work, the Brockton Company, has just merged with another, somewhat smaller firm. All the routines that your firm follows must be taught to the supervisors in the new firm so that they, in turn, can inform the employees in their departments. Approximately three hundred employees in the newly absorbed firm will need training. The two firms will use the same forms, letterhead, format for letters, and telephone-answering technique. These are the first areas in which training is to be conducted. You have been asked to coordinate the training for these areas of information. You will be coordinating the work of about ten supervisors from the parent firm who are responsible for training employees at the smaller firm.

What factors have to be considered in developing a plan of action for all this training? Explain.

FURTHER READING

Foy, Nancy. "Action Learning Comes to Industry." *Harvard Business Review*, September–October 1977, pp. 158–68.

Describes an in-house training program for managers that allows them to tackle real problems in unfamiliar situations.

Glazer, Rollin. "The Management Development Job: Why It Never Gets Done." *Personnel News and Views*, Winter 1977–78.

Explains that the difficulty of setting standards and getting agreement on them stalls many programs, but that the need to manage human resources more effectively requires that action be taken.

Kerzner, Harold. "Training Systems Managers." *Journal of Systems Management*, December 1978, pp. 23–27.

Reports how adults participate in evening training programs that colleges and industry develop jointly and how new curriculums are analyzed by questionnaires that are directed to systems and project managers.

McLagan, Patricia A., Raymond E. Sandborgh, et al. "Computer-Aided Instruction." *Training*, September 1977, pp. 48–57.

Explains the advantages of CAI training, and discusses how to get started, how to aid individuals, and the costs involved.

O'Donnell, Margaret, and Lee Colby. "Developing Managers Through Assertiveness Training." *Training*, March 1979, pp. 36–41.

Describes how the training program at Minnesota Mutual Life helps managers to voice their thoughts better, thus improving the company's team spirit.

Ricklefs, Roger. "Milquetoasts Unite! For $425 You Can Learn to Be Pushy." *Wall Street Journal*, September 19, 1977, pp. 1, 28.

Describes how a course given by an outside organization prepares one to be assertive on the job.

"Train More for Less with Models, Mock-ups, and Simulators." *Training*, December 1978, pp. 63–69.

Reports how the use of special audiovisual aids allows more people to be trained in less time.

Whiteley, John M., and John V. Flowers. *Approaches to Assertion Training*. Monterey, Calif.: Brooks/Cole, 1978.

Discusses various approaches to assertion training that use unique techniques with various populations and the assessment of them.

8
motivating
employees

After studying and analyzing this chapter, you should be able to:

Define "motivation," and explain why it is important for employees to be motivated.

Discuss the following theories and concepts about motivation, and explain how supervisors can apply the desirable ones: the carrot and the stick, the Hawthorne experiments, change theory, job redesign, Theory X and Theory Y, hierarchy-of-needs theory, theory of hygiene-motivator factors, Transactional Analysis, participative management, managerial grid, and management by objectives.

Explain the supervisor's role in motivation.

UPERVISORS ARE judged both for their own ability and productivity on the job and for that of their staffs. Supervisors, therefore, have a double interest in the achievements of their departments—an interest in their own personal standing in the organization due to their departments' overall productivity and an interest in the rewards their subordinates receive as a result of their individual effort.

What is motivation ?

Motive comes from the Latin word *motio*, meaning "to move." A *motive* is something within a person that makes him or her act in a certain way. To *motivate* means to provide with a motive, that is, to move toward action; *motivation* is the process of doing so.

Note particularly that motives come from "within a person." Throughout history, some people believed that they could motivate other people to work harder and produce more. Many ideas about motivation have flourished at various times. Owners of slaves believed fear was a motivator. Many parents believe that fear motivates children to be obedient. People believe that fear of jail deters thieves, muggers, or burglars from their pursuits. Some also believe that the fear of being fired will move the worker to accomplish more on the job. This is the "stick" concept.

Another strongly held belief is that money motivates people to work harder. Unions have frequently supported the idea that for more pay, workers will produce more. This is the "carrot" concept.

That these ideas are incorrect is shown by the fact that children are not always obedient; thieves, muggers, and burglars continue to pursue their illegal acts; and workers continue to be fired for inefficiency, low production, laziness, absenteeism, and a host of other reasons. The carrot and the stick concepts generally do not work.

The traditional motivators, fear of punishment and rewards in the form of added pay, do not work with all people under all circumstances. Some people perform well without being afraid of the consequences of doing otherwise. Many perform effectively even though pay is given not on a merit basis but through some formula that does not award individual initiative or output. Some people work at jobs that pay very little just because they enjoy that particular occupation. Motivation, therefore, is quite obviously something that comes from within a person and cannot truly be imposed by outside authority. As Leo F. McManus, an industrial psychologist, stated, "No one motivates anyone. All we can really do is create a climate with another individual in which that individual motivates himself or herself."[1]

Although supervisors are constantly being told "to motivate" employees, they must understand what causes people to act in certain desirable ways. Supervisors cannot motivate as such, but they can help employees to motivate themselves. Supervisors can help to create situations that will encourage employees to want to achieve and produce more.

In virtually all enterprises, the ultimate purpose of motivation is to get higher productivity at lower cost and to maintain employees' goodwill. Until a person desires to improve his or her performance on the job, little the supervisor does will effect any change in that person. Therefore, the supervisor's role is to help the worker to want to do the job effectively.

Theories and concepts about motivation

Research into the causes of job satisfaction, worker productivity, and worker motivation has led to many theories and concepts that reveal what impels workers to react positively or negatively to the supervisor's actions. Because each person reacts differently from others, no one theory or concept covers all situations.

Studies on productivity

Until the development of general psychology, usually credited to Wilhelm Wundt in 1879 at the University of Leipzig, observation and intuition had been the ways human problems were analyzed. Few studies, however, applied to workers. Some studies about the health of workers and vocational guidance were conducted, but until the period before World War I, no scientific and detailed study of job efficiency, including time and motion studies of workers, was performed. Frederick Taylor (1856–1915) was the first to do so. Taylor's desire was to have laborers make a "decent livelihood through increasing the productivity of work."[2]

Taylor's investigation was based on the concepts of selection, training, and motivation: "To select the best men for the job. To instruct them in the most efficient methods, the most economical movements, to employ in their work. To give incentives in the form of higher wages to the best workers."[3]

By following Taylor's scientific management methods, each person capable of doing the work as Taylor mandated was able to increase productivity and thus become virtually a "mechanical man" and make more money. However, only a few workers could meet the standards set by Taylor, and several others were downgraded or thrown out of work. Taylor believed workers inherently disliked work but that they were motivated by money to work harder. Many people thought Taylor's methods exploited workers for the benefit of the firm's owners.

The time and motion studies begun by Taylor were continued by Henri Fayol (1841–1925), a French industrialist. Fayol believed in having one person in charge of an organization, each worker responsible to only one boss, and authority equal to responsibility for each employee. Fayol thought that organizing work in that way would motivate employees to be productive.

Frank B. Gilbreth (1868–1924) and Lillian Gilbreth (1878–1972) also experimented with time and motion studies. They advocated that workers use fewer motions and increase the speed of the needed motions in accomplishing physical work. Their studies were done using high-speed photography to record the exact details of work movements. Careful analysis of these movements resulted in the improvement of workers' activities. The Gilbreths agreed with Taylor that employees who could produce more and therefore made more money were the ones who were motivated.

The Hawthorne experiments

The first studies of workers that attempted to have all conditions controlled except those being tested have become known for the name of the plant at which they were conducted, the Hawthorne plant of the Western Electric Company near Chicago. These studies were carried out from 1927 to 1933. General discontent among workers who had satisfactory wages and fringe benefits led to this investigation, which was conducted by George Elton Mayo, of the Harvard Graduate School of Business, and his associates, Fritz J. Roethlisberger and W. J. Dickson.[4]

Following the generally held beliefs of that period, this team selected a group of workers and varied the physical environmental factors that might affect their work: lighting, rest periods, and hours of work. In one part of the experiment, the lights in the work station were dimmed slightly each day until seeing became difficult. Production, however, increased each day until the dim lighting made the work too difficult to perform. Only then did productivity fall.

Similarly, rest periods were lengthened slightly. Even though employees had less time at their work, production continued to climb. Again, the researchers noted that the time allotted to work did not determine output as much as did the desire of the workers to be productive. Even when the workers were allowed to leave work one-half hour earlier than usual, production did not fall. They were so motivated by their feeling of being special persons that they worked harder during the day to offset the early-leaving time.

The results of the experiments showed that the attitudes of the workers, not their physical environment, controlled their production efforts. Because the workers were aware that they had been chosen for the experiment and their opinions were sought, they therefore felt special, adopted a more constructive attitude toward their work, and greatly increased their production. This finding—that productivity increases when workers know they are receiving special attention—is called the *Hawthorne effect*. Revolutionary at the time, this concept has become a consideration in all subsequent research with people who know they are subjects in a study. Supervisors who are aware of the Hawthorne effect may take steps to make their entire staff feel special and important. As a result, those employees will probably put forth additional effort on behalf of the group.

Another phenomenon that was observed was the formation of a *group mentality*. Each person changed his or her concern for self to that of concern for the group. Peer pressure became more important as a result of this interest in the group than the supervisory pressure of the assigned boss.

The group members were friendly not only during working hours but also in their leisure time. The awareness of the development of a group mentality led to further observations of workers who were not aware that they were being watched. In all groups that worked together, this same group cohesiveness was noted. Informal leaders within the group had more authority with group members than the supervisors. The group, rather than the supervisor, controlled production, and the informal leader determined the minimum and maximum production. The incentive of more pay for more production did not change the level of production of the workers in the group. Supervisors who are aware of this group mentality can work with the informal leader to channel efforts toward the objectives of the organization.

Change theory

In using any theory of motivation, the supervisor must realize subordinates' ability to and interest in change. Kurt Lewin[5] and Edgar H. Schein[6] have developed a theory of change that proposes three stages through which any alteration in the actions of a person or a group must go:

- o First, the former way of acting or thinking must be brought to the level of awareness. The person or group needs to understand that the former thought or action is not necessarily either the best way or even as good as other methods. This stage is known as *unfreezing*. The person or group must be motivated to change.

o Second, the new beliefs, attitudes, values, and behavior patterns must be actually implemented. In this stage, known as *changing*, the person or group accepts a new way of thinking or acting and practices it.

o Third, the new methods of acting or thinking must become the ones used all the time and must be accepted as the ones that will be continuously used. This stage is known as *refreezing*. Until it has occurred, the person or group can well slip back into the original way of acting or thinking. Refreezing stabilizes and integrates the new beliefs, attitudes, and values into the person's behavior patterns.

Any theory of motivation that a supervisor accepts and decides to implement with subordinates is subject to the three stages of unfreezing, changing, and refreezing.

Job redesign

Job redesign is a process of structuring jobs so that tasks are more varied and employees have more responsibility for their work. It may involve *job rotation* (moving from one assignment to another), *job enlargement* (adding more tasks), or *job enrichment* (making a different combination of tasks).

Subordinates' boredom on the job should be a cause of concern to all supervisors. Workers who are bored cannot do their jobs in the most productive way and therefore cannot contribute optimally to the goals of the enterprise. Boredom is often caused by repetitious work. As one worker said, "I think most of us are looking for a calling, not a job. Most of us, like the assembly-line workers, have jobs that are too small for our spirit. Jobs are not big enough for people." [7]

Routine jobs became common during the Industrial Revolution, when owners of firms envisioned the worker as a mechanical being who could learn one job and do it with increasing speed and effectiveness. Today, however, as workers become better educated and want to have a greater voice in their work, they find tedious jobs less and less desirable. And although technology has allowed people who do repetitive work to be replaced by machines and to do work requiring more thought, not all jobs are satisfying.

Job redesign is a way to eliminate boredom and other dissatisfaction. Initially used in Europe in the late nineteenth century, it was revived in the 1940s by the then president of IBM, Thomas Watson, when he learned that what workers disliked was the repetitive nature of their jobs. The assembly-line job at IBM was subsequently expanded to include setup of the work and inspection of the item produced.

When various dimensions are added to a job, some workers become more responsible and enjoy the job more. Many even find improved ways to do the job that save time and money for the firm and in the end produce either a better or an equally satisfactory product or service.

The supervisor who plans to redesign jobs to make them more interesting and to involve employees more completely may be helped by asking these four questions:

- o *Should the employee be involved in more initial decision making?* If employees were included in the planning stages, when decisions were being made about the tasks needed to accomplish the work, would their interest in their jobs be heightened?

- o *Should employees share some of the supervisor's responsibilities?* Could some of the work the supervisor does, such as checking, revising, arranging, and evaluating, for example, be assigned to employees to make their jobs more meaningful?

- o *Are some of the tasks so routine that they could be automated and thereby release employees to do more creative tasks?* Routine clerical filing, typewriting, cutting and pasting, and record keeping may be allocated to areas where word processors or data processors can handle the work more efficiently. This would free some employees to do less routine tasks.

- o *Should tasks that are performed at a later stage by other people be included as part of the tasks of this group of employees?* If projects are only partially completed in one unit and move on to other units for completion, the employees in the original unit may believe that their tasks are of little importance. They view those who work on the final production as having more satisfaction in work. For example, one department was assigned to develop brochure materials. Their copy was sent to another department that decided on the size, shape, color, and illustrations to be used. When the two departments were merged, each person responsible for copy also could be included in decisions on layout, color, and illustration. Workers' enthusiasm for their jobs was greatly improved.

Peter Drucker, a well-known management theorist, observed that in order for a worker in a job-redesign program to achieve satisfaction, he or she must first take responsibility for the job. "This requires (1) productive work, (2) feedback information, and (3) continuous learning."[8]

During the 1970s, new support for job-redesign ideas made them commonly used motivation methods. Supervisors who adopt their use must provide employees with the necessary training to make them even more knowledgeable and competent about their expanded duties.

Theory x and theory y

By the end of World War II, views of human motivation were moving far from Taylor's belief in "the carrot and the stick" concept. Douglas McGregor, of the Massachusetts Institute of Technology, explained that the supervisor's view of the worker determined how the supervisor directed behavior. McGregor called the assumptions that underlie the two different attitudes of supervisors *Theory X*, for the traditionally held beliefs, and *Theory Y*, for the emerging concepts:[9]

Theory X	**Theory Y**
o Management is responsible for directing employees' efforts, motivating them, controlling their actions, and modifying their behavior to fit the needs of the organization.	o Management is responsible for making it possible for people to recognize and develop their abilities to achieve organizational goals.
o The average person is by nature lazy and works as little as possible.	o The motivation, potential for development, capacity for assuming responsibility, and readiness to direct behavior toward organizational goals are all present in people.
o People lack ambition, dislike responsibility, and prefer to be led.	o Management should arrange organizational conditions and methods of operation so that people can achieve their own goals best by directing their own efforts toward organizational objectives.
o People are inherently self-centered and indifferent to organizational needs.	o People are not by nature resistant to organizational needs.
o People are by nature resistant to change.	o When people understand the need for change, they readily adapt themselves to that change.

Despite McGregor's insistence that Theory Y produces the best results with people, many supervisors have not accepted that set of assumptions. Drucker, who advocated a theory that paralleled Theory Y, noted that "to manage worker and working by putting responsibility on the worker and by aiming at achievement made exceedingly high demands on both worker and manager."[10]

All workers respond individually. Those who are self-motivated work well under the Theory Y concept. Those who are not self-motivated and do not really have an interest in their job may not work noticeably better under Theory Y supervision than under Theory X supervision.

Theory X continues to be a concept that is followed in many organizations. Autocratic supervisors often use the Theory X approach with employees. Some supervisors vary their approach to employees by using Theory Y with those employees who respond positively to assignments, who are enthusiastic about their work, and who bring creative ideas to their jobs. Those employees who respond to work assignments with indifference, who appear anxious to leave work as soon as possible, and who do their work by expending only minimal effort often evoke a Theory X attitude on the part of their supervisors.

In general, supervisors who have respect for their employees' ability follow a Theory Y approach in working with them.

Hierarchy-of-needs theory

In the mid 1950s, another view of what motivates people was presented by Abraham H. Maslow, a noted psychologist.[11] Maslow explained that each person has basic needs that act as motivators, that these needs are built one upon the other, and that no higher need can be satisfied until the one before it has been (see Figure 8–1). The lowest needs in the hierarchy are *physiological needs*. These are basic biological needs that must be satisfied to exist—hunger, thirst, sleep, and shelter. If a person is hungry, for example, food will act as a motivator and the person will be unable to function effectively at higher levels until he or she is fed. Once the hungry person's need for food has been satisfied, food is no longer a motivator nor a deterrent to other needs.

The second level in the hierarchy is *safety* or *security needs*. A person who is afraid is unable to function effectively. Security must be ensured before a person can turn attention to other matters. Once a person feels secure, the need for safety no longer serves as a motivator.

The third level in the hierarchy is *social* or *love needs*, or the need to belong, to be accepted, and to be liked by and to like other people. A closely knit group, as Mayo found in the Hawthorne experiments, helps to meet social needs. Social needs act as a motivator after physiological and safety needs are satisfied.

FIGURE 8–1
MASLOW'S HIERARCHY OF NEEDS

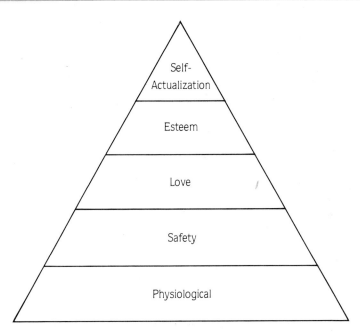

Source: Data based on Hierarchy of Needs in "A Theory of Human Motivation" in Abraham H. Maslow, *Motivation and Personality*, 2nd ed. (New York: Harper & Row, 1970). Copyright © 1970 by Abraham H. Maslow. By permission of Harper & Row, Publishers, Inc.

After a person has been accepted by a group, *ego needs* emerge and serve as motivators. They include the needs for recognition, respect, admiration, and status. Many people will strive very hard to achieve this appreciation of their work. Supervisors can express appreciation for work well done.

The highest level in the hierarchy is the need for *self-fulfillment*. This is the need to live up to one's potential, to realize one's own ability, and to be creative in any way that one can.

The three lower levels in the hierarchy—physiological, safety, and social needs—are the minimum needs that motivate people. To function adequately and to have any measure of enjoyment on the job, people must have them met. People who seek to have ego needs met usually aspire to do their job more proficiently or more creatively.

Theory of hygiene-motivator factors

In the 1960s, additional motivational research enlightened supervisors about the attitudes and interests of employees. Frederick Herzberg, a psychologist at Case Western Reserve University, proposed a two-factor theory of motivation, based on interviews with two hundred engineers and accountants.[12]

Herzberg found that there were five strong determinants of job satisfaction: achievement, recognition, work itself, responsibility, and advancement. These satisfiers, which were therefore called *motivator factors*, were all related to the actual work being done.

Herzberg also observed that there were other factors that rarely led to positive job attitudes: company policy and administration, supervision, salary, interpersonal relations, and working conditions. These factors were all dissatisfiers. That is, they had to exist at an adequate level or dissatisfaction would result. But by themselves they did not motivate people. The dissatisfiers all related to the environment in which the job was done and were preventive. Therefore, they were called *hygiene factors*.

Herzberg's findings contradict Taylor's belief that salary is the main motivator for work. They indicate that salary has to be adequate or workers will be discontented. However, once a raise has been given, it no longer moves a person to greater productivity but rather only keeps him or her from being dissatisfied. Almost as soon as a raise has become effective, workers may be ready to demand an even higher salary. Similarly, improved working conditions, interpersonal relations, administration, and policies serve only to allay dissatisfaction, not to stimulate harder work. Increased productivity results from the opportunities a job provides for increasing achievement, responsibility, advancement, sense of personal worth, and individuality.

Transactional analysis

Transactional Analysis (TA) is a method of examining human behavior. The importance of social intercourse, or communication, is the basis of this theory, which was developed by Eric Berne, a psychiatrist.[13] Because this theory is explained so that the average person can easily understand it, people can gain personal awareness of their own behavior and, when it is undesirable, change it. In explaining his theory, Berne defined certain terms:[14]

o *Stroke*—Any sign of recognition of another's presence.

o *Transaction*—An exchange of strokes, or a unit of social intercourse. If one person speaks to or acknowledges another person, a *transactional stimulus* has occurred. If the second person acknowledges the stimulus, a *transactional response* has taken place.

o *Programming*—The operational aspect of time structuring.

o *Game*—Individual programming sequences. "An ongoing series of transactions progressing to a well-defined, predictable outcome."

Berne explained that "significant social inter[change] most commonly takes the form of games." [15] When people function effectively, they are said to be "OK." When they do not function effectively, they are said to be "not OK." Berne further explained that in social activity, people show behavioral changes that reveal shifts in their feelings. These are called *ego states*. Each person has three ego states: parent (P), adult (A), and child (C). These three ego states may be displayed at any time in social interchange. Every normal person exhibits all three of them at various times.

The *parent* in every person takes care of routine matters, often stresses doing things in the traditional way because that is the way things are done, and is concerned with the survival of the human race. The parent exhibits prejudicial, critical, and nurturing behavior, and often talks in an authoritarian, judgmental manner aimed at putting others down.

The *adult* considers the facts, assesses the situation as it exists, and determines how best to react under those circumstances. For the adult, who brings objective judgment and analytical ability to any transaction, virtually every activity requires evaluation. Even crossing the street necessitates judgments about when it is safe to do so.

The *child* provides "intuition, creativity, and spontaneous drive and enjoyment." [16] The child in every person may be anxious and insecure, but is often interested in fun and making up stories. The child ego state may be revealed as obedient, manipulative, or impulsive.

Transactions between people may be complementary, crossed, or ulterior. Whether these transactions involve the adult-adult, parent-child, or other combination determines how natural and healthy they are. *Complementary transactions* are those that elicit predicted responses from the same or different ego state (see Figure 8–2A). For example, a parent complementary transaction occurs when a person states, "I suppose you have to live up to the equal employment rulings on hiring people?" and the responder states, "Oh, yes. We keep out of trouble with the government that way." An adult complementary transaction occurs, for instance, when a person, in discussing a new job, asks, "What are the hours of work?" and the employer explains, "The hours are from 9:00 A.M. to 5:00 P.M. daily, Monday through Friday, with one hour for lunch plus appropriate rest periods during the day." A child complementary

FIGURE 8–2
TYPES OF TRANSACTIONS

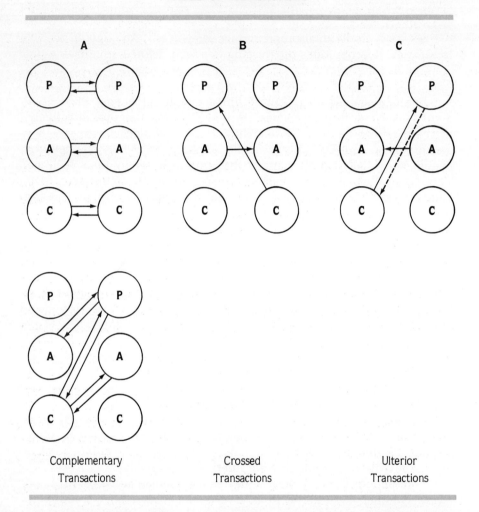

Complementary	Crossed	Ulterior
Transactions	Transactions	Transactions

transaction occurs when a new employee says, "I'm going to have fun making lots of changes in this department," and a co-worker states, "I'll love seeing those prissy workers squirm when you get going."

The important consideration in complementary transactions is that the response carries forward the initial statement in an anticipated manner. Thus, for example, if an employee in a child ego state said to a supervisor, "I am so angry, I could tear up this report," and the supervisor in an adult ego state replied, "Something did make you angry, didn't it?" the transaction would be complementary. Or if an employee in an adult ego state said, "I've worked on this report consistently for three hours. I'd better take a break before my fingers become numb," the supervisor might reply from the parent ego state by saying, "You should take a break and relax for a few minutes so you feel refreshed."

Crossed transactions occur when the adult of one person is faced by the parent or child ego state of the other (see Figure 8–2B). These transactions begin at one level but are received at a different level, and the response bypasses the sender's level. If, for instance, the person who asked about the hours of work received a parental answer—"If all you care about is the time you have to spend on the job, then maybe you really aren't interested in this position"—the transaction would be difficult to bring back to an even keel. The parent of this transaction might be answered by the child saying, "All my friends get out of work at 5:00 P.M., and I want to be sure I can meet them as they leave." Similarly, an employee in the adult ego state might say, "This might be a good way to handle this job," and the supervisor in the parent ego state might reply, "I'll tell you what to do and how to do it."

Ulterior transactions occur when the real motive for a person's actions differs from what the person says or implies, and when any response, regardless of how well intentioned, is unacceptable unless it gives full approval to the action (see Figure 8–2C). Ulterior transactions originate in two or more ego states. "A hidden message is sent disguised as a socially acceptable communication."[17] Words and behavior in such a message are in conflict. For example, a secretary who is a poor typist submits a letter to a supervisor without bothering to proofread it, saying, "This is all done and it's okay." The supervisor glances at it, finds several errors, and returns the letter in an obviously annoyed manner, saying, "Retype this and proofread it before you give it to me to sign." Or an employee who knows the standards for promptness in a firm is habitually late and uses obvious rationalizations for this tardiness. Even though employees know they are wrong, they are subconsciously seeking parentlike approval of the misdeed.

The principles of Transactional Analysis may be applied in any place where people deal with other people. All three ego states exist in each person, but the more the adult state takes over, the more reasoned and intelligent conversations will be. Understanding the theory of transactional analysis is, therefore, important both for supervisors and those they supervise.

Transactional Analysis is a teaching-learning device. The supervisor may use it to understand the employees in the department better, to observe their varying ego states as they interact with one another, and to communicate on a one-to-one basis more effectively with them. By perceiving employees' responses, the supervisor can raise the level of interaction and improve relations in the entire department. Instead of becoming annoyed at an employee who makes a request from a child ego state, for example, the supervisor would be aware of that condition and be able to counter it either with a parent or an adult ego-state response to the problem. Similarly, an employee who takes a parent ego-state approach to other employees could be brought to an adult level of interaction more effectively by a knowledgeable supervisor. Through this means, the individual employee would be motivated to more productive interaction and work.

Participative management

Participative management means that workers take part in making decisions about a range of matters, including production methods, internal distribution of tasks, recruitment, additional tasks to undertake, and hours of work.

Being allowed to participate in such important decisions permits workers to develop and sustain a sense of personal worth and importance, to grow, to motivate themselves, and to be recognized and approved for their activities. Participation encourages employees to identify more closely with the organization, its plans, and its accomplishments. According to this concept, when employees have had a voice in the decision about work, they are more concerned with its success than when they are viewed only as workers on a project.

Participative management is a relatively recent approach to supervising workers. Joseph Scanlon, of the Massachusetts Institute of Technology, advocated a plan in the late 1950s based on his belief that people not only can be more productive but actually want to produce more.[18] His ideas were born out of the Depression years. Scanlon believed that employees should be told what the problems of a firm are in terms they can understand and that any benefits that accrue by their improved performance should be shared equitably. He was particularly concerned about the friction between line and staff workers. He believed staff workers often impose their standards on line personnel who have specific knowledge that enables them to know how well a plan will work.

For the *Scanlon Plan,* as he termed it, teams of employees composed of both management and nonmanagement representatives serve on committees that discuss the problem before them and make suggestions. Before participation begins, employees have been given guarantees against layoffs arising from improved technology. Therefore, they are completely free to suggest innovations and the purchase of new equipment that will increase productivity.

Rensis Likert of the University of Michigan, also advocates participative management.[19] He developed the concept of *interlocking work teams.* Whereas in the usual line organization several people report to one boss, in the interlocking work team one member serves at the next highest level and acts as a liaison for both groups on which he or she serves.

One study of what participative management is and how it gets results was conducted by Larry E. Greiner.[20] He surveyed two groups of managers, totaling 318 people, who revealed the following:

o The most important facet of participative management is giving subordinates a share in decision making.

o Subordinates should be kept informed of the true nature of the situation.

o Everything should be done by the supervisor to keep the morale of the organization high.

Greiner also found that participative management works best when supervisors are easily approachable; counsel, train, and develop subordinates; communicate effectively; are thoughtful and considerate; are willing to change ways of doing things; support subordinates even when they make mistakes; and commend subordinates who do a good job.

This participative management concept reflects the theories of Maslow and Herzberg.

Managerial grid

In the mid 1960s, Robert Blake and Jane Srygley Mouton developed a grid to analyze whether supervisors are primarily concerned about production or people.[21] The managerial grid is two-dimensional, having nine horizontal lines and nine vertical lines. The horizontal line shows low to high concern for production, while the vertical line shows low to high concern for people. By analyzing the supervisor's actions and attitudes on this grid, the supervisor's primary disposition may be determined. The supervisor may then work to change that posture if it does not appear to be the most effective one.

The grid allows for eighty-one different combinations of supervisory style. These range from the 1–9 "country-club manager," who encourages satisfying relationships among people and is less concerned with production; to the 5–5 "organization person," who balances the performance of people with their production; to the 1–1 "do nothing manager," who exerts only the minimum amount of effort to get work done; to the 9–1 "production pusher," who favors production over people; and to the optimum 9–9 "team builder," who is equally concerned with production and with developing trust and respect among the employees.

Supervisors who want their staffs to be motivated for optimum productivity will attempt to develop their own abilities as team builders. Supervisors who are concerned with both subordinates and productivity are the ones who succeed in creating a departmental climate that encourages employees to self-motivation.

Management by objectives

A method that has been used whenever goals were set and people attempted to achieve them gained a formal name and some structure when the term "management by objectives" was coined by Peter Drucker in 1954.[22] *Management by objectives,* or *MBO* as it is commonly called, is a technique used by many enterprises to help the management team decide specifically what measures it will take to implement the overall objectives of the firm. Each manager confers with the people in his or her department, asks each person to set objectives that will help the firm achieve its overall plan, has those objectives discussed, and finally uses the finished statements at a later date to determine whether or not the plan has been met.

Through management by objectives, each person becomes accountable for the activities he or she has agreed with the supervisor to accomplish within a given time period. In this way, both the subordinate and the supervisor know how effectively the specified objectives have been met. For example, if a firm decided to add five thousand new accounts to its books within a five-week period, one department might agree to be responsible for five hundred of those new accounts. If twenty people were working in that department, each might contract to develop twenty-five new accounts, or five accounts each per week. Some workers might attain more than the five new accounts per week, while others might get only three or four per week. Each person would be able to determine exactly what his or her role had been in the achievement of the department's objective, and the supervisor would know which employees made the largest contribution to the total. At the conclusion of the five-week period, the executives of the firm would be able to judge the value of that particular department to the overall objectives of the company.

Not all plans are as easily quantified as those in this example. Other objectives might pertain to lowering the number of complaints, to improving the quality of work, to speeding output, or to developing new products, processes, or services for the firm. Whatever the objectives, each person is involved in specifying what measures he or she will take to help to meet the specific objective.

MBO requires that records be established when objectives are set and that those records be checked subsequently in evaluating the attainment of those objectives. For this reason, some supervisors find MBO to be time-consuming and cumbersome. However, MBO takes the guesswork out of evaluating the employee and the group. No longer need people be judged on such various traits as cooperativeness, appearance, and attendance, for example. Rather they can be judged on the specific accomplishment of objectives they have helped set for themselves. Moreover, because workers have an opportunity to aid in setting their own objectives and because supervisors meet with them to agree on the aims and again to check on the outcome, MBO often results in both increased production and increased satisfaction on the job. These are the measures of the motivation of the individual employee.

The supervisor's role in motivation

Getting employees to produce effectively requires knowledge of people and of how they respond to varying challenges. Each person reacts differently from the way others react. What inspires or moves one employee may not work for other employees. However, certain factors are known about people and their responses, and these provide the supervisor with various means to aid employees toward self-motivation.

Through the Hawthorne experiments, supervisors know the value of making people feel needed and important in their jobs. Allowing people to attain their potential on a job, giving them responsibility, and allowing them to innovate follow the theories of both Maslow and Herzberg and should produce desirable results. Wherever possible, Theory X attitudes should be avoided and Theory Y attitudes adopted. When employees are interested, concerned, and knowledgeable, management by objectives and participative management are both helpful concepts.

Job redesign, when feasible, gives people more control over their work and adds to their feeling of importance.

Awareness of Transactional Analysis helps supervisors to improve their interpersonal relations with employees.

The supervisor can check his or her own inclinations and abilities by using the managerial grid as proposed by Blake and Mouton. The supervisor also needs to remember the concepts introduced by Lewin-Schein, that new ways of doing things require "unfreezing, changing, and refreezing" if they are effectively to be integrated into the workplace.

SUMMARY

o Through the ages, fear (the stick) and money (the carrot) have been the traditionally held concepts of worker motivation. Motivation is today understood to come from within each individual.

o Frederick Taylor believed that productivity was increased by careful selection and training of employees and by using money as a motivator.

o Henri Fayol and the Gilbreths continued research on productivity along the lines begun by Taylor.

o The Hawthorne experiments revealed that workers' attitudes affected their production. People who feel important are more likely to produce more than others who have not been treated in a special way.

o Change theory, proposed by Lewin and Schein, requires that people who are to alter permanently their way of performing must go through unfreezing, changing, and refreezing stages.

o Job redesign may be achieved by rotating tasks, adding more tasks, or making a different combination of tasks.

o According to McGregor, Theory X supervisors believe that they are responsible for their subordinates' actions and behavior and that people dislike work, lack ambition, are self-centered, and are resistant to change. Theory Y supervisors believe that they can help people to develop their abilities and that people seek responsibility, like to set their own goals, work toward the needs of the organization, and are basically ready to change when change is desirable.

o Maslow's hierarchy-of-needs theory reveals that certain needs must be satisfied before other needs become important. In ascending order, they are physiological needs, safety needs, love needs, esteem needs, and self-actualization needs.

o Herzberg's hygiene-motivator factors theory reveals that job satisfiers (achievement, recognition, work itself, responsibility, and advancement) are positive motivators. Hygiene factors (company policy, administration, supervision, salary, interpersonal relations, and working conditions) must exist at an adequate level, but they do not motivate a person to greater productivity.

o Berne's Transactional Analysis theory helps people to react in socially useful ways with others by understanding how the parent, adult, and child ego states exist in each individual.

o Participative management calls for workers to help to make decisions that affect their work. These employees usually work harder to have those projects succeed.

o The managerial grid developed by Blake and Mouton is a device that helps supervisors to analyze their styles of working with subordinates and to determine whether they are more concerned with people or productivity.

o Management by objectives is a motivational method that helps both the supervisor and the employee to set specific amounts and the quality of work to be done and later to evaluate their accomplishment.

REFERENCES

[1] Quoted in Samuel Feinberg, "From Where I Sit," *Women's Wear Daily*, October 2, 1979, p. 12.

[2] Peter F. Drucker, *Management: Tasks, Responsibilities, Practices* (New York: Harper & Row, 1973), p. 24.

[3] J. A. C. Brown, *The Social Psychology of Industry* (Harmondsworth, England: Penguin Books, 1954), p. 13.

[4] Fritz J. Roethlisberger and William J. Dickson, *Management and the Worker* (Cambridge, Mass.: Harvard University Press, 1939).

[5] Kurt Lewin, *Field Theory in Social Science* (New York: Harper & Bros., 1951), pp. 224, 228.

[6] Edgar H. Schein, *Professional Education* (New York: McGraw-Hill, 1972), pp. 76–84.

[7] Quoted in Studs Terkel, *Working* (New York: Avon Books, 1974), p. xxix.

[8] Drucker, *Management*, p. 267.

[9] Douglas McGregor, *Adventure in Thought and Action*, Proceedings of the Anniversary Convocation of the School of Industrial Management (Cambridge, Mass.: Massachusetts Institute of Technology, April 9, 1957), pp. 23–30.

[10] Drucker, *Management*, p. 232.

[11] Abraham H. Maslow, *Motivation and Personality* (New York: Harper & Row, 1954).

[12] Frederick Herzberg, *Work and the Nature of Man* (New York: Mentor, 1966), pp. 78–85.

[13] Eric Berne, *Transactional Analysis in Psychotherapy* (New York: Grove Press, 1961).

[14] Eric Berne, *Games People Play* (New York: Grove Press, 1964), pp. 15, 16, 17, 29, 48.

[15] Berne, *Games People Play*, p. 19.

[16] Berne, *Games People Play*, p. 27.

[17] Dudley Bennett, *TA and the Manager* (New York: AMACOM, 1976), p. 50.

[18] Frederick G. Lesieur, ed., *The Scanlon Plan: A Frontier in Labor-Management Cooperation* (Cambridge, Mass.: MIT Press, 1958).

[19] Rensis Likert, *New Patterns of Management* (New York: McGraw-Hill, 1961).

[20] Larry E. Greiner, "What Managers Think of Participative Leadership," *Harvard Business Review*, March–April 1973, pp. 111–17.

[21] Robert Blake and Jane Mouton, *The Managerial Grid* (Houston: Gulf Publishing Company, 1964).

[22] Peter F. Drucker, *The Practice of Management* (New York: Harper & Bros., 1954).

REVIEW AND DISCUSSION QUESTIONS

1. Why should supervisors be concerned about the motivation of workers in a firm?
2. Why are the studies of Frederick Taylor and Frank and Lillian Gilbreth less important today than they were in the early part of the twentieth century?
3. How do the Hawthorne experiments contribute to our understanding of what motivates employees?
4. How does job redesign differ from Taylor's methods of increasing production?
5. If you were a supervisor, would you find Theory X or Theory Y easier to use? Give reasons for your answer.
6. What role would a supervisor be able to play in satisfying the ego needs of an employee as explained by Maslow's hierarchy-of-needs theory?
7. Contrast Taylor's concept of the importance of wages with Herzberg's theory of their importance.

8. According to the theory of Transactional Analysis, how can the concept of the parent, adult, and child ego states be used to help employees accept directives?
9. How does the use of participative management motivate employees?
10. Explain the advantages and disadvantages of using MBO.

ASSIGNMENTS

1. Read an article from the Further Readings section in this chapter, or select an article on some aspect of motivation from another current publication. What ideas did you obtain from the article? Did they agree or disagree with the ideas in this chapter? Write a report of your findings.
2. Interview five students in your school who excel in scholarship, sports, music, art, or another endeavor. What motivates them to do so well? Write a summary of your findings.

PROBLEM FOR RESOLUTION

The secretary in a small department was a superior worker—speedy, accurate, interested in the job, and gracious and charming to all the people who had contact with that office. Her one fault was that she always came late to work. She was not a clock-watcher, however, and she often stayed after closing to complete work that was not yet done. However, her tardiness caused other workers and bosses to have to answer the telephones and do routine errands until she arrived each morning. The supervisor had talked to her about her lateness on several occasions, and she had always promised to try to get in on time. However, she had not changed her ways.

As supervisor, how would you attempt to get her to come to work on time?

CASE STUDY

The staff of one department in a retail firm included the buyer; the assistant buyer; the department manager, who was the supervisor; and six salespersons. The department sold televisions, expensive radios, and hi-fi equipment. The ratio of goods sold to those returned had been increasing over the past year, thus lowering profits, causing inventory gluts, and reducing commissions of the salespersons.

Everyone blamed everyone else in the department for the high number of returns. The salespersons said the merchandise the buyer purchased was not right; the buyer and the assistant buyer blamed both the department manager and the salespersons for poor placement of merchandise and low sales. The department manager said the buyer bought the wrong merchandise and the sales force used high-pressure selling techniques.

Actual analysis of the returns found that:

o Approximately 60 percent were due to overoptimistic promises given by the salespersons.

o Over 10 percent were due to operations failures (merchandise not delivered on time or damaged in delivery).

o About 30 percent were due to deficient qualities of the merchandise.

If you were the supervisor in the department, what steps would you take to try to remedy this situation?

FURTHER READING

Denny, William A. "Ten Rules for Managing by Objectives." *Business Horizons,* October 1979, pp. 66–68.
    Presents step-by-step procedures to develop an MBO program with written objectives that reinforce commitments and the efforts of subordinates.
Ford, Robert N. "Job Enrichment Lessons from AT&T." *Harvard Business Review,* January–February 1973, pp. 96–106.
    Reports how seven years of experience with job enrichment demonstrate that both productivity and morale rise when a worker can claim "a thing of my own."
Foy, Nancy, and Herman Gadon. "Worker Participation: Contrasts in Three Countries," *Harvard Business Review,* May–June 1976, pp. 71–83.
    Explains how patterns of participation differ in Sweden, Great Britain, and the United States, but the trend toward worker participation is growing in all three.
Harris, Thomas A. *I'm OK—You're OK: A Practical Guide to Transactional Analysis.* New York: Harper & Row, 1967.
    Explains the vocabulary needed to understand the field and the transactions at all levels, from the you and I are not OK, through one of us is OK but the other is not, to we are both OK as applied to life at various stages.
Herzberg, Frederick. "Herzberg on Motivation for the '80s." *Industrial Week,* October 1, 1979, pp. 58–63.

Discusses how managers must try to develop a consistent philosophy of motivation and job satisfaction.

———. *Work and the Nature of Man.* New York: New American Library,
1966.

Reports on research that leads to an understanding of the motivation of people on jobs and to a reinforcement of the hygiene-
motivator theory previously developed.

Levinson, Harry. "Asinine Attitudes Toward Motivation." *Harvard Business Review,* January–February 1973, pp. 70–76.

Discusses how employees know the difference between motivation and manipulation. The carrot and stick concept does not
work any more.

Schaffer, Robert H. "Demand Better Results and Get Them." *Harvard
Business Review,* November–December 1974, pp. 91–98.

Explains how failure to establish high performance expectations causes organizations to settle for mediocre achievements.

Quible, Zane K. "Use of Participative Management in Supervising Office
Employees." *Delta Pi Epsilon Journal,* August 1974, pp. 13–22.

Reports on research that shows the nature of selected managerial activities determines the extent to which administrative office
managers use participative management.

9

conducting meetings

After studying and analyzing this chapter, you should be able to:

Explain the advantages and disadvantages of meetings.

Describe general, departmental, and committee meetings.

Discuss inspirational, informational, evaluational, problem-solving, explorational, reorganizational, educational, and combination meetings.

Discuss the guidelines for holding effective meetings.

Explain why evaluation of meetings is needed and how it may be accomplished.

MEETINGS ARE AS natural to human beings as any other physical or mental activity. Ancient tribes had council meetings and the Sermon on the Mount was given to a large assemblage of people. Today, many kinds of people with common interests—politicians, teachers, parents, students, musicians, artists, actors, writers, poets, athletes, lawyers, doctors, and dentists, for example—gather together to exchange ideas. Business people and union members have long found the meeting to be an indispensable means of accomplishing certain types of work.

Visions of a world of service institutions, business, and industry with no meetings have been advanced by technology-minded people who foresee telephones, television consoles, and other communications technology making face-to-face meetings obsolete. For example, the telephone company has developed the *conference call,* by which one person can conduct business from his or her office with two or more other people in their offices many miles away without ever seeing them. In addition, Peter F. Drucker has said that *"too many meetings* attended by too many people" is a common symptom of poor organization, and that "the human dynamics of meetings are so complex as to make them very poor tools for getting any work done." [1]

The attempts to supplant face-to-face meetings and the negative comments about their effectiveness have not been successful in doing away with them. Although the conference call has been widely used and accepted, it has not taken the place of the face-to-face meeting, and even Drucker maintains that personal meetings are absolutely essential.[2] As Antony Jay, a noted evaluator of the business scene, has said, "A meeting still performs functions that will never be taken over by . . . technological instruments of the information revolution."[3]

Meetings exist in every enterprise. Supervisors are involved in meetings in many ways: as subordinates, as supervisors, and as peers (either within or outside the organization). Therefore, to be effective, supervisors must understand the nature of meetings, meeting groups, the kinds of meetings, and how to hold and evaluate meetings.

The nature of meetings

As noted, meetings take place in all firms. In large organizations, they are held at every level down through each department, until every person in the firm is involved in some way. Small firms also have meetings. However, because more face-to-face interaction is possible in small firms, meetings are usually less frequent.

Informal get-togethers, such as huddling (see Chapter 5) or dropping into a boss's or peer's office, are not considered to be meetings. Meetings are more than chance encounters. They have defined populations and are called at designated times.

Meetings can vary in a number of ways. They may be large, small or medium in size. They may be short, lengthy, or of moderate duration. They may be held in the morning, at noon, in the afternoon, or in the evening. They may include the service of full meals, snacks, or just soft drinks, or they may include no food or drink. They may bring together people whose jobs are similar or people whose interests vary widely. They may include just peers, or subordinates and supervisors as well. They may have formal agendas or no apparent structure. They may be regularly scheduled, thus allowing attendees to plan their calendars months in advance, or held only when a need arises, thus not ensuring the attendance of those most involved.

Only one common denominator pertains to all meetings—people are brought into person-to-person contact with one another to consider a topic or topics of mutual concern.

Group meetings

Meetings in organizations can range in size from a very few people to all the people in one location of the enterprise. Meetings can be categorized as general, departmental, or committee meetings. Supervisors can be involved in all of them (see Figure 9–1).

General meetings

Assemblages of all the people within the enterprise who are available to attend are *general meetings*. They are rarely held because few topics are so important that all employees need to be informed at one time. Most general information filters through supervisors at each level, who pass it on to their subordinates in departmental meetings. The head of the organization usually presides at general meetings.

Departmental meetings

Enterprises that are divided into departments, divisions, or other work groups hold meetings that involve the members of that unit rather frequently. Some hold weekly meetings; others hold meetings once or twice a month; and still others find that meetings every two or three months are sufficient. Usually the supervisor presides at these meetings. The members mainly discuss concerns about the operation of the department or the people within the department, or the supervisor reports on information received from superordinates or teaches subordinates to use some new form or device.

FIGURE 9–1
THE SUPERVISOR IS INVOLVED IN
MANY KINDS OF MEETINGS

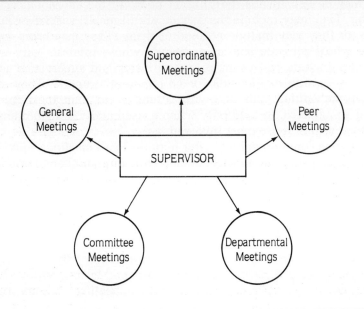

Committee meetings

Committees are composed of designated persons (volunteers, elected persons, or appointees) from one or more departments who confer on assigned matters and report back to either superordinates or the entire body of persons from which they have been drawn. Usually committee members perform their committee work in addition to doing their assigned jobs.

On occasion, special committee groups are set up to analyze important all-organization matters. They may be given special designations, such as task force, conference group, council, forum, senate, president's group, research group, or board. If such a group is assigned to work on an especially urgent matter, the members may be excused from their regular jobs for a specified period of time to spend all their efforts on this committee. (If they devote full time or a large portion of their time to this work, the assignment resembles the matrix organization discussed in Chapter 3).

Committees vary in size from as few as one person to as many as fifty or more. Groups, regardless of size, may in turn assign individuals or two or more members to obtain certain facts and to report back to the other committee members. These appointed groups are known as *sub-committees.*

Committees may be standing or ad hoc. *Standing committees* are those whose functions continue year after year. The membership, however, may change periodically. Committees on policies, finances, personnel, or work rules may be standing committees, whose members continue deliberations at stated intervals.

Ad hoc committees are usually short-term and are brought into existence to deliberate and report on one specific issue. An organization considering putting in new equipment, for example, might designate an ad hoc committee to investigate types of equipment, charges, and special features. When the final report is made, the committee is usually dissolved.

Because committees, except for those composed of just one person, have meetings, the information about the conduct of meetings is important for members and conductors of them.

Kinds of meetings

The reasons for calling meetings are as diverse as the people who plan and attend them. Meetings may be held to inspire, inform, evaluate, solve problems, explore, reorganize, or educate, or to perform two or more of these tasks in combination.

Inspirational meetings

Meetings intended to spur employees to be enthusiastic and loyal to the firm are called *inspirational meetings.* They may be called to announce an unusual service recently provided or about to be provided by the organization for its employees or customers; the successful launching of a new product; or the unique achievement of an employee, several employees, or the entire enterprise. Inspirational meetings usually include subtle urging to continue the high standards set by these examples or people and to pursue excellence through additional accomplishments.

Usually, all the employees available are called to these meetings. Some other business may be conducted briefly, but the main portion of the time is devoted to one stirring message from a speaker—either a well-known person from outside the firm or one of the top executives of the firm, such as the chairman of the board, the president, or an executive vice-president.

Both before and after inspirational meetings, time is allowed for people from different divisions to meet and mix. They thereby get a sense of togetherness. Questions may be allowed at the end of these meetings, but they are usually addressed only to matters raised by the main speaker.

Informational meetings

Meetings held to give facts and figures to a group are called *informational meetings*. The information presented may concern new products, new ways of processing data, new company rules, new laws, changed policies, planned moves, or any other area about which employees need to know. The size of informational meetings can vary from small, involving only one department, to large, involving all employees.

An informational meeting is usually conducted by the supervisory executive most knowledgeable about the matter or by supervisors who have been briefed earlier and then pass along the information to their staffs. To be sure that the information has been both completely disseminated and understood, the supervisor usually encourages questions at the end of the meeting. The more detailed and complex the information, the smaller the group should be to ensure that each person absorbs the information and interprets it correctly.

Evaluational meetings

Meetings held to discuss employees' ratings, salary increments, promotions, transfers, and related matters are called *evaluational meetings*. They are attended by the employees' immediate supervisor and other relevant people in the firm—usually representatives from the personnel and financial departments and the supervisor's superordinate. In some firms, supervisors from related departments also attend. Evaluational meetings are not held in all enterprises, but when they are, they usually occur once or twice a year.

Following an evaluational meeting, the supervisor meets individually with each of the employees assessed to explain what decisions were made.

Problem-solving meetings

When difficulties or new opportunities arise that call for answers or actions, *problem-solving meetings* may be called with people whose expertise can contribute to their resolution. Problem-solving may occur at any level of the hierarchy—among peers or among superordinates and subordinates. Such matters as how to price products, meet competition, increase production, or make a system work effectively are among the types of considerations that may necessitate problem-solving meetings.

Because business is constantly changing, as soon as one problem appears to be solved, another looms in importance and needs resolution.

With participatory management, employees may be invited to analyze the problem and offer solutions. For employees who enjoy being involved, and for those who have unique expertise, this type of meeting is helpful to both the participants and the firm.

Some employees, however, have been known to resent this type of meeting and to consider that "the bosses are paid to make the decisions." Regardless of this attitude on the part of a few employees, the benefits of participatory decision making far outweigh the disadvantages. Meetings of this type are used to get expressions of opinion and to have employees share their specialized knowledge. The final decision must be made by the person charged with the responsibility, but the input from the various well-informed people will help that decision to be sound.

Explorational meetings

Enterprises prosper when their employees create new products, think of new ideas, and find new and better ways of performing tasks. This creativity is not accidental but is the result of a constant search to improve some aspect of the business.

Meetings held to spur creativity are called *explorational meetings.* Explorational meetings are not held in all firms, and no pattern exists for them because each depends on the needs of the individual firm. In general, though, they are forums for discussing and analyzing the way certain functions are carried out. They are attended by people who perform the tasks under consideration, who are best able to suggest better ways of accomplishing those tasks, such as shortcuts or other productivity-increasing methods. For example, in one small sportswear shop with just seven employees, shoplifting was cut over 40 percent by holding meetings among the employees to discuss creative ways to stop the problem.

Another example is in the federal government, where, since 1921, employees used paper that measured 8 by 10½ inches, which had been mandated for all work. The Bureau of Efficiency at that time determined that size was economical because its use saved more paper than the use of the standard 8½-by-11-inch size commonly used by everyone else. In 1979, a government committee's assessment of the "text area" size of the 8½-by-11-inch sheet showed that fewer pages were needed for jobs, resulting in the saving of millions of dollars in clerical labor and reduced handling, storage, and mailing costs.[4]

Brainstorming, an idea-gathering game, has been used in some firms since the mid 1940s to spur creative ideas among people in a group. For a brainstorming session, people holding positions at the same level are brought together. The group, if large, may be divided into subgroups and each group may compete against the others. A problem is introduced, and the people within each group suggest ways of handling it. Outlandish ideas are encouraged, and anyone who says, "That's silly," "That won't work," or any similar negative remark is immediately out of the game. The ideas are recorded, and a subsequently appointed committee is asked to judge their worth. Many new ways of viewing a product or a project have been inspired by this freewheeling type of idea gathering. For example, elimination of extra forms, development of streamlined forms, ideas for advertising and promotion, and creation of new and improved products have all resulted from brainstorming sessions.

Reorganizational meetings

No enterprise is stagnant. All are constantly changing either by expanding or, in some cases, diminishing in size. Employees need to be aware that change occurs in all firms. Most people resist change, and many fear that change will affect their job. Indeed, few people remain in a firm for a prolonged period without experiencing substantial changes in the scope of their job and in the composition of the work force. *Reorganizational meetings* are held when changes in the structure of the hierarchy, the staff, or assignments will affect employees and, therefore, need to be discussed.

Change signals movement of some type for almost everyone. Sometimes it involves movement just within the firm itself for a few people. In extreme cases, it may mean movement to other geographical areas and involve the private as well as the working lives of the employees. Change may bring promotion and expanded responsibility to some employees, signify lateral moves for others, or mean a reduction of responsibility for others.

Regardless of the impact that change will have on the members of a firm, they are entitled to know what is planned. Wise supervisors will carefully consider how best to broach the subject and how to deal with the various reactions that undoubtedly will occur.

If meetings pertaining to change are held just among top and middle managers, rumors will filter throughout the organization, and fear and resistance will build among the other people in the firm. Therefore, carefully structured meetings should be held to discuss and plan reorganization. Meetings about reorganization must include all employees, supervisory and nonsupervisory, affected by the proposals. If the change affects only one part of the enterprise's personnel, that group should be so informed. However, the others should be reassured that, at least for the present, no further reorganization is planned. Rumors will thereby be either lessened or entirely eliminated, and fact will replace fiction.

Because some people are extremely apprehensive about change, when possible the supervisor should reassure them that the change will not disrupt their working lives too much. If the change is to be a major one, the supervisor should advise the employees that the company will do everything possible to help them adjust to their altered job status. Reorganizational meetings give employees a chance to express and share their feelings, and thus help to reduce their animosities and fears.

Educational meetings

Meetings held to teach a chosen group of employees specific new facts or processes are called *educational meetings.* They are conducted by the supervisor or some other person knowledgeable in the area under consideration. If general routines are being changed or if new laws necessitate different ways of handling work, an educational meeting may include all employees.

Improving one's knowledge or skill has become essential in today's technology-oriented world. Employees who have shown, through tests, to have an aptitude for working in a different field or with different machines may be invited to join a class to study the technology that will prepare them for a position in a different or more advanced area. Information systems, data processing, computer analysis, word processing, and systems analysis are all examples of areas that have opened to people in recent decades. The classes may be given in the firm or in special schools. They may be held during working hours, after working hours, or on weekends. Being chosen to attend educational meetings may be viewed as an honor by those who participate.

Combination meetings

Meetings held to achieve more than one goal—for example, to inspire and present information, to evaluate through problem solving, or to explore through education—are called *combination meetings.* Combinations of purpose are common, especially if assembling people at one time and place is difficult.

How to hold effective meetings

Holding a meeting entails more than just calling people together. The supervisor must consider many factors, such as costs, planning, scheduling, complex issues, and techniques.

Consider the costs

Meetings are costly to hold. Depending on the situation, the supervisor must consider the costs for materials and equipment, use of the space, lighting, air conditioning or heating, outside experts, and transportation. In addition to the money paid directly for these items, the supervisor must consider such indirect costs as the time taken from the work of the people involved, the value of the material presented, the time needed for the meeting, and the frequency with which such a meeting should be held. If a meeting lasts for half an hour and involves fifty people whose average salary is $8 per hour, the cost of their time alone is $200.

In the end, thousands of dollars may be spent on just one meeting if many of these costs are involved. One of the first questions the supervisor has to ask is, "Is the meeting worth the money it will cost?"

Consider the planning

Planning a meeting that is to achieve certain goals requires careful thought. To make a meeting effective, the supervisor must consider the why, who, when, where, and how of the meeting.

Why. The purpose for which the meeting is to be held must first be assessed. Is a meeting the best way to accomplish what needs to be done? Would other means of communication be equally satisfactory? Could the same message be sent as effectively via a bulletin board, a loudspeaker, or videotape? If none of these media would provide the desired results, a meeting may be the answer to the present need.

Who. Does this meeting concern the entire work force or just certain segments of it? The decision about which employees are to attend is important, since it not only narrows attendance to those most concerned but also determines the size of the meeting. Large meetings require different facilities and a different format than small meetings. Also, large meetings require that notices be sent well in advance if they are to be well attended.

When. What date and what time of day are best to hold the meeting? Different enterprises have different considerations. Schools have to reckon with scheduled classes; hospitals must determine when nurses are free; offices must consider when employees are able to leave their desks; marketing firms must decide when customers will not need the services of the salespersons.

Where Does the firm have conference rooms or other areas that are available? Are those rooms large enough for the group? Are there sufficient chairs and tables? If not, how can these be transported to the meeting place? Is a loudspeaker system needed? If so, does the available room have one? Will visual aids be used? If so, how large must they be to be readily visible? Will projectionists or other technicians be needed to set up and run the equipment? Is the software ready for use in the machines? Is the meeting place relatively quiet? Will other employees need to pass through the area while the meeting is in progress? Will telephones be ringing, thus distracting the speaker or the audience? Will refreshments be served? If so, how can these be obtained and handled expeditiously, and where will they be placed? Will meeting attendees be able to reach the meeting place easily? If not, what transportation will be needed, or what information should they be given to reach the meeting place?

How. In what manner will the meeting be conducted? What is the agenda? What items should be considered first, second, last? How can attention be maintained at the highest level throughout the meeting? How can participation be obtained? How will people who are responding from the audience be heard? How will questions be handled? How will the meeting be conducted to have an adult-adult relationship among all attendees? How will attendees know what to do to prepare for the meeting?

Many of these "how" questions may be resolved by the agenda, which should be prepared and sent to attendees ahead of time. People sometimes become apprehensive about meetings, or rumors may precede them. An agenda allays these fears. Also, knowing the agenda permits participants to prepare certain questions or statements ahead of time, and encourages more people to be involved in the meeting.

Consider the scheduling

In firms in which meetings are held frequently, meeting times may be set as much as six months ahead. Doing so permits attendees to plan their calendars, setting aside the required time for the meeting. If meetings are held sporadically, the amount of prior notice needed depends on the difficulty of getting people together. Most meetings are planned for at least a week or two ahead of time. Occasionally, an urgent problem arises that necessitates an immediate meeting. If the firm is well run, such emergency meetings will be kept to a minimum.

Consider the complex-issue meeting

In some cases, meetings are called to resolve issues that are exceedingly complex. In such complex-issue meetings, the time needed just to explain the details so that each person can understand all the various ramifications and make intelligent judgments may take many hours. The knowledgeable supervisor facing such a complex-issue meeting may take advantage of huddling (see Chapter 5) to inform attendees about the matter. In this way, attendees will need less time to understand the complex issues and will be able to consider the problem at their leisure. Consensus is usually arrived at with considerably less trauma when huddling is used before complex-issue meetings than when it is not.

Consider the techniques

In developing a meeting, the supervisor should follow certain guidelines that will increase the possibility that the meeting will produce effective results:

- o Write an agenda for the meeting. If possible, distribute copies of it before the meeting. If not, give out the copies as people enter the meeting room or leave one at each person's place.

- o Start and end the meeting at the announced times.

- o Assign the amount of time that will be devoted to each item on the agenda. Doing so allows every topic to be covered, keeps everyone alert, and satisfies people that the meeting is moving ahead.

- o Guide and control the discussion so that the matters at hand are those talked about and considered.

- o Allow only one person to talk at a time, and make sure every person who wants to has a chance to express an opinion. Do not let one person or a few people dominate.

- o Inject humor to relieve the tenseness and apprehension that sometimes build up during a meeting. Pertinent jokes can ease boredom, get people to relax, and make people laugh at a situation that might otherwise be stressful.

- o Attempt to foster an "I'm OK, you're OK" atmosphere. Urge people to listen to others and make positive suggestions rather than argue or belittle others' opinions.

- o Make sure the ideas put forth are understood by having them repeated or restated by attendees before counterarguments are presented.

- o Move the meeting forward by encouraging people to express points of view not previously stated.

- o Bring the meeting to a close by attempting to get a consensus. If a vote is needed, it should be taken according to the parliamentary rules followed by the firm. Vote taking is more time-consuming than merely getting an agreement on the ideas presented.

o Prepare a summary of the meeting to distribute to all attendees within one week. Restate the date and time of the meeting, the members present, and the actions agreed upon. If assignments resulted from those agreements, note them.

Evaluating meetings

For most attendees, meetings have advantages and disadvantages. On the positive side, meetings serve to encourage desirable actions, obtain agreement on new proposals, get suggestions, inform, educate, stimulate, bring people together so greater understanding can be obtained, let employees know the wealth of talent that resides within an organization, and give status to those who are included.

However, meetings also cost both time and money, result in consensus usually only by compromise, encourage passivity in most attendees, dilute authority, spread out responsibility, and delay decisions.

To determine whether the strengths outweigh the weaknesses, meetings should be evaluated by both those who conduct them and those who participate in them. Assessment may be informal or formal. Conductors of meetings can make *informal assessments* by asking attendees whether or not they considered the meetings to be of value and by reviewing the accomplishments of the meetings themselves.

Conductors and attendees can make *formal assessments* through checklists, short reports, or a small committee. People making formal assessments should consider how the meeting was conducted as well as the results. How effectively the speakers presented their ideas, how well visual aids supplemented the messages, how expeditiously time was used, and how valuable the results were are all factors that should be considered in determining the worth of a meeting.

Tables 9–1 and 9–2 show two suggested checklists for formal assessments. They may be used for different types of meetings. Before the next meeting of a particular group is planned, any assessments should be carefully analyzed to ascertain how subsequent meetings can be improved.

SUMMARY

o Meetings occur in every kind of enterprise. Supervisors are frequently involved in meetings and they play roles both as meeting leaders and meeting attendees.

o Meetings are time-consuming and costly. They vary in every organization. No one formula exists for determining meeting time, place, size, or format.

TABLE 9-1

SUPERVISOR'S SELF-RATING SCALE FOR MEETINGS

	Yes	No	Not Appli-cable
1. Meeting was planned well in advance.			
2. Meeting's date and time were announced to all attendees sufficiently in advance.			
3. The purpose, date, time, and place of meeting were stated in the notice.			
4. An agenda was prepared and distributed to all attendees.			
5. The meeting started on time.			
6. Over 90 percent of invited persons attended.			
7. The purpose of the meeting was presented clearly and succinctly.			
8. Interchange of ideas among attendees was friendly.			
9. All persons who volunteered had an opportunity to partic-ipate in the discussion.			
10. No one individual or group dominated.			
11. Audiovisual aids were easily visible and audible through-out the meeting place.			
12. Speakers could be heard easily by all attendees.			
13. Attendees appeared to be interested in the agenda.			
14. An attempt was made to ensure that attendees under-stood one another's viewpoints.			
15. Attendees' questions were answered.			
16. Summaries were developed for all to see as the ideas were presented.			
17. Consensus was obtained.			
18. Assessment sheets were distributed.			
19. Meeting concluded as scheduled.			
20. Summary of meeting decisions was made and distributed to all attendees within five working days.			
21. Evaluation sheets of meeting were analyzed to improve on meeting's weak points.			

TABLE 9–2

RATING SCALE FOR ATTENDEES AT MEETING

	Yes	No	Not Appli- cable
1. Meeting notice arrived in time to fit the meeting into schedule.			
2. Meeting notice stated purpose of meeting.			
3. Meeting notice stated date and time of meeting.			
4. Meeting notice stated place of meeting and gave adequate directions for getting there (if off the premises).			
5. Meeting started on time.			
6. Agenda was presented.			
7. Meeting was well attended.			
8. Purpose of meeting was clearly and succinctly stated.			
9. Visual aids were well developed and visible.			
10. Audio reception was clear.			
11. Supervisor stimulated discussion.			
12. Supervisor made sure members understood one another's point of view.			
13. Supervisor encouraged everyone to participate.			
14. Summaries were developed as meeting progressed.			
15. Consensus was obtained.			
16. Assessment sheets were distributed.			
17. Meeting concluded on time.			
18. Meeting notes were received within one week after the meeting.			
19. The meeting was worth the time and effort to attend it.			
20. Overall, the meeting was (check one) ___ Excellent ___ Very good ___ Average ___ Poor ___ Not worth attending			

o Meetings may be general, departmental, or committee meetings. Standing committes are continuing, while ad hoc committees exist to perform basically one important assignment.

o Meetings are diverse in purpose. Inspirational meetings are held to build enthusiasm and loyalty. Informational meetings present news, facts, or innovations. Evaluational meetings are held to rate employees' performances. Problem-solving meetings are held to find solutions to some dilemmas. Explorational meetings search into new, creative ways to perform tasks or to develop services or products. Reorganizational meetings occur when changes in the relationships of people, departments, or assignments are needed. Educational meetings are held when instruction in how to do something or how to understand some idea is needed. Combination meetings have two or more purposes.

o When contemplating holding a meeting, supervisors must take into account costs, planning, scheduling, complex issues, and techniques.

o Meeting evaluations make subsequent meetings more effective. Informal assessments merely ask opinions orally, whereas formal assessments are recorded and may be carefully analyzed.

REFERENCES

[1] Peter F. Drucker, *Management: Tasks, Responsibilities, Practices* (New York: Harper & Row, 1973), p. 548.

[2] Drucker, *Management*, p. 408.

[3] Antony Jay, "How to Run a Meeting," *Harvard Business Review*, March–April 1976, p. 44.

[4] "More Is Less, More or Less," *New York Times*, January 1, 1980, p. 18.

REVIEW AND DISCUSSION QUESTIONS

1. Explain why meetings are so diversified in character.
2. List the various ways in which supervisors may be involved in meetings.
3. What is the primary purpose of an inspirational meeting?
4. What is the primary purpose of an informational meeting? How do informational meetings differ from educational ones?
5. What is accomplished by evaluational meetings, in which employee performance is discussed?
6. What may be achieved through a problem-solving meeting?
7. What is the purpose of an explorational meeting? How might brainstorming be used in an explorational meeting?
8. Why are reorganizational meetings necessary?
9. What considerations should be undertaken in developing an effective meeting?
10. Why should meetings be evaluated?

ASSIGNMENTS

1. Attend a meeting at your school. Use Table 9–2 to evaluate the meeting. What would you do to improve the meeting? Give reasons for your suggestions.
2. For several years, the college in which you are a student has been concerned with the role of students in governing the school. Recently, your school received an invitation to send a representative to a state convention of students who are to discuss "The Role of Students in College Governance." Your class has voted to raise the money to send a member to attend this convention. You have been appointed as the chairperson of the committee, which includes four other people. Your committee is charged with determining how much money needs to be raised to send a delegate, how that amount can be raised, and how a contest can be devised to choose the class member who will attend the convention.

   Detail the procedures you, as the chairperson, would go through to assemble the other committee members, gather the information needed, make the proposal, and present the proposal to the class.

PROBLEM FOR RESOLUTION

Your school debating team has won all the intercollegiate competitions in the state. The team now wants to debate other state winners. There are nine members on the team, and six additional students in the society, each with his or her own debating expertise. All are anxious to represent the team, but only three can go to the state competition.

As the president of the debating society, you have been asked by the members to try to work out a solution to this dilemma. You believe a meeting of the officers of the society plus all interested debaters may provide some answers.

What kind of meeting would you plan? Detail how you would set up the meeting.

CASE STUDY

A group of three men in the accounting department of the Saugerties Company has come to you, their supervisor, to complain that the federal law that requires hiring and promoting minority-group members and women will void their right to seniority promotions. They tell you that the entire staff of twenty-five white males feels threatened by the newly hired Puerto Rican woman, Maria Caraballo-Perez, a certified public accountant, who is working for her M.B.A. degree at a local university during the evenings. This woman is considered to be one of the foremost young accountants to have been employed in the firm.

How would you handle this situation?

FURTHER READING

Anthony, William P. "Management for More Effective Staff Meetings." *Personnel Journal,* August 1979, pp. 547–50.
> Analyzes staff meetings and vital communication devices on the basis of cost-benefit effectivenss.

Duncan, W. Jack. "Small Groups and Interpersonal Communication." In *Essentials of Management.* Hinsdale, Ill.: Dryden Press, 1975, pp. 170–99.
> Analyzes small groups; explains their important characteristics; and notes the role of cohesiveness, conformity, and problem solving in those groups.

Dunsing, Richard J. *You and I Have Simply Got to Stop Meeting This Way.* New York: AMACOM, 1978.
> Explains how meetings work best, the environment in meetings, the games people play at meetings, and how to analyze and diagnose meetings.

Jay, Antony. "How to Run a Meeting." *Harvard Business Review,* March–April 1976, pp. 43–57.
> Presents guidelines on how to run meetings: how to define objectives, make preparations, and conduct a meeting.

Prince, George M. "How to Cope with Too Little Time—and Too Many Meetings." *Training,* October 1977, pp. 39–40.
> Discusses how meetings waste a lot more time and energy than they should, and how a few ground rules, such as planning, clarifying directives, keeping attitudes positive, and having an open-minded evaluation, help.

Schwartz, David. "Group Dynamics and Committees." In *Introduction to Management: Principles, Practices, and Processes.* New York: Harcourt Brace Jovanovich, 1980, pp. 314–51.
> Explains why people form groups, the nature of committees, and guidelines for maximizing the effectiveness of committees.

Zeltin, John D. "Planning the Small Meeting." In *Meetings and Conventions.* New York: Ziff Davis, 1979, pp. 131–32ff.
> Describes how to make small meetings effective.

10

evaluating employees

After studying and analyzing this chapter, you should be able to:

Discuss objectivity, subjectivity, and the "halo effect" in evaluating employees.

Explain how employees may be evaluated informally, including the role of the actions of the supervisor.

Define "reliability" and "validity" in terms of evaluation.

Describe the various kinds of formal evaluations.

Explain how supervisors are evaluated.

Discuss how formal evaluations are used and employers' problems with them.

List and explain the guidelines for effective evaluation.

FROM THE TIME a person is employed by a firm until he or she leaves it, evaluation takes place. *Evaluation*, sometimes called *performance appraisal*, is the determination of an employee's value to the company in which he or she is employed.

Assessing abilities of employees occurs for many reasons. For the new employee, appraisals take place during the probationary period, when the worker's ability to do the job is determined. After the probationary period, which is usually about three months, appraisals may be made for other reasons, including salary raises, job transfers, promotions, demotions, dismissals, or just helping the employee do a better job. *Help employee do a better job.*

Evaluations may be both objective or subjective, formal or informal. What these are and how they are used are discussed in the pages that follow.

Objectivity, subjectivity, and the "halo effect"

Evaluations of people are based on both objective information and subjective feelings or insight. The more objective appraisals are, the easier they are to explain and defend. *Objectivity* is the impersonal establishment of truth based on facts. Objective appraisals are external to the rater and not affected by his or her own ideas or biases.

For example, if productivity can be measured, an objective evaluation of a person's contribution to the organization's goals can be determined. The number of letters typed, accounts entered, customers contacted, errors made, or days late or absent are all objective measures of a person's performance. The more an employee can be evaluated on such measures, the more objective the appraisal will be.

Subjectivity is the application of personal, internalized impressions, biases, thoughts, and feelings. Subjective appraisals, instead of using facts, are based on remembrances or opinions about the people being evaluated. Because bias may be part of the reaction, subjective evaluations are not likely to be as useful as objective ones. Statements such as "The person seems to work hard," "That worker is easily upset," or "She has apparent interest in her job" are subjective judgments that have little meaning unless they can be backed up with objective facts.

One type of subjective judgment is the *halo effect*. This is the supervisor's tendency to form an early impression of a person that influences all subsequent ratings. Thus, a person whom the supervisor likes personally will be perceived as being cooperative and interested in the job, while another whom the supervisor dislikes is viewed as being uncooperative and disinterested in the job. Or an employee recommended as a hard worker is viewed as productive, while another thought to be lazy is viewed as unproductive, even though they accomplish similar amounts of work.

Informal evaluations

When people greet one another, one often says, "How well you look" or "You must be doing well, you look so prosperous (or happy or well dressed or contented)" or "What is the matter? You look depressed (or ill or unhappy or as though you have lost weight)." These statements are all evaluations of one person by another. Even if the words were not stated, the evaluation would be made. Every time we see a person we know, we make some value judgment about him or her. Similarly, when a supervisor sees an employee, the supervisor makes some estimate of the employee's appearance or performance on a particular task.

These unstructured appraisals of appearance or performance are known as *informal evaluations*. They take place whenever people come into contact with others. Informal evaluations build up over time into fairly definitive judgments of an employee. They may be the only type of appraisal used in a small firm. In larger firms, informal evaluations may be included in the overall formal evaluations.

While a supervisor is informally evaluating an employee, that employee, in turn, is evaluating the supervisor. Whether or not subordinates' ratings of supervisors are subsequently used in a formal evaluation depends on the policy of the firm.

form opinion in informal basis — highly subjective

Actions of supervisors

Employees get feedback about their job performance both by what the supervisor says and by the way the supervisor acts. For example, Jack, a newly appointed assistant in a department, was preparing some defective goods for return to the manufacturer. This was a time-consuming job that entailed getting the merchandise to the returned-goods section on the lower floor, lining the items up by manufacturer, and filling out a form for each manufacturer that asked for detailed information about each item being returned. When the job was about two-thirds done, the supervisor called to say that Jack was wanted upstairs in his office immediately. Jack explained that the returned-goods job was well underway, that he needed only a short time to complete it, and that the goods could not be left because he was responsible for them. The supervisor's reply was, "I said to come up now, and I want you here now." With that, the supervisor hung up the telephone.

Jack rushed to have all the forms that had been carefully filled out in triplicate voided, repacked the merchandise in boxes, and ran up to the office, sure that something momentous was at hand. When Jack arrived, the secretary said, "Oh, the boss left, but he wants you to tell this reporter about our new line of goods."

Jack was dumbfounded. He knew that the secretary could have answered all the reporter's questions as well as he. After the interview, he went back to the returned-goods section angrily muttering, "Apparently my time and effort count for nothing in the eyes of the supervisor." The supervisor's actions told Jack how his job was regarded, what value the supervisor placed on his judgment, and how the time expended by him was esteemed.

Similarly, a secretary who transcribes and types a lengthy letter that the boss has hurriedly dictated and that needed a great deal of editing before it could be submitted in final form may, instead of being praised, be reprimanded for one minor erasure or for an unimportant punctuation omission. Employees who handle customers with tact and discretion may be criticized because their record keeping is tardy. Employees may notice that the ones who get praised are those who trade jokes with the boss when he or she is in a good mood.

Informal evaluations as demonstrated by the supervisor's actions may tell employees what is and what is not important in the eyes of the supervisor. They may be conscious or subconscious. Often they are done without any intention of using those judgments, but simply because one is aware of how others look, speak, react, and perform.

Formal evaluations

Formal evaluations are assessments that are prescribed by the policies of the organization and based on specific criteria. They necessitate examination of and a written report on the employee's quantity and quality of work and personal characteristics, and are done at specified intervals.

Formal evaluations are undertaken purposely. They are used to develop information that may be helpful to the members of the organization in many ways and to the person being evaluated, who needs and wants to learn what particular strengths and/or weaknesses he or she has for the job.

Specifically, they:

o Serve as feedback to let the employee know what the supervisor and other members of the management team think about his or her performance

o Allow both the employee and the supervisor to know if the objectives of the job for a certain period of time have been met o Help the supervisor set merit raises and determine if the employee should be transferred, promoted, warned about job performance, or in extreme cases, dismissed

o Provide a basis for comparing the output of employees doing similar work and for developing standards for a particular job

o Give the employee an opportunity to express opinions about the firm and its activities that may be be helpful in the future

o Furnish both the supervisor and the employee with proof about any need for further training or for discipline or counseling

o Aid the employee in career planning

o Assist the employment staff in knowing how well its screening procedures for selecting and placing employees are working

o Supply proof of reasons for promotion, transfer, or dismissal of an employee in case of challenges by the employee, other employees, a union, or a government agency

o Help in inventorying the human resources of a firm

may see a potential supervisor ...
can see qualities of people.

For formal evaluations, most firms use some type of written method, chosen from a wide variety. Each kind has somewhat different uses, so selectors can choose or devise those that are most pertinent for the particular enterprise.

Reliability and validity

For appraisal forms to be effective, they should be both reliable and valid.

Reliable means that the form measures the same qualities consistently each time it is used. Two measures of reliability are commonly used. These are test-retest and split-half. In addition, two different raters may compare their ratings of one person to check reliability.

Test-retest requires that the same form be used twice for the same person with a period of time, usually about two weeks, between ratings. If the ratings are virtually identical, the form is deemed reliable. *Split-half* is a speedier method of testing reliability. The answers are divided in half, and each half is checked to see that the ratings total the same. If the ratings are different for each half, reliability is in doubt. If two *different raters* evaluate one person, reliability is ensured if their judgments are quite similar. If their judgments are quite different, the form has to be redesigned.

Valid means that the form measures what it was meant to measure. Thus, if a person's performance is being appraised, all elements of that person's performance should be examined. To obtain validity, people familiar with the worker's job are asked to look at each item on the form and to make sure that a representative sample of all tasks performed is included. Thus, if a secretary was being evaluated and no question was asked about transcription skills, the rating would not be valid.

For formal evaluations, employers may use productivity charts, graphic rating scales, ranking, sociograms, checklists, forced-choice checklists, critical incident reports, written reports, management by objectives, multiple-person assessment, or a combination of these methods.

Productivity charts

Productivity charts are useful for jobs for which output can be measured. If a factor like the number of sales made, customers handled, invoices or other forms processed, persons interviewed, patients administered to, or transactions completed can be tallied, a rating of productivity can be attained and used to judge performance.

This is both an accurate, objective, and relatively easy method of evaluation. The productivity figures, however, only give one measure of a person's value. Other characteristics may be considered in the annual or semiannual performance appraisal. Thus, if a person is a top producer but also causes trouble among other workers, disobeys rules, or is guilty of some misdemeanor, he or she may not receive a good overall rating in spite of an excellent productivity record.

Graphic rating scales

A *graphic rating scale* is an evaluation method by which the supervisor rates various qualities of subordinates on a scale of sliding values. The scale may range from poor to excellent, from 1 for poor to 5 for excellent, or, with a wider base of numbers, from 1 for poor to 10 for excellent. The qualities evaluated may include work habits, judgment, maturity, accuracy, flexibility, promptness, attendance, cooperation, sensitivity, quantity and quality of work, dependability, initiative, appearance, interest in the job, ability to organize work, and effectiveness of time management (see Figure 10–1).

Because they often provide a numerical rating, capsulize the judgments made about each subordinate, and are simple to use and understand, graphic rating scales are popular. However, the apparently definitive rating that may be derived from totaling the individual ratings should be viewed with some apprehension. Individual raters interpret each quality somewhat differently. In addition, some supervisors tend to rate subordinates as average in most categories, while others may give either all high or all low ratings. Also, supervisors may use the "halo effect." Therefore, the numbers that result from graphic rating scales are not as informative as they appear to be.

Ranking

When using *ranking,* the supervisor places the employees on a list ranging from best to poorest in performance. If all the employees in a department perform the same job, ranking is relatively useful and informative. Thus, tellers in a bank, salespersons in a department, typists in a typing pool or word-processing center, data processors, and warehouse employees, for example, can be ranked from the top performer to the lowest producer. However, in departments in which people do quite different tasks, the supervisor may be inclined to rate the importance of the task rather than the quality of performance. When people do different work, accurate ranking is virtually impossible and may lead to subjective rankings.

Sociograms

To determine which employees are the leaders among their peers, the supervisor may wish to develop a *sociogram, or a map of the social interplay within the office during working hours.* To do this, the supervisor makes a diagram of the positions of the different employees—their desks, stations, or other assigned posts—and then charts the movement of employees to and from one another's positions. Usually one or two employees turn out to be "stars," those people sought by others for advice, consultations, comment, or other reasons. In Figure 10–2, out of twenty different interactions, twelve are to or from B. B, therefore, is the informal leader of the group.

Although a sociogram does not give an overall rating of a person's qualifications, it does indicate the informal leadership within a group and is helpful to the supervisor in judging the value of different people in the section. A sociogram may also be used to determine which employees to recommend for promotion to supervisory jobs.

Checklists

A *checklist* presents many brief descriptive statements applicable to traits, behaviors, and actions pertinent to the job being performed. The supervisor checks those items that apply to the employee being evaluated. Different items on the checklist may be assigned various values, allowing for an overall score. When completed, the checklist may be

FIGURE 10–1
GRAPHIC RATING SCALE

Employee Name _____

Job Title _____

Department _____

Period From _____ To _____

Number Days Absent _____

Number Days Late _____

Directions:
Fill in this form by placing an X in the box that most nearly reflects your careful, objective, accurate judgment of the employee's work.
Consider the typical performance, not unusual ones. Rating; 5 = Best to 1 = Poorest

	5	4	3	2	1	RATING
1. *Good Work Habits*—How quickly and efficiently job is done	Eager and able to work hard ☒	Willing to work hard ☐	Usually works hard ☐	Needs prodding to get things done ☐	Poor—Rarely finishes tasks on time ☐	_____
2. *Quality of Work*—How well work is done	Virtually perfect ☐	Very well done ☒	Average quality ☐	Often makes errors ☐	Poor—Needs to redo most assignments ☐	_____
3. *Quantity of Work*—How much employee produces	Top producer ☐	Among top producers ☐	Average producer ☒	Below-average producer ☐	Lowest producer ☐	_____
4. *Personal Appearance*—How neat, clean, and well groomed employee is	Always neat and well groomed ☐	Usually neat and well groomed ☒	Neat and well groomed about half of the time ☐	Rarely neat and well groomed ☐	Always appears ill kempt ☐	_____
5. *Sociability*—How willing employee is to talk with and work with others	Always friendly and willing to work with others ☐	Generally interested in others ☒	Occasionally interested in others ☐	Rarely interested in others ☐	Grumpy and unsociable ☐	_____

6. *Mental Alertness*—How quickly employee learns and how well information is retained	Thinks quickly and retains well ☐	Usually understands and retains information ☒	Occasionally understands and retains information ☐	Slow to understand and has to be reminded often ☐	Unable to understand unless material is repeated and rarely retains information ☐
7. *Organizing Ability*—How well employee arranges work and uses time efficiently	Unusual ability to arrange work and time ☐	Usually organizes work and time efficiently ☒	Occasionally is able to organize work without help ☐	Often needs help in determining how to plan job ☐	Always needs help in getting work organized ☐
8. *Cooperation*—How employee is willing to share knowledge and to help others to get work done	Marked ability to work with and help others ☐	Usually willing to share know-how and help others ☒	Occasionally helps others ☐	Rarely cooperates with others ☐	Never helps others ☐
9. *Emotional Control*—How able employee is to retain composure under stressful conditions	Unusual calmness under stress ☐	Usually well balanced ☐	Controls self about half the time ☒	Usually becomes upset under stressful situations ☒	Easily depressed and irritated ☐

TOTAL RATING _____

Remarks: _____

Date _____   Rated By _____   Discussed With Employee _____   Signed _____
                  Title _____   Date _____   Date _____
                                                                             (Employee)

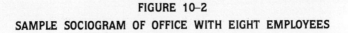

FIGURE 10–2

SAMPLE SOCIOGRAM OF OFFICE WITH EIGHT EMPLOYEES

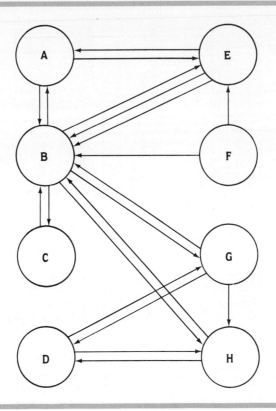

used to develop a profile showing the person's strengths and weaknesses or to compare the worth to the company of various employees in similar positions.

Figure 10–3 illustrates statements that might appear on a checklist for a general office worker. To use the checklist, supervisors check those statements that most closely identify the work or attitudes of the employee. Each positive statement has a negative counterpart. Positive statements get a rating of 1, and negative statements a rating of −1. The higher the positive score (25 is the highest), the better the rating. To get the final rating, the negative total is subtracted from the positive total.

Forced-choice checklists

With forced-choice checklists, the supervisor is required (forced) to check each of the various items, telling whether it is most descriptive or

FIGURE 10-3
CHECKLIST FORM FOR EMPLOYEE EVALUATION

_____   _____   _____
Name of Employee   Job Title   Date

_____   _____
Name of Supervisor   Department

Check the following behaviors that best characterize the employee being rated.

___ Is a hard worker
___ Is often late returning from lunch and rest breaks
___ Avoids problem solving
___ Manages time well
___ Often arrives late to work
___ Has poor health
___ Is self-reliant
___ Does work in a slipshod manner
___ Keeps calm when problems arise
___ Is well liked by peers
___ Avoids gossiping during working hours
___ Is unusually accurate
___ Arrives promptly in the morning
___ Files materials promptly
___ Has frequent absences
___ Has very good health
___ Has lone-wolf attitude
___ Organizes work well
___ Dislikes being told how to improve work
___ Takes criticism well
___ Wastes time
___ Shows leadership qualities
___ Has very good attendance
___ Never suggests ways of improving work
___ Has only fair productivity
___ Has generally untidy appearance
___ Keeps work area neat and clean

___ Usually cooperates with others
___ Becomes easily upset when things go wrong
___ Is generally avoided by peers
___ Accepts new assignments willingly
___ Frequently asks for time off
___ Is enthusiastic
___ Makes frequent errors
___ Gets work done promptly
___ Delays filing
___ Has excellent productivity
___ Is usually neatly groomed
___ Enjoys analyzing jobs and solving problems
___ Avoids helping others
___ Tends to be lazy
___ Usually returns promptly after lunch or rest breaks
___ Work area is untidy
___ Generally acts bored on the job
___ Likes to gossip with co-workers
___ Depends on others for help
___ Resents being given new assignments
___ Never asks for special favors, such as time off
___ Is often late with assignments
___ Frequently suggests ways of improving the job

Has this report been discussed with employee?   Yes___   No___
If not, explain why:

_____

If yes, note employee's comments:

_____

Date Reviewed with Employee:

_____   _____
Supervisor's Signature   Employee's Signature

least descriptive of the employee. No values are attached to the statements. These are determined later by a statistician using a weighted value that has been assigned to each item.

The advantage of the forced-choice method is that it is fairly objective because the rater is reporting observed behavior rather than measuring it on a sliding scale. Each item must be checked, thus eliminating the more subjective method of selecting items that is used with ordinary checklists.

The disadvantages result from the time needed to construct the list and the complicated scoring. Each different position within an organization needs a separate checklist. Computation is difficult, requiring knowledge of statistics to scale the items for final scoring. Figure 10–4 shows a forced-choice checklist for an office worker.

Critical incident reports

A more difficult to perform and less frequently used method of evaluation is the critical incident report. A *critical incident report* is a written record of the details of particularly good, particularly bad, and/or mediocre performances of an employee. For example, two employees' bickering over the time each would take for a rest period would be a critical incident. If an employee accepts an urgent assignment from the supervisor and then wanders off to take an extra coffee break before doing the work, the supervisor could record the event as a critical incident. If a customer stopped into an office and one employee immediately approached the person saying, "Good morning. How may we serve you?" that event could be chronicled as a critical incident.

After the records are completed over a period of a month or more, a comparison is made of the good versus the bad. The reports provide a basis for either continuation training or retraining.

This is a time-consuming way of evaluating employees and is considerably less objective than even graphic rating scales, ranking, and checklists. The supervisor must be present, observe in detail how each part of an operation is handled, and then record the performance accurately. Not all supervisors have the talent for writing that this method requires.

Written reports

Another form of evaluation that is not popularly used is the *written report.* For this, the supervisor writes a general overview of the job performance of each employee in a department. Not only is this method time-consuming, but it lacks objectivity, since a supervisor may be influenced by some recent event or by certain characteristics of the employee rather than thoroughly review all the facets of the person's performance.

FIGURE 10–4
FORCED-CHOICE CHECKLIST

Employee Name _____   Supervisor _____   Date _____

Title _____   Department _____

For each of the following statements, indicate by a check mark whether it is most like the person being evaluated or least like that person.

Most	Least	
____	____	Is self-confident
____	____	Is not always punctual
____	____	Receives constructive criticism well
____	____	Is always neat and orderly
____	____	Understands directions and follows through well
____	____	Interrupts other workers frequently
____	____	Dominates other employees
____	____	Is calm and relaxed under pressure
____	____	Is frequently absent
____	____	Generally observes rules and regulations
____	____	Wastes time
____	____	Likes to keep busy
____	____	Is innovative in doing job
____	____	Takes care of personal business during working hours
____	____	Gets work done on time
____	____	Complains a great deal
____	____	Has poor health
____	____	Organizes work efficiently
____	____	Makes frequent errors
____	____	Has excellent skills

- -

Has employee seen this finished rating?   Yes ___   No ___
If yes, does employee agree with rating?   Yes ___   No ___
If no, comments: _____
_____

Signed:
  Employee _____   Supervisor _____   Date _____

Moreover, the people who are responsible for granting promotions, increasing salaries, or dismissing personnel have to read the written reports and draw conclusions based on them. These factors add to the time-consuming and subjective nature of written reports.

Management by objectives (mbo)

For firms that use <u>management by objectives</u>, the system for evaluating productivity is built in. Together with the supervisor, the worker has set the objectives for a given period. At the end of that time, the worker's accomplishments are examined and checked against the objectives that were set. If the objectives have been met, the job is reanalyzed and new objectives are set and recorded. If the objectives have not been met, the reasons are analyzed and a decision is made about the worker's ability to do the job. If the decision is reached that the objectives were too ambitious, new objectives that are more realistic are set for the next period.

Most advocates of this system claim that its job-related nature makes it both objective and accurate. Critics contend that subordinates are often pressed into setting unrealistic goals; that performance in some jobs, such as those in training or public relations, cannot be measured so precisely; and that goal setting prods some people to achieve their objectives to the exclusion of every other desirable activity.

Multiple-person assessment

To eliminate subjectivity in evaluations, one firm used *multiple-person assessment.*[1] In this method, each employee is rated by a group of fellow workers, including the immediate supervisor, two or three higher-level managers, and one or two subordinates. This method is considered to give a better-rounded indication of a person's performance than an evaluation by a single supervisor can.

Morale surveys

Surveys about morale assess the degree of satisfaction of the individual employees with the various aspects of the job, including supervision. Results of these surveys are important to supervisors because they tell how the employees feel about their job, the organization, the policies of the organization, the supervisor, other employees, their opportunities for future growth on the job, their salary, and their working conditions.

In addition, more specific questions may deal with factors over which the supervisor has some control: efficiency of the department, adequacy of communication, fairness, interpersonal relations with the supervisor, technical competence of the supervisor, work load of employees. Morale surveys may also include questions on status of the employee; recognition of the employee by peers, subordinates, and supervisor; interpersonal relations with fellow employees; technical competence of fellow employees; and fringe benefits.

Morale surveys are difficult to administer because employees often fear honestly appraising their supervisor and their job lest someone take offense. For that reason, many organizations have morale surveys administered by outside agencies. In answering questions, employees identify only their departments. In that way, no individual can be singled out.

Supervisors receive only totals on each item, and they have no way of knowing how individual employees rated each question.

Combination of methods

To get the most accurate evaluation possible of employees, some firms use a combination of methods—productivity charts and graphic rating scales, rankings based on those charts and scales, or written reports reinforced by critical incident reports, for example. This is a time-consuming method of evaluation, but combinations are more likely to give a total picture of employees than any single method.

Evaluation of supervisors

Supervisors may be evaluated by their own supervisors in any of the ways previously discussed. The productivity and the general morale of the employees in the supervisor's unit as well as the supervisor's relationship with people are of particular interest to the firm's management. Morale surveys also give a measure of supervisory effectiveness.

   Another valuable way to evaluate supervisors, but one that is infrequently used, is to have them appraised by the subordinates in their departments. Although subordinates constantly evaluate their supervisors informally, a formal evaluation procedure gives supervisors the benefit of subordinates' thinking and allows them to correct their behavior and gain workers' support.

   To develop an effective evaluation instrument that subordinates can use, supervisors should first help them define the criteria by which their judgments will be made. Then an evaluation form using those criteria should be constructed. This will probably include factors such as how well the supervisor supports them in their work, how well their work is facilitated by the supervisor, how well the supervisor backs them when dissent arises, and how well training and development are carried out.

Using formal evaluations

As the numbers of laws have increased throughout the United States, people have demanded that their records, including evaluations, be open to them. One survey revealed that in seventy-four big companies, 76 percent of the employees had access to some personnel records, but only 16 percent of the companies let employees see their supervisors' files on them.[2]

   However, evaluations that are made secretly or that are not used to help workers improve are of limited use to a firm. Therefore, enterprises that use formal evaluations should not only make them available to employees but also help employees plan their future growth with them. Little improvement or development can be expected from workers who are not shown their evaluations. Sharing and discussion are the essence of the well-run evaluation system. Some firms even require that employees sign evaluation forms as an indication that they have been read and discussed with the supervisor.

Employees who have been shown their evaluations may respond in one of three ways:

o *They may agree completely*—In this case, they would sign the evaluation form, and the discussion with the supervisor may help them understand how to improve in certain phases of the work.

o *They may think the evaluation is too praiseful*—In this case, they would sign the form and may or may not wish to indicate those areas in which the work could really be better done to merit the evaluation given.

o *They may think the evaluation is too condemning or even unfair*—In this case, they would sign and may, after discussion with the supervisor, appeal the evaluation or write in detail why they do not agree with it. In the latter course of action, an intermediary may be brought in to discuss the situation, or the employees may be asked to submit proof that their performance differs from that assessed. One supervisor, in evaluating an employee, noted that the worker needed "close supervision." The employee objected and stated that she could accomplish satisfactory work without being closely supervised. She was asked to submit her request for a change of evaluation in writing. Her letter, which was less than a page long, contained five grammatical and spelling errors and proved that she needed "close supervision."

Employers' problems with formal evaluations

Regardless of how carefully they are planned and conducted, formal evaluation systems have several shortcomings:

o Most forms are cumbersome and tedious to fill out, and the process is time-consuming. Time is needed to complete the necessary forms, to consult with employees about their evaluations, and then to discuss the evaluations with top management personnel who will make the ultimate decisions concerning them.

o With the exception of the use of actual productivity figures, subjectivity creeps into evaluations no matter how objective they are designed to be.

o Sometimes supervisors are criticized by their bosses for the poor evaluation of a subordinate. This criticism may affect the way the supervisor evaluates an employee in subsequent evaluations.

o When evaluations are tied to salary raises, supervisors may be loathe to give a poor one that would prevent a person's receiving a raise.

o Supervisors who feel threatened by unusually creative or able subordinates may give them evaluations that do not accurately reflect their talents.

o Some otherwise good workers are afraid of taking jobs because of the threat of evaluations.

o For many white-collar jobs, determining what to measure and how to measure it is difficult.

Guidelines for effective evaluation

Any evaluation system presents some problems. However, to make the system as effective as possible, the following guidelines should be considered:

o *Keep the system as simple as possible*—The more complex the system, the less chance that everyone will understand it and be able to use it effectively.

o *Inform supervisors and subordinates of the purposes of the appraisal system*—Do raises, promotions, transfers, or discharges result from appraisals? Are they used primarily to help employees improve their performance? The more positive the reasons for evaluation systems, the more readily they will be accepted and implemented.

o *Make the system as objective as possible*—With the openness to scrutiny that has increasingly become part of all evaluation systems, some supervisors have been more hesitant about evaluating subordinates forthrightly. Some supervisors fear reprisals from employees; others think that poor evaluations reflect their own failure to lead; and some think that any evaluation, whether good or bad, may reflect a personal bias. To minimize this problem, an evaluation system should be as impersonal as possible. Supervisors should strive to avoid bias, personal feelings, or the halo effect when rating employees.

One way to achieve objectivity is to evaluate all employees on one trait at a time when using productivity charts, graphic rating scales, ranking, checklists, or forced-choice lists. By doing this, each employee is appraised against every other employee on single components of the evaluation. Personal biases are not as likely to contaminate evaluations when each characteristic is considered separately.

Another way for supervisors to be objective is to have groups of them meet together before evaluations are performed to discuss the importance of avoiding biases or the halo effect. If supervisors are aware of the pitfalls of subjectivity, fewer ratings will be based on subjective impressions.

o *Keep time to complete appraisals short*—Supervisors and subordinates dislike having to spend large amounts of time on evaluations. In addition, employees in personnel offices or other superordinates who analyze the evaluations after they have been made should not have to spend inordinate amounts of time on this task. The total time needed to run an effective system should be determined before adopting it.

o *Plan how often evaluations are to occur*—New employees are usually evaluated more frequently than those who have served for a long period of time. For new employees, an evaluation must be made before the probationary period ends, usually two to three months after employment. These employees need to know how well the job is being done and where improvement is needed. The evaluation also helps the supervisor to determine whether or not the employee should be retained. For employees who have passed the probationary period, evaluations are usually made once or twice a year. For employees who are only marginal in performance, additional evaluations may be needed.

o *Discuss evaluations with each worker*—The supervisor may or may not find holding discussions with each employee a difficult chore to perform. Employees with good appraisals are often the ones who are most ready to accept suggestions for further improvement. Those with questionable ratings may dislike criticism and see evaluations as a threat. Therefore, the supervisor has to approach them in a manner that suggests that positive results may be achieved. If the supervisor is eager to help the employee improve his or her productivity, attitude, or behavior, the employee will react more agreeably than if the supervisor appears to want only to berate him or her for a poor performance.

o *Have employees rate themselves on the instrument being used*—A chance to rate oneself often helps an employee to be more objective about his or her own performance. This also smooths the way for an agreement between the employee and the supervisor. If, however, the employee is not aware of his or her own shortcomings, the supervisor may wish to use techniques such as critical incident reports or MBO to help the employee realize the need for improvement on the job.

o *Create a usable evaluation system*—For positions in which productivity is not a matter of measurable items, many firms have asked the workers themselves to design an evaluation system that applies specifically to the work they do. This approach may be undertaken in several ways. A firm may:

1. List the various tasks of a job, judge the relative difficulty of each, and give each a ranking. Employees are then evaluated on which tasks they perform effectively and are given higher ratings for the more difficult ones.
2. Analyze the backlog of workers' unresolved problems and the number and kinds of errors made by workers. This analysis may reveal the difficulty of various tasks.
3. Analyze the primary qualities needed by workers in a specific job. This analysis may result in changing the required skills and abilities of people hired for the positions. For example, one bank always hired people with technical expertise until appraisal showed that it mainly needed people who were able to work effectively with others.
4. Analyze all the details that employees go through to complete a job. This analysis may result in a streamlined method of handling the job.

After the jobs have been thoroughly analyzed, the measurements have to be tried out and then discussed with the employees. Only when workers know what is expected of them can they be relied on to improve their performance. Employees need to know what is to be done and how it is to be done, and then need feedback on whether or not the job has been done correctly.

The only evaluation systems that work effectively and continuously are those that are planned, carried out periodically, monitored carefully, improved constantly, and involve the cooperation of workers.

SUMMARY

o Evaluations of employees in some form, although scheduled to occur only periodically, take place constantly.

o Objectivity, a factual look at people or events under consideration, is essential in evaluating employees. Subjectivity, including personal impressions and biases, has no place in effective evaluation. The "halo effect" is one type of bias that makes a person appear better or worse than he or she actually is.

o Informal evaluations, which are unstructured and based on no specific criteria, occur whenever two people meet. Both what supervisors say and their manner of acting reveal their informal evaluations of a worker.

o Formal evaluations are written reports based on specific criteria about the employees in an organization. They provide a record that may be used in many ways by the supervisors.

o Evaluations must be reliable, meaning that they must consistently test the same factors each time they are used, and valid, meaning that they must test the factors that measure a person's performance on the job.

o Formal evaluations make use of many types of instruments: productivity charts (devices that permit objective measures of the volume of work accomplished), graphic rating scales (forms on which judgments about productivity, attitudes, and characteristics are rated on a scale from excellent to poor), ranking (the determination of which employees are best to poorest in overall performance within a given work area), sociograms (maps that show both the amount of interaction among employees and which employees interact most often with other employees), checklists (forms that present brief descriptive statements), forced-choice checklists (similar to checklists except that each item must be rated for each worker), critical incident reports (written notes of events that occurred on the job that reveal how an employee reacts in given situations), written reports (summations of job performance based on the supervisor's overall judgment), management by objectives (the selection of specific objectives by the supervisor and employee and the decision at the end of a given period about the success or failure to achieve those objectives), multiple-person assessment (the analysis by several persons of one individual), morale surveys (assessments of the degree of satisfaction about the job), and combination methods (the use of two or more assessment reports or evaluations).

o Supervisor evaluations are made by both their superordinates and their employees.

o Formal evaluations should be available to employees, who can benefit from them.

o Supervisors have varying attitudes about filling out evaluation forms.

o Guidelines for effective evaluations include: keep the system simple, inform employees of their purpose, make the system objective, make evaluations short, plan how often they are to occur, discuss them with workers, have employees rate themselves, and create a usable evaluation system.

REFERENCES

[1]Harry B. Anderson, "The Rating Game," *Wall Street Journal,* May 23, 1978, pp. 1, 23.

[2]Robert W. Merry, "Labor Letter," *Wall Street Journal,* July 24, 1979, p. 1.

REVIEW AND DISCUSSION QUESTIONS

1. Why is objectivity in the rating of employees important?
2. How do informal evaluations sometimes play a part in the formal evaluations of employees?
3. How may a supervisor's actions tell employees the value that is placed on the job they are doing?
4. Why do firms use formal evaluations?
5. List the unique features of the following types of evaluation: graphic rating scales, ranking, sociograms, checklists, forced-choice checklists, productivity charts, critical incident reports, and written reports.
6. How might a firm use the following evaluation methods: combination evaluations, management by objectives, multiple-person assessment, and objective appraisal trait by trait?
7. Explain how employees can evaluate their supervisors.
8. After evaluation has been completed, what added value may be obtained from having the employee and the supervisor discuss the evaluation together?
9. How does an evaluation provide feedback to the employee? to the firm?
10. What are some of the guidelines involved in the development of formal evaluation systems?

ASSIGNMENTS

1. If you work for a firm, obtain one of the forms used for evaluating people. Classify the form according to the types discussed in the text. Does the form lend itself to objectivity on the part of the evaluator? Does the firm ask the supervisor to discuss the worker's evaluation with him or her? If so, discuss your reaction to the discussion you last had with your supervisor. If not, explain how you reacted to having an evaluation with no feedback.

   If you do not work for a firm, refer to one of the forms in the text. Can the evaluator be objective using that form? How do you rate yourself (on the job or in school) on that form? Do you think your superior (teacher or supervisor) would rate you differently? Why? Would you like your superior to discuss your rating with you? Explain.

2. Draw a sociogram for five to eight of your classmates who sit where you can observe them in your class. Label your friends on the sociogram either by name or by letter. Which student has the most interaction with other students? Which student has the least interaction? Is the interaction among the various students fairly evenly distributed? What conclusions would you draw from your sociogram? Write a short report of your findings.

PROBLEM FOR RESOLUTION

Construct a useful, objective evaluation system for tellers in a bank. Base the plan partly on your experience in depositing and withdrawing money and in receiving monthly records from the bank.

CASE STUDY

Betty Wing left her supervisory job after five years. Her successor, Sam Johns, had previously reported to Ms. Wing. He inherited the secretary whom Ms. Wing had initially hired, trained, and worked with for five years, Sue Cohen.

   Six months after he became supervisor, Mr. Johns was required to evaluate Ms. Cohen's work. After he had completed his analysis, he saw a file copy of Ms. Wing's evaluation of Ms. Cohen. Ms. Wing had given the secretary an excellent evaluation on all characteristics except two: neatness and promptness. For these she had given fair ratings.

   Mr. Johns, by contrast, had given the Ms. Cohen only one excellent rating, for transcription ability. He gave all the other characteristics previously evaluated as excellent only a fair rating, and neatness and promptness a poor rating.

The executives of the firm had considered Ms. Wing to be an outstanding supervisor. Her reputation had been that of a most capable person and one whose department was excellently run. Mr. John's personal experience with her had proved all this to be true. He could not understand why his judgment of Ms. Cohen, who performed the same tasks in exactly the same way that she previously had, should be so different. He wondered what his evaluation would mean to both Ms. Cohen and management.

* What factors might have caused the differences in these two supervisors' evaluations of the same person?

* What reaction do you think Ms. Cohen would have to the poorer evaluation? What reaction might management have to the change in the evaluation?

* Assume you are Mr. John's superior. You have received his rating of Sue Cohen. What questions might you want to ask him about his rating before you make a final decision about Ms. Cohen's work with the organization?

FURTHER READING

Anderson, Harry B. "Formal Job Appraisals Grow More Prevalent but Get More Criticism." *Wall Street Journal,* May 23, 1978, pp. 1, 23.
    Explains that some consultants, workers, and executives find appraisal systems unfair, subjective, and cumbersome.
Cummings, L. L., and Donald P. Schwab. *Performance in Organizations: Determinants and Appraisal.* Glenview, Ill.: Scott, Foresman, & Co., 1973.
    Discusses the major determinants of human behavior and key concepts in constructing an effective appraisal system. Analyzes the frequency of conducting appraisals, who should receive feedback, and how feedback should be given. Presents three systems for evaluation and development of employees.
Kellogg, Marion S. *What to Do About Performance Appraisal.* Rev. ed. New York: AMACOM, 1975.
    Analyzes the ethics of appraisal, how to appraise, types of appraisals, and results of appraisals.
Lazer, Robert I., and Walter S. Wikstrom. *Appraising Managerial Performance: Current Practices and Future Directions.* Lynbrook, N.Y.: Conference Boards Division of Management Research, 1978.

Reports on a research study. Compiles forms from large industrial firms for organization management appraisal.

Levinson, Harry. "Appraisal of *What* Performance?" *Harvard Business Review,* July–August 1976, pp. 30–46.

Explains that appraisal systems must accommodate the "how" as well as the "what" in performance, and that people are judged on how they get things done as well as on what they produce.

Patz, Alan L. "Performance Appraisal: Useful but Still Resisted." *Harvard Business Review,* May–June 1975, pp. 74–80.

Discusses how, although problem-ridden, performance appraisals are nevertheless considered to be important assessment tools by executives.

Smith, Howard P., and Paul J. Brouwer. *Performance Appraisal and Human Development: A Practical Guide to Effective Managing.* Reading, Mass.: Addison-Wesley, 1977.

Explains that since people are an organization's most important resource, performance appraisal helps to achieve full human resource utilization.

Yuzuk, Ronald Paul. *The Assessment of Employee Morale: A Comparison of Two Measures.* Bureau of Business Research Monograph Number 99. Columbus, Ohio: The Ohio State University, 1961.

Analyzes the use of descriptive versus evaluative scales. Relates productivity, absenteeism, and personnel turnover to various measures of morale.

11

counseling
employees

After studying and analyzing this chapter, you should be able to:

Define "counseling," and list the signals of counseling need and the ways the supervisor can bring a problem out.

Describe the initial counseling interview.

List and explain the guidelines for conducting successful counseling sessions.

Explain directive, nondirective, and combination counseling, and the steps the supervisor may take to resolve problems.

Discuss the problems that the supervisor does and does not anticipate.

Explain the role of counseling for stressful situations.

Explain how and why counseling programs are evaluated.

List the advantages and disadvantages of counseling.

THE EVALUATION OF employees is closely allied to the counseling of employees. Evaluation first helps to show strengths and weaknesses, and counseling may then be used to help counteract the weaknesses. Counseling is a "deliberate, formal effort to help the employee to become more valuable to the company by means of personal discussions."[1] In terms of Transactional Analysis (see Chapter 8), counseling is meant to assist employees to reveal and strengthen their adult ego state. Counseling means helping people—and usually doing it by helping them help themselves—and is intended primarily to benefit employees.

Firms first began to offer some type of counseling to employees during the early 1900s. Counseling grew in importance in business and industry after World War II, when psychologists in sizable numbers became available for counseling. Although research has shown counseling to have many advantages, some firms still hesitate in providing it. Counseling for job-related problems is usually viewed as part of a company's responsibility. But many enterprises are not eager to become involved in personal-problem counseling, which in most cases necessitates the use of trained psychologists. Yet, if an employee is under stress or is unhappy due to personal problems, the difficulty can affect his or her work and therefore does involve the company if the employee is to continue to be effective on the job.

Although supervisors and firms are interested in having all employees function at their peak level of ability, they intrude beyond the area of the worker's job only as the employee shares outside experience with the supervisor or if that employee is unable to function on the job because of outside problems.

Counseling is an aid to both the employee and the organization. It helps the employee either to regain, retain, or increase his or her ability. It helps the organization, which has expended both money and time to hire and train employees, to have workers who can function effectively on the job.

Signals of counseling need

The supervisor must be alert to signs that employees within his or her area of responsibility need help. The need for counseling for individual employees may be shown by any of the following:

○ Evaluations that are less than satisfactory

○ Productivity that has fallen

○ Sudden changes in work habits, such as previously unshown tiredness, boredom, lateness, absenteeism, sloppiness in appearance, and proneness to accidents o Constant complaining, abrasiveness with others, anger over small matters, rudeness, indifference to departmental needs, or defiance of orders

o Changes in status within the organization, such as transfer, promotion, demotion, imminent retirement, or outplacement (discharge)

o Appeal for counseling help. A direct appeal may be made by a request from the employee. An indirect appeal may be made by the employee's use of alcohol or other drugs during working hours or by apparent depression or negative reaction to stress.

Once the need for counseling has been observed, the problem must be brought out into the open.

Bringing the problem into the open

Once a supervisor is aware that a problem exists, the difficulty cannot be ignored. The supervisor and the employee may become involved in counseling in several ways. The supervisor may:[2]

o Wait for the subordinate to ask for help. People usually seek help when they know their behavior falls short of the goals set. They also may seek help if their progress in a firm has not been as rapid as they anticipated.

o Expose the subordinate to situations that will reveal his or her inadequacies or that will present new challenges and open new lines of thinking so that he or she will beome aware of certain weaknesses.

o Approach the subordinate and simply assert that a problem exists.

Any of these three ways of bringing the problem out in the open leads the supervisor and the employee to the counseling interview.

The initial counseling interview

Once a supervisor becomes aware that a problem exists and brings it out in the open, he or she conducts the *initial counseling interview*. This is a face-to-face discussion with the employee about the problem. It is a channel of upward communication that reinforces the employee's awareness of the company's interest.

In the initial counseling interview, the supervisor determines what the employee's problem is, the extent of it, and whether the worker can be helped through further discussion. This interview will be successful only if the relationship between the supervisor and the employee is one of trust. Only if the supervisor has at all times been fair, open, and truthful with the employee will he or she reveal innermost thoughts. Moreover, the subordinate has to be sure that the information given will be held in the strictest confidence by the supervisor.

Some firms have established counseling programs with one or more assigned counselors. In such a firm, the counseling interview will be the supervisor's last involvement in the counseling process. If, during the interview, the supervisor determines that the employee needs more help, the subordinate will be referred to an official counselor, who may be a clinical psychologist or a social worker. The initial interview takes place with the supervisor, with whom the employee has an established rapport, and therefore the interview is easier to schedule and less threatening than it would be with an official counselor, whom the employee may not know. However, complex personal or family problems, alcohol or other drug abuse, or severe withdrawal due to extreme stress, for example, should be handled only by those experienced in such matters—the official counselors. In this case, the supervisor's job is to help the subordinate accept the idea of referral.

Other firms do not have assigned counselors. In these firms, the supervisor undertakes the role of counselor for those problems that he or she is trained to handle. If the employee needs further help but the supervisor is unskilled in dealing with the problem, the employee is referred to a preselected social agency, hospital clinic, or other local source in accordance with the firm's policy (see Figure 11–1).

How to conduct successful counseling sessions

The supervisor who holds counseling sessions with employees indicates interest in those employees and a concern to help them do a good job. Certain steps are desirable for these sessions to be effective:

○ *Discuss with the employee a suitable time* for the session—If you arbitrarily set the time, the employee will not react as positively as if you both agree on a mutually available time.

○ *Familiarize yourself with the employee's previous evaluations and work record*—If you analyze the employee's file for the first time in his or her presence, your interest appears to be routine rather than personal.

FIGURE 11-1
FLOW CHART SHOWING COUNSELING DECISIONS

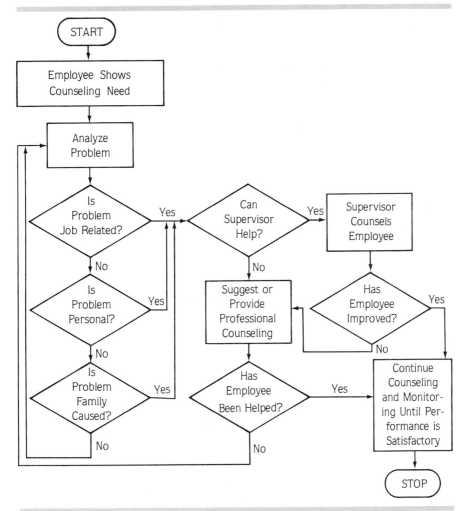

o *Be punctual*—If you arrive late for the interview, you give a negative impression to the employee about his or her importance to the organization.

o *Allow sufficient time for the session*—The employee should not feel rushed. If not enough time is available, a second counseling session should be arranged.

o *Meet where privacy may be ensured and where interruptions may be kept to a minimum*—An employee is not likely to

feel comfortable or want to discuss sensitive matters if part
of the conversation can be heard by others. Similarly, if the
supervisor is constantly interrupted with telephone calls or
with people coming in and out of the office, the employee
would understandably be upset.

o *Personalize the counseling session*—Initially, the employee
should be greeted pleasantly, called by name, and asked to
sit down. To put the employee at ease, some comments unrelated to the job, about such matters as the weather or local
items of interest, may be made. The purpose of the counseling session may then be broached. If this is an appraisal interview, the employee should be advised that organizational
policy requires that the supervisor talk with each employee
about the evaluation. If the counseling session has arisen for
some other reason, it should be mentioned to the employee.
The employee should be reassured that the supervisor and
other superordinates want to know how the employee feels
about the job, the department, and the organization. The employee should feel that he or she is a member of a team.

o *Be as relaxed and informal as possible*—If you constantly
look at a watch, act nervous, or appear to have other matters
of concern, you soon convey to the employee a feeling of dis-
interest.

o *Be forthright and honest in reply to any questions* the employee asks—An atmosphere of mutual understanding and
trust must be maintained.

o *Avoid arguing with the employee*—Being angry or upset will
not accomplish the aims of the counseling session and will
only bring it to an untimely conclusion.

o *Listen carefully to the employee*—Nod your head, smile, or
indicate assent whenever possible. Avoid interrupting the
employee. Use comments such as "I see," "That's interesting," or "I didn't know that." These remarks are not viewed
as interruptions but as positive feedback.

o *Treat pauses in the session positively*—If an employee pauses
after making a statement and you wish to pursue the point
further, you may repeat some part of the last statement in the
form of a question. For example, if the employee ended a series of comments with the remark, "Some of our equipment
is very old and outdated and slows my production," the supervisor could ask, "How do you think the old equipment
slows your production?" Sometimes the supervisor may wish

just to give the employee time during the pause to collect his or her thoughts for the next idea to be presented. In this case, the supervisor would not interrupt the pause.

o *For an appraisal interview, inform the employee about his or her record and standing in the organization*—Commending the employee before condemning him or her is almost always desirable. Strong points should be enthusiastically praised. The employee's point of view on weaknesses should be elicited. If the employee agrees on the weak points that need strengthening, the main task is to discuss how those areas might be improved. If the employee does not agree on the weak points, you have to devise ways of getting the employee to become aware of unproductive behavior.

o *Maintain a calm, objective point of view throughout the session*—If the employee becomes emotional during the session—angry, defiant, tearful—allow him or her time to regain composure before continuing the discussion.

o *Help the employee build a plan for improvement*—Listen attentively to the ideas the employee suggests and express agreement with those you believe can be implemented. Suggest ways you think the employee could overcome difficulties if you believe the employee is willing to improve performance.

o *Close the counseling session courteously*—If time permits, ask the employee if any additional material should be discussed. If needed, arrange for a subsequent meeting to continue the counseling or suggest that the employee have more professional counseling with a specialist. A summary of the highlights covered in the session is a desirable way to conclude the counseling.

o *Make a written record of the counseling session*—As laws pertaining to the protection of the rights of employees have increased, firms have realized the need to keep detailed records about each person employed by the firm. Because counseling is part of the work of a firm, notes of the facts surrounding counseling interviews, usually called *case records*, should be made by the supervisor and placed in the employee's file. A case record should include the date of, improvement plan time length of, and topics covered during the counseling interview. If a referral has been made, it should be noted along with any pertinent details. The case record should also note any follow-up that would be desirable to aid the employee further. In recording facts about counseling interviews, don't include any confidential material, since the record may be read by other people. This written record may be checked with the employee both to reinforce what has been said and agreed to and also to reassure the employee about information entering his or her formal record.

Methods of supervisory counseling

When supervisors serve as counselors to employees, they undertake a series of counseling interviews in which one of three methods may be used: directive counseling, nondirective counseling, or the combination method.

Directive counseling

Counseling that includes advice from the supervisor is called _directive counseling_. The supervisor first elicits information from the employee about the problem. After determining what is troubling the employee, the supervisor suggests the action that the employee may take to work out a solution. In some cases, the supervisor may suggest two or more solutions and advise the employee to choose the one that appears to be the most readily workable.

For example, Michael Curtis held a first-level supervisory position in a sales department of a firm that prepared improved office systems for companies. He enjoyed being involved in every activity of the firm. He frequently boasted to his co-workers about the number of meetings he had attended during the previous week. He was generally well liked, although he was considered to be less thorough in doing his job and less productive than he should be. Recently, Michael had annoyed his boss, Melba Delaney, by not having a proposal ready when it was needed. At annual evaluation time, Michael was ranked last in productivity among the salespersonnel. The counseling session included the following exchange:

MELBA: Michael, your review shows some good points. Let's talk about those first. Your customer relations are rated very good. Your customers like you and generally want to continue to do their business with you.
MICHAEL: Thank you, I enjoy working with them.
MELBA: You also have high marks on your energy for the job and your enthusiasm.
MICHAEL: Well, I do work harder than most other people.

MELBA: Unfortunately, we have some problem areas that we must address.

MICHAEL: Such as what?

MELBA: First, you are rarely around the office even when you are not on assignment elsewhere. Whenever I enquire about where you are, the secretary tells me you are at a meeting. I appreciate the importance of your participation in firm events, but you appear to be in meetings at the expense of your own department.

MICHAEL: Well, I consider meetings important. I get to know other people in other departments of the firm, and I learn a lot about inside workings that I miss when I don't attend the meetings.

MELBA: We all like to meet people and hear about other facets of the firm, but our own department's work must come first. You appear to have reversed the order of importance of the tasks. The company newsletter tells us what other departments are doing. You need to do less meeting and more follow-up work with your clients.

MICHAEL: But other departments invite me to attend their meetings.

MELBA: Your job is sales productivity. If that is not good, the other departments are ultimately affected, and so you help them most by doing your own job well. And you were to submit a proposal for extending our territory for our latest office system materials. As yet, I haven't seen it.

MICHAEL: I've just been too busy to do it.

MELBA: Why not try omitting some of your meetings? That will give you time to get your reports done and also time to improve your sales record.

MICHAEL: You really do want to change my role here.

MELBA: Only to improve it. Think this over and let's talk again next week.

Nondirective counseling

First used in industry at the Hawthorne plant of the Western Electric Company with great success in the late 1920s, nondirective counseling casts the supervisor in the role of an attentive, empathic listener who offers no advice or solution to a problem. The supervisor is passive, sympathetic, and occasionally repeats what the subordinate has said to ensure complete understanding of the problem. The employee directs the discussion and is the one who must come up with any solution. Nondirective counseling is based on the belief that an employee can best develop insight and willingness to solve a problem if he or she is

permitted to discuss it openly with a supervisor who allows free expression with no show of disapproval.

The job of the nondirective counselor is to become familiar with the
employee's problems and to reflect the employee's feelings so that the
person can be free to express them. By being passive, the supervisor
encourages the employee to express feelings and then to develop new
insight into the problem. The nondirective approach, with its permissive
atmosphere, allows the employee to view the problem clearly. Instead of
being defensive and believing that everyone else is at fault, the subordinate comes to see that his or her own behavior needs to be changed.
Only by this recognition can change be effectively achieved. The employee has to be self-motivated to modify the nonproductive behavior.

If the interview between Melba and Michael had been nondirective,
it may have gone as follows:

MELBA: Michael, I'm delighted we could get together for this talk.
Although we work together, we rarely have time to chat
about anything except the daily tasks. How do you consider your work has been going?

MICHAEL: Very well. I'm busier than anyone else in the department.
I'm involved with many things outside the department,
and everyone appears to seek my expertise.

MELBA: You say you are busier than anyone else.

MICHAEL: Well, I didn't mean my production was better—just that I
am busier. I am out of the office meeting many people in
other parts of the organization, and that should pay off in
time.

MELBA: You say that should pay off eventually?

MICHAEL: Yes. The more I know about their problems, the more I
can work that knowledge into proposals from our department.

MELBA: You say the meetings help you in making proposals?

MICHAEL: Yes, I know that my last proposal is overdue, but I think
I have some ideas that will make it very good when I sit
down to do it. For example, at a meeting yesterday, I
learned that the organization is preparing materials especially for banks. I can work that into the proposal. Only
thing is, they have the material ready, and my proposal is
going to take time to write.

MELBA: Yes.

MICHAEL: Gee, I have two meetings this afternoon, and one tomorrow morning. That means I can't start work on the proposal until tomorrow afternoon, and then I have
appointments with two clients. That means I am still not
getting time for the writing I have to do. Maybe I'll have

to rethink the importance of some of those meetings I've scheduled.

MELBA: Maybe you have come to an important decision.

MICHAEL: Yeah. Maybe I have gotten off the beaten path a bit. Maybe I could spend more time on my job and less on outside meetings. I'll think about that a bit.

MELBA: I'm glad we had this chance to talk.

MICHAEL: So am I. Maybe my production will be better next time.

The combination method

In bringing together directive and nondirective counseling, and thus using the combination method, the supervisor listens, accepts, and then helps the employee to arrive at a solution. In some cases, the employee asks for suggestions and the supervisor responds to the requests. The combination method may be effective when the problem does not involve interpersonal conflicts.

If Melba were using the combination method for the counseling session with Michael, it might parallel the nondirective session to the point where Michael admitted the too heavy schedule of meetings and client appointments that would again delay his report:

MELBA: You have just illustrated your main problem. Perhaps if you rated the importance of each of your activities, you would direct your efforts more specifically to your sales productivity.

MICHAEL: I have been doing what I thought was important.

MELBA: Try making a chart of all you do at work. Rate those activities that directly affect your sales productivity as essential, those that aid you as helpful, and those that are really not directly helpful as not necessary. This might change your work plan.

MICHAEL: Yes, I could try that.

Steps the supervisor may take to resolve problems

If in analyzing the problem the supervisor decides that with the cooperation of the employee it might be resolved, no outside counselor needs to be involved. Under those circumstances, four different ways of developing solutions might be undertaken:

o *The supervisor may suggest solutions to the problem*—If the frustration of the employee involves money, a loan might be

arranged, a way of consolidating debts and scheduling payments might be devised, or strict adherence to a budget
might be planned. If a person has been denied a promotion,
a change of job or job enrichment might be undertaken. If a
conflict exists between employees in the department, a clari-
fication of job duties might alleviate the situation. If the employee feels "put upon" in the job, an analysis of tasks might
be undertaken to see if the attitude is justified.

- *The supervisor may help the employee to reanalyze the situation that caused the problem*—If the employee resents some
  company policy, the supervisor might explain the reasoning
  behind the need for the policy. If the employee resents being
  treated in a certain way by other people in the firm, pointing
  out that he or she has not been singled out for such treatment
  or talking with the abusive people to urge them to change
  their treatment of the employee who feels wronged may help
  to lessen the problem.

- *The supervisor may help the employee to unleash aggression
  in harmless ways*—If the employee is angry or hurt at someone in the organization, the supervisor may suggest the employee write a retort and later tear it up. This may help the
  employee even though the note does not reach the person
  who caused the initial anger. Once the emotion has been expressed, it may be relieved and the potentially frustrating situation may no longer pose a threat. Even expressing the
  resentments to the supervisor may relieve the person's anger.
  An employee who expresses emotions through verbalizing
  them, shedding tears, or using other emotional outlets may
  feel relieved of the pressure of that emotion and be able to
  view the entire situation more objectively.

- *The supervisor may suggest that the employee role play a
  similar situation*—By acting the part from another's point of
  view, the entire circumstance may take on a more whole-
  some, less threatening aspect.

Problems the supervisor anticipates

Counseling is needed not only for problems that arise unexpectedly but
also for problems that the supervisor is aware are pending for the employee. Four of the most persistent of these, and all stressful, are transfer, promotion, outplacement, and retirement.

Transfer

Transfer to another department in a firm is common, especially in large companies. However, any move to another job entails some trauma or stress for the employee. The person may be moving not only to a different part of the firm but to a different geographic area. The latter may necessitate the moving of household goods and family.

The supervisor's job is to prepare the employee for the new surroundings and for a new and different job. Talking over the transfer, discussing its advantages and disadvantages, and helping the employee make a necessary move greatly diminishes the stress that results from a transfer.

Firms in which many geographical transfers take place sometimes employ consultants who help the employee sell the old home and find suitable new housing. The employee's spouse and children may also need help from the consultant to find appropriate schools, shopping areas, and community services.

Promotion

Promotion is stressful because the employee must undergo many changes before settling into a new position. The supervisor should discuss the new job, the new people with whom the employee will work, the new working conditions, and the new expectations of achievement in order to orient the employee to the increased responsibility and the work force.

If the promotion is within the same department, the subordinate will no longer have the same relationship with peers. Therefore, counseling is desirable to prepare him or her for the anticipated change in other people's attitudes. Training for the new job will further prepare the person.

Outplacement

The termination of an employee from the job he or she has been doing is called *outplacement* or *discharge*. *Outplacement counseling*, or smoothing the way for the person to leave the firm and and find another job, has become quite common, especially for people who have been with a firm for a number of years. People who hold temporary jobs are not usually given outplacement counseling.

Losing a job that has been held for a long time can be an extremely traumatic event. The loss not only deprives a person of salary and benefits but may also deal his or her self-esteem a severe blow. Unemployment insurance may cushion the financial setback, but it does not lessen the suffering of acknowledging the failure to perform adequately on the job. The supervisor, therefore, needs to help the employee rebuild confidence, restore a feeling of self-worth, and reinstate the belief that another job can be found and success will be achieved.

The supervisor faces another task when outplacement occurs. Most employees who are discharged are antagonistic toward the firm and its representatives. The supervisor must therefore also help the person continue to feel loyalty to the firm. This is an important challenge to the supervisor, who has to have particular sensitivity in this situation.

Retirement

Terminating one's work life ranks high as being stressful. Individual employees, however, react in a wide variety of ways to the idea of retirement. Some prepare for it, anticipate it, and accept it when the time has arrived. Others take retirement as a matter of course and move through it mechanically. Still others refuse to admit that they must retire and totally resist the idea of getting too old to work at a job that they have held successfully for many years. Before attempting to help a person who is going to retire, the supervisor should hold a nondirective counseling session with him or her to determine which point of view is held.

Ideally, retirement counseling should begin several years before the event so that the employee can plan income, housing, and activities to fill his or her time, as well as deal with feelings. As the date of retirement approaches, the person who looks forward to leaving work or the one who is indifferent may not need much counseling to counter traumatic feelings but may need help in planning for future income and other facets of retirement.

The employee who resents having to retire presents the biggest problem to the supervisor. He or she may need special counseling sessions to be reassured that self-worth does not diminish even when that person is not reporting to the job each morning. During counseling, the supervisor should explain the benefits available to retirees—medical insurance (Medicare), Social Security, and pension. If company policy permits, the supervisor can ease a person into retirement in several ways:

- o Introduce the employee to various types of work available in volunteer groups or community organizations
- o Reduce the amount of work required during the last year on the job to allow the person to have more time in which to develop hobbies
- o Transfer the employee to another, less arduous job for the final months on the job
- o Give the person extended vacations to allow him or her to adjust to living away from the job

- o Allow the employee to work somewhat shorter hours for a few months before retirement

- o Arrange for the person to serve, after retirement, on one of the firm's committees about which he or she has special knowledge

- o Arrange for the person to be employed, after retirement, in temporary jobs for which he or she has skill

- o Form a club of retirees from the firm who meet with those about to retire

The supervisor should be alert to how other employees treat the about-to-retire person. Some say, "Oh, are you still here? I thought you had retired already." Others compete for the person's desk or some of his or her duties; they appear to push the employee into retirement even faster than desired. Under these circumstances, the supervisor may wish to discuss the trauma of retirement with other people in the department to avoid unpleasant situations.

After the person retires, the firm should keep his or her name on mailing lists so that notification of changes in the working status of long-time employees and newsletters or other publications of general interest can be received. An occasional letter or card from still-employed friends is also a welcome gesture from them that the supervisor can encourage.

Problems the supervisor does not anticipate

The need for counseling may arise from unanticipated problems that erupt suddenly or that unexpectedly become overwhelming for an employee. Among these are stress, alcohol and other drug abuse, and depression.

Stress

Stress is the response of the body to any demand made on it. If we are cold, we shiver; if we are hot, we perspire; if we run, our hearts beat faster; if we stretch or reach, our muscles ache; if we are sorrowful or joyful, our body chemistry changes. Medicines produce changes in our pulse rate or blood sugar or cause other reactions. The body has to adapt to any change. Mild changes necessitate little adaptation; vast changes require considerably more adaptive ability. All of these changes are known as the "fight or flight" response that endowed the cavemen and women with their ability to overcome their environment.

Job-related factors that may contribute to stress include fear of job loss, change, new technology that will displace workers, evaluation, or new assignments; lack of use of skills and abilities; perception of the job as boring; unclear or conflicting assignments; assignments that demand higher ability levels than the employee has; close scrutiny of work by a supervisor; lack of feedback from the supervisor; problems with the supervisor or co-workers; inadequate income; overloads of work; and excessive noise or poor lighting. The thoughtful supervisor will, through counseling, attempt to help the employee prepare for or adjust to these stressful job situations.

Stress is also believed to contribute to increased vulnerability to illness. Doctors Thomas Holmes and Richard Rahe, professors of psychiatry at the University of Washington, published a chart as a result of their research with groups of people.[3] They gave a life-change unit (LCU) value to stress for various events (see Table 11–1). They found a positive relationship between the value of the LCUs and the severity of subsequent illnesses people suffered. They determined that if the ratings add up to more than 300 in one year, the accumulated stress could result in depression, a heart attack, or another serious ailment.

Subsequent research has substantiated these findings but has also shown that if a person can continue customary interests, affiliations, and activities during a stressful period, adverse reactions may be reduced.[4] No research has been published to date showing how LCUs affect a person's performance on a job.

Supervisors who have good rapport with their employees will know when particularly stressful life-change units occur, will do what they can to lessen problems on the job, and will counsel employees or arrange special counseling for them.

Drug abuse and depression

The abuse of any drug, including alcohol, and depression are evidenced by abnormal behavior, which alerts the supervisor that counseling is needed. Abnormal behavior may be expressed by unusual happiness or even giddiness for short periods, withdrawal or noncommunicativeness, a physically changed appearance, frequent unexplained absences from the work station, persistent tardiness in arriving at work or in returning from lunch or rest breaks, inability to concentrate, recurring sleepiness on the job, or sudden emotional reactions to ordinary events.

In a few instances, the supervisor's concern and work with the person to realize his or her problem may help to resolve the situation. Only if the employee is ready to acknowledge that a problem exists, however, is any change likely to take place.

If the firm is small or if the problem is chronic, the supervisor should encourage the employee to see an experienced counselor or psychiatrist who specializes in the difficulty. In the case of alcoholism, Alcoholics Anonymous has helped some people to change by having them

TABLE 11-1
THE HOLMES-RAHE SCHEDULE OF RECENT LIFE EVENTS

Life Event	Value
Death of a spouse	100
Divorce	73
Marital separation	65
Jail term	63
Death of a close family member	63
Personal injury or illness	53
Marriage	50
Fired from work	47
Marital reconciliation	45
Retirement	45
Change in family member's health	44
Pregnancy	40
Sex difficulties	39
Addition to family	39
Business readjustment	39
Change in financial status	38
Death of close friend	37
Change to different line of work	36
Change in number of marital arguments	35
Mortgage or loan over $10,000	31
Foreclosure of mortgage or loan	30
Change in work responsibilities	29
Son or daughter leaving home	29
Trouble with in-laws	29
Outstanding personal achievement	28
Spouse begins or stops work	26
Starting or finishing school	26
Change in living conditions	25
Revision of personal habits	24
Trouble with boss	23
Change in work hours, conditions	20
Change in residence	20
Change in school	20
Change in recreational habits	19
Change in church activities	19
Change in social activities	18
Mortgage or loan under $10,000	17
Change in sleeping habits	16
Change in number of family gatherings	15
Change in eating habits	15
Vacation	13
Christmas season	12
Minor violation of the law	11

Source: T. H. Holmes and R. H. Rahe, "The Social Readjustment Rating Scale," *Journal of Psychosomatic Research,* 1967, pp. 213–18. Copyright 1967, Pergamon Press, Ltd. Reprinted with permission.

take responsibility for changing themselves. The supervisor's role is to encourage the employee to change and to support him or her during the period of change, at which time both tension and anxiety will be evidenced. After rehabilitation, the employee will continue to need constant encouragement or reinforcement of the changed behavior.

Evaluating the counseling program

Because counseling is time-consuming and keeps both the supervisor or counselor and the employee from other productive activity for a period, it must be evaluated.

In large firms, records made before and after the counseling program was initiated may be compared to determine the program's benefits. Employees may be asked to express their attitudes toward management and the employee benefits on morale surveys. If the counseling program is well run, the evaluations should show that it has helped to reduce nonproductive behaviors (such as absenteeism) and to improve morale.

In small firms, where fewer people are involved, the benefits of a counseling program may not be measurable. However, if the program is well handled, it will undoubtedly improve the way in which people interact with one another and with customers.

Advantages and disadvantages of a counseling program

Several advantages accrue to the company that develops a counseling program. Counseling:

- o Demonstrates the enterprise's interest in employees—all people like to believe that the firm for which they work is concerned about their welfare

- o Indicates that a company intends to be fair in its treatment of employees

- o Reinforces the loyalty of employees to the firm

- o Increases the productivity of employees who believe in the concern shown by the firm's management

- o Compels supervisors to pay more attention to their subordinates than they might if no counseling program existed

- o Improves morale, since people are given a chance to talk and air grievances

However, even a good counseling program may cause some problems for the firm. For example, it:

o Consumes time for both supervisors and employees

o May harm the ego of both supervisors and workers, since supervisors are often cast in the role of judge and this might make working together difficult in the future

o May have detrimental effects on the company. People do not change unless they become uncomfortable about themselves or their situation. This discomfort may make them react negatively to the company and to those who counseled them[5]

o Makes many supervisors unhappy because they dislike having to perform counseling duties

SUMMARY

o Counseling is a deliberate, formal effort to help an employee to become more valuable to the organization, accomplished through personal discussions. Counseling helps the employee to regain productivity, retain it, or increase it.

o Supervisors become aware of the counseling needs of employees through evaluations, productivity records, changes in work habits, complaints, changes in the job the employee has, or requests for help.

o To bring the problem into the open, the supervisor may wait for the employee to ask for help, force the employee into a situation in which he or she must seek help, or confront the employee with the fact that a problem exists.

o The initial counseling interview explores what problem or problems exist and determines if specialized help is needed to resolve them.

o For counseling to be effective, the supervisor should set meeting times jointly with the employee; preanalyze the employee's records; be punctual; allow ample time for the session; meet where privacy is ensured; personalize the interview; be relaxed; be forthright and honest; avoid arguments; listen carefully; allow the employee to reflect during the session; inform the employee about his or her record, giving commendation for the good points first; maintain a calm, objective point of view; help the employee plan for improvement; close the session courteously; and make a written record of the essential features of the session.

o Supervisory counseling may be directive (suggestions are made by the supervisor), nondirective (the employee is encouraged to analyze the problem and suggest remedies), or combination (the supervisor listens and then helps the employee arrive at a solution).

o The supervisor may help the employee to resolve problems by making specific suggestions, helping the employee to reanalyze the situation, allowing the employee to unleash aggression or other emotions, or urging the employee to role play a similar situation.

o Employee problems for which the supervisor anticipates counseling will be needed include transfer, promotion, outplacement, and retirement.

o Unanticipated problems for which counseling may be needed include unusual signs of stress, alcohol or other drug abuse, or depression.

o Periodic evaluation of the counseling program should be undertaken to monitor its value to the firm.

o Advantages of a counseling program are that it demonstrates the interest of the organization in its employees, indicates fairness in the treatment of employees, reinforces the loyalty of the employees, increases productivity, makes supervisors pay more attention to employees, and improves morale.

o Disadvantages of a counseling program are that it uses much time, may harm supervisors' and workers' egos, may make employees react negatively, and may make supervisors unhappy.

REFERENCES

[1] Saul W. Gellerman, The Management of Human Relations (New York: Holt, Rinehart and Winston, 1966), pp. 85–86.

[2] Harold J. Leavitt, Managerial Psychology, 2nd ed. (Chicago: University of Chicago Press, 1964), pp. 195, 196.

[3] T. H. Holmes and R. H. Rahe, "The Social Readjustment Rating Scale," Journal of Psychosomatic Research, 1967, pp. 213–18.

[4] Alan A. McLean, Work Stress (Reading, Mass.: Addison-Wesley, 1979), pp. 65–71.

[5] Leavitt, Managerial Psychology, p. 195.

REVIEW AND DISCUSSION QUESTIONS

1. Why are evaluation and counseling related activities?
2. Why are some firms hesitant to counsel employees?
3. What are some signals of the need for counseling?
4. Under what circumstances would a supervisor refer an employee to a professional counselor?
5. What caution should a supervisor observe in making case records of counseling interviews?

6. What are the differences among directive, nondirective, and combination counseling?

7. Why do employees who are being promoted sometimes need counseling?

8. What is outplacement? Why is counseling needed when a person is outplaced?

9. What are some stressful situations that occur to cause emotional problems for individuals?

10. What are the advantages and disadvantages of a counseling program?

ASSIGNMENTS

1. Read an article in a current magazine or one of the readings at the end of this chapter about outplacement (discharge) or retirement. What information did you learn that supplements your study of this chapter? What kind of counseling might have been used for the people or the situations discussed in the article? Write a short report of your analysis.

2. If you have had a counseling session in school or at work with a teacher, supervisor, or counselor, write a report explaining what kind(s) of counseling was done, who initiated the counseling, how long the counseling session lasted, and how the follow-up to the counseling was handled. To your knowledge, was a written report made of the counseling session? Did you see the report? Did you consider the counseling helpful? Write a report of your experience.

    If you have not had a counseling session, interview one of your friends who has. Answer as many of the previous questions as possible based on your interview.

PROBLEM FOR RESOLUTION

Assume a school organization of which you are the president has a vice-president who, after being elected, has not attended any of the four meetings held to date nor done any of the work assigned.

What actions would you as the president take in the matter?

Do you think counseling would be effective? Give reasons for your response.

What questions would you ask the vice-president about the nonattendance record?

Counseling
Combination
good points
bad points
solutions

(272)   COUNSELING EMPLOYEES

⨯**CASE STUDY**

Ruth Doody was hired five years ago as a secretary for a department by Katherine Griffiths, head of the department. Two years later, Kurt Blanding and Fred Schmidt joined the department as assistants to Ms. Griffiths. Ms. Doody did work for all of them, but she considered Ms. Griffiths to be her real boss.

Ms. Doody was an unusually fine worker. She was particularly good with clients on the telephone, and whenever Ms. Griffiths met with clients, they praised Ms. Doody. Moreover, Ms. Doody liked to work, enjoyed taking shorthand and typing letters, and generally ran the department where routine clerical tasks were concerned.

She did have some faults, however. She disliked filing. This resulted in her desk's being the dumping ground for anything she had pulled from the files as she answered queries or looked up for work she was doing. Also, mail and other material that arrived during the day would be added to the piles. About once every one or two months, when the desk became totally unmanageable, she would take a day to clear everything up, get it all in perfect order, and then proceed to repeat the process of piling it up.

Her second fault was that she did not come in on time. Day after day, she came to work from a few minutes to half an hour late. She never owed any time, however, because she often worked until 6:30 or 7:00, since she waited to meet friends with whom she was having dinner or to leave for classes that she attended. Because clients often called after 5:00 and because Ms. Griffiths and the other bosses often met clients in the office after official closing hours, having Ms. Doody there was quite convenient.

Therefore, Ms. Griffiths did not complain about Ms. Doody's lateness. From time to time, she did confer with her about the neatness of her desk and about the need to replace folders that everyone needed for reference. Ms. Doody would improve for a few days and then slowly return to her usual way of handling file materials.

The day arrived for Ms. Griffiths to retire. Mr. Schmidt was appointed to head the department. His work habits were different from Ms. Griffiths's. He did not arrive early at the office each day as she had. He preferred to go directly from his home into the field to meet clients. Therefore, no one was in the office early to answer telephones, take messages, or look things up, since Mr. Blanding also went directly into the field. Because Ms. Doody was not in to answer calls that came before 9:30, other clerical workers in nearby offices tried to cover for her, but they could never find anything, so they gave up trying and just asked people to call back later.

Mr. Schmidt and Mr. Blanding complained about this system to Ms. Doody, but she did little to change. Finally, she misplaced an order and did not give Mr. Blanding an important message that she had left in the disorder on her desk. Both of them were very upset over her newest errors. Although she continued to perform other facets of her job excellently, they believed her sloppiness in handling her desk and her irritating lateness were hampering their efforts to increase productivity in the office.

If you were Mr. Schmidt, what would be your next step? What plan of resolution do you think might work?

How would you proceed to resolve this situation? Detail the steps you would take and the measures you believe would be necessary to make this office efficient while still retaining the strengths that Ms. Doody brought to it.

FURTHER READING

Benson, Herbert, and Robert L. Allen. "How Much Stress Is Too Much?" *Harvard Business Review,* September–October 1980, pp. 86–92.
> Explains that stress can be both helpful and harmful. Presents top executives' views on how to cope with stress.

Cassell, Frank H. "The Increasing Complexity of Retirement Decisions." *MSU Business Topics,* Winter 1979, pp. 15–24.
> Discusses how retirement attitudes are changing as workers take early retirement or extend the usual work life.

Cooper, Cary L., and Roy Payne, eds. *Stress at Work.* New York: John Wiley, 1978.
> Reports on various aspects of occupational stress.

Levinson, Harry. "The Abrasive Personality." *Harvard Business Review,* May–June 1978, pp. 86–94.
> Analyzes the problems of people who work with others who are sharp-tongued and blunt.

McLean, Alan A. *Work Stress.* Reading, Mass.: Addison-Wesley, 1979.
> Explains that the role of stress at work has been proven by research, and that both psychological and physiological changes result from stress.

McQuade, Walter. "What Stress Can Do to You." *Fortune,* January 1972, pp. 102–41.
> Describes how mental stress is transmitted to the brain and how the body rallies in defense by pouring adrenalin into the bloodstream.

Monat, Alan, and Richard S. Lazarus, eds. *Stress and Coping.* New York: Columbia University Press, 1977.

Discusses, in an anthology of articles on stress, three basic types: physiological, psychological, and social. Investigates how to cope with stress and the links between stress and illness.

Rosen, Benson, and Thomas H. Jerdee. "Too Old or Not Too Old." *Harvard Business Review*, November–December 1977, pp. 97–106.

Discusses how some supervisors have stereotyped views that "older" means less able to change and be creative, and thereby lose valuable employees' services.

Selye, Hans, and Laurence Cherry. "On the Real Benefits of Eustress." *Psychology Today*, March 1978, pp. 60–70.

Discusses the modern use of the word "stress" and how to convert negative stress into a positive experience.

Sirota, David, and Alan D. Wolfson. "Pragmatic Approach to People Problems." *Harvard Business Review*, January–February 1973, pp. 120–28.

Explains that solving problems is the supervisor's responsibility and that solving people problems is more an enigma than solving other managerial problems.

Warren, E. Kirby, Thomas P. Ference, and James A. F. Stoner. "Case of the Plateaued Performer." *Harvard Business Review*, January–February 1975, pp. 30–38.

Describes what happens when older employees block bright young subordinates and how such situations might be handled.

Warshaw, Leon J. *Managing Stress*. Reading, Mass.: Addison-Wesley, 1979.

Discusses how supervisors can recognize, appreciate, and control stressors in the workplace and how counseling programs, among other methods, work to alleviate stress problems.

12

rewarding
and
disciplining
employees

After studying and analyzing this chapter, you should be able to:

Define "reward," and differentiate between intrinsic and extrinsic, and financial and nonfinancial, rewards.

Explain how the award system should be evaluated.

Define "discipline" and "punishment," and discuss the concepts about discipline.

Differentiate between the judicial approach and the human relations approach to discipline.

Explain the concept of "discipline without punishment" and the four steps involved in this process.

List and discuss the situations that result in disciplining employees and the actions supervisors take for each.

List the guidelines for taking good disciplinary actions.

Explain how the discipline system should be evaluated.

THE SUPERVISOR IS IN the position to reward employees who do good jobs and to withhold rewards or to discipline those who do not perform satisfactorily. Reward and discipline were referred to in Chapter 8, on motivation, as the carrot-and-stick, or the Theory X, approach to handling employees. Although there are other approaches to achievement, rewards and discipline are so commonly used that the methods by which these are given to employees need to be understood.

Rewards, represented by the carrot, are desirable, and most, if not all, people seek them. Discipline, represented by the stick, is generally considered to be undesirable by workers but thought to be essential by most supervisors. The supervisor controls only some types of rewards. Discipline, however, is usually under the control of the supervisor.

Rewards

Rewards are pleasurable objects or conditions given to employees in return for good work or service for the organization. Rewards meet a need or fulfill a desire for the employee involved.

Intrinsic and extrinsic rewards

Rewards can be intrinsic or extrinsic. *Intrinsic rewards* are those that come from within a person as a result of the job that is done. They correspond to the motivators as explained by Frederick Herzberg, discussed in Chapter 8. A person's feelings of security, belonging, responsibility, achievement, competence, and self-esteem on a job are all intrinsic rewards. If a person completes a very difficult task, he or she feels a glow of pride—an intrinsic reward. Having responsibility for a job, being allowed to determine how a job should be done, finding a better way to accomplish a task, having the satisfaction of being challenged by difficult assignments, all of these are intrinsic rewards.

Extrinsic rewards are those that are not part of the job itself but that result from it. Increased pay is the most obvious extrinsic reward. Promotion, praise from the supervisor or one's peers, time off to celebrate some special achievement, and awards are examples of extrinsic rewards. The supervisor who recommends rewards observes the policies of the organization regarding them. Extrinsic rewards can be financial or nonfinancial.

Financial rewards

Financial rewards are those that involve payments of money. They are tangible, real rewards that a person can see, understand, and use. They may be awarded in several ways: additional pay, bonuses, commissions, profit sharing, pension plans, employee stock ownership plans, awards for suggestions, and other fringe benefits. Some of these are more directly seen as rewards. The supervisor has direct input only into salary increases and suggestion awards.

Salary increases. Putting additional money in an employee's pay envelope is a tangible way for a supervisor to say "Well done" to an employee. Salary increases are obvious, immediate rewards for the worker. Pay increases are of two types: those given for cost of living and those given for merit.

Cost-of-living increases are usually given across the board, meaning to all employees regardless of the quality or quantity of their work. Merit increases are based on the important achievements and contributions of an individual employee. Some organizations base their merit pay increases on ratings or job-performance levels. Employees considered most deserving would receive possibly a 5 to 7 percent increase above the cost-of-living increase; those in the middle category, a 3 to 4 percent increase; and those in the lesser category, a 1 to 2 percent increase. Employees who did not merit an increase would receive just the cost-of-living increase. Barring an economic recession or a cutback in money for everyone in a firm due to financial reverses of the organization, salary increases are permanent for the people to whom they are awarded.

Bonuses. Extra payments, in addition to salary, based on some defined measures are bonuses. They are established either for an individual worker or for an entire department. Bonuses may be awarded in any department in which productivity can be measured or other features, such as reduced absenteeism or decreased waste, can be observed. Bonuses are obvious to employees at the point of payment. If they are given to an entire department for its achievement, they are usually allotted on the basis of the relative salary each worker gets. Bonuses are not permanent increases, however. Each year or each season, new standards are set for achieving one. For example, an employee may be given a bonus of one day's pay for having no absences during a six-month period.

Commissions. One method of paying people in departments or organizations where productivity is measurable is the commission. Sometimes people in sales departments work on a commission of a percentage of their sales, ranging from a fraction of a percent to as much as 11 percent. This may be all their pay, or they may work for a base salary plus an additional commission of a fraction of a percent to as much as 4 percent over a certain minimum amount of production. Because commissions are directly related to the number of sales made, the reward for doing good work is built in. If sales slump, commissions also go down.

Profit sharing. Paying employees a percentage of the profits of the firm based on their salaries is called *profit sharing*. Employees who make larger salaries get a larger share of the profits. In theory, because all employees are rewarded on a proportionate basis, this method rewards all employees jointly for doing good work. In profit-making concerns, employees may be well rewarded by such payments during good years. In poor years, when no profit is made, employees get no money beyond their regular salaries.

Pension plans. Payments made by the organization and sometimes also by the employee into retirement funds that ensure a person a certain amount of income after serving for a given number of years in the organization and reaching retirement age are *pension plans* (see also Chapter 14). Sometimes they entice employees to remain with the organization and to do a good job so that they can continue with the firm. Because pensions are a delayed payment, the employee sees little relationship between the hopes of a pension and his or her current productivity.

Employee stock ownership plans (ESOPs). Available in some corporations, ESOPs provide for up to 15 percent of an employee's salary to be placed into stock of the company. The employee may buy additional amounts if desired. In some cases the stock may be bought below the regular price. The employee owns the shares, which may be cashed in as needed or held until retirement or beyond. If the stock of the organization goes up in price, the stock-owning employee gains. If the price goes down, the employee may get little or nothing. The employee who owns stock in the enterprise may be motivated to work harder in the hope that the organization will be more successful. However, the employee can see little direct relationship between his or her performance and the ultimate reward.

Awards for suggestions. To spur employees to consider ways of improving the activities of the organization, *awards for suggestions* may be given. If the firm can save money, increase productivity, simplify operations, or eliminate unnecessary tasks as a result of suggestions made by employees, the supervisor is delighted to reward them for the help. Cash awards are often given for accepted ideas. The award process helps to involve all employees in thinking of ways to improve the procedures used in the enterprise, and the reward is obvious when it is received.

Other fringe benefits. Nondirect payment for services or protection for employees that is determined by management and reflected in organizational policies or that is obtained through bargaining by a union is known as *fringe benefits*. They include such features as pension plans, employee stock option plans, vacations, health plans, insurance plans, and Social Security.

Fringe benefits are available in most organizations to employees who have satisfied certain conditions of employment. They range in total value from approximately 11 percent to as much as 25 percent of an employee's salary. However, fringe benefits are not viewed as rewards by most employees but rather sometimes are an important consideration in joining a particular enterprise. Supervisors are responsible for seeing that employees understand fringe benefits.

Nonfinancial awards

Rewards that do not involve money are nonfinancial awards—for example, promotions, status symbols, additional assignments, special awards, and commendations.

Promotions. The most tangible nonfinancial reward that an employee can achieve is promotion from one job level to another. If a person is ambitious and is planning a career with that or a similar organization, promotion is proof that the person is doing a good job and that job standards have been met. Most promotions are also accompanied by salary increases, and so the employee who wins a promotion gets both a financial and a nonfinancial reward.

Status. The evident rank or standing of a person within the organization is status. It may be evidenced in many ways: by a person's being assigned a larger office, having a more attractive office, having the use of a company car, having a special telephone and telephone number, being assigned an assistant, or being granted an expense account privilege. Sometimes a new title is an indication of increased status, as when a secretary is called an administrative aide. One joke refers to obtaining the "keys to the executive wash room" as an indication of status.

Status symbols may bring no monetary advantages, but they do attest to the improved well-being of the employee within the enterprise.

Additional assignments. These sometimes serve as awards, especially if they replace more routine tasks. A person who runs seminars, for example, and also takes care of mailing lists may have the latter job removed when additional seminars are planned.

Although a person's salary may not reflect such additional assignments immediately, salary level is eventually increased for handling the more difficult tasks. Therefore, taking on additional assignments often results in both financial and nonfinancial rewards.

Other assignments employees may consider to be rewards are inclusion in special committees or on task forces or representing the organization in meetings of outside groups.

Special awards. Longevity at work, excellence in some phase of work, or some unique contribution may be rewarded by a *special award,* such as a badge, pin, plaque, scroll, or gift. Sometimes competitions are held among departments that do similar work. The winning department may be treated to a dinner by the losers, and a trophy may be given to the winners. When such events become traditional within organizations, employees sometimes vie with one another enthusiastically to win. Retirement parties for employees who have both given long years of service and reached ages in the 60s or 70s are also frequent. Expensive gifts may be presented at these parties.

Commendation. Praise from one's supervisor or peers is another type of reward that helps to reinforce one's own image of self-worth. Commendation also makes a person feel needed and wanted in an organization. Such a nonfinancial reward may be as effective as a financial one in keeping the employee loyal to the organization.

Evaluation of rewards

Periodically, to make sure the reward system is fair, it should be reviewed. Questions such as the following might be considered:

o How many rewards were given during the previous six-month period?

o How many different employees received rewards?

o What productivity increase appeared to be due to the reward system?

o Was the reward system fair, that is, did those who merited the award actually receive it?

o Did the reward system honor the work that should be rewarded?

o How did the other members of the department react to those who received awards?

o Were there any improvements that should have been considered in the reasons for awards?

o Were there any improvements that should have been considered in the kinds of awards given?

Discipline

Every action taken in a firm should be directed toward the accomplishment of the goals set by top management. If employees do not work efficiently to achieve the utmost productivity, changes may need to be made among them. Before those changes are made, the supervisor attempts to alter the attitudes and actions of the employees who are not meeting the goals.

Discipline implies orderliness as opposed to confusion. It also implies punishment. Discipline means that people are trained to act in accordance with rules and that if they do not perform in that way, punishment is inflicted by way of correction.

When a supervisor states that an employee needs disciplining, he or she means that the worker is required to adhere to rules and regulations with the implied threat of punishment or penalty for not doing so.

Punishment in organizations involves warnings, threats, suspensions, demotions, or ultimate discharges. For some, threats alone may change behavior, but in many people punishment "creates anger and hostility and a desire to get even. We know that punishment destroys self-respect and feelings of confidence. And we know that punishment more frequently teaches people to avoid getting caught than to change their ways."[1]

Concepts about discipline

The initial idea of discipline was that it should be harsh, incorporating the concept of the stick. People did the job as it was to be done, or else! "Or else" usually meant the loss of the job or, at the least, the loss of pay for the work that was not properly done. For example, when money was missing in the cash register in retail stores, it was subtracted from the pay of the employees who handled that register. Bank employees were similarly required to make up shortages in their tills. Lateness in coming to work was offset by having the employee work overtime or docking the employee's pay for the time missed. Absenteeism meant no pay for that day regardless of the reason.

This punitive concept of disciplining employees resulted in fear and resentment among the workers. Morale was lowered and production often fell, making these penalties undesirable to both the firm and the worker.

Methods of taking disciplinary action

Supervisors approach the problem of discipline in different ways. Some observe the rules that the organization has established and they use

FIGURE 12–1

BOTH REWARDS AND DISCIPLINE ARE THE SUPERVISOR'S RESPONSIBILITY

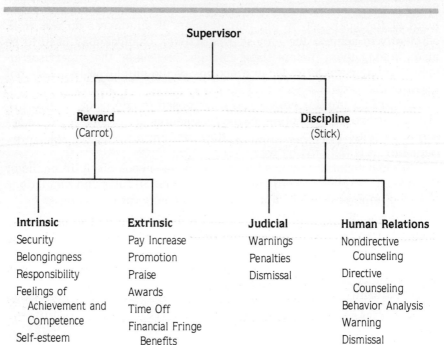

them as the approach to the problem. Others view the individual in relation to those rules. These two methods have been called the judicial
approach and the human relations approach, respectively (see Figure
12–1).

The *judicial approach* compares the specific action of the employee
to the rules of the firm, and the penalty prescribed therein is the penalty
imposed by the supervisor. The *human relations approach* views the
employee's incorrect or nonproductive action as a problem to be solved,
and seeks to improve the employee's behavior rather than to punish him
or her.[2]

The supervisor cannot ignore behavior that deviates from that expected from an employee. If supervisors do not "deal effectively with
those who violate rules, the disrespect for order will spread to the employees who would otherwise prefer to comply. . . . A supervisor has to
take action to counteract misconduct so that the offender either comes to
realize and accept the standard of conduct necessary for his [her] continued employment, or demonstrates that he [she] will not do so and, therefore, must be discharged."[3]

The supervisor cannot overlook behavior that is harmful to the well-being of the rest of the staff. Employees are the first to notice if someone is ignoring rulings or is guilty of unproductive behavior. The supervisor must take some action in such a situation; at this point the supervisor must decide whether to use the judicial or the human relations approach to the problem.

In a role-playing study in which the two types of approaches to a disciplinary problem were used with 172 groups, slightly over one-half of the supervisors used the human relations approach. This approach was deemed more satisfactory by all who participated in the project.[4] For this reason, the human relations approach should be considered by the supervisor.

Discipline without punishment

In 1964, John Huberman first reported on the method he had previously developed, called *discipline without punishment*, to reduce troublesome behavior of employees in a Canadian plywood mill.[5] Eleven years later, in 1975, he reported that many firms were using this method which closely follows the human relations approach to discipline.[6]

In Huberman's view, when the need to discipline an employee arises, the supervisor should take four sequential steps to resolve the problem:

o *When the objectionable behavior is observed, explain to the employee casually and in private that the action is not productive*—In this step, a nondirective, counseling-type interview may be used, concluding with a reminder about the undesirable behavior. For example, in the case of repeated lateness for arrival at work, the supervisor may say, "Is anything troubling you? Would you like to talk about some problem that has arisen recently?" After this interview, the date of the talk is noted in the employee's personnel file, together with mention of the topic(s) covered.

o *If the incorrect behavior persists, discuss it further with the employee*—This interview is more direct than the first, very casual talk. Again, a note is made of this conversation and includes the date, time allotted, and topic covered.

o *If the behavior does not improve, call the employee in to analyze the reason for his or her lack of improvement*—Questions may be raised about the worker's attitude toward the job, the work he or she does, or the reasons at the place of work that may have caused this behavior. The intention of the employee to abide by the rules should also be discussed.

All of this information should be put into a letter that is either given or sent to the employee and a copy of which is put in the employee's file. To avoid any possible embarrassment, the supervisor should be sure the employee, and not a member of his or her family, receives the letter.

o *If the undesirable behavior persists, have a discussion with the employee and your boss*—At this point, suggest that the employee take the rest of the day off with pay, go home, and make a decision about the intention to conform in the future. Inform the employee that one more failure to meet requirements will, regretfully, result in termination. This conversation should be recorded in a letter that the employee receives and a copy of which is placed in the employee's file. If termination results at a later date, the records clearly indicate what actions were taken on the specific dates to try to help the employee. If the employee opts to return and abide by the rules of the organization, the record is cleared, one step at a time as months of trouble-free behavior continue.

In Huberman's experience with plant and factory personnel, this system was responsible for reducing dismissals and for rehabilitating the majority of employees who reached steps three or four. This record reinforced the belief that "disciplinary action should be designed to correct the conduct of the employees involved rather than to punish."[7] Huberman further recommended that in addition to using this counseling approach to discipline, the supervisor should also use reinforcement by letting the employee know that the changed behavior is appreciated.

Because it allows supervisors to be supportive rather than punitive, Huberman's method also helps them to confront problems earlier, further reducing the amount of undesirable behavior.[8]

Situations that result in disciplining

Reasons to discipline employees may occur both because of situations that are not the fault of employees but about which they neglected to alert the supervisor, or because of situations employees themselves have caused.

Situations that are not the fault of the employee.   These include faulty communications, unreasonable orders, nonunderstandable orders, and misplacement on the job:

o *Faulty communications*—These cause errors to occur. For example, the marketing department of a firm may not have been told soon enough about a new product the manufacturing de-

partment was about to have ready for sale, and sales, therefore, of that product lag.

o *Unreasonable orders*—For example, a large job may have
been scheduled to be finished during the vacation period,
when many employees would not be around to accomplish
the work. Those left in the department would not be able to
carry out the assignment.

o *Nonunderstandable orders*—For example, an employee may
have been told to prepare an agenda for a forthcoming meeting without being advised what the meeting was to cover or
what people were to attend. Or an employee may have been
told to order some supplies without being given the details
needed to place the order. Such omissions make it impossible
to carry out the assignment.

o *Misplacement on the job*—For example, a person who likes
to be around others may have been isolated. Conversely, one
who dislikes working with people may have been placed
near many other workers. In some cases a person who has no
sales ability may have been asked to present products to prospective buyers, or those who have sales ability may have
been assigned to desk jobs.

When situations that are not the fault of the employee occur, those
situations need to be brought to the attention of the supervisor as soon
as the employee is aware of the problem. Otherwise the supervisor may
accuse the employee of being remiss when the job is not done properly.

Situations that are the fault of the employee. These include lack of skill,
ignoring rules, incompatibility, refusal to follow orders, forgetfulness,
personal offensiveness, tardiness, absenteeism, theft, and alcohol and
other drug abuse:

o *Lack of skill*—For most jobs that require skills in handling
machines or filling out special forms, or that need knowledge
of English, grammar, spelling, and proofreading, pretests are
given prior to employment. However, pretests can only reveal
some of the person's abilities. Judgments are also made on
the basis of the experiences and education the employee
claims to have had. If those were misrepresented, the person
may prove to be unqualified. Misrepresentation of skills and
abilities is a serious offense.

o *Ignoring rules*—Rules that ensure safety of workers, economy
of materials, or productivity must be observed. When the supervisor is sure that the rules are reasonable and have been

established fairly, and that employees understand the rules, he or she has no alternative but to insist that they be observed.

o *Incompatibility*—Employees' inability to get along with others or with the supervisor may cause problems. Because a place of business must be harmonious if work is to be productive, people who do not get along with others reduce the chance for work to be successfully completed.

o *Refusal to follow orders*—When specific directives have been given about doing a job, the entire job may need to be redone if the employee does not follow them. This not only wastes time and effort but also usually causes friction within the department.

o *Forgetfulness*—A person who is forgetful is usually one who lacks interest in the job. When an employee is asked to fulfill a certain assignment and later says, "I forgot to do it," others may be seriously inconvenienced. Forgetfulness may delay a project slightly, or it may seriously disrupt the work that many people are doing.

o *Personal offensiveness*—A person may offend others in many ways. Uncleanliness, foul language, derisive statements, loud talking, sloppiness in attire, being argumentative, gossiping about others, or actually misrepresenting facts about peers or bosses are among the ways people offend others in the organization.

o *Tardiness*—Being late in reporting for work or in returning from lunch periods or rest breaks or departing from work early are all disrupting behaviors that affect productivity.

o *Absenteeism*—A person who takes unauthorized time off just to satisfy personal wishes damages the productivity of the enterprise and may also lower the morale of the other workers. Even those who are absent for illness or for other reasons over which they have no control may also disrupt the work of the firm. The work of the organization cannot wait until people get well, and so employees must meet attendance standards unless the firm can supply temporary workers to do their jobs while they are absent.

o *Theft*—"Employee theft is the most critical crime problem facing business today,"[9] stated one authority. Theft of billions of dollars, estimated to be 35 to 40 percent of all shortages, is committed by employees each year in firms in the

United States.[10] Employee theft ranges from the taking of office supplies, the mailing of personal letters through the office, and the making of unauthorized personal telephone calls to the stealing of money and merchandise. Computers have added a new inroad for theft by the programmer, who can siphon vast reserves into personal accounts. Careful controls, watchful supervision, and frequent discussions with employees may help to cut down on these offenses.

o *Alcohol and other drug abuse*—Estimates indicate that as many as 5 to 10 percent of employees in large organizations have alcohol or other drug-related problems.[11] In most instances, the offending employee is careful to hide the use of drugs from both the supervisor and the other employees. However, erratic behavior, unusual appearance, frequent absenteeism from either the job or the work station, drowsiness, increasing errors, and general unreliability are some of the characteristics that alert the supervisor to the problem.

Kinds of disciplinary actions supervisors take

Supervisors have direct responsibility for the work employees perform in their departments. Therefore, when employees are not performing satisfactorily, the supervisor has the responsibility to take the necessary steps to ensure adequate performance. Any of the previously mentioned problems result in the need for some type of disciplinary action.

For situations that are not the fault of the employee.   The supervisor needs to take remedial action for these. If communications are faulty, the supervisor must determine who is responsible and do the necessary training or counseling to ensure that communications are properly handled in the future. If orders are unreasonable, the supervisor needs to be more careful in the future either in accepting assignments from superiors or in making assignments to subordinates.

If orders are nonunderstandable, the supervisor again may be at fault and care must be taken to make sure all orders are properly presented in the future. If the employee is misassigned, the supervisor usually tries to arrange for a transfer to an appropriate department. If that is not possible, the supervisor may have no recourse other than to discharge the employee.

For situations that are the fault of the employee.   The supervisor should take the human relations approach to the problems. If the employee lacks necessary skills, the supervisor may arrange for added training or for reassignment. As a last recourse, the employee who is incapable of doing the job would be discharged. Usually only temporary employment is offered when people first join a firm, and the first few months are used to determine if the employee is qualified for the job.

For the employee who ignores rules, the supervisor usually makes sure first that he or she knows the rules. If the employee continues to ignore rules, the supervisor may first warn him or her of the danger that results. If the progressive human relations method of handling and counseling the employee does not work, the supervisor may have to discharge the offending employee.

Employees who are incompatible with others may need counseling-type interviews to help them to adjust. If after going through the four-step approach of rehabilitation the employee continues to be incompatible, the supervisor may suggest transfer and, failing that, may discharge the employee.

Similarly, employees who refuse to follow orders may be taken through the four steps to help them. If they continue to disobey orders, discharge may be the only recourse left.

Forgetful employees may similarly be taken through the four steps in the hope that they will be induced to pay more attention to the job.

Employees who are personally offensive in some way would be counseled by the supervisor. If counseling does not work, stricter disciplinary action, resulting ultimately in discharge, needs to be taken.

For employees who are chronically late, the supervisor would usually discuss the problem and attempt to help them resolve the situation. If the organization uses flexible time scheduling, tardy employees may be permitted to select the hours they will work. Not all organizations have that flexibility, however. If tardiness persists, employees should be either reassigned to work that allows more time latitude or dismissed.

Similarly, if after repeated absences and repeated counseling sessions an employee continues to be absent, he or she may be advised to obtain a position for which being on the job daily is not so important, such as with a firm that makes temporary assignments.

Theft requires immediate disciplinary action. If the theft is substantial, the employee is discharged immediately and criminal charges may be brought against the former worker. Minor thefts are also cause for dismissal, but the supervisor may prefer to use a series of counseling interviews in the hope that the employee's attitudes will change. Stealing is a serious offense, and if small thefts are tolerated, they may lead to others.

Because most supervisors are not trained to handle alcohol- and other drug-abuse problems, the supervisor should refer the offending employee to the company psychologist, psychiatrist, or medical doctor. If the firm is small and no such help is available, referral should be made to an outside service. Today, with the help of professional counselors, as many as 80 to 85 percent of alcoholics and other drug abusers are able to be rehabilitated and to take their place again in the work force.[12] The supervisor, of course, should treat the whole affair with the greatest confidentiality. Offenders who refuse rehabilitation are dismissed.

Handling dismissals in small versus large organizations

The ultimate penalty for poor performance, not following orders, or deviant behavior is dismissal. In small organizations, the supervisor may actually dismiss an offending employee after carefully chronicling each step taken in the disciplinary process. In large organizations, the supervisor recommends dismissal to his or her superior. When agreement is reached about dismissal, the actual firing is handled by the staff in the personnel office. These people make sure that all records are on file and that all legal procedures are observed.

Guidelines for taking good disciplinary actions

To ensure that the most productive results are obtained under disciplinary situations, the supervisor should:

- o Inform all employees when they are first hired of all the firm's rules and regulations. These may be available in booklet form.

- o Discuss any new rules as soon as they are formulated.

- o Attempt initially to correct the employee's incorrect behavior rather than to punish the person.

- o Hold disciplinary sessions in private so that only the offender is aware of the reprimand.

- o Plan the disciplinary session for a time when emotional tensions have abated. Calm appraisal on the part of both the supervisor and the supervisee is essential for a fair and impartial analysis of a complaint.

- o Discipline all employees who commit the same offense equally. One person should not be made the scapegoat for action that should be departmentwide.

- o Criticize the act performed and not the employee in any personal way.

Evaluation of disciplinary actions

Once every six months the supervisor should review the disciplinary actions that have been taken and consider the results that have been obtained. Questions such as the following should be answered in doing this evaluation:

Know some

o How many disciplinary measures had to be taken during the six-month period?

o How many of those measures went to the first interview stage only?

o How many went to the second interview stage?

o How many went to the third interview stage?

o How many went to the fourth interview stage?

o How many of the people who were disciplined were rehabilitated?

o How many of the disciplinary situations resulted in firing of the employees involved?

o Were any of the situations badly handled? How could those situations have been handled better?

o Were any of the situations well handled? Could those methods be applied in other cases?

o Are the rules and regulations of the firm reasonable or do some need change?

o What method of discussing the rules and regulations with the staff was used?

o How do staff members regard the disciplining that has occurred in their department?

Careful study and analysis of the results of previous disciplinary actions can help the supervisor to improve on the handling of problem situations in the future.

SUMMARY

o Both rewards and discipline are used to improve the productivity of workers. Rewards, known as the carrot, are sought by employees. Discipline, known as the stick, is disliked by employees but considered essential by supervisors.

o Rewards, pleasurable repayments for good work or good service, may be intrinsic (those the person senses about his or her achievement on the job, such as security, belonging, responsibility, competence, and self-esteem) or extrinsic (those that result from doing a good job, such as increased pay, promotion, or praise).

o Extrinsic rewards may be financial (increases in salary, bonuses, commissions, profit sharing, pension plans, employee stock ownership plans, awards for suggestions, and other fringe benefits) or nonfinancial (promotions, status, additional assignments, special awards, and commendations).

o The reward system should be evaluated periodically.

o Discipline seeks to have employees conform and produce as expected with the implied threat of punishment for not doing so.

o Judicial discipline is the imposition of penalties for any infraction of the rules. Human relations discipline is a method of seeking to improve the employee's behavior rather than to punish the employee.

o A four-step method of disciplining employees without punishing them is an example of the human relations method.

o Situations that result in discipline include those that are not the fault of the employee (faulty communications, unreasonable orders, non-understandable orders, misplacement on the job) as well as those that are the fault of the employee (lack of skill, ignoring rules, incompatibility, refusal to follow orders, forgetfulness, personal offensiveness, tardiness, absenteeism, theft, alcohol and other drug abuse).

o For problems that are not the fault of the employee, the supervisor should examine the procedures and modify and improve them. For those that are the fault of the employee, the four-step process may be used or employees may be referred to specialists. The last recourse when the employee does not improve is dismissal.

o Periodically, disciplinary actions should be evaluated.

REFERENCES

[1] Richard D. Grote, "Positive Discipline: Keeping Employees in Line Without Punishment," *Training*, October 1977, p. 43.

[2] Norman R. F. Maier and Lee E. Danielson, "An Evaluation of Two Approaches to Discipline in Industry," *Journal of Applied Psychology*, October 1956, pp. 319–23.

[3] Paul Pigors, Charles A. Myers, and F. T. Malm, *Management of Human Resources* (New York: McGraw-Hill, 1969), p. 468.

[4] Maier and Danielson, "An Evaluation of Two Approaches," pp. 319–23.

[5] John Huberman, "Discipline Without Punishment," *Harvard Business Review*, July–August 1964, pp. 62–68.

[6] John Huberman, " 'Discipline Without Punishment' Lives," *Harvard Business Review*, July–August 1975, pp. 6–8.

[7] Huberman, " 'Discipline Without Punishment' Lives," p. 8.

[8] Jack Horn, "Discipline Without Tears: Be Positive, Not Punitive," *Psychology Today*, November 1977, pp. 34, 38.

[9] "Employee Theft," *Personnel News and Views*, Winter 1977–1978, p. 17.

10 "Employee Theft," p. 16.
11 Ian Elliot, "Drunks, Drugs . . . and Trainers," *Training*, May 1975, p. 35.

12 Elliot, "Drunks, Drugs . . . and Trainers," p. 36.

REVIEW AND DISCUSSION QUESTIONS

1. What is a reward? How do intrinsic and extrinsic rewards differ? Give examples of each.
2. What financial rewards are available to employees? Which of these rewards are most directly the result of good work?
3. What nonfinancial rewards are available? In your opinion, should both financial and nonfinancial rewards be available for employees?
4. Why might disciplinary actions be needed in a firm?
5. Why is the supervisor involved in disciplinary actions?
6. What are the major differences between the judicial approach and the human relations approach to discipline?
7. What is the four-step disciplinary approach suggested by John Huberman?
8. What procedures should be followed by the supervisor in disciplining employees who have been involved in the theft of the firm's money or material?
9. What procedures should be followed with employees who have alcohol- or other drug-abuse problems?
10. What is the supervisor's ultimate responsibility in discharging employees?

ASSIGNMENTS

1. Review your own school or work experiences. Have you ever received an award? Did you appreciate it? Did you work harder as a result of it? Have you ever been disciplined? How harsh was the discipline? Did you improve your behavior as a result of the discipline? Write a report of your experiences and the results attained.
2. Read one of the references in the Further Reading section or another article on rewards or discipline in a current publication. What method did it recommend? Write a review of the article and tell whether you agree or disagree with what the author said. Give reasons for your opinion.

PROBLEM FOR RESOLUTION

A bank guard, John Paul, had been employed by the bank for five years. He ate his lunch in an area where bank books were received, updated, and mailed back to customers. An employee was assigned to oversee that work. The employee weighed the envelopes using an automatic stamping machine that placed the correct postage on the envelopes and then dumped them into mailbags ready for the post office. When no one was in the room as Mr. Paul ate his lunch, he fed his personal mail through the machine.

One day, when the employee in charge of the machine returned from his lunch break, he noticed that the number of letters posted was greater than it had been when he left the room. He reported this discrepancy in the numbers to the supervisor of the section.

What should the supervisor do about this matter?

CASE STUDY

A large office of the Erstwhile Book Company was divided into sections for specialized work. The one that dealt with financial publications had an office staff of three people, Rory, Eva, and Jessie. Rory and Eva had worked in the office for more than twenty-five years, while Jessie had been on the job just one year.

Hours at the firm were from 9:00 A.M. to 5:00 P.M. daily, Monday through Friday, with one hour for lunch. No formal rest periods were assigned, but the employees were allowed considerable latitude. They all sent out for coffee or tea daily, and they sat at their desks talking and sipping the morning refreshment at their convenience.

A new supervisor, Sue, was assigned when the previous supervisor was transferred to another area. Sue found the following situations in existence when she had been in the area for about a week. Rory arrived at 8:40 or 8:50 A.M. daily. She did not start work until 9:00 A.M., but if the telephone rang before that time, she did answer it. Her lunch period was scheduled from 1:00–2:00 P.M., but at 12:00, she opened up her newspaper at her desk and read it or did the crossword puzzle. When her lunch time arrived, she moved into a small adjacent room, ate her lunch, and continued to work on the puzzle. At 2:00 P.M. she returned to her desk. At 4:00 P.M. promptly, she proceeded to the ladies' room to prepare to leave for the day. She slipped out between 4:15 and 4:20 P.M. daily. In checking on Rory's work, Sue found that many times she was late in getting in reports, was always complaining that she was being pushed, and never had time to get her work done before something else was demanded of her.

Eva arrived daily at 9:30 A.M. or slightly thereafter. She worked industriously even during coffee break until 1:00 P.M., when she went with Rory to the small room for lunch. Daily, at 4:40 P.M., she left the office to wash up before leaving for the day. She usually closed the office at

5:00 P.M. promptly. Occasionally, when her work was backed up, Eva would take a shortened lunch period to catch up on the backlog.

Sue noticed that both of these employees answered telephone calls if necessary during their lunch period, since Jessie was relatively new and did not always know the answers to questions that came into the office.

Jessie had physical problems that necessitated that she be able to sit a great deal of the time. Therefore, she liked both to arrive early at work to avoid crowds and to leave early. Jessie arrived daily at 8:30 A.M. and left the office promptly at 4:30 P.M. Her lunch period was from 12:00–1:00 P.M. She left the office during lunch period. Although she arrived one-half hour early each morning, she accomplished little before 9:00 A.M. because her work was dependent on the tasks assigned by the experienced employees, Rory and Eva, and by activities that occurred during regular hours.

Sue noticed that someone was covering the office throughout the day except from 4:40–5:00 P.M. However, when telephone calls came in, Sue had to handle them and to resolve problems that should have been taken care of by staff members. One afternoon, Sue's boss called her to a spur-of-the-moment meeting at 4:40 P.M. No one was in the office, and so she had to lock it and leave it unattended. Another day, an urgent complaint came in that only Rory could handle, but she had been gone since 4:15 P.M. and could not be reached.

What action, if any, should Sue take about the work schedules that the office staff had developed over the years?

FURTHER READING

Cooper, M. R., B. S. Morgan, P. M. Foley, and L. B. Kaplan. "Changing Employee Values: Deepening Discontent?" *Harvard Business Review*, January–February 1979, pp. 117–25.

Reports on a study done over a twenty-five-year period that revealed that managers, clerical, and hourly employees rate their jobs differently and that generally managers are the most satisfied, clerical employees are fairly satisfied, and hourly employees are least satisfied.

Cummings, L. L., and Donald P. Schwab. "Motivational and Organizational Variables as Performance Determinants." In *Performance in Organizations*. Glenview, Ill.: Scott, Foresman, 1973, pp. 21–44.

Explains that task design, leader behavior, and rewards have a substantial impact on how employees perform their jobs, and that linking pay to productivity and using performance appraisal are two ways of rewarding employees.

Flowers, Vincent S., and Charles L. Hughes. "Why Employees Stay." *Harvard Business Review*, July–August 1973, pp. 49–60.

> Discusses how the employee's satisfaction on the job and environmental pressures inside and outside the organization affect his or her determination to continue or terminate.

Hinriche, John R. *Practical Management for Productivity*. New York: Van Nostrand Reinhold/Work in America Institute Series, 1979.

> Explains how the right skill levels of employees must be combined to achieve production objectives and how financial incentives plus praise and recognition help to sustain productivity.

Katzell, Raymond A., and Daniel Yankelovich. *Work Productivity and Job Satisfaction*. New York: Psychological Corporation, 1975.

> Reports the findings of a research study concerning productivity and job satisfaction: Financial compensation of workers must be linked to their job performance, and work must be diversified and matched to workers' abilities so that workers are challenged.

Sweeney, Herbert C., and Kenneth S. Teel. "A New Look at Promotion From Within." *Personnel Journal*, August 1979, pp. 531–35.

> Concludes from a study of various types of organizations that most organizations promote from within but are not taking full advantage of motivational techniques to improve morale and performance.

13

handling employee grievances

After studying and analyzing this chapter, you should be able to:

Differentiate between a complaint and a grievance.

List and explain the reasons for grievances.

Define "grievance procedure," and explain what steps should be included in a nonunionized and unionized firm's established grievance procedure.

List the guidelines that a supervisor should follow to prevent or resolve grievances.

Explain the changing attitudes toward discharging employees.

EVERY SUPERVISOR strives to have a smoothly functioning, relatively contented work force. Not only is this state beneficial to employees, but the organization's goals and objectives can most efficiently be met when there is harmony in the workplace. This state is achieved when:

o Employees have the abilities and skills needed to perform their jobs adequately.

o Assigned tasks are understood by the employees and can be accomplished as planned.

o Everyone works together in relative harmony.

The ideal state is seldom wholly attained, for several reasons. People do not always function in the manner that is expected, snarls in the flow of work cause delays and other problems, and people react to others in ways that cause conflict. Employees may view promotions of their peers as unwarranted, and demotions, transfers, discharges, and disciplinary actions as unfair. Some employees say nothing, but they become discontented when they believe actions are not beneficial to them. Other employees express their opinions openly. Both the silent and the vocal employees may express their discontent in complaints and grievances.

Complaints and grievances *know difference between them*

Usually, when employees believe that an action taken by the supervisor, another employee, or the firm itself is unfair or detrimental to their well-being, the first step is to lodge a complaint. A *complaint* is an informal expression of annoyance, frustration, discontent, or resentment about the matter. Complaints are usually made orally to the immediate supervisor unless they involve that supervisor. Then the employee may prefer to go to a personnel representative. If the complaint is justified and the problem can be resolved easily, making extensive records or formalizing the procedure is not necessary. The supervisor or the personnel representative tries to resolve the problem. In fact, part of the supervisor's success depends on the ability to deal with problems at their source rather than to pass them up to a higher level, and to do so in a timely manner.

If a complaint is not resolved or if the matter is very serious, the employee may believe that such informal handling will not produce the desired result. In this case, the employee may wish to lodge a grievance. A *grievance* is an official charge against a supervisor, another employee, or the firm's management. Grievances, to be acted upon, should be in writing.

Reasons for grievances

If the supervisor handles subordinates with tact and consideration, if the organization's policies are fair, and if other employees are cooperative, few complaints should occur and even fewer should become formal grievances. When complaints arise, the supervisor should react as previously discussed in the chapters on counseling and rewarding and disciplining.

The employees' right to present a formal grievance is one that must be protected at all times. In organizations, many conditions exist about which employees may have real or imagined grievances.

Broken promises

When employees are first hired or after they have been working for a firm for a while, they may be promised certain conditions that do not eventually hold to be true. Promises made about duties, hours, pay, working conditions, and promotions may sometimes be broken.

About duties.   Duties are discussed with the employment manager or the supervisor when a person is first hired. They may prove to be different once he or she starts work. For example, Wilma Blake was hired as a secretary for two managers, Mr. Bowen and Ms. Shact. When Ms. Blake reported for work, she found that Mr. Bowen and Ms. Shact were rarely in the office because their assignments took them on frequent trips. They did, however, send in tapes of material to be transcribed, and she had other routine work to perform for them. In their absence, Ms. Blake reported to Francine Torres, the office manager. When no special work from Mr. Bowen or Ms. Schact was received, Ms. Torres put other assignments on Ms. Blake's desk. Ms. Blake resented these other assignments and complained that she had been hired to work for Mr. Bowen and Ms. Shact only.

About hours.   Initially stated hours may differ from the actual hours that an employee is expected to put in once he or she begins work. For instance, when Brooks Martin was hired, she was told the hours were from 9:00 A.M. to 5:00 P.M., Monday through Friday. However, she found that one of her bosses was frequently out of the office during the afternoon and that he needed her there to take dictation and get letters out when he returned. She often worked until 5:30 P.M. and occasionally until 6:00 P.M. He would then suggest that she take compensatory time off the next morning so that her hours would not exceed the thirty-five per week for which she was paid. This late working time, however, disrupted her home life, made evening appointments difficult to keep, and occasionally interfered with her attendance at evening college classes.

About pay. Initially promised pay may also differ from that which the employee receives. For example, Bob Duer was making $160 per week when he applied for a new job that paid less to begin with but offered a better future. The outgoing employee had made $145 per week, but Mr. Duer was promised $155 because he had considerable experience and would not require much training. However, communication broke down between the personnel office and the payroll office. When his first weekly check arrived, it was for $145.

About working conditions. For a variety of reasons, promised working conditions may not materialize. For example, Brian Biggs was employed in a shipping room that he was told was to be automated in the near future. Within a month or two, he was promised, he would no longer have to roll merchandise in wheelers because the goods would move automatically on overhead racks. He was told that his work would then consist primarily of record keeping and checking. Several months passed, and the architects found new problems that would take more and more money to resolve. Finally, the automation plans were abandoned, and Mr. Biggs continued to fill wheelers and roll goods to the areas where they were packed for shipment.

About promotions. Another source of broken promises is promotions. For instance, Molly McRae had a fine record as an executive secretary. She had also done the budgets for the department, acted as the overseer for the other employees, and kept the office running smoothly when the boss was away for weeks at a time. He appreciated her efforts. One day, just as she was preparing to leave on her annual vacation, he called her into his office and told her that on her return, she would become the assistant manager of the department. She was delighted and proudly told all her friends and co-workers. When her vacation was over, however, she was dismayed to find that she was still classed as an executive secretary. After another month had passed and no promotion was in evidence, Ms. McRae reminded her boss of his promise. "Oh," he replied, "I've changed my mind about that."

Inequitable pay

Employees also have a right to complain or make a grievance if their pay is not the same as that of others who do comparable work. Jane Stewart had worked for a firm for three years. One lunch hour, when she was with a new employee who held a similar job to hers, she found that the new employee made several dollars a week more than she did. Ms. Stewart was astonished to find that the new employee worked the same hours, had a similar background, and less experience.

Personal harassment

Personal harassment, resulting from jealousies, vindictiveness, or lack of appreciation for work done, may result in a grievance. For instance, Beverly Burke had been the only secretary in an office for ten years. She prided herself on her speed and efficiency. However, she had been inundated with work recently. She did not complain, but the managers noticed that she was taking short lunch hours and working overtime to get the work done. Without consulting her, they hired a young, attractive high-school graduate to help. Jill Ember was eager to work, but she was careless. This carelessness annoyed Ms. Burke, who, on several occasions, left snide notes on Ms. Ember's desk about errors or work left undone that Ms. Burke had to complete. Although Ms. Ember was upset by the notes, she plunged ahead without changing her ways, but she was increasingly nervous when Ms. Burke was around.

One day, after Ms. Ember arrived home, she received a telephone call from Ms. Burke, who threatened to report her for failing to lock her desk when she left the office. Ms. Ember realized she had made an error, but she did not think that she should be abusively treated for it.

Sexual harassment

Although sexual harassment on the job is not new, it has become newsworthy of late both because more women are joining the job market and because the Civil Rights Act (see Chapter 14) gives a measure of protection to people who charge that they have been sexually harassed.

Sexual harassment is any unwelcome action by a co-worker or superior, ranging from a requirement to wear revealing clothing, as in the case of waitresses or hostesses, to comments related to sex, to unwanted embraces, or to a demand for sexual favors. Both men and women may be subject to sexual harassment, but most of the grievances and lawsuits that have occurred have been initiated by women. Some women have claimed that when sexual favors are denied, some bosses have sabotaged their work or even dismissed them. Studies of women at work have revealed that as many as 70 percent claim to have been sexually harassed at some point in their careers.[1]

For example, Ms. Malgren, recently divorced, was anxious to get a job. She considered herself very fortunate to be employed as a data processor in a large company, but she was surprised to find that she was the only woman in the department. All of her co-workers were helpful and treated her just as one of the team.

A supervisor from an adjacent department, however, treated her very differently. Every time he came into the data-processing office, he made a point of stopping at her desk, leaning over her, putting his arm across her shoulder, and making some comment such as, "How's the glamour girl today?" She attempted to ignore these gestures and comments, but she was annoyed by them.

One day he sat by her in the lunch room and made several offensive remarks. She moved away to sit with another group. When she left work, he was waiting for her. When she explained she did not want him to bother her, he remarked, "I carry a lot of clout around here with your supervisor and with the head office. I think you should be a little more cooperative with me."

Company policy manuals rarely include any statements about sexual harassment. It is difficult to prove, and claims that demotion, non-promotion, or dismissal resulted from resisting sexual advances are also hard to confirm.

If any such incident occurs, the employee should go first to the supervisor unless the supervisor is the one being accused. Once the supervisor is alerted, other measures may be taken to detail occurrences and to compile a file of evidence. Co-workers should also be enlisted to corroborate the incidents. If the supervisor is the offender, the employee should take the grievance to a personnel representative or to the supervisor's boss.

Hazardous working conditions

Defective electrical equipment, improperly lighted stairs, nails protruding from furniture or railings, and slippery floors are only some of the hazards that may be present in work or recreation areas. For example, a section of stairs, worn from years of use, had several deep dents on the steps. Employees were warned to be careful when using those stairs. One day, Jeff Stewart was carrying an armload of materials. The elevator was stuck on an upper floor, and so he decided to use the stairway. Halfway down, he stumbled on one of the dented parts. He fell to the bottom, injuring his arm as he landed.

Employees have a responsibility to report such dangers, and supervisors should be constantly alert for these threats to the safety of the work force.

Unjust demotion or discharge

The supervisor's perception of an employee's work may be different from that of the employee, resulting in what the employee perceives as an unjust demotion or dismissal. For example, Denise Boland thought that she was a superior employee. She worked very hard and fast and was an excellent organizer. However, she snooped into the work of the other employees, read their mail, looked through their files, and was openly contemptuous of the way they worked. She constantly reminded them that she did more and better work than they.

Somehow, she was almost always the first to answer the telephone, and even when the call was not for her, she would try to take care of the request. She rushed to open the mail so that she could see what came in for various workers, and then she acted as though she were their boss in distributing it. When the supervisor was not around, she was even more offensive to the other workers.

Tensions in the department grew. Ms. Boland was warned twice by the supervisor that her attitude toward the other employees was causing problems. Her reply was, "Then why don't they work the way I do?" The complaints about her grew, and she was finally dismissed with an extra two weeks of salary in lieu of notice.

Discrimination

Discrimination on the basis of age, religion, or race is another cause of grievances. For instance, Julio Diaz was the first Puerto Rican employed in a firm as a word-processing specialist. He noticed that his co-workers all went out to lunch together, but they never asked him to join. He tried to be particularly friendly, but except for superficial greetings, the others continued to ignore him. Aside from work-related encounters, Mr. Diaz was overlooked. Even the supervisor paid little or no attention to him and did not include him in meetings. Mr. Diaz became increasingly depressed over his isolation on the job.

A peer's unmerited promotion

Employees who work together daily usually know what their peers do, and they can compare their own productivity and work records with others' in the department. When someone who other employees believe is not deserving is promoted, a complaint or grievance may be lodged against the action.

For example, Mary Ellen and Louise worked in a public-relations office. Both of them served as aides to the director, Mr. Beckworth. Mary Ellen had been an aide for two years and Louise had been hired just a few months ago. Louise kept asking Mary Ellen for ideas about various public-relations campaigns, and Mary Ellen, wanting to help a new person to learn, was generous with her ideas and time.

One morning, Mary Ellen came in all agog with a new public-relations idea. Louise begged her to share the idea with her. Mary Ellen explained it in detail, saying that as soon as she could see the boss, she would suggest it to him. During the morning, Mary Ellen was busy with clients, and so she did not get in to see the boss. To her surprise, she saw Louise and the boss return from lunch together.

The boss called the office staff together and announced that Louise would be the new public-relations assistant director. Her new idea, he said, was sensational, and she was being promoted because of it. Later, Mary Ellen found it was her idea that Louise had claimed as her own.

Grievance procedures

A firm that has an enlightened personnel policy will also have an established *grievance procedure,* which is the formal, step-by-step process that an aggrieved employee may follow to air and resolve the grievance. Small firms usually try to resolve grievances by a face-to-face meeting with the supervisor. Large firms usually have a grievance procedure that is outlined in the company manual. If a firm has a union, a grievance procedure is developed and written as part of the union contract.

Grievance procedures usually state the following:

o *The need for ensuring fairness to all employees*

o *The role of the person's supervisor in the grievance procedure*

o *The hierarchy, in ascending order, to which the employee may go to resolve the grievance*—For example, if the grievance is about the supervisor and unless the matter is something that can be resolved between the supervisor and the employee, the employee may prefer to go to the supervisor's superior to resolve the problem. Sometimes the employee would rather talk with the personnel office representative before approaching either the supervisor or the supervisor's boss. Regardless of the person or persons with whom the grievance is discussed, confidentiality must be assured to the grievant. If a grievance is not resolved at the first level of the hierarchy, it may then be carried to the person next higher in rank.

o *The action to take if the grievance cannot be resolved*—The firm may have an impartial committee analyze and pass judgment as arbitrators. These committees may be established in many ways. In nonunionized firms, one or two supervisors from unrelated departments, a personnel representative, and an employee designated by the grievant may comprise the committee. Committees may also be composed of only personnel representatives and an employee designated by the grievant. The policy manual should detail the composition of the committee. In a unionized firm, the committee's composition will be designated in the union contract. It usually includes an equal number of union designees and organization designees plus an outside arbitrator. This committee hears both sides of the case, examines the evidence presented, and makes its final recommendation. This decision is binding upon both sides.

Usually, an appeal for arbitration must be in writing and

must be made within a specified number of days after the first official grievance.

o *The final recourse*—If the employee refuses to accept the arbitration decision, he or she always has the right to go to the courts for resolution of the matter. This, however, is a costly, time-consuming procedure.

Some firms, such as educational institutions, have an ombudsman (or ombudsperson), whose role is to hear grievances and to try to resolve them. This person usually intercedes before the steps outlined for a formal grievance are taken.

No one in a firm likes a complaint to become a formal grievance. The supervisor does not like it because it is a condemnation of the way he or she has handled the people or the situation that led to the grievance. The aggrieved employee does not like it because it means that some unsolved problem has been festering in his or her mind and that a number of appearances may have to be made in front of other people and an arbitration committee to resolve the grievance. Other employees and members of management do not like it because they may have to judge impartially the claims and counterclaims made by each side and be taken from their jobs while the grievance procedure is conducted.

However, in the interest of fair play, grievance procedures have been developed to ensure that an aggrieved employee has an opportunity to present his or her side of the case, has an impartial jury of peers and bosses to hear the grievance, receives the same treatment as other employees in the same situation, and knows to whom to go and what steps to take to get the grievance before the hearing bodies in the firm.

Grievance procedures in unionized organizations

Unions, discussed further in Chapter 15, were initially established because of employees' dissatisfactions with one or more conditions of work. Grievance procedures are, therefore, an important part of every union contract. In unionized firms, aggrieved employees may turn to the union representatives (sometimes called *shop stewards*) for their first appeal. In turn, the union representative discusses the problem with the supervisor. Thereafter, for unresolved grievances, specific steps are stipulated in the union contract. Union agreements end with binding arbitration as the final step. This procedure usually is performed by an arbitration panel or committee represented by a union official, a management executive, and an outside arbitrator. This outside member is agreed on by both sides, selected from a special list of arbitrators, and paid by both the union and the organization.

Table 13–1 summarizes nonunion and union grievance procedures.

TABLE 13–1
COMMONLY USED STEPS IN GRIEVANCE PROCEDURES
IN NONUNIONIZED AND UNIONIZED ORGANIZATIONS

Steps	People Involved at Each Stage		Approximate Resolution Percent*
	Nonunionized Organization	Unionized Organization	
First: Formal grievance submitted by employee.	Grievant Supervisor or personnel representative	Grievant Union representative Supervisor	75–90%
Second: Unresolved grievance goes to second stage.	Grievant Ombudsperson or supervisor's superordinate and/or head of personnel	Grievant Union representative Union head Supervisor's superordinate or head of personnel	9–20%
Third: Unresolved grievance goes to third stage.	Grievant Head of organization or specially designated person or group to hear difficult cases	Grievant Established grievance committee of union and management representatives Personnel head or industrial-relations head	1–4%
Fourth: Final step.	Grievant Special hearing committee with impartial representatives selected from both employee and management groups	Grievant Arbitration board with union-selected member and impartial member selected under rules of American Arbitration Association or Federal Mediation & Conciliation Service	0–.02%

*The fraction of a percent not settled may or may not become lawsuits. Figures range widely depending on the company involved and the way in which each grievance is handled. Supervisors try hard to resolve the grievance at the first step.

Source: Approximate percentage resolutions based on "The Antiunion Grievance Ploy," *Business Week*, February 12, 1979, pp. 117–20, and on author's experience.

Grievances that become lawsuits

As a result of the Civil Rights Act of 1964, some women, members of minority groups, and people who believed "reverse discrimination" needs to be redressed have filed lawsuits against employers. Large retroactive wage payments have been awarded to grievants when the courts found that the firms had not lived up entirely to the spirit of the law. Lawsuits over promotion, testing, and training policies have also increased dramatically in recent years.

To attempt to counter lawsuits like these, firms are developing personnel manuals and affirmative-action manuals that supervisors are required to follow. Courts are also tending to consider written personnel policies as contracts. If a firm fails to follow the policies, the courts see that as a reason for a grievant to win a suit.

Employees have also sued for libel, slander, and invasion of privacy. These suits have made employers more careful than ever about giving information about previous employment when references are requested. Such suits have also caused firms to avoid firing an employee "on the spot." Instead, firms are using a cooling-off period to ensure that the case is thoroughly investigated before the employee is dismissed.

The supervisor's role in the grievance procedure

A supervisor plays many roles in relation to the employees who report to him or her. In addition to assigner, trainer, motivator, evaluator, and discipliner, the supervisor is also an arbitrator, friend, counselor, adviser, judge, and listener. The supervisor is in the position to know most intimately the role the employee plays in the firm and how effectively his or her work is carried out.

An employee who has a grievance usually approaches the supervisor first. The supervisor, therefore, has important responsibilities in the grievance procedure. Most executives believe that the supervisor should be able to resolve problems that arise in his or her department and that these problems should not have to be handled by people above.

To achieve this goal, the supervisor needs to follow certain guidelines:

o *Maintain an open door*—An open door is one of the most desirable conditions for a supervisor to have. If the supervisor is too busy to see an employee, further frustration may set in, and what might have been an easily resolved problem may fester and grow out of proportion to its initial significance. When an employee wishes to talk to a supervisor, the supervisor should make every effort to see the worker promptly.

o *Listen attentively*—As discussed in the chapter on communication, attentive listening is especially important when an
employee has a problem to be discussed. The supervisor
should listen without interrupting except to state, "Let me be
sure I understand this point. You said . . ." By repeating
what the grievant said, the supervisor indicates both that the
idea was received and that it was understood.

o *Be prompt*—The supervisor's promptness in hearing and responding to a grievance is also essential. Once an employee
has lodged a formal complaint, some action should be taken
quickly to solve the matter. If a resolution cannot be accomplished speedily, the grievant should be kept informed that
the matter is under consideration and that it will be resolved
as soon as possible. If a grievance drags on interminably, a
more serious grievance may be filed or the discontent of the
aggrieved employee may spread to the other employees.

o *Maintain confidentiality*—The information imparted by the
grievant should be considered a dedicated trust by the supervisor. If the grievant finds that the supervisor cannot be en-
trusted with confidential material, he or she would never
again be willing to consult with the supervisor about important matters. This lack of trust would soon spread to other
employees.

o *Be objective*—In viewing the evidence presented, the supervisor must be impartial. If the supervisor sees the issue only
from the firm's point of view, the employee will be short-
changed. Keeping an open mind and seeing the evidence
from the employee's side as well as from the company's side
is a requisite for success in supervising people who have
problems.

o *Be fair and consistent*—*Fairness* means that all employees
are treated the same—no individuals or groups are favored
over others. *Consistency* refers to the meting out of the same
rewards or penalties for the same actions by different people.
If some people are treated better or worse than others, or if
some are rewarded more or are penalized more severely than
others, the bias of the supervisor will make future dealings
with other employees difficult.

o *Respond clearly and specifically*—Once an employee has
made known the problem over which the grievance has been
lodged, the supervisor must state specifically and clearly
what actions may result. The supervisor cannot equivocate in

such a matter. The grievant must know exactly what to expect as a result of the response of the supervisor. For example, Alice Long did not come to work the day after an official "snow day," when employees were allowed to be absent without penalty. The rule of the organization was that regular penalties were to be imposed for absence beyond the one day allowed. Alice explained to her supervisor that she could not get out of her street because of piled-up snow, but she was docked for the day's absence. The supervisor, in turn, had to explain that regardless of her reason, when the organization was open, she had had no choice but to be present or to be penalized.

o *Take all possible steps to solve the problem*—To save time, satisfy the employee, and spare the hierarchy of bosses the work of reviewing the grievance, the supervisor should, whenever possible, handle problems without passing them on to other executives in the firm.

o *Keep accurate, detailed records*—From the first counseling interview through all the steps of the grievance procedure, detailed, accurate records are a requisite. Initially, the supervisor is charged to keep accurate records of all infractions of rules by employees, of the discussions or reprimands given to employees, and of employees' responses. In grievance procedures, every meeting and every person involved should be noted with as many details as possible. If a grievance is not resolved within the firm and if a lawsuit is brought subsequently, all the records about the case must be available.

Changing attitudes toward discharging employees

In the early days of the entrepreneurs in this country, most businesses were owned by the people who started them. Employees could be fired for infractions of any rules, for irritating personal qualities, or just at the whim of the boss. As rules protecting workers became more prevalent, as professional managers replaced owners in the running of firms, as laws required firms to pay unemployment compensation based on the number of employees they discharged, and as organizations with union agreements became more prevalent, firing people, except for incompetence, serious behavioral problems that affected their work or that of other workers, or other just cause, has somewhat diminished. However, unjust dismissals still occur at all levels of some firms. The common law protects the right of the employer to fire a person without reason if no discrimination is involved. (This is discussed further in Chapter 14.)

Many firms that are large enough to absorb workers in other areas try to transfer those who cannot do one job into another less demanding area of work or to move disruptive employees to sections of the firm where they will have less opportunity to interfere with the work of others.

The government's intrusion into the hiring and firing of employees is further changing the rules in many enterprises. As firms with more enlightened policies monitor their own practices more carefully, and as the government makes penalties for noncompliance with the 1964 Civil Rights Act more severe, discharging employees without just cause will become increasingly difficult.

SUMMARY

o The supervisor's aim is to have a smoothly functioning work force. Conflict, however, sometimes arises in spite of good supervisory practices.

o Complaints are informal expressions of annoyance or discontent. Grievances are official written charges brought by an employee against someone in the organization.

o Grievances may be brought against an organization, a supervisor, or another employee because of broken promises, inequitable pay, personal or sexual harassment, hazardous working conditions, unjust demotion or discharge, discrimination, or unmerited promotion of peers.

o A grievance procedure is a formal, step-by-step process that an employee may follow to air and resolve a grievance.

o In unionized firms, union representatives, in addition to supervisory personnel, take part in the grievance procedure, and an impartial arbiter is jointly agreed upon for the final arbitration step.

o New laws have given employees an opportunity to sue for long-standing inequalities in pay and promotion.

o Supervisors play a vital role in employee relations. They need to maintain an open door, listen attentively, be prompt in taking care of problems, maintain confidentiality, be objective, be fair and consistent, respond clearly and specifically to complaints, take all possible steps to solve the problem when it first arises, and keep accurate and detailed records.

o As attitudes toward employees have changed, organizations have become more careful about their procedures for hiring and firing em-

ployees. Recent laws are particularly causing organizations to review
'carefully their methods of dealing with employees.

REFERENCES
[1]"Sexual Harassment Lands Companies in
Court," *Business Week*, October 1, 1979,
p. 120.

REVIEW AND DISCUSSION QUESTIONS

1. How do complaints differ from grievances?
2. What are the common reasons for grievances?
3. Why should a firm have formal procedures established for handling grievances?
4. What are the basic steps in a grievance procedure?
5. Why is the supervisor so important in the grievance procedure?
6. What is meant by maintaining an "open door"?
7. Why should the supervisor listen attentively to grievances?
8. What role does the supervisor's fairness play in the grievance procedure?
9. Why are detailed records necessary in grievance procedures?
10. What grievances have increased since the mid-1960s?

ASSIGNMENTS

1. In a personnel journal, find a complaint or grievance filed by an employee. What would you do to resolve the grievance if you were the supervisor? Write a report of your analysis.
2. Ask your friends and relatives about any complaints or grievances they have had at their place of work. Make a list of them. How serious are they? How difficult would they be to resolve? Write a report of your findings.

PROBLEM FOR RESOLUTION

Before January 1981, the basic pay for three beginning levels of employees in your section was as follows: level-5 employee—$3.20 per hour, level-6 employee—$3.35 per hour, level-7 employee—$3.60 per hour. Then, in January 1981, the minimum wage was raised to $3.35 per hour. Therefore, the newly employed level-5 people had to have $3.35 as the minimum—but that was the pay for temporary workers and students who worked on a part-time basis. Finally, the firm decided to give the level-5 employees $3.45 per hour.

To avoid a grievance, what adjustment, if any, would you suggest for the level-6 and the level-7 employees' base pay?

CASE STUDY

John Maggin was employed six months earlier in a social welfare office as a social worker. In the period of his employment, his work was acceptable. After he had been on the job for two months, however, he took unauthorized time off without calling the office. The company policy manual specified that employees who were ill or who planned to be absent from work for other reasons should call the office no later than the morning of the day they were to be out to report to their supervisor about the absence.

The supervisor rebuked John for being absent without reporting to the office and reminded him about the specific policy concerning absenteeism. Two months later, he was again absent without notifying the office. This time, he was warned in writing by the supervisor that repetition of this action would result in dismissal. The third offense on his part in another few weeks resulted in his dismissal for "frequent absences without excuse."

John filed a grievance. In it, he stated that he was not "frequently absent" as the notification had said and that he should have another chance.

If you were the supervisor, how would you reply to this grievance?

In your opinion, did John have sufficient warning about his behavior?

What other steps could the supervisor have taken before dismissing John?

FURTHER READING

"The Antiunion Grievance Ploy." *Business Week*, February 12, 1979, pp. 117–20.

Reports on procedures for settling grievances in nonunion companies.

Dullea, Georgia. "Female Workers Protest Scanty Uniforms." *New York Times*, June 30, 1980, p. B14.

Describes how employees claim sexual harassment results from the requirement to wear revealing clothes.

Hubbartt, William S. "Sexual Harassment: Coping with the Controversy." *Administrative Management*, August 1980, pp. 34–36.

Explains how unwelcome advances of a sexual nature that affect employment or interfere with a person's work are covered by Equal Employment Opportunity guidelines.

"A Productive Way to Vent Employee Gripes." *Business Week*, October 16, 1978, pp. 168–71.

Describes how surveys are used to let employees express opinions on such things as pay, benefits, recognition, and assignments, and how discussions that allow employees to understand the situation reduce complaints.

"Sexual Harassment Lands Companies in Court." *Business Week*, October 1, 1979, pp. 120–22.

Explains how Title VII of the Civil Rights Act has given people more opportunity to reject harassment and to use law courts for resolution of such actions.

supervisory
restraints

14

supervising within the bounds of federal laws

After studying and analyzing this chapter, you should be able to:

Differentiate between common law and civil law.

Detail the major emphases of laws pertaining to equal opportunity, federal insurance contributions, fair labor standards, equal pay, federal unemployment tax, age discrimination, occupational safety and health, consumer credit, fair credit reporting, rehabilitation, privacy, Vietnam-era veterans, and employee retirement income security.

Analyze the role of the supervisor in relation to the effective administration of the laws within a firm.

ANALYSIS OF THE enactment of federal laws in the United States reveals a constantly expanding awareness, beyond that of common law, of the basic rights granted under the Constitution. This awareness is particularly applicable to the fields of business, industry, and government, where enormous growth was sometimes accompanied by abuses in hiring, placement, promotion, transfer, pay, and discharge, based on race, religion, color, sex, age, national origin, or physical condition. As these cases have come to the attention of legislators, laws have been increasingly passed to ensure that all people have rights to jobs and that they are protected from discrimination.

In addition, legislation has been enacted to guarantee workers certain other rights that pertain to the workplace. Thus, today there are many laws that protect workers: the Civil Rights Acts (passed over a period of more than one hundred years), the Federal Insurance Contributions Act, the Fair Labor Standards Act, the Equal Pay Act, the Federal Unemployment Tax Act, the Age Discrimination in Employment Act, the Occupational Safety and Health Act, the Consumer Credit Protection Act, the Fair Credit Reporting Act, the Rehabilitation Act, the Privacy Act, the Vietnam Era Veterans Readjustment Assistance Act, and the Employee Retirement Income Security Act.

Because supervisors are involved with much of the work of employees, they need to know these laws, be able to explain their impact, and know what to do to ensure fair treatment of all employees (see Figure 14–1).

The heritage of common law

Originated in England and adopted by the American colonies, *common law* is based on accepted customs, usages, and traditions. Grounds for deciding cases brought into the courts are found in the precedents set by past decisions. Common law contrasts with *civil law,* which is based on statutes and prescribed texts. Common law makes the decision of the highest court in the jurisdiction binding on all other courts in that sphere of authority.

Common law provides for trial by jury. It also upholds the doctrine of supremacy of the law. This means that even government agencies and officials are subject to scrutiny in ordinary legal proceedings.

As the United States has grown, common law has failed to keep pace with social developments, necessitating the enactment of statutes to bring about needed changes. However, common law is still the basis of legal decisions that are not covered by other specific statutes. Under common law, employers have the right to dismiss an employee with or without a reason for doing so.

FIGURE 14–1

THE SUPERVISOR MUST OBSERVE AND EXPLAIN
THE MANY LAWS THAT AFFECT EMPLOYEES

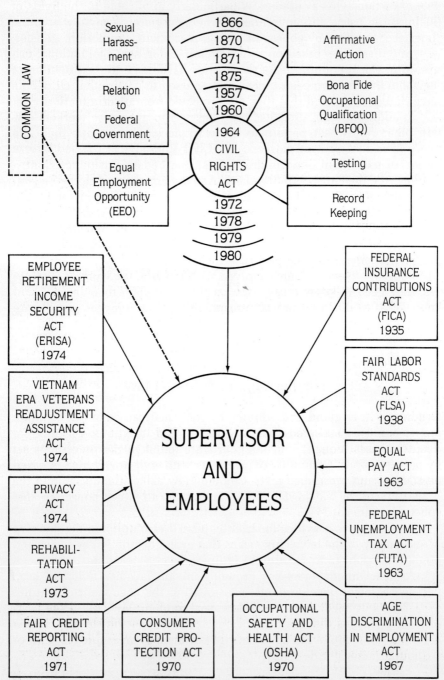

The civil rights acts

Although various legislation and rulings regarding discrimination had been in effect since 1866, the Civil Rights Act of 1964 was the most comprehensive. The first Civil Rights Act was passed in 1866, just after the Civil War. Subsequently, in 1870, 1871, and 1875, additional Civil Rights Acts were passed in an attempt to grant blacks political and legal equality to whites. These various acts gave blacks the rights to sue and be sued, give evidence, and own property. However, blacks did not gain equal rights to the use of public conveyances and public accommodations on the federal level until the Civil Rights Acts of 1957 and 1960 were enacted.

Passed during the presidency of Lyndon Johnson, the Civil Rights Act of 1964 prohibits discrimination for reason of color, race, religion, or national origin in public accommodations affected by interstate commerce, such as theaters, restaurants, hotels, and transportation. *Discrimination* is any practice that has or tends to have an unequal effect that is unfair or injurious to a person or a group of persons based on some factor characteristic of that person or group.

Title VII of this act specifically forbids any discrimination, including that based on sex, in employment by employers, public and private employment agencies, joint labor-management apprenticeship programs, and labor organizations. It applies to all employers who have fifteen or more employees. An *employee* is defined as one who, regardless of hours worked, is employed for twenty or more consecutive weeks.

In 1972, the equal employment opportunity guidelines were amended by stating that excluding applicants or employees from employment because of pregnancy, childbirth, or related medical conditions is a violation of Title VII. Pregnancy was to be treated as any other temporary disability.

That amendment, however, did not ensure that working women were protected against all forms of employment discrimination based on sex. A new amendment, passed in 1978, makes clear that distinctions based on pregnancy *per se* are violations of Title VII and states that women are to be treated the same as men for all employment-related purposes, including receipt of fringe benefits.

A further amendment in 1979 reinforced the requirement that benefits for men and for women must be equal.

Affirmative action

The Equal Employment Opportunity Commission (EEOC) was established by the Civil Rights Act of 1964 to monitor the legislation. Under the EEOC's guidelines, while all firms must practice nondiscrimination, only those firms that have government contracts are required to have affirmative-action programs. *Affirmative action* is defined by the EEOC as "those actions appropriate to overcome the effects of past or present practices, policies, or other barriers to equal employment opportunity."[1]

According to the EEOC, the essence of the affirmative-action program should be to:[2]

- o Establish strong company policy and commitment

- o Assign responsibility and authority for the program to a top company official

- o Analyze the present work force to identify jobs, departments, and units where minorities and females are underutilized

- o Set specific, measurable, attainable hiring and promotion goals, with target dates, in each area of underutilization

- o Make every manager and supervisor responsible and accountable for helping to meet these goals

- o Reevaluate job description and hiring criteria to assure that they reflect actual job needs

- o Find minorities and females who qualify or can become qualified to fill goals

- o Review and revise all employment procedures to assure that they do not have discriminatory effects and that they help attain goals

- o Focus on getting minorities and females into upward-mobility and relevant training pipelines to which they have not had previous access

- o Develop systems to monitor and measure progress regularly. If results are not satisfactory to meet goals, find out why and make necessary changes.

Thus, for every new person employed in a firm, the number of people who applied, the methods of announcing the opening, and the criteria for selection are analyzed to ensure that a firm that does business with the government is offering equal employment opportunity. Affirmative action is meant to encourage all employers to hire more women and minorities voluntarily.

No part of the 1964 Civil Rights Act requires firms to hire nonwhites or to give preferential treatment to nonwhites. The requirement is that equal opportunity be given to everyone. However, firms that have aggressive affirmative-action programs will take steps to seek out minority employees and to move them as rapidly as possible into management positions. These firms usually state their policy on application blanks and literature describing employment opportunities within the firm by saying "_____ is an Equal Opportunity Employer."

To establish affirmative-action programs, firms first analyze all phases of their business, including:

o Percentage of males and females in each category of employment

o Percentage of blacks and other minorities in each category of employment

o Age of employees in different levels of employment

o Skills needed by employees in different areas of the company

o Specific job titles within the company

o Educational achievement of employees in each category of employment

o Turnover in each specific job category within the company

o Number of "dead-end" jobs in the company and turnover in each

o Number of employees considered for promotional positions

With this information, companies are then able to develop policy statements that conform to equal employment opportunity legislation. Training sessions are then held to ensure that every section within the company has both management and nonmanagement employees who are aware of the equal employment opportunity policy.

Even the best affirmative-action plan, however, does not ensure equal access to jobs for women and minorities. Seniority rules in company policy and union guarantees of seniority often mean that when the number of employees is cut back, the newly hired are the first to be released. This leaves the firm with the initial imbalance among employees.

Bona fide occupational qualifications

The Civil Rights Act of 1964 prohibits discrimination in employment with regard to race, color, religion, sex, or national origin except where there is a *bona fide occupational qualification* (BFOQ), or an actual need based on the character of the job. Race, color, or national origin can never be a BFOQ. Religion may not be used as a job qualification unless the job entails work with a specific religious group. Sex may not be used unless the job specifically requires a male or a female, for example, a male model for men's clothes. Age may be a factor only when apprentice training needs to be given or when the job specifically requires a person of a certain age (for instance, when a young person is needed for modeling).

To ensure that no discrimination occurs, employment interview questions must be carefully restricted to those pertaining specifically to the job. The interviewer and the application form *may* request the following information: name, address, educational background (if pertinent to the job), previous work experience, health factors or conditions that would prevent a person from performing the job as required, convictions for crimes, references, and citizenship.

The interviewer and the application *may not* ask questions on age (except whether the applicant is under eighteen or over seventy), race, religion, birthplace, marital status, children, whether or not the applicant lives alone, habits (such as smoking or drinking), maiden name or alias, parents' names, arrest record, and names and addresses of relatives.

Testing for employment and/or promotion

According to Title VII of the Civil Rights Act of 1964, testing is permissible as long as the tests are not designed, intended, or used to discriminate on the basis of race, color, religion, sex, or national origin and as long as they are related to the jobs for which applicants are applying. The tests used must have been professionally developed so that they ask questions about the material intended, thus making them *valid*. Moreover, the tests must be tested against actual job performance, and test results must indicate those people who have a greater chance for success on the particular jobs under consideration.

One form of test used requires that the employee supply data pertaining to time employed on the job and is known as the *bio-data exam*. The applicant is asked for a self-rating on questions such as, "How fast do you work compared to other people?" and "How would your former employer rate your performance?" Applicants have been found to answer such questions with surprising frankness.[3]

Record keeping under title vii

The 1964 Civil Rights Act requires that records be kept completely and exactly to prove that lawful employee practices have been maintained. The government does not accept reports made from memory. Records must be kept for a minimum of three years.

For people who have been employed, certain questions may be asked only after hiring, and other data result from hiring: name, address, birth date, occupation, days worked each week, and hourly pay and/or weekly compensation are the data required to be kept about each employee. Organizations also need to know the person to notify in case of an emergency.

Moreover, tests administered, test results, applications, documentation of disciplinary actions, salary history from the day of present employment, and reason for termination must be recorded for all permanent employees who have been discharged. For people who apply for a job and are not employed, records must be kept to show why they were not hired. In addition to personal data, information about the job; the means of recruitment; and the policies, practices, and general benefits provided by the firm must be available.

In addition to records about initial employment, records must also be kept about training and advancement in pay and responsibilities. Documentation in these areas is required in case any employee charges the firm with discrimination. Performance appraisal forms should be kept on file and augmented by reports of incidents pertaining to each employee.

An *incident report* should include the name of the employee(s) concerned and of the person(s) making the report; the relationship of these people; the date of the report; the date and time of the incident; the names of all people involved in the incident; reference to any relevant policy, rule, or regulation; a description of what occurred; and a note of the action taken. Commendations as well as condemnations should be covered. Supervisors are responsible for incident reports.

Although a firm is restricted from asking any personal and possibly discriminatory questions before employing a person, after employment a firm must obtain data of a personal nature.

The firm's relationship to the federal government

The federal government offers advisory, investigative, and disciplinary services pertaining to the effective administration of equal employment opportunity in firms:

o *Advisory*—Interpretation of statutes, analysis and discussion of the implementation of equal employment opportunity, and recommendation of certain courses of action are among the advisory services offered.

o *Investigative*—For those firms that have government contracts, alleged violations, discriminatory acts, and biased procedures are investigated by the government.

o *Disciplinary*—If violations are found and not corrected, the government may reprimand a firm, fine a firm, or cancel government contracts.

Sexual harassment

The Equal Employment Opportunity Commission regulations on sexual harassment were issued on April 11, 1980. These apply to federal, state, and local government agencies and to private employers with fifteen or more employees, which have an affirmative duty to prevent and eliminate sexual harassment, which may be either physical or verbal. Sexual harassment, like harassment on the basis of race, religion, and national origin, is a violation of the Civil Rights Act.

The rulings state that harassment on the basis of sex is a violation of Section 703 of Title VII of the Civil Rights Act of 1964, as amended. It includes unwelcome sexual advances, requests for sexual favors, and other verbal or physical conduct of a sexual nature when:

- o Submission to such conduct is made, either explicitly or implicitly, a term or condition of an individual's employment.

- o Submission to or rejection of such conduct by an individual is used as the basis for employment decisions affecting the person.

- o Such conduct has the purpose or effect of substantially interfering with a person's work performance or creating an intimidating, hostile, or offensive working environment.

On January 13, 1981, the United States Court of Appeals for the District of Columbia ruled that "a woman could sue her employer to stop sexual harassment on the job without having to prove that she lost job benefits by resisting the harassment."[4] This ruling is considered by legal experts to be an important added protection against sex discrimination.

Both men and women are protected under the law, although the rules were issued mainly in response to concerns expressed by women. How extensive sexual harassment on jobs is has never been documented, mainly since employees are often reluctant to make formal complaints because they fear embarrassment or retaliation by employers.

Federal insurance contributions act

Known as the Social Security Act, the Federal Insurance Contributions Act (FICA) of 1935 mandates contributions by both the employer and the employee to the Social Security program. Originally, the law provided for retirement benefits only. Modified payments are given to retired workers from age sixty-two on. Full payments are given to retirees at age sixty-five. Restrictions are placed on the amount of additional money that may be earned until the retiree reaches age seventy-two, at which time all restrictions are lifted. In 1939, dependents and survivors of eligible workers became covered under the act, and in 1956 the system was expanded to include disabled workers.

Fair labor standards act

The Fair Labor Standards Act (FLSA) of 1938, also known as the Wage and Hour Law, provides for a forty-hour workweek for employees who work in firms that are engaged in interstate commerce, the payment of time-and-a-half for certain employees who work over forty hours in one week, and a minimum wage. The minimum wage increases at stated intervals. In 1979 it was $2.90 per hour; in 1980 it became $3.10; and in 1981 it became $3.35.

Exempt and nonexempt employees

With the federal government's provision for a minimum wage and with payment of overtime for certain employees who work beyond forty hours per week has come a need to specify which employees are exempt from those regulations and which are not. *Nonexempt employees* have few or no supervisory responsibilities; would, in general, be classified as "rank and file" employees; and must be paid overtime and the minimum wage or more.

Exempt employees are determined by several qualifications:

o They must supervise two or more employees.

o They may not spend more than 20 percent of their time (40 percent in a retail firm) performing the nonexempt work of those they supervise.

o Their work includes directing jobs to be done; setting and adjusting pay rates and hours; and interviewing, selecting, and training employees.

Exempt employees are paid a minimum weekly salary as specified by the Department of Labor. This is changed almost yearly, but at all times it is about twice the minimum hourly wage for nonexempt employees. Exempt employees are not entitled to overtime pay regardless of the number of hours they work.

Effects of the minimum wage

The minimum wage has been viewed in different ways by management and labor. While it sets a floor, it is not much above the poverty level.

For people who live at home or with other wage earners, the minimum wage may be sufficient. For those who have to maintain a household, it may not be.

In business firms, the minimum wage limits the market for extras and for students who want to earn money while still in school. Because the minimum wage applies to virtually all workers, firms are reluctant to employ unskilled workers or to offer any but the most essential employment. Moreover, young people also lose out to more mature employees because the same wage must be paid to each.

Furthermore, as the minimum wage is increased, the raise has a "ripple effect" on other wage scales. For example, an experienced person making $3.50 when the minimum wage for beginning workers is $3.35 expects an immediate raise when the minimum wage goes up. If production does not increase commensurately, the employer's costs skyrocket and prices for the same amount of product or service must be raised to pay for the increased costs. Thus, the minimum wage has been viewed by some people as being detrimental.

Companies whose products or services compete with those of foreign firms are also hurt by the minimum wage. Usually, foreign firms can hire workers for a fraction of the cost that companies in the United States can. U.S. workers are thrown out of jobs when our products cannot compete on a price basis with products manufactured in other countries. Those who object to the minimum wage maintain that if no minimum were set, less unemployment would exist among workers in the United States.

Equal pay act

Equal pay for employees who perform identical or equivalent tasks has been a subject of controversy since World War I, when large numbers of women were employed in the same jobs as men. The Equal Pay Act of 1963 makes discrimination in wage rates solely on the basis of sex illegal. Thus, men and women doing equal work must be paid the same. *Single-unit businesses* (firms in only one location) with an annual volume of $250,000 or more and *multiunit businesses* (those in two or more locations) with an annual volume of $1 million or more are covered by the law.

Equality of jobs is determined by equality of the following factors: skill, effort, responsibility, and working conditions. Different pay may be given for factors other than sex, however. Seniority pay, pay based on a merit system, shift differentials, incentive payments, and bonuses are all permitted as long as they are given in an equitable manner to all employees.

Federal unemployment tax act

Both the federal government, beginning in 1963, and the state governments, beginning before then, have collected taxes for unemployment insurance. To ensure that workers who have been fired will not be without funds during the period that they seek another job, each state imposes a tax on employers. The federal government also imposes a small tax that is used for the overall administration of the program. The federal law applies to all employers who employ at least four or more workers on at least one day in each of twenty different weeks during the year. Over 70 percent of workers are covered under state laws.

Age discrimination in employment act

The Age Discrimination in Employment Act was passed in 1967. It protects people above the age of forty, and as amended in 1979, to the age of seventy, against discrimination on the basis of age. This act prevents employers from specifying age as a requirement for employment and from using an above-forty age as a reason for nonpromotion unless age is a bona fide requirement for the job. Employers having twelve or more employees are affected by the act.

In addition to firms, labor unions and employment agencies may also not discriminate on the basis of age. Apprenticeship programs, for example, which are considered a continuation of a person's education, may be restricted to younger people. Advertisements that by the nature of their phrasing discriminate, however, may not be used. "Office boy," "gal Friday," and "junior clerk" are examples of terms that imply age discrimination and cannot be used.

Nothing in this law prevents physical fitness from being a requirement for a job or prevents a firm from setting age requirements for people under forty years of age. Airline flight attendants, for example, for years worked in that role until only age thirty-two. After that age, they were usually offered other employment within the firm, but that restriction is now being changed.

Firms that have generous pension arrangements with management employees may also mandate that these workers retire before they are seventy years old.

Occupational safety and health act

The Occupational Safety and Health Act (OSHA) was passed in 1970 to protect every working person in the nation from hazards in the workplace. Because few dangerous chemicals or machines exist in firms in which white-collar jobs are performed, this act has had only minimum impact on people in most such firms. However, certain aspects of the law are pertinent to all work sites.

According to the act, employees must be advised of any hazards in the workplace. For example, fire is a danger that firms work hard to avoid. Fire exits must be well marked, and fire drills must be held on occasion to check the effectiveness of the routine for evacuating a building.

Safety rules must also be specified. The rules must be designed to prevent safety violations, and they must be communicated to employees. Through observations, the firm must be able to check whether or not employees are violating safety rules. If violations are discovered, a procedure for enforcement of the rules must be established.

Other OSHA specifications that affect the white-collar worker apply to:

- o *Entrances, exits, stairways, and other walk and work areas—* These must be adequate in size and be safe for the use for which they are intended.

- o *Lighting levels*—These must be adequate for work and walkway areas, and *electrical connections* must be safe to use.

- o *Noise levels*—These are regulated at a maximum of ninety decibels for an eight-hour period. (One decibel is the lowest sound detectable by the human ear.) A noisy office usually registers about seventy decibels, while an average office registers about fifty decibels. Noise over eighty-five decibels can damage hearing if that noise level is sustained.[5]

- o *Work areas*—These must be uncluttered.

- o *Ventilation*—Adequate ventilation must be provided so that the air is free from contamination.

The supervisor must not only be familiar with the requirements of the OSHA legislation but also is responsible to see that the work area under his or her control is safe from hazards and is maintained in an adequate manner.

The term "hazardous" may be interpreted rather broadly. One woman claimed office tobacco smoke made her sick. She won her case, and the company was required to transfer her to a smoke-free working environment. If smoking is permitted in a work area, the supervisor needs to arrange for a smoke-free area for nonsmokers.

Consumer credit protection act

Through its Title III, the Consumer Credit Protection Act of 1970 protects a portion of an employee's pay from garnishment. *Garnishment is* a legal process that requires an organization to withhold part of an employee's wages or salary to pay debts owed by that employee to an outside individual or enterprise. Such legal action is usually taken only after persistent delay or refusal of the employee to repay those debts.

Only up to 25 percent of *disposable earnings* (earnings after tax withholding) can be garnisheed. Also, no one can be fired for having a salary garnisheed unless at least two separate garnishments have been made in one year.

Fair credit reporting act

The Fair Credit Reporting Act of 1971 regulates the methods of obtaining an applicant's credit bureau report. Through this act, people are ensured of adequate protection by the following requirements:

- o The person must receive prior notice that his or her record is being sought.
- o The person must be informed about what information is being requested.
- o The name and address of the reporting agency must be given to any person who is denied credit, insurance, or a job based on information in a report.
- o The person must have access to the agency, to the files the agency used in reporting on him or her, and to the names of the firms to whom the information was reported.
- o If any incorrect material is in the file, the agency must not only correct the data but must also supply the corrected information to any client who had previously received the incorrect data.
- o A job applicant who is denied a job solely on the basis of a credit report must be so advised.
- o In general, information becomes obsolete after seven years.

Rehabilitation act

The Rehabilitation Act of 1973 protects the hiring of handicapped persons if they can do a job. It applies, however, only to firms that get federal money. A few states have similar laws. For those firms affected by this act, affirmative action is required in the hiring of a handicapped person unless the handicap would interfere with job performance or would be dangerous.

Privacy act

The Privacy Act of 1974 further deters the collection and dissemination of personal information about employees, students, and other persons. Concern for the misuse of personal information gathered and maintained and the increasing use of masses of data about individuals kept in computer records caused the passage of this law. The right to privacy of individuals is fundamental under the Constitution. The Privacy Act permits any person to:

o Determine what records are collected, maintained, and used

o Prevent records' use for other than the particular purpose for which they were established

o Gain access to information that is pertinent to him or to her and to get copies of and, where incorrect, amend such records

o Keep such records up to date and to protect against their misuse

Exception to this act is permitted only for important public policy, such as security of the country. As a result of this act, many firms give no references and no employment data other than dates of employment. For example, if a former employee asked a firm to send a reference to a new employer, the firm might respond as follows: "Ms. Judith James was employed by us from 9–1–76 until 10–2–80." No further explanation would be included in order to prevent any claim of giving private information to others.

Vietnam era veterans readjustment assistance act

This act, passed in 1974, pertains to firms that have government contracts. It requires these firms to take affirmative action in the hiring of qualified veterans of the Vietnam conflict, including those who were disabled.

Employee retirement income security act

The Employee Retirement Income Security Act (ERISA) of 1974 provides greater security, mobility, and tax advantages for workers. Prior to the passage of this act, some employees who had worked for many years for organizations that provided pension benefits found, at the time of retirement, that they had no money in their pension account. For that reason, ERISA was enacted. It applies only to employers who offer pensions.

This act requires affected organizations to allow people who are twenty-five or more years old and who work one thousand or more hours a year to be covered by a pension after one year of service or after three years if the pension funds are fully vested. *Vested pension funds* are those that must be set aside by the organization and protected so that they will be available to the employee at the time of retirement. Vesting (protecting) the funds is done both on those funds the employee pays into the account and on those funds the employer pays into the account on behalf of the employee.

The law also requires employers to disclose fully information about the pension plan, including workers' accrued benefits. ERISA also affects any medical, disability, life and accident, retirement and savings, or thrift plans that a company provides by requiring that any promised services be available.

For employees who receive benefits, vesting is advantageous if they choose to change employment after, say, five, ten, or fifteen years of service. Even though their income from this work period may be small, upon retirement they will be able to draw retirement pay. Thus, people no longer have to remain with one employer until retirement to receive their money. ERISA also ensures some pension payment to retirees who worked for firms that have gone out of business.

The employee's right to accrued benefits derived from his or her own contribution is nonforfeitable, and after five years of service the employer's part of the pension plan is also partially to totally nonforfeitable. ERISA guarantees the nonforfeitable part of the employer's contribution to be as shown in Table 14–1.

The supervisor's responsibility

Laws are constraints upon those to whom the laws apply. Because the laws discussed in this chapter exist, firms must be familiar with them and must see that their supervisers know and abide by them. Supervisors in all types of occupations have a responsibility to work within the framework of these laws in all their dealings with employees. If a supervisor is proved guilty of breaking one or more of these laws, the firm is liable for conviction. Court cases are usually lengthy and costly, and firms attempt to inform all their employees of the law so that no infractions occur.

The economic welfare of individuals, communities, states, and the nation is closely tied to the activities of business and industry. If prejudice exists for any group of people, they become economically disadvantaged and this, in turn, affects all Americans. Only through equal

TABLE 14–1
EMPLOYEE'S YEARS OF SERVICE
RELATED TO RETIREMENT PAY

Years of Service	Nonforfeitable Percentage of Employer's Contribution to Pension
5	25%
6	30%
7	35%
8	40%
9	45%
10	50%
11	60%
12	70%
13	80%
14	90%
15	100%

opportunity in employment can everyone in the United States become part of the economic community that has enabled us to have the highest standard of living in the world.

SUMMARY

o Protective legislation in the United States has increasingly supplemented the common law that was used by the early colonists in this country. Common law is based on accepted customs, usages, and traditions.

o The first Civil Rights Act, in 1866, gave some measure of protection against discrimination to blacks. Additional Civil Rights Acts, passed from 1870 to 1960, increased that protection.

o The Civil Rights Act of 1964 erased all discrimination for reasons of color, race, religion, or national origin in public accommodations. Title VII of that act forbids discrimination, including that based on sex, in employment in firms employing fifteen or more workers. Additions, in 1972 and 1978, to the Civil Rights Act banned discrimination on a basis of the pregnancy of a woman.

o Affirmative action to overcome effects of unfair past employment practices and to move minority persons and women into jobs on an equitable basis is required of all enterprises that have government
  contracts.

o Bona fide occupational qualifications may be used to hire people on a
  basis of religion, sex, or age in certain specified occupations.

o Tests used for employment must specifically apply to the tasks to be
  performed.

o Records showing how the enterprise conforms to the mandates of the
  law regarding employees must be meticulously kept.

o Equal employment opportunity must be assured to all applicants and
  employees.

o The federal government offers advisory, investigative, and disciplinary services to ensure effective administration of the Civil Rights Act
  within firms.

o Elimination of sexual harassment in jobs was mandated in 1980.

o The Federal Insurance Contributions Act (FICA) established the Social
  Security system and mandates contributions from both employees and
  employers into a retirement system that pays retirees after age sixty-
  two.

o The Fair Labor Standards Act (FLSA) provides nonmanagerial (nonexempt) employees with a minimum wage and overtime for work beyond forty hours in one week.

o The Equal Pay Act makes discrimination in pay on the basis of sex
  illegal.

o The Federal Unemployment Tax Act (FUTA) provides support to the
  various states in collecting and distributing money for unemployed
  workers.

o The Age Discrimination in Employment Act protects employees between the ages of eighteen and seventy against discrimination on the
  basis of age.

o The Occupational Safety and Health Act (OSHA) protects employees
  from hazards in the workplace.

o The Consumer Credit Protection Act protects a portion of an employee's pay from being garnisheed and further protects that employee
  from being fired for having his or her salary garnisheed unless two
  such garnishment actions occur in one year.

o The Fair Credit Reporting Act protects the confidential credit reports of persons from being distributed to other persons or firms without permission, and requires that a person be told why credit, insurance, or a job has been denied.

o The Rehabilitation Act requires that jobs supported by federal funds be available under affirmative action to handicapped persons who are able to perform the job without being endangered.

o The Privacy Act further ensures the right to privacy of employees by permitting them access to files about them and the rights to amend incorrect records and prevent the use of the records for any purpose other than that for which they were obtained.

o The Vietnam Era Veterans Readjustment Assistance Act ensures non-discrimination in the hiring of qualified veterans of the Vietnam conflict, including those who were disabled.

o The Employee Retirement Income Security Act (ERISA) protects employees' rights to the pensions into which they have paid and/or into which employers have paid after specified intervals of time and at the point of retirement. It also permits employees, after a specified number of years, to change jobs without losing their pension rights.

o Supervisors are responsible for knowing the laws, upholding the laws, and informing their employees about their rights under the laws.

REFERENCES

[1]"EEOC Adopts Final Guidelines Covering Hiring," *Wall Street Journal*, December 12, 1978, p. 2.

[2]United States Equal Opportunity Commission, *Affirmative Action and Equal Employment*, Vol. 1, January 1974, p. 3.

[3]Lee Smith, "Equal Opportunity Rules Are Getting Tougher," *Fortune*, June 19, 1978, p. 156.

[4]"U.S. Appellate Court Hands Down a Key Ruling on Sex Harrassment," *New York Times*, January 14, 1981, p. A16.

[5]Jerome Gates, "Finding a Cure for the Noisy Office," *Office Products News*, May 16, 1975, p. 31.

REVIEW AND DISCUSSION QUESTIONS

1. What personal characteristics have laws against discrimination particularly sought to redress?
2. Which persons have benefited from the Civil Rights Acts of 1964 through 1980?
3. What is affirmative action?
4. What questions may be asked when a person is applying for a job? What questions may not be asked?
5. What additional questions need to be asked after employment?

6. What rules must be observed in using tests for employment or promotion?
7. How is equality of jobs determined in figuring equal pay?
8. In the same firm, what are the differences in work assignments for nonexempt and exempt employees?
9. How does OSHA affect people in white-collar jobs?
10. How is a worker's privacy protected when his or her records are sent to third parties who request such data?

ASSIGNMENTS

1. A small firm that did little hiring has just merged with a nearby firm. This action more than doubles the number of employees and the volume of business with which the small firm previously had to deal. Suddenly, the firm's management realizes that it is now subject to many more laws than it was before. You, as the supervisor, have been given a copy of the previously used application blank and have been asked to redo it in conformity with the present laws. What changes would you make?

EMPLOYMENT APPLICATION

Full name _____ Tel. No. _____

Address _____ ZIP Code _____

Educational Background: High School ___ Beyond High School _____

Are you: Single___ Engaged___ Married___ Widowed___ Divorced___ Separated___

Spouse's Name and Address _____

Spouse's Employer _____

Father's Name and Current Address _____

Mother's Maiden Name and Current Address _____

Do you smoke? ___ Drink? ___ Use drugs? ___

Have you ever been arrested? ___ If yes, give details: _____

Have you ever been convicted? ___ If yes, give details: _____

Religion _____

Personal References (two)

I certify the facts set forth in this application for employment are true.

_____
Signature

---

2. Visit a local jeweler or a bank to find out the law in your state pertaining to the use of polygraph tests, a means by which some employers check for honesty when hiring employees. Are these tests

used? If so, do they find the results helpful? Write a report of your findings.

PROBLEM FOR RESOLUTION

Fred Brown was the only black man working in an office with seven whites and one Chinese. The office rules required good attendance; frequent absenteeism was a reason for being dismissed. Mr. Brown had been absent from work on five different occasions over the past two months. The supervisor dismissed him from the job.

> Before terminating Mr. Brown for absenteeism, what facts about the policy of the firm should the supervisor check?

> What records would the supervisor have to have to support a charge of nondiscrimination for this dismissal?

CASE STUDY

Martin Bechman had just had his fifty-eighth birthday. He was hopeful that, at last, he would be promoted in the company for which he worked. His supervisor was taking a better job in another firm, and that would leave a vacancy that Mr. Bechman thought he was the most able to fill. His work records were excellent, and his ratings showed how efficiently he performed his job. He was a dedicated person, always coming to work on time and frequently being the last to leave. After twenty years on the job, he could see no reason for not being promoted. Whenever his supervisor had to be away, he relied on Mr. Bechman to handle all the problems. Mr. Bechman was the logical successor, therefore, to fill the supervisor's job.

When the day came for the announcement of the replacement, the job was given to Bennett Fodor, a man who had been in the department just two years and who was thirty-six years of age. Mr. Bechman knew Mr. Fodor's work records could not be as good as his. He knew that the firm's routines were not as well known by Mr. Fodor as they were by him. He decided to appeal the promotion.

> Under what law could Mr. Bechman appeal?

> What kinds of records would be needed to prove the case for or against Mr. Bechman?

> What reasons might the company have under the law for promoting someone other than Mr. Bechman to the position of supervisor?

FURTHER READING

Addlestone, David F., Susan Hewman, Fredric Gross. *The Rights of Veterans.* New York: Avon Books. 1978.
> Describes the rights of veterans under the various laws.

Antieau, Chester J. *Federal Civil Rights Acts: Civil Practice.* Rochester, N.Y.: Lawyers Co-operative Publishing Co., 1971.
> Analyzes the various Civil Rights Acts and decisions based on them through the courts.

Davis, John W., Esquire and Bern L. Gentry. *Affirmative Action Manual.* Tulsa, Okla.: Human Resource Consultants, 1977.
> Explains that affirmative-action programs include methods of implementation; responsibility; qualifications and selection; affirmative recruitment; pay policies; equal pay review, benefits, goals, and timetables; program dissemination; and grievance procedures. Includes forms and parts of the law.

Loomis, Carol J. "A.T.&T. in the Throes of 'Equal Employment.' " *Fortune,* January 15, 1979, pp. 44–57.
> Explains how the nation's biggest private employer has been forced to meet specified targets for hiring and promoting women and minorities.

Mood, Lester E. "Coping with Anti-Discrimination Laws." *Administrative Management,* July 1980, pp. 31–33+.
> Explains the variety of federal and state antidiscrimination laws and the ways in which actions are resolved.

Pear, Robert. "Sexual Harassment at Work Outlawed." *New York Times,* April 12, 1980, pp. 1, 20.
> Describes how employers have a duty to prevent and eliminate physical and verbal sexual harassment.

Priestland, Sue. "Association Salaries: Equal Pay for Equal Work?" *Association Management,* April 1979, pp. 42–47.
> Reports on evidence that shows women are paid less than men for the same jobs.

Schwartz, Lloyd. "Age Bias Persists Despite Raise in Retirement Age." *Supermarket News,* June 16, 1980, p. 17.
> Reports on 1978 Harris Poll that found that 87 percent of both working and retired persons agreed that mandatory retirement should be abolished, although employer bias against older workers persists.

Summers, Clyde W. "Protecting All Employees Against Unjust Dismissal." *Harvard Business Review,* January–February 1980, pp. 132–39.
> Explains how approximately 70 percent of the work force in the private sector has no contractual protections from arbitrary or unjust discharge and how a system should be set up to prevent discharge except for just cause.

15

supervising
the job-protected
employee

After studying and analyzing this chapter, you should be able to:

Define "union," and explain the role that laws have played in helping unions to develop and in restraining some of their power.

Differentiate among open shops, agency shops, union shops, and closed shops.

Trace the development of blue-collar and white-collar unions in the United States.

Define "civil service," and differentiate between the classified and the unclassified civil service.

Describe the legislation that has been enacted regarding civil service in the United States.

Define "tenure," and describe its development in the United States.

Detail the restraints put on the supervisor who works with job-protected employees.

WAYS OF PROTECTING employees' jobs have developed throughout the history of employment as workers have been exploited by some unscrupulous or unthinking bosses. Favoritism in hiring or promoting, firing without cause, dismissal with a change in management or to employ a less costly worker, overwork, unreasonable demands of employers, low pay, and unhealthy working conditions are among the problems that caused employees to agitate for job protection.

As discussed in Chapter 14, laws have given some defense against unfair employer practices. In addition, certain workers have been given job security through enlightened policies of their organizations or through unions, civil service, or tenure. These workers are *job protected*. That is, they have assurances that they will retain their jobs unless they perform acts that break the agreements under which they work, their unit of work is abolished, or their own specific job is eliminated. Even then, through a system of seniority, some job-protected employees may be able to "bump" others with less seniority out of jobs in other segments of the organization. In general, however, job protection means that the worker has security in the work force as long as his or her job continues to exist and the worker performs adequately.

Unions

Through unionization, employees have been retaining their jobs, improving their working conditions, and getting improved pay and fringe benefits for over two hundred years. *Unions* are voluntary associations of employees that are formed to maintain or further employees' rights and interests within the organizations for which these people work. Unions may be *independent* (organized for just the local group of workers they represent) or *national* (representing workers across the country).

Unions have officers who are responsible for running the union and for helping workers improve their working conditions. A union representative, known as a *union* or *shop steward*, is present in an organization to see that the union's agreements with management are kept and to help workers who have complaints or grievances against the employer. This person is also an employee of the enterprise.

Unions assess dues for membership, and in some cases, nonmembers also have to pay dues. Unions have several strategies for accomplishing their goals in bargaining with management. First, after determining what standards concerning employees they want management to agree to, union members may pursue formal bargaining sessions, institute slowdowns of the work force, call a strike if demands are not met, or boycott an organization so that outsiders will not do business with it. Two types of boycotts have been used by unions. *Primary boy-*

cotts deter employees and customers from dealing with the firm. *Secondary boycotts* attempt, through picketing, to have people withhold their business from suppliers to the firm or to keep retailers from selling the firm's products. The latter is now deemed to be an unfair labor practice.

Legal steps to deter or force certain actions of unions against employers or of employers against unions are known as *injunctions*. These are decrees issued by a court that, if negative, command the employer or union to refrain from committing certain actions or, if affirmative, that require them to perform certain actions.

Legislation about unionization

Legislation has alternately hampered and helped union activity. In general, legislation has followed the attitudes of Americans toward union activity. Through the years, strikes and boycotts have been severely limited by the belief of the courts that business interests represent property rights that cannot and should not be abridged by employees. These attitudes have changed somewhat in more recent times.

Lloyd-LaFollette Act.   Enacted in 1912, this law permitted federal postal employees to affiliate with national labor unions. It gave considerable stimulus to the movement for public-employee unionization. This law was enacted after the *American Federation of Labor*, a national organization of craft unions, did much work on behalf of federal employees.

Clayton Act.   Enacted in 1914, this act was hailed initially by many as the liberator of labor from restrictive rules. Under this act, labor unions were no longer subject to the *antitrust laws*, which had claimed that unions were guilty of restraint of trade. The act further provided that restraining orders or injunctions could not be granted by a federal court in cases involving labor disputes except when necessary to prevent injury to persons or property. It also prevented employers from terminating a person's employment because of peaceful or lawful union activity.

Railway Labor Act.   In 1926, this act provided for mediation and arbitration of wage disputes for railroad employees and required the railroads to recognize unions of workers and to bargain with them.

Federal Antiinjunction Act.   In 1932, this act, better known as the *Norris-LaGuardia Act*, strengthened the previously passed Clayton Act. The Norris-LaGuardia Act ensured workers full freedom to organize and power to designate representatives of their own choosing to negotiate terms and conditions of employment. It also ensured employees that employers could not interfere, restrain, or coerce them from their right to collective bargaining. This act outlawed *yellow-dog contracts*, which had previously been used to get workers to agree, when hired, that they would not join unions. Moreover, it ruled out injunctions against peaceful picketing.

National Labor Relations Act.   Better known as the *Wagner Act*, this act, in 1935, established a national labor policy and created a National Labor Relations Board (NLRB) to interpret and enforce labor laws. It gave workers in the private sector the rights to "self-organization; to form, join, or assist labor organizations; to bargain collectively through representatives of their own choosing; and to engage in concerted activities, for the purpose of collective bargaining or other mutual aid or protections."[1] It also prohibited employers from interfering with employees' union activities and from discriminating against employees who were union members. These actions were determined to be unfair labor practices.

As a result of the Wagner Act, labor unions grew rapidly and gained a great deal of power. However, that power needed to be balanced between labor and management.

Labor-Management Relations Act.   Also known as the *Taft-Hartley Act*, this act of 1947 helped to balance the power between labor and management. It still protected workers who wished to organize, prevented employers from discriminating against unionized employees, and required that both employers and unions bargain in good faith. However, it also designated certain union practices as unfair: *coercing employees* (trying to force them to join the union), *conducting secondary boycotts* (picketing against employers that merely carried products made by or who did business with other firms where strikes were in progress), charging excessive fees for membership, and *featherbedding* (requiring employers to pay for services not rendered). The Taft-Hartley Act also prohibited any strikes by workers employed by the United States or any of its agencies.

Except for garment industry workers, building trades employees, and longshoremen, the Taft-Hartley Act prohibited unions from requiring union membership of people being hired for jobs. It also included a *right-to-work section*, which enabled individual states to pass legislation that guaranteed workers who did not wish to belong to a union the right to work. The *dues checkoff* (the deduction of dues for the union by the employer from an employee's wages) was also declared illegal unless it was agreed to in writing by the employee.

Labor-Management Reporting and Disclosure Act.   In 1959, this act, also known as the *Landrum-Griffin Act*, was passed when the entire labor movement found itself on the defensive. Disclosures had been made regarding improper activities, such as *collusion* (cooperating to act in a fraudulent way), *extortion* (attempting to get money in an unlawful way), the use of violence, and the misuse of funds on the part of some labor leaders. As a result, this act was passed to correct abuses in the relations between labor union leaders, the employees they represented, and the managements of the firms with which they dealt.

The Landrum-Griffin Act required that union officers be elected by the members, that votes be taken on union matters, and that elections and votes be open to all union members. It also established guidelines for the handling and reporting of union funds. Moreover, this act required that a union report any loans it made to union officers in excess of $250 and all conflicts of interest by union officers in any business dealing they conducted when using union funds.

Executive Order 10988.   Issued by President Kennedy in 1962, this order extended collective-bargaining rights to government employees. Formerly, these rights had been given only to employees in the private sector, except for postal employees, by the Wagner Act. Although some government employees had joined unions previously, this new order encouraged increased unionization among government employees.

Types of union membership agreements

Union contracts include various standards for union membership in firms and industries. These are known as closed shops, union shops, agency shops, and open shops.

Closed shop.   This standard requires that only union members be hired and that only union members in good standing—those who have paid their dues and who have abided by union rules—be retained in their jobs. This type of shop was outlawed for all workers except garment industry employees, building trades employees, and longshoremen by the Taft-Hartley Act.

Union shop.   The union shop gives the union control over all the people hired in a firm after a specified period of time, usually thirty days. Management may hire any people it wishes, union or nonunion, but after a specified period of employment, all nonexempt workers must join the union and pay dues. If an employee quits before the specified grace period, he or she does not have to join the union. The grace period, therefore, allows a worker to find out whether or not the job is desirable and whether he or she is competent to handle it before joining the union and paying dues. States that have right-to-work laws do not permit union shops.

Agency shop.   This shop allows management to hire any employees it wants, and no employee is later required to join the union. All employ-

TABLE 15–1

CHARACTERISTICS OF UNION MEMBERSHIP AGREEMENTS

| Type of Shop | Membership in Union | | Payment of Dues | Voting Privileges |
	Before Employment	After Employment		
Closed shop	Nonexempt applicants must be members.	Nonexempt employees must be members in good standing.	All members	All members
Union shop	Nonexempt applicants may or may not be members.	Nonexempt employees must join after a specified period of time.	All members	All members
Agency shop	Nonexempt applicants may or may not be members.	Nonexempt employees may or may not join.	All nonexempt employees	Only members
Open shop	Nonexempt applicants may or may not be members.	Nonexempt employees may or may not join.	Only members	Only members

ees, however, are required to pay dues to the union, which gets benefits for all workers. Employees who are not union members cannot attend union meetings to express opinions or vote on issues taken up by the union.

Open shop.   The open shop gives management the right to hire any person it wishes, and employees have the option of joining or not joining the union. Employees who do not join do not have to pay dues. Union members dislike this type of shop because employees who are not union members get the same raises and other benefits as union members without paying their share of the costs of achieving those benefits.

Table 15–1 summarizes the characteristics of these various types of shops.

Development of blue-collar unions in the United States

The concept of unionization grew from the inability of individual workers to effect change in the workplace. By uniting in their efforts to improve working conditions, employees found greater strength against those managements that were reluctant to improve plants, equipment, hours or wages or to give fringe benefits.

Formal unions did not exist in the United States until the Industrial

Revolution. With the establishment of factories, many employer practices that penalized workers began to be noticed by the workers. Pay was withheld on the grounds that there were flaws in the finished product even though no flaws were present when it left the worker's station; workers were compelled to work many hours overtime with no additional compensation; hazardous conditions sometimes existed at the place of employment and no corrective steps were taken; rest periods were nonexistent; people could be fired at the whim of the employer; and fringe benefits were unheard-of luxuries.

By 1786, when the printer's union held the first recorded strike for higher wages, the union movement was beginning to grow. The printer's union was an example of a *craft union*, which represented all the workers in one trade, such as printers, carpenters, tailors, or weavers. Each group had its own organization representing the craft of all its workers.

Workers were not content, however, just to be in small, isolated groups. The first *labor federation*, the joining of different union groups, was founded in 1827. It was made up of local unions in Philadelphia and was known as the Mechanics Union of Trade Associations. It sought ten-hour days for workers; free, universal education; and the elimination of property qualifications for voters.

Nationalization of unions had its formal beginning in 1886 with the creation of the American Federation of Labor (AFL). Through this federation, the job security of the craft workers was sought by limiting the number of apprentices, avoiding the use of convict labor, refusing work to people who were not union members or ready to join the union, and setting minimum pay for certain jobs.

In 1890, the carpenters were the first union group to get the eight-hour day accepted. By 1909, the typographers had also won an eight-hour day.

Between 1910 and 1912, the labor unions were successful in getting the government to create the Department of Labor, a government agency that gave labor a much more important voice in the country than it had prior to the formation of the agency.

A song, written by Ralph Chaplin in 1915, became the anthem of the American labor movement. It was sung to the tune of *John Brown's Body* and explained the power of unionization:[2]

Verse:	When the union's inspiration through the worker's blood shall run,
	There can be no power greater anywhere beneath the sun.
	Yet what force on earth is weaker than the feeble strength of one?
	But the union makes us strong.

> *Chorus:* Solidarity forever! Solidarity forever!
> Solidarity forever! For the union makes us strong.

By 1920, five million people, primarily blue-collar workers, were in labor unions in the United States. This number diminished sharply during the Depression years that followed the stock market crash of 1929.

After 1933, legislation was passed that was favorable to unions and enabled them to attract many new members. John L. Lewis, a famous union leader, sought to organize workers within industries, as opposed to the craft union idea espoused by the AFL. Lewis established the Congress of Industrial Organizations (CIO) in 1935. The might of these two great federations was brought together in 1955, through a unification agreement, to form the AFL-CIO.

Development of white-collar unions in the United States

Although some unionization of white-collar workers occurred in the 1800s, most unionization of these workers has taken place since the 1960s.

Retailing employees. Retailing employees were the initiators of unionization in the white-collar fields. By 1882, the first of the Early Closing Societies, which sought to reduce the twelve-to-sixteen-hour days that retailing employees worked, was formed. In 1889, the Retail Clerks International Protective Association was founded. In 1947, its name was changed to the Retail Clerks International Association.

In June 1979, the Retail Clerks International Association, which had 735,000 members, joined with the Amalgamated Meat Cutters and Butcher Workers, which had 520,000 members, to make the largest union in the AFL-CIO, the United Food & Commercial Workers International Union.

Unionization in retailing has occurred mainly in large department stores in urban centers, where unions have successfully organized other industries, and in large supermarket chains, where employees have to work hard at jobs with only modest hope of future promotion.

Government employees. In 1888, the postal workers union, one of the first of the government employees' unions to be formed, brought about the passage of the so-called eight-hour law for government workers. Other craft workers' groups also began to form unions of government workers.

In 1896, the National Civil Service Association, a labor-oriented employee group, was formed, but it did not last. After passage of the Lloyd-LaFollette Act in 1912, white-collar government clerks joined with employees of the Bureau of Printing & Engraving to form a federal employees' union. Thereafter, seventy similar groups joined forces to form, in 1917, the National Federation of Federal Employees (NFFE). This national group was part of the AFL. A later split in the ranks of the NFFE, however, resulted in some units' withdrawing from the AFL. Therefore, in 1932, the AFL chartered a new union group, the American Federation of Government Employees (AFGE). The NFFE continued as an independent union.

The greatest growth in unionization in government agencies developed at the local level. In 1936, the AFL chartered the American Federation of State, County, and Municipal Employees (AFSCME). As of 1980, it had approximately one million members, of whom approximately 300,000 were white-collar workers.

Teachers.   Teachers also have sought the protection of unions or of associations that provide union services. The American Federation of Teachers, an affiliate of the AFL, was organized in 1916. By 1920, it had a membership of almost three thousand teachers. Today, the United Federation of Teachers (UFT), an affiliate of the AFL-CIO, has members from all levels and from educational institutions across the country. The National Education Association (NEA) enrolls elementary- and high-school teachers, and the American Association of University Professors (AAUP) has a membership of college and university faculty from both public and private colleges and universities. Unionization in private colleges and universities was slowed in 1980 by a ruling of the National Labor Relations Board that acknowledged that professors took part in the decision-making process and, therefore, were ineligible to unionize.

Office employees.   Unionization of office employees, other than those in government, has been less successful than that of workers in any other white-collar field. Moreover, those white-collar workers who have joined unions usually work in organizations in which unions exist for the blue-collar workers, such as factories. For example, railroad employees have a union, and those who work in the offices of the railroads also belong to a union, known as the Railroad Clerks Union.

By 1960, about 6 percent of two thousand large firms had office workers' unions. These represented approximately 13 percent of clerical workers. About 20 percent of clerical workers were unionized as of 1975.

The Office and Professional Employees International Union was started in 1945. It later became an affiliate of the AFL-CIO. As of 1980, it had approximately 125,000 members. The members of this union are mainly white-collar workers in private industry and include clerical and professional members, such as engineers.

By 1980, of the approximately fifty million people in the white-collar work force of the country, only six million were in unions.

Attitudes toward unionization

Traditionally, most enterprises have preferred to employ nonunionized workers. Many firms believe that a nonunionized work force gives them more freedom to hire, fire, promote, and award merit raises. However, federal and state laws concerning civil rights, equal opportunity, unemployment compensation, and minimum wages have made management's role less and less comprehensive in these areas. To work effectively with subordinates, supervisors today must be aware of the rights of employees as well as the rights of management.

Analysis of why employees sometimes seek unionization of their firms also helps supervisors work more effectively with employees:

- o Large firms often lose the personal touch with employees, who then turn to unions so that they have someone to listen to their problems and to consult about their special concerns.

- o Unions are quite persuasive in marketing their services to employees, especially if other workers in the company are unionized or if the company is located in an area of great union activity.

- o Some firms are slow to meet their competitors' salary increases or to adapt to the salary standards for comparable work.

- o Some firms are reluctant to provide generous fringe benefits.

In spite of the pressure that may be exerted on white-collar employees to join a union, many resist such persuasion because:

- o They still associate unionization with blue-collar jobs.

- o Women in white-collar jobs, until the recent decade, were little interested in unionization. Many worked either for short periods of time or held part-time jobs, neither of which were affected by unionization.

- o Those who work closely with management, such as secretaries, tellers, accounting employees, and salespeople, do not usually identify themselves as unionizers.

- o People seeking to be promoted into the ranks of management are rarely concerned about joining unions.

- o Many firms have neutralized the advantages of belonging to a union by improving salaries, fringe benefits, and working

conditions for white-collar workers to match blue-collar
workers' gains.

Supervisors in firms that are not unionized may help to avoid
unionization of employees by:

o Making sure that treatment of employees is fair and that
  working conditions are good

o Checking salary and fringe-benefit policies to make sure that
  they are fair and equitable with those for comparable work in
  other firms

o Being interested in employees, encouraging them to participate in decision making, and showing appreciation for their
  work

Supervisors in firms that are unionized will help to avoid job actions by:

o Consulting the union steward or union representative whenever an employee is not doing a job properly

o Consulting the union steward when an employee has complaints about some facet of the job

o Being familiar with the union contract so that they know
  what their rights are

Civil service

To be in the *civil service* of a country means to be employed in government work. Therefore, everyone who is elected, appointed, or assigned
to a government post is in the civil service of his or her country.

The term "civil service" also has another, more definitive meaning.
In this second meaning, it refers to just those employees who are permanently assigned to their jobs and who have attained those jobs
through special examinations and/or credentials. These two categories of
government employees are in either the unclassified service or the classified service. The *unclassified civil service* includes all the elected and
appointed government workers, such as the president, vice-president,
cabinet officers, congresspersons, other heads of departments, and some
of their staffs. The *classified civil service* includes those government employees who are job protected by having attained their jobs through the
special testing procedures established under the various civil-service
acts and who retain their jobs irrespective of the political party in power.

The classified civil service grew out of the *spoils system,* which was the practice of regarding all government positions as available for newly elected officers to assign to the people who had helped them to get elected. This practice so disrupted the work of the government every time a new election was held that laws were eventually passed to prevent this wholesale reassignment of persons to jobs.

Within the classified civil service, workers are assigned to jobs according to *grade levels.* Each grade has a range of salary and specific qualifications that have been established as essential to perform the work in that grade.

Legislation about civil service

As noted, the shift after each election in all federal jobs came to be viewed as disruptive of government work. Gradually, some people were retained in their jobs even though a new administration had come into power. Congress's concern for more government efficiency resulted in the Senate's request, in 1851, that cabinet officers submit their recommendations about testing, promotion, classification, and pay of clerks in the federal government. By 1853, Congress required that applicants for clerical positions in the government pass examinations before being employed. Also in 1853, Congress instructed the directors of every department except the Department of State to categorize their clerical employees in four grades according to their duties. Subsequently, salary ranges and duties were set for these four grades.

The most complete sweep of government employees from their jobs occurred in President Lincoln's first term (1861–1865). During his second term (1865), however, he refused to remove people. This decision signaled the decline in the spoils system.

President Grant pressed for civil-service reform before his first inauguration, in 1868. In 1870, he requested civil-service legislation. In a rider to another bill, the president was authorized to prescribe rules and regulations for the admission of people to the classified civil service. The purpose of this reform was to promote efficiency and to ascertain the fitness of each person with respect to age, health, character, knowledge, and ability to do the job that he or she was seeking. In 1871, President Grant, in an attempt to devise an equitable system, appointed a Civil Service Commission, composed of seven people. Although two years later Congress refused to renew the small appropriation for the commission and it ceased operations, it had laid down procedures and devised terminology that are in use to this day.

The separation of government employees from party politics had been developing as the spoils system declined. In 1877, President Hayes issued an executive order stating that federal officers should be neither required nor permitted to take part actively in politics.

The public, through the years, had become increasingly aware of the inefficiency of government workers under the spoils system and had clamored for reform. President Garfield took on the cause of the reformers. He was, however, constantly harassed by office seekers, and a disappointed one, Charles J. Guiteau, shot Garfield on July 2, 1881.

Civil Service Reform Act of 1883.   Better known as the *Pendleton Act*, this act was overwhelmingly passed after Garfield's death in September 1881. It created a new Civil Service Commission on a firm basis to oversee the act. It also had provisions to neutralize the effects of the spoils system. This law established the classified civil service of people under the merit system. This meant that employees, other than those who were elected or appointed, were selected and promoted on an objective basis using specified criteria and were assigned to salary groups or classes.

President Harrison extended the classified civil service to include more positions. By the end of President Cleveland's second administration (1896), civil-service reform was a reality and the merit system had been effectively established.

The Civil Service Commission supervised the administration of civil-service examinations for entrance to the classified service. These included tests of general intelligence and special skills. The early examinations required that people be able to write a correct letter; do arithmetic; demonstrate ability in bookkeeping, accounting, orthography (spelling), syntax (sentence structure), history, and geography; and answer questions about government. The commission also developed special examinations for particular positions. Women, blacks, and other minorities were increasingly brought into the civil service through this merit system. By 1911, 75 percent of federal employees were in the classified civil service, and 70 percent of those were under the merit system.

Under President Theodore Roosevelt, the concept of personnel administration emerged. A full study of the economy and efficiency of the civil service was started in 1911. This study recommended amending the civil-service law to broaden its scope. The executive branch was subsequently given a bureau of personnel in charge of examinations, certification, efficiency records, classification of positions, inspections, arbitration of disputes, and representation of the interests of individuals.

Classification Act of 1923.   The federal government had long applied the principle of "rate for the job" to its own employees. The Classification Act of 1923 established a uniform salary range for each of fifteen grades of work regardless of the sex of the workers.

Hatch Acts.   The Hatch Act of 1939 prohibited nearly all federal employees from using their official authority or influence for the purpose of interfering with an election or affecting the results of one. The Hatch Act of 1940 extended the prohibitions against political activity to state and local employees who were paid in full or in part by federal funds. This act does permit expressions of opinion and voting but forbids partisan political activity.

Ramspeck Act.   In 1940, this act authorized the president to extend the merit system rules to nearly two hundred thousand positions previously exempted. It also required federal employees to pass noncompetitive tests before they received permanent status in the public service. By 1940, the civil-service system was virtually completely centralized. By 1947, the percentage of people in the service within the continental United States who were under the merit system exceeded 92 percent.

Veterans Preference Act.   In 1944, this act required that the person chosen for a job in the civil service be from among the top three in rank on the examination for a position. It further required that five points for able veterans or ten points for disabled veterans be added to the overall scores of honorably discharged veterans who took the examinations. An agency of the government may not appoint a nonveteran from among the three top applicants if one of them is a qualified veteran.

Classification Act of 1949.   This law replaced the 1923 act and created three new top grades—16, 17, and 18—known to most as "supergrades." These new grades also carried higher rates of pay than any previously authorized. Congress kept control over them by placing a ceiling of four hundred such jobs that could be established. No ceilings exist for grades of 15 and below. In 1962, Congress lifted the ceiling for appointments of people to research and science positions but retained it for other categories.

Public Law 330.   Some of the laws concerning unionization applied to government employees. Enacted in 1955, Public Law 330 specifically prevented federal employees from participating in any strike or asserting the right to strike against the government.

Executive Order 10577.   Under this order, effective in 1955, nonelected (appointed) job holders were categorized as indefinite, career-conditional, or career. The *indefinite* category included people who had been hired for temporary positions or who had not yet taken the competitive examination for the position held. *Career-conditional* employees were those who had qualified for the position but had served for less than three years and, therefore, had not yet become permanent employees. *Career* employees were those who had served for three or more years and who enjoyed all the rights and privileges of permanent and continuing employment with the right, if their job was discontinued, to have the first chance for jobs in other agencies for which they were qualified.

New Careers Program. By 1960, civil service was being challenged by community groups that believed that the entrance requirements and examinations discriminated against minority-group candidates. The New Careers Program of 1966 offered jobs, training, and remedial education to disadvantaged people so that they would have a career ladder into civil-service jobs or be trained for better jobs in special programs. No civil-service standards, however, were changed.

Griggs v. Duke Power Company. In 1971, in the precedent-setting case of *Griggs v. Duke Power Company,* the U.S. Supreme Court ruled that job applicants must be rated on the basis of skills related to job performance. Title VII of the Civil Rights Act of 1964 placed the burden of showing the relationship of job requirements to the job on the employer.

Testing as a whole came under serious scrutiny. Were the tests really valid for the positions, or were they being used to eliminate some groups of applicants? The civil-service system was initially designed to provide security for employees, who had been carefully selected for their jobs. However, the standards that had been developed appeared subsequently not to meet the changing needs of society.

The Equal Employment Opportunity Commission stated that there was "a decided increase in total test usage and a marked increase in doubtful testing practices which, based on our experience, tend to have discriminatory effects. In many cases . . . candidates are selected or rejected on the basis of a single test score. Where tests are used, minority candidates frequently experience disproportionately high rates of rejection."[3]

In 1981, members of minority groups charged that the Professional and Administrative Career Examination (PACE), a test used to screen applicants for 118 separate white-collar jobs, discriminated against blacks and Hispanic Americans. "Over the last two years, 42 percent of the whites who took the examination passed it, compared with 13 percent of the Hispanic Americans and 5 percent of the blacks."[4] This dispute was resolved in the challengers' favor. Under the settlement, tests keyed specifically to each of the 118 job classifications skills will be developed.

Civil Service Reform Act of 1978. This act established an Office of Personnel Management to develop plans for the merit pay and promotions that had been approved by Congress.

A survey among federal civil-service workers in 1979 revealed that most of them were satisfied with their jobs. However, 56 percent of them thought that their getting a promotion or a raise based on merit was unlikely. The Office of Personnel Management is charged with analyzing the replies from fourteen thousand persons out of the twenty thousand who were mailed questionnaires.

Civil service in state, county, and municipal governments

Governments in states, counties, and cities usually use standards similar to those of the federal government's for their positions. Therefore, civil service dominates the field of public hiring throughout the nation. By the early 1970s, approximately 80 percent of nonfederal government employees were covered by some form of job-protected civil service.

Because government employees may also join unions, many have double job protection given by both the civil service rules and the union contracts.

Supervising government employees under civil service

Supervisors of job-protected civil-service workers may have attained their own positions in one of three ways. They may have:

o Been elected to the position by their constituents

o Been appointed to the position

o Taken a competitive examination or been promoted within the civil service

Regardless of the means by which supervisors have attained their job, many of the employees who are to be supervised will be career civil-service employees with job protection. Usually appointed and elected officials serve somewhat limited terms, while career civil-service employees have continuous service in an agency. Thus, the elected or appointed supervisor may know less about the running of the agency or department than the employees who are being supervised. The elected or appointed supervisor, therefore, needs time to learn the routines and thus cannot always immediately establish the standards believed to be most desirable for attaining maximum productivity. Employees who have stabilized their routines are often less willing to change than those who have not been doing the job for a considerable period of time.

This limitation on the supervisors requires that they exhibit both tact and patience while adjusting to the system that has been in use. After the supervisors have mastered the many facets of their jobs, they must evolve creative ways of energizing the workers, encouraging self-motivation, determining ways to get employees to accept change, and figuring how to develop new and better ways for employees to perform their jobs.

Tenure

Other job-protected employees are those who have tenure. Tenure is job protection granted to an employee who has met hiring standards and served satisfactorily in a position for a specified number of years (usually between three and seven). Employees with tenure have job security and cannot be released unless their job ceases to exist, they develop a disability that prevents them from performing their job, or they are guilty of gross misconduct. Tenure is most common among school-system teachers and college and university professors.

The concept of organizing to get tenure grew slowly. In the colonial period, teachers usually didn't think that they were a group with common professional concerns and problems. Therefore, they did not have professional organizations.

By 1857, the National Teachers Association had been founded. This association joined with other groups and in 1870 they became the National Educational Association. This organization lobbied for tenure, stating that "only when teaching offered salaries and security commensurate with other professions would men of strong capability be attracted to it."[5] Teachers argued that tenure would free them of political pressures from the community and would give them the security to help make teaching their life's work. These expressions of opinion laid the groundwork for the institution of tenure.

The American Association of University Professors, formed in 1915 to defend faculty rights, supported the idea of granting tenure after a probationary period. It also fought for academic freedom for college teachers.

By 1918, seven states and the District of Columbia had provided for tenure as long as good service and behavior were offered. Finally, by 1951, the National Education Association formed a Committee on Tenure and Academic Freedom.

Although attacks were made on the tenure system during the 1970s, tenure is part of the agreement with teachers in most public schools and public and private colleges in the nation. Schools and colleges that do not grant tenure may instead offer teachers contracts for a period of three to five years. These contracts are renewed at the pleasure of the board of trustees or the school board if the service has been satisfactory. However, teachers have no guarantee of contract renewal.

The supervisor's relationship to the job-protected employee

Civil service, unions, and tenure are ways of protecting workers' jobs. Unions strive for better salaries, increased fringe benefits, shorter working hours, more holidays, and seniority in hiring and retaining employees. Civil service stands for job classification, hiring and promotion standards, and job security based on seniority and level of position. Tenure stands mainly for security of job after a given period of satisfactory employment. Because no system offers all the security and advantages that workers seek, some civil-service and tenured employees have also joined unions (see Figure 15–1).

Whatever form it takes, job protection affects employees in different ways. Some view job security as only an assurance of a steady job, and they continue to work as hard as ever to achieve and excel in their work. Others relax and do only the minimum needed to remain on the job.

Because some teachers who have tenure do only what is needed to hold their jobs, many school districts have agitated to have tenure eliminated. Similarly, because some civil servants and unionized employees have taken advantage of their job protection to do only the minimum work required, some people believe that the protective systems themselves are at fault. The history of these movements, however, proves the need that workers have for job protection.

Supervisors have the same relationship to job-protected employees as to any other employees except for the one right of dismissal. Job-protected employees may be dismissed for cause, but the causes for dismissal are specifically stated in the employment agreement and must be proved by evidence.

Because supervisors have little control over the productivity of job-protected workers who choose to do just the minimum required to hold the job, they have a challenge to help job-protected workers put forth their best efforts. One method of helping workers be more productive is to give merit raises based on performance evaluations.

In 1979, the New York State Civil Service Employees Association, for example, proposed a four-category system of rating: "outstanding," "highly effective," "satisfactory," and "needs substantial improvement." Employees who maintained an "outstanding" rating would get a $300 bonus above the regular raise given all workers. If any bonus money was left over, it would be awarded to those in the "highly effective" category. Both state and union officials hope that the modified merit system will improve employee morale and productivity.

Some supervisors have found that letting job-protected workers participate in decision making helps to motivate them to put forth their best efforts to increase productivity or to improve the quality of the product or service provided.

FIGURE 15–1
TYPES OF JOB PROTECTION

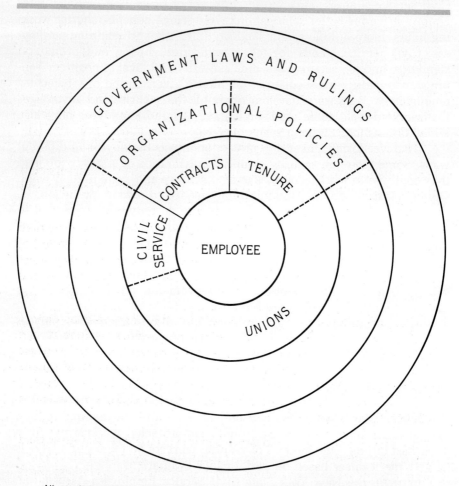

All employees have some measure of protection under government laws and rulings.

All employees have some measure of protection under the organizational policies of enterprises.

Civil service gives some measure of protection to government workers.

Tenure gives some measure of protection to teachers, as granted under organizational policy.

Contracts give a limited-time protection to persons working under them. They are granted under organizational policy.

Unions give certain types of job protection and other advantages to their members. Civil-service, contract, and tenured employees may also seek the added protection of unions.

SUMMARY

o Job protection means that employees have security in the work force as long as the job they hold continues to exist and they perform adequately. Job protection comes from company policy, unions, civil service, and/or tenure.

o Unions are voluntary associations of employees formed to further workers' rights and interests. A union representative in a firm oversees the complaints or grievances of employees and checks the compliance of management to the demands of the union contract.

o Government legislation has both spurred the growth of unionization and restrained unfair labor practices on the part of management and labor unions.

o Union contracts call for either closed shops (only union members may be hired), union shops (employees must join after a certain period of employment), agency shops (nonmembers may work but they must pay dues), or open shops (nonmembers may work without paying dues).

o Blue-collar unions were established with the beginning of factory work in the United States. Craft unions represented workers in one trade, while industrial unions represented workers in organizations regardless of their individual skill or craft. Nationalization of unions began in 1886 with the formation of the American Federation of Labor (AFL), which joined with the Congress of Industrial Organizations (CIO) in 1955 to form the AFL-CIO.

o White-collar unions were slower to become established and grow than blue-collar unions. Since 1960, government workers and teachers have greatly swelled the ranks of white-collar union workers. Both employers and employees have positive and negative views of unionization for white-collar workers.

o Civil service refers to all persons who work for the government. Job-protected civil-service workers are employed under the classified section of the civil service. They attain their jobs through examinations and/or special qualifications, and they gain permanency in their jobs after a specified period of time.

o In 1883, the first legislation was passed that gave some job protection to government employees. Since then, various laws and rulings that further defined the role of the civil service have been enacted.

o Federal, state, county, and municipal governments all have standards of job protection for classified civil-service workers.

o Tenure, another form of job protection, usually found in the teaching profession, ensures a competent teacher a job after a given period of trial employment, usually three to seven years. Tenure does not set salary standards or provide fringe benefits.

o Unionization is often sought by tenured and civil-service employees to gain advantages not otherwise available. Thus, seniority rights, wage or salary increases, and fringe benefits may not be included in the other job-security rights employees have.

o Supervisors of job-protected employees are restricted in dismissing employees, but they may employ a number of methods to encourage employees to be more productive on their jobs.

REFERENCES

[1] *Congressional Record Proceedings and Debates*, February 21, 1935 to March 12, 1935, p. 2369.

[2] Edith Fowke and Joe Glazer, *Songs of Work and Freedom* (Garden City, N.Y.: Doubleday, 1961), p. 13.

[3] *Equal Employment Opportunity Commission Guidelines*, Section 1607.1(b).

[4] David E. Rosenbaum, "U.S. Set to Replace a Civil Service Test," *New York Times*, January 10, 1981, p. 16.

[5] Ida B. Haslop, "How May a Professional Spirit Be Acquired by the Secondary Teachers of America," *National Education Association Proceedings*, 1894, pp. 758–64.

REVIEW AND DISCUSSION QUESTIONS

1. What categories of employees have job protection?
2. How have the National Labor Relations Act and Executive Order 10988 affected unionization?
3. What are the benefits of unionization to the worker? What are the disadvantages of unionization to the worker?
4. Differentiate among a union shop, a closed shop, an open shop, and an agency shop. Why do union members dislike open shops?
5. Why did unionization occur rather slowly in the white-collar job category?
6. Which white-collar group was the first to unionize in strength? Explain why it sought unionization earlier than other white-collar groups.
7. Why did civil-service protection develop for government workers? How does civil service differ from unionization?
8. What is tenure, and how does it differ from unionization?
9. What induces tenured and civil-service workers to unionize in some instances?
10. How does the relationship between the supervisor and the subordi-

nate differ depending on whether or not the subordinate has job protection?

ASSIGNMENTS

1. Interview a union steward in a local firm to find out his or her opinions of the advantages of unionization. Then, if possible, interview a manager in the same firm or in a similar type of firm to find out his or her opinions about the advantages of not having a union. Contrast these two points of view, and write a report of your findings.
2. Read an article on unionization in the white-collar field in a recent publication. Were the views expressed for or against unions? What arguments were given for the point of view stated? Write a report of your findings.

PROBLEM FOR RESOLUTION

A large nonprofit service organization in a central city had an influx of new employees who were neither loyal to the firm nor appreciative of the raises that had been given on merit to the staff over the years. When a union approached the office employees to organize, the newer employees particularly agitated to have the union accepted.

The union promised substantial across-the-board salary increases, especially for beginning workers, to bring their salaries up to par with those paid by profit-oriented organizations in the community. The union also promised to fight for substantial monetary fringe-benefit gains.

In addition to giving merit raises, the firm had been especially generous in granting employees special leaves, days off, personal days, and other amenities, such as paid-for pension plans and health and accident insurance. The employees especially enjoyed extra days off from work. For example, they had annually been granted a day off on the Friday after Thanksgiving, three to four days off immediately after Christmas, and two personal days, in addition to regular vacation time and sick leaves. These extra days off, however, were not written into company policy but had been granted as long as the employees who had been in the organization for ten or more years could remember. Each time those specific amenities had been discussed, however, the organization's management had stressed that they were not part of the formal policy but were granted yearly as a special concession to employees.

In August, the union succeeded in getting an election scheduled. That was the time when employees arranged for their Thanksgiving and Christmas time off. When they asked about those days, the personnel officers replied that no word could be issued until the union vote had been taken.

On investigation, the employees found that none of the firms represented by this particular union granted such liberal time off and that all pay raises were strictly "across the board," not granted on merit as theirs were.

What arguments are there for and against a union for this organization's office employees?

CASE STUDY

A new manager, Ms. Valerie Stone, was informed that the employees in her department, who had long been unionized, worked from 9:00 A.M. to 5:00 P.M., with an hour for lunch and time for coffee breaks in both the morning and the afternoon.

Ms. Stone noticed on several occasions that many of her workers were massed at the elevators at 4:45. They had their coats on and were ready to leave. On examining the union contract, she found that the workers were allowed "wash-up time" before leaving at 5:00. However, they were not permitted to leave before that hour.

The next time she found a group waiting for the elevators at 4:45, she took their names and reported them to the personnel office.

Was this an appropriate action? Defend your response.

FURTHER READING

Beal, Edwin F., Edward D. Wickersham, and Philip Kienast. *The Practice of Collective Bargaining*. 4th ed. Homewood, Ill.: Richard D. Irwin, 1972.

> Reports how vigorous unionization took place after World War II among federal, state, and local public employees.

Blum, Albert A. *Management and the White-Collar Union*. AMA Research Study 63. New York: American Management Association, 1964.

> Explains how, beginning in 1961, the AFL-CIO determined to take the unionization membership drive into the white-collar field, where it was largely unknown.

Chamot, Dennis. "Professional Employees Turn to Unions." *Harvard Business Review*, May–June 1976, 119–27.

> Discusses how unionism among teachers has increased manyfold

since 1965, especially since collective bargaining rights were granted to government workers.

Cohen, Sanford. *Labor in the United States.* 3rd ed. Columbus, Ohio Charles E. Merrill, 1970.

Presents the history of the labor movement in the United States.

Foulkes, Fred K. *Personnel Policies in Large Nonunion Companies.* Englewood Cliffs, N.J.: Prentice-Hall, 1980.

Describes how lower turnover, higher productivity, lower resistance to technological change, and less time spent adjusting grievances are characteristics that add up to less costly operations overall in nonunion companies.

Fulmer, William E. "When Employees Want to Oust Their Union." *Harvard Business Review,* March–April 1978, pp. 163–70.

Explains that although both managers and union leaders may take the offensive in an election to oust a union, both need to consider whether winning is worth it.

Mills, D. Quinn. "Flawed Victory in Labor Law Reform." *Harvard Business Review,* May–June 1979, pp. 92–102.

Reports how relations between business people and labor leaders have been harmed by business managers' reaction to the Labor Law Reform Bill of 1978, which was not passed.

Nevin, Jack, and Lorna Nevin. *AFGE—Federal Union: The Story of the American Federation of Government Employees.* Washington, D.C.: American Federation of Government Employees, 1976.

Presents the story of how the AFGE grew and how it serves the federal employees.

"On Trial: A Union's Fairness." *Business Week,* August 13, 1979, pp. 76–78.

Explains that employees are increasingly accusing unions of failure to defend the rights of members under labor agreements.

Van Riper, Paul P. *History of the United States Civil Service.* Westport, Conn.: Greenwood Press, 1976.

Describes the development of laws that led to the creation of the civil-service system in government in the United States.

supervision
in the future

16

trends affecting tomorrow's supervisor

After studying and analyzing this chapter, you should be able to:

Detail how increasing automation and better communications technology will contribute to changes in the workplace.

Describe how the changes in size and complexity of firms and the multinational character of many firms will have an effect on the workplace.

Explain how laws change the work of the supervisor.

Discuss how supervisors might have to cope with changing work hours, changing age groups, more women and minority members, and better-educated people in the workplace.

Detail how the increasing use of matrix organization will affect the workplace.

Describe the role of participative management in the future.

HE INDUSTRIAL REVOLUTION DECISIVELY changed the laboring activities of blue-collar workers, who moved from handwork to machine work and then to mass production. As work became more mechanized, workers became alienated from their jobs. Extensive studies were performed to determine what motivated workers and what aspects of their jobs offered satisfaction. Many blue-collar workers unionized to offset some of the problems brought on by the industrialization of the workplace.

Some of the same changes are affecting white-collar workers today. Technology that alters white-collar jobs has arrived at a lightning-fast pace. The introduction of television in the 1940s and of computers in the 1950s signaled the beginning of the communications revolution. Since then, television has improved dramatically and its uses have multiplied. Computers have decreased in size from huge cabinets to miniaturized desk-top models. Typewriters have become increasingly mechanized to perform in amazingly flexible ways as word processors. That technology unknown to us today will be developed for our use in the future is certain. No one can wholly foresee the marvels that await us or the changes they will make in business and service occupations in the future.

People in the United States, which has an unusually high standard of living, have during the past decades begun to compete more strongly for the world's supply of goods. Other nations, their financial coffers swelled by oil money and by payments for their lower labor-cost products (such as automobiles and electronic goods), have been able to purchase large amounts of goods in world markets. This purchasing ability combined with the lowered productivity in the United States and the greatly increased energy prices has resulted in an inflation rate that has changed the ratio of spendable income to costs. In the United States, the cost of imports has been greater than that of exports for years, making dollars worth less in foreign countries and adding to our inflation rate. Conversely, real estate, products, and travel in the United States have been a bargain for foreign visitors.

All of these technological and economic changes have an effect on the white-collar field. Moreover, the future is likely to see increasing automation, larger and more complex enterprises, increasing foreign-job opportunities, more government regulation, changing work hours, a growing and changing population, more minorities and women in the work force, better education of employees, increasing use of matrix organization, and more employee participation in management. Projecting these anticipated changes into the twenty-first century shows that the supervisor's job will change and grow in importance and that beneficial effects will emerge from the increased interaction of employees within a firm.

Increasing automation

For many decades, the technological changes that affected white-collar workers were modest. Typewriters were electrified, copiers were improved, and electric calculators were introduced. Then great innovations began to take place. Computers, developed in the 1950s, began to speed the work of computation and to take over the record keeping for bankers, tax collectors, and accountants.

Word-processing machines, which moved communications technology directly into the secretary's office, were also initially developed in the 1950s but did not have any appreciable impact on business or government until the 1970s. With the introduction of the microprocessor in the form of a *silicon chip*—a flake of silica (sand) on which tiny electronic circuits are etched—both computers and word-processing machines have become more flexible. Sales of them are slated to increase every year for the foreseeable future. Word-processing machines allow changes in typed material to be made easily, spelling errors to be corrected automatically, and records of corrected material to be kept on disks or tapes that can be used as masters for subsequent automatic typing. Computers are used for a variety of tasks—computation, record keeping, text processing, and information storage and retrieval, for example. Wedding the computer to the word-processing machine will further mechanize filing and record keeping. In addition, various electronic devices are being used in distributing mail, making bank deposits and withdrawals, filing, and otherwise altering the usual way of doing business.

Video-display terminals (VDTs) are another technological innovation. They are machines with typewriter keyboards and televisionlike screens that exhibit the typed text; permit portions of it to be changed, deleted, or replaced with the touch of a few buttons; transfer the text to paper; and store large amounts of copy.

Business satellites, designed for high-speed business communications, called *telecommunications*, were launched initially in November 1980 to be ready for network operations in 1981. Messages conveyed from user terminals go through senders to earth stations and then to the satellite. They reverse that order in being received. Telecommunications facilitate global interaction (see Figure 16–1).

All these machines are in use now and will become more commonplace.

Another innovation that will speed up communications is electronic mail. Mail going from one firm to another will bypass the post office and take less than a minute to transmit. Messages sent from word processors or terminals will proceed through local telephone lines to special centers where they will be converted into computer code and transmitted by means of cables or microwaves to a switching center near the desti-

FIGURE 16-1

TELECOMMUNICATIONS

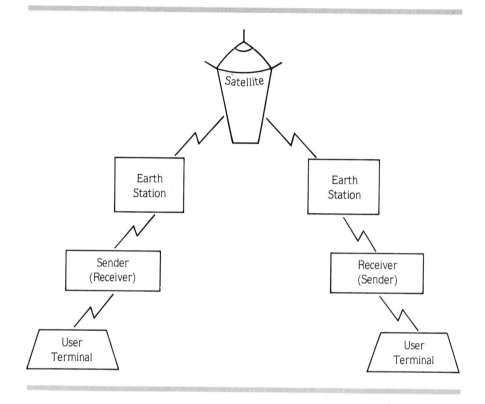

nation area. At this switching center, the messages will be reconverted into words and automatically typed out for receipt.

These developments in telephone technology will increase productivity because they will improve the efficiency and output of workers. One caution, however, needs to be observed for the future. People create machines and other technology. But once these products are introduced into the workplace, the technology tends to take control of the workers. Certain routines must be followed if the equipment is to perform correctly. Therefore, the worker becomes, during working hours, wedded to the machine. He or she also becomes a specialist in handling a particular device. Specialization tends to routinize work; discipline a worker by forcing him or her to perform certain tasks in a required order; and somewhat alter, after training has been completed, the relationship of the worker to the supervisor. Depersonalization may result because the worker, of necessity, must be concerned with the routine of working with the machines that produce the finished output. Thus, interaction with other people is often reduced.

Therefore, as work becomes more automated, the workplace must become more humanized. The supervisor, in constant interaction with employees, will need to develop judgmental abilities that will help workers adjust to a more impersonal atmosphere. More concern for workers, more participatory activities, and more opportunities for interchange in small groups will be necessary to relieve some of the monotony and impersonality that mechanization imposes and some of the fear that technology produces.

In addition, as technology is used more by first- and middle-level managers, this same impersonality will afflict them. Their supervisors, in turn, will find the same need to involve their employees in decision-making phases of the firm's activities.

Larger and more complex enterprises

The economic development of the United States has demonstrated that successful firms often grow to become giant-sized firms. Many large firms also absorb smaller firms by purchasing them or outperforming them. Thus, in some industries, there is a *monopoly*, or a situation in which one large firm, such as the American Telephone and Telegraph Company, virtually dominates the market for a product or service. An *oligopoly*, by contrast, exists when a few large firms share the market. The U.S. automotive industry is a good example of this, with American Motors, Chrysler, Ford, and General Motors producing cars.

Government's antitrust laws prevent firms from buying competitors if, by so doing, competition is lessened. No restraint, however, is placed on those firms that buy noncompeting organizations. Thus, *conglomerates*, companies that produce different, totally unrelated products and/or services, may be created by one corporation that buys noncompeting companies and merges them under one top management as a diversified organization.

As firms create new products or services or as they merge with others that offer different products or services, their managerial structures become increasingly varied. Firms with branches also have complex structures that offer diversity in jobs, opportunities for growth and development of personnel, and challenges to the executives to mesh the workings and to synchronize the activities of the employees so that the goals of the organization are met. Municipal, state, and national government offices; universities; hospitals; and other service organizations similarly have complex structures that require constant analysis so they can continue to function effectively.

Large corporations employ many workers, pay substantial salaries, and offer desirable fringe benefits. Even so, smaller firms with unique entreprenurial-minded talent have been able to lure workers to join. The opportunities the small firms often give to workers to participate in decision making, to see the results of their labors, and to innovate have made them able to compete in the employee marketplace. Some of these smaller firms have, in a comparatively short time, joined the giants in producing innovative products and creating new markets. This has been particularly true in recent years in the electronics industry.

As firms increase in size, they need both additional workers and more supervisors to oversee those workers. Promotion from within presents opportunities for entry-level employees to advance to managerial positions. Workers' effective growth and increased productivity require that supervisors constantly improve their techniques and approaches to their staffs.

Increasing foreign-job opportunities

Multinationals are firms that have "producing branches or subsidiaries located in more than one nation."[1] If a company merely sells its products or services in another nation or nations, it is still considered to be just a national company. If, however, it establishes branches in which its products or services are produced in another country or countries, then it becomes a multinational. Today, hundreds of large corporations have branches in six or more nations.[2]

Multinationals open many new opportunities for workers to take jobs in other countries. The U.S. government also employs people to work for embassies and other offices in foreign nations. Even some state governments have commerce divisions that operate overseas. These firms and government agencies offer opportunities for people who have appropriate foreign language skills, knowledge of business and government record keeping, and interpersonal skills to live abroad for a period of two or more years. People applying for foreign positions must be able to adapt to the customs of the country in which they will be working.

Wherever workers are needed, supervisors are also needed. Supervisors in multinationals often oversee the work not only of U.S. workers but also of nationals from the country. Supervisors, too, need to be knowledgeable about the country in which they work.

More government regulation

Since the Depression of the 1930s, the federal government has increasingly intervened, through laws and rulings, in the economic life of individuals, partners, and corporations. Taxes and laws restrict enterpreneurs and established firms. Employees have benefited from laws establishing employer liability, minimum age limits, collective bargaining, civil rights, affirmative action, and social insurance. Everyone has benefited from environmental protection. The explosive growth of federal legislation affects pricing; wages and salaries; hiring, retention, and promotion of employees; fringe benefits; and safety on the job. According to a report by the Center for the Study of American Business, twenty new federal regulatory agencies have sprung up since 1970. The government has 116 agencies and programs that now regulate business.[3]

Little likelihood exists that the government will retreat from its legislative barrage on the economic life of the country. All indications are that government influence will continue to expand as the need to serve as a watchdog over private enterprise persists. Although experts anticipate that the economy will continue to move ahead, some suggest that business and government will need to be more cooperative and less counteractive.[4]

Therefore, this increase in government regulation has necessitated the creation of new jobs and offices within firms to deal effectively with these laws and rulings, which cannot be ignored. It has also stimulated firms to find ways to work more skillfully with government agencies. Many enterprises are hiring employees who have had government experience so that they can better interpret laws and ensure both the government and the public that they are acting within the law. In addition, to deal with anticipated government actions and to attempt to stop conflicting legislation, which causes a firm that abides by one ruling to be guilty of evading or breaking another ruling, some companies have established offices in Washington, D.C. The people who staff these offices attempt, through lobbying, to have a say in the legislation that is and is not enacted.

Thus, new workers and new supervisors are needed for this work. Additionally, all the supervisors already within a firm are affected because they need to know the law, how to interpret it, and how not to infringe on it. Firms need knowledgeable people to train the supervisors to ensure that they will properly handle situations within their jurisdiction.

Changing work hours

The five-day, forty-hour week (thirty-five or thirty-seven and one-half hours in some firms), which has been traditional for white-collar workers for several decades, has been repeatedly challenged in recent years. Some firms have tried four-day weeks with nine- to ten-hour days. Others have tried *flextime*, which permits employees to choose, within certain limits, the daily hour of arrival and departure. Others have tried *schedules that rotate,* which allow some employees to work early shifts for a given period of time, then to be assigned to later shifts, and finally to rotate back to the early shift.

Others have tried *platoon systems,* especially designed for complete complements of part-time workers and part-time supervisors who work four hours a day in either the early morning, the early or late afternoon, or the evening or night. One hospital that had difficulty keeping nurses and supervisors because of constantly changing schedules developed special bonus work-time groupings that paid a premium to those nurses and their supervisors who took the least desirable time assignments. A week's pay, for example, was given to nurses and supervisors who worked two twelve-hour days each Saturday and Sunday. This was advertised, to attract applicants, as "a weekend of nursing and a week of free time." [5] People on the night shift, similarly, were paid more. The other nurses worked regular Monday to Friday shifts of forty hours for their week's pay.

Recently, firms that specialize in supplying temporary workers have found greatly increased demands for their personnel, as workers choose to have variety in work assignments rather than to be attached to just one enterprise. In many instances, companies have found that their fluctuating needs are better served by nonpermanently assigned employees.

All these methods of assigning time and work are of mounting interest to both employees and management. New time arrangements and work assignments need to be considered for various reasons. First, energy conservation has encouraged increased use of mass transit. This, in turn, makes a nine-to-five workday difficult for those who need to take trains, buses, or subways to work. If large numbers of workers are scheduled for the same hours, transportation systems become overloaded at certain times and underused at others. By staggering beginning and ending work hours for large segments of workers, firms can help to alleviate the problems of lines, overcrowding, and insufficient equipment at peak periods and to make all employees more comfortable.

Second, for the increased number of single-parent households, odd-hour scheduling is helpful in seeing children off to school before leaving for work or in being home when the schoolday ends. Third, inflation has resulted in some people's needing to hold more than one job, and flexible scheduling helps them to do so more easily.

Fourth, some people need to upgrade their knowledge by attending school while they hold a full-time job. Again, flexible scheduling helps make this possible. Fifth, leisure-time activities may also be accommodated more conveniently if a person can alter a schedule to permit blocks of time for special hobbies.

Supervisors who can train new workers quickly and easily, hold meetings with employees at odd hours, adapt to constant employee changes, and remain flexible, amenable, competent, and concerned are needed to fit into variable-time patterns. Effective supervision becomes even more essential to a firm when the work force comes and goes at different hours.

Growing and changing population

The size of the population of the United States has changed radically in the past several decades. During the Depression, there was a relatively small population increase. During the 1940s and 1950s, a veritable population explosion occurred. The 1960s and 1970s saw a return to an almost zero population growth.

With the increase and decrease in population growth, the number of people in each age group keeps changing. In the 1950s, almost half the population was twenty-five years old or under. Now, the population is rapidly maturing. The more mature, experienced, and work-oriented population will help productivity to increase. Also, the retirement laws that were changed in 1979 to allow people to remain in their jobs until age seventy will further add to an experienced work force. Experts predict that these demographic changes will reduce expenditures for crime prevention, welfare, and education and will accelerate progress for minority groups.[6]

Because of these changes in the population, business will not have enough experienced managers to handle the many workers born in the 1940s and 1950s. Therefore, increasing opportunities will exist for supervisors, who will have more mature people to work with in white-collar jobs. These people tend to be more stable in their jobs, more satisfied with their jobs, less rebellious in their attitudes, and a bit more inflexible toward change. More mature people also tend to seek intrinsic rewards in their work. Supervisors will find increased acceptance in their role if they approach these workers from an adult-ego state.

More minorities and women in the work force

In the 1960s, the labor force was composed of over 30 percent women. The percentage grew to over 40 percent in the 1970s. Spurred by the need for extra income, the equal employment laws, the equal-pay-for-equal-work legislation, the proposed Equal Rights Amendment, the demand for equality by groups of feminists, the increased enrollment in institutions of higher education, and the affirmative action of businesses to hire eligible women for or promote them to management positions, women have entered or reentered the work force in large numbers.

Many women, however, did not enter the so-called traditional fields. Therefore, shortages of personnel developed in such conventional areas as secretarial services and nursing.[7] But the growing technological development in the secretarial field began to attract men. As a few men have entered the field and many women have shunned it, the personnel shortage caused salaries to rise.[8] This attraction, plus the fact that secretarial jobs will be viewed by both men and women as stepping-stones to managerial positions, is likely to draw more people to the secretarial field.

Both women and men from minority groups—blacks, Hispanics, and American Indians—have been given new employment chances by the Civil Rights Act of 1964. This law requires employers to give equal opportunity to all potential workers. Minority-group members bring not only talents and abilities to the workplace but also some different cultural attitudes and customs that enrich those who have the opportunity to interact with them on the job. Supervisors need to understand any cultural differences that may affect people's on-the-job behavior.

As both members of minority groups and women are given opportunities, they will exhibit talents that make them eligible for promotion. Thus, supervisory and managerial positions will be increasingly filled by people who had little opportunity in previous decades to hold those jobs. These new supervisors will bring refreshing points of view that will lead to many innovative ways of handling situations.

Better education of employees

The revolution in technology and communication not only brings more mechanization to white-collar jobs but also necessitates more preparation on the part of job holders. Nonexempt, entry-level workers need at least a high-school education for most white-collar jobs, and firms are increasingly seeking two-year-college graduates. Many firms seek four-year-college graduates to fill their management-training positions. For more specialized jobs, people with master's degrees are often employed.

As the educational background of workers is upgraded, the job of the supervisor will change. The supervisor will be working with people who have studied humanities, psychology, sociology, and other social sciences, in addition to the technical skills needed. In addition, an educated work force is knowledgeable about current events, interested in social change, aware of government regulations, and often interested in broadening its opportunities for advancement. Therefore, supervisors' education must change as that of their subordinates does.

This constant educational upgrading of the work force may lead to "virtues unknown in the '60s and '70s—self-control, self-discipline, stoicism, decorum, even inhibition and a little puritanism."[9] These attitudes will spill over into the workplace. Supervisors will be training and advising subordinates who have different values, aspirations, concepts,

FIGURE 16–2
DIMINISHING THE AUTHORITY OF THE SUPERVISOR
INCREASES THE DECISION-MAKING POWER OF SUBORDINATES

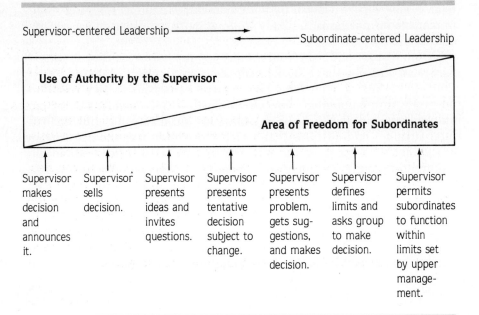

Supervisor-centered Leadership ────────▶
                                    ◀──────── Subordinate-centered Leadership

Use of Authority by the Supervisor

Area of Freedom for Subordinates

| Supervisor makes decision and announces it. | Supervisor sells decision. | Supervisor presents ideas and invites questions. | Supervisor presents tentative decision subject to change. | Supervisor presents problem, gets suggestions, and makes decision. | Supervisor defines limits and asks group to make decision. | Supervisor permits subordinates to function within limits set by upper management. |

Source: Adapted from R. Tannenbaum and W. H. Schmidt, "How to Choose a Leadership Pattern," *Harvard Business Review*, May–June 1973, p. 164. Copyright © 1958 by the President and Fellows of Harvard College; all rights reserved.

and attitudes from the workers of earlier decades. Theory X methods of dealing with people will increasingly need to be replaced by Theory Y, MBO, and participative management concepts. Supervisor-centered leadership will diminish and subordinate-centered leadership will increase (see Figure 16–2).

Increasing use of matrix organization

As explained in Chapter 3, *matrix organization* is a way of drawing together people from different departments or specializations within a firm to work on new projects or to devise new ways of doing business for a limited period, thereby rearranging the work force. A supervisor in one area may become a subordinate in the new matrix, or a specialist from another area may suddenly become the supervisor of the new group. This situation creates a novel set of interactions for each of the people.

Furthermore, they are aware that they have a limited assignment in this new group, and that once the group's mission is accomplished, the various members will return to their original departments. They are also aware that the new assignment will be enriching, place them in a new spotlight within the company, and forever change them.

The new supervisor needs considerable talent to weld this disparate group into a productive unit. Because the assignment is limited (usually from a few weeks to as much as six months or more), the supervisor has only a short time to get to know the people in the group, make assignments, share ideas, and get the work done and into proposal or final report shape. Thus, the supervisor is challenged to function even more efficiently than he or she did when working with the regular staff.

Participatory management is one way to get everyone in the new group involved quickly and to assess their abilities and potentialities. The talent of the supervisor to enlist the support of the group, to get the people to bring their best efforts to the solution of the problem, and to work effectively with the group as a team largely determines the success of the group. Developing supervisory ability for short-term work teams will increasingly be a challenge to supervisors in the future.

More employee participation in management

All of the trends that have been discussed—increasing automation, larger and more complex enterprises, increasing foreign-job opportunities, more government regulation, changing work hours, growing and changing population, more minorities and women in the work force, better education of employees, and increasing use of matrix organization—will necessitate increased employee participation within firms. As enterprises employ more specialists, managers will find that more joint decision making is desirable. This interaction is needed to ensure that technology is most effectively used and that employees get recognition for their input.

People who want to advance in their jobs have a different attitude toward their work than people who want no further responsibility. Therefore, among their subordinates, supervisors will find greater challenges to their authority, increased competence, and more willingness to accept added assignments. Upwardly mobile workers seek to be part of decision making. Participative management, which involves employees in management decisions, results in both increased productivity and cost savings.[10] Thus, worker's aspirations may result in improving white-collar occupations in the future.

One way for management to involve workers is to use *quality circles*.[11] These are small groups of workers who meet regularly and are trained to identify and solve production problems in their departments. Quality circles bring employees together, involve them, allow them to express ideas, and then reward them when their ideas are accepted. This participative-management concept has been implemented in many firms at various levels and will increase with added technological advances.

For white-collar employees, such plans are of considerable significance. Because of the rising educational level of employees, the changed attitude toward work as a vital part of their lives, and the knowledge people have of their importance to the success of a firm, the only direction that will provide a vital, productive work force is one that involves each person in decision making at his or her level of operation.

Furthermore, the person who is involved and rewarded from time to time for unique input to the system becomes more interested in the company that offers that opportunity. Loyalty to the firm is increased, turnover of personnel is reduced, and the abilities of this motivated employee continue to be realized by the company.

People like to be involved. They enjoy discussing facets of their jobs about which they are expert. They appreciate opportunities to express their points of view and to share their knowledge with others. Giving employees a chance to participate and rewarding them for meaningful contributions are ways of ensuring a concerned work force. The supervisor is one of the key members in this dynamic arrangement.

SUMMARY

o Increasing automation is changing not only the speed with which information may be assembled and communicated but also the manner in which employees interact with one another. Increased technological development at the work station necessitates increased humanization of the organization. More opportunity for decision making will help to offset the impersonality brought on by increased mechanization.

o Complexity enters into any organization that becomes large in size— government, service enterprises, or product-oriented firms. Successful, growing organizations constantly seek new workers and new supervisors to oversee those workers.

o Enterprises may sell their products or services in foreign countries, or they may actually establish branches of their firms in other countries, thus becoming multinationals. Workers and supervisors are needed for these foreign branches. Such employees should have knowledge of both the language and the culture of the country in which they will be employed.

o Since the 1930s, government has increasingly passed laws that protect workers. Employees are needed within enterprises to interpret these laws and to train others to abide by them.

o Changing life-styles will increasingly be accommodated by flexible working hours. Altered work schedules aid mass transportation, scheduling for single-parent households, opportunities for holding more than one job, educational opportunities, and leisure-time activities. Supervisors need flexibility to adapt to these changed work patterns.

o The aging of the population will necessitate supervisors who have the ability to relate to more mature workers.

o Minority workers, including women, will take increasingly important positions in organizations. Supervisors will need to understand cultural differences and ways of working effectively with them. Moreover, minority workers will also become supervisors and need, in turn, to know how to work with their staffs.

o Educational advancement of employees will require that supervisors consider newer ways of working with people, such as Theory Y, MBO, and participative management.

o More specialization in complex organizations will require the increasing use of matrix organization. This will necessitate that employees be flexible in both accomplishing work and energizing groups to complete their tasks.

o A more enlightened work force increasingly seeks a chance to have its say in the activities of the organization. Use of quality circles will help management to improve work within departments. The more supervisors involve employees in a meaningful way in their work, the more the employees will enjoy the work they do.

REFERENCES

[1] Robert L. Heilbroner, *The Making of Economic Society*, 5th ed. (Englewood Cliffs, N.J.: Prentice-Hall, 1975), p. 223.

[2] Heilbroner, *The Making of Economic Society*, p. 224.

[3] Vasil Pappas, "More Firms Upgraded Government-Relations Jobs Because of Sharp Growth in Federal Regulations," *Wall Street Journal*, January 11, 1980, p. 42.

[4] "Higher Hurdles for the U.S. Economy," *Business Week*, September 3, 1979, p. 175.

[5] "Hospital Offers Nurses a Two-Day Work-

week," *New York Times*, November 30, 1980, p. 55.

[6] "Population Changes That Help for a While," *Business Week*, September 3, 1979, p. 181.

[7] Hillel Levin, "Where There's a Skill There's a Way," *New York*, December 17, 1979, p. 54.

[8] Urban C. Lehner, "Labor Letter," *Wall Street Journal*, January 29, 1980, p. 1.

[9] Lance Morrow, "Back to Reticence!" *Time*, February 4, 1980, p. 86.

[10] Earl C. Gottschalk, Jr., "U.S. Firms Worried by Productivity Lag, Copy Japan in

Seeking Employee's Advice," *Wall Street*
Journal, February 21, 1980, p. 48.

[11]Gottschalk, "U.S. Firms Worried by Productivity Lag," p. 48.

REVIEW AND DISCUSSION QUESTIONS

1. In what ways does the technological revolution of the last part of the twentieth century reflect the Industrial Revolution?
2. What is meant by the statement, "As work becomes more mechanized, the workplace must become more humanized"?
3. Why have small firms often been able to operate successfully in competition with giant-sized firms?
4. What special skills are needed by supervisors in multinational companies' foreign-location jobs?
5. Is government interference in business increasing or decreasing? How are employees helped by government's interference?
6. How is the supervisor affected by government regulations?
7. How do shifting work hours and the hiring of nonpermanent employees affect the supervisor's job?
8. How does the influx of women and minority-group members into the workplace affect the supervisor's job?
9. What changes will the supervisor of the future have to adjust to in supervising better-educated workers?
10. What problems does a supervisor under matrix organization face?

ASSIGNMENTS

1. Interview an experienced supervisor in a bank, an insurance office, a hospital, or a retail store. Ask him or her to explain how the job of supervising employees has changed over the past year or two. Compare the changes detailed with the changes discussed in the text. Write a report of your findings.
2. Analyze the kinds of white-collar jobs advertised in the help-wanted sections of your area's newspaper. What proportion requires a fairly high level of skill—a high-school or better educational background? Write a report of your analysis.

PROBLEM FOR RESOLUTION

In the department over which you are the supervisor, one handicapped employee had been hired after showing aptitude for machine operation. When training that was planned to take two weeks was given, she needed almost double that length of time to become proficient because of her handicap. However, once she learned to operate the machine, she was able to function effectively in producing documents. In addition, she has been a model employee in every way.

Recently, in your discussions with other supervisors, you have been aware that the machine on which she works has been replaced in several departments by a more sophisticated model that takes additional skills to operate. You believe, from what you hear through the grapevine, that within a period of a year or less your own department will also have such a machine installed. On enquiry, you learn that the people running this more sophisticated model have all taken a special course at a nearby community college. The cost of this course was subsidized by the company.

Should you advise the handicapped employee to take this training to run the more sophisticated machine? Why or why not?

Is considering the career path of an employee the responsibility of the supervisor? Explain your response.

CASE STUDY

Professional Applied Science (PROAPSCI) was a small professional organization and a division of a larger enterprise. PROAPSCI had a staff of eight people. Six worked strictly on organizational business, while the two others, an editor and a business manager (who held the rank of administrative assistant), produced the organization's quarterly literary publication. Articles for this publication were solicited from professional people who wished to share their knowledge with others. The publication had a subscription list of approximately three thousand people and firms.

The general manager of PROAPSCI also served as the head of the editorial board of the publication, which included people from outside the organization who volunteered their services. The editor, but not the business manager, also served on the editorial board.

The business manager, Ms. Duncan, had four main functions: to obtain paid advertisements for the quarterly, to keep records of subscribers and deposit their subscription money, to increase the number of subscribers, and to prepare the labels for the mailing of the publication. These labels were prepared by typing quadruple copies as subscriptions were renewed or added each quarter. Thus, approximately eight hundred names and addresses had to be typed every three months to update the lists and to prepare enough labels for each subscriber to receive four copies of the publication.

The business manager had held the job for about ten years, and she was a dedicated, concerned worker. She kept careful records, and under her direction the publication had had steady, small increases in subscribers. These had risen from about two thousand when she took it over to the three thousand currently on the list. She was proud of the lists she kept, the accuracy of the accounts she kept and of the labels she typed, and of the constant small but steady increases in the number of subscribers.

At the editorial board's annual meeting, one member suggested that the lists be computerized and that the labels be printed out automatically for each edition. Ms. Duncan was not consulted about this change. She had previously resisted computerization of the records, and so the general manager of the organization asked another administrative assistant, who had no connection with the publication, to ascertain the costs and to arrange for the computerization.

When all plans had been completed and approved, the administrative assistant presented the business manager with the facts and stated that the business manager would now have to carry the plan through to completion. The business manager was shaken with rage when she was presented with this approved plan by a peer.

Would you have accomplished this change as the general manager did? Give reasons for your response.

Assume that the general manager left the firm and you were assigned as the new general manager. How would you handle the irate business manager? Give reasons for your response.

FURTHER READING

Bruno, Jim N. "Electronic Mail: It Gets There Fast." *Administrative Management*, September 1979, pp. 28–29.

   Describes how "electrical impulse communication" has recently become a business buzzword.

Byron, Christopher. "Now the Office of Tomorrow." *Time*, November 17, 1980, pp. 80–82.

   Reports how technology's dazzling breakthroughs shake up the white-collar world.

Connell, John J. "How Your Job Will Change in the Next 10 Years." *Administrative Management*, January 1979, pp. 26–28.

   Explains that supervisors will be required to manage technology, information, and people in the future.

Foegen, J. H., and Talmer E. Curry, Jr. "Flextime: The Way of the Future." *Administrative Management*, September 1980, pp. 27–29.

   Presents a discussion and a case problem that show that

changes from traditional scheduling create many problems but may evoke positive employee reactions.

Herzberg, Frederick. "Herzberg on Motivation for the 80s." *Industry Week,* October 1, 1979, pp. 58–63.

Explains that workers can best be motivated when they see their work as serving a meaningful purpose and that the need for personal growth and development through participation is enhanced through service on the job.

Lippin, Paula, "Telecommunications: Where It Is and Where It's Going." *Administrative Management,* September 1980, pp. 34–37.

Reports that many experts agree that digital transmission is the technology of the future but that they do not agree when it will be in general use.

Mills, D. Quinn. "Human Resources in the 1980s." *Harvard Business Review,* July–August 1979, pp. 154–62.

Explains how women, minorities, and illegal aliens will test the ability of organizations to meet demands and to change the business climate for these new work groups.

Schuyten, Peter J. "G.T.E.: The Promise of Electronic Mail." *New York Times,* November 2, 1980, pp. 1, 22–23.

Discusses how electronic mail, although still in its infancy, is considered a key component of the automated office of the future.

Toffler, Alvin. *The Third Wave.* New York: William Morrow, 1980.

Explains how, from the First Wave (the agricultural revolution) and the Second Wave (the Industrial Revolution), we have emerged into the Third Wave, which is creating different jobs, life-styles, work ethics, life concepts, and economic structures.

"Voice Mail Arrives in the Office." *Business Week,* June 9, 1980, pp. 80–84.

Describes five ways that voice mail can save time on the telephone.

glossary

action learning A form of project training in which employees resolve an actual problem and then communicate the solution to management.

ad hoc committee *See* committee.

affirmative action Those actions taken to overcome the negative effects of past or present discriminatory employment practices.

agency shop A union agreement with a firm that allows management to hire any employees it wants, does not require employees to join the union at a later date, requires all employees to pay union dues, and does not permit nonmembers to vote on union concerns.

application A printed form that requests information permitted by law from those persons who seek a job within an enterprise.

aptitude test A test used to determine an applicant's ability to learn a particular skill or concept.

assertiveness training A method of training that helps employees to balance their behavior between passivity and aggressiveness and emphasizes self-responsibility.

assessment center A place where job applicants are given a series of tasks to perform and problems to resolve in order to determine their potential as managers.

assigning A supervisory aspect of managing in which a supervisor distributes tasks to subordinates.

audiovisual aid Supplementary viewing and/or hearing equipment or materials used to reinforce or illustrate information or to provide specific practice.

authority The right to give job-related orders to subordinates, to make decisions, and to take goal-directed actions. Authority may be *centralized* (retained by top management) or *decentralized* (delegated to subordinates).

autocratic leader A leader who makes decisions and gives orders without consulting subordinates.

behavior modeling A method of training in which trainees observe a person performing a task correctly, discuss the demonstration, and then practice the behavior.

blue-collar worker An employee who performs manual tasks and generally wears protective clothing.

body language The use of facial expressions or movements of the body to communicate.

bona fide occupational qualification (BFOQ) A requirement for a job based on the nature of the job, with the exception of race, color, or national origin.

bonus A financial reward by which an employee receives an extra payment based on some defined measure in addition to salary.

brainstorming An idea-gathering method in which people suggest unusual ways to achieve desired results for a problem or project.

case study A method of training in which problematic situations are presented and trainees suggest ways to resolve them.

centralized authority *See* authority.

centralized training Formal training that takes place under the direct jurisdiction of the training staff and is usually given to employees from different parts of the firm simultaneously.

chain of command The path that orders and directives follow from top through middle to lower-level managers until they reach the workers who will carry them out.

change theory A theory developed by Lewin and Schein that proposes that any alteration in behavior goes through three stages: unfreezing, changing, and refreezing.

channel of communication The path that communication follows in a firm. It may be *downward* (from supervisors to subordinates), *upward* (from subordinates to supervisors), *horizontal* (between peers), or *diagonal* (from a supervisor of one unit to a subordinate in another or vice versa).

checklist A method of formal evaluation that presents brief, descriptive statements about the traits, behaviors, and actions pertinent to employees and their jobs, and on which the supervisor checks those items that apply to the employee.

civil service The people employed by the government. They may be *classified* (job protected and permanently assigned to jobs through special tests and/or credentials) or *unclassified* (elected or appointed).

classified civil service *See* civil service.

client organization The division of work based on the clients served by an enterprise.

closed shop A union agreement with an organization that requires that only union members in good standing be hired or retained. Legal today only for garment industry workers, building trades employees, and longshoremen.

commission A financial reward by which employees receive payment depending on their production.

committee A group of people assigned to confer, make decisions, and report to a larger body on specific matters. A committee may be *ad hoc* (short term) or *standing* (long term).

communicating A supervisory aspect of managing in which a supervisor gives and receives ideas through speaking, writing, symbols, or body language.

communication The process of exchanging information or ideas between a sender and one or more receivers through speaking, writing, symbols, or body language. Communication is only effective when the receiver understands the message as intended.

complaint An employee's informal expression of annoyance, frustration, discontent, or resentment.

computer-assisted instruction (CAI) A method of individual training that provides programmed learning through a computer.

computer game analysis A method of training in which teams of trainees are given data about costs and expenditures for a part of an enterprise and repeatedly program decisions about the data into a computer. The team whose profits are the highest according to the computer wins.

consolidating The management function of strengthening and holding the position of part or all of an enterprise against infringement by a similar entity.

continuation training Formal training given to keep employees up to date in their jobs, to present more advanced information, or to improve attitudes.

controlling The management function of measuring the performance of employees to ensure that plans are effectively carried out.

coordinating The management function of meshing all tasks so that a smooth flow of work and a unified project will result.

counseling A supervisory aspect

of managing in which a supervisor advises or discusses a problem with a subordinate to help him or her become more valuable to a firm. Also, a method of individual training.

counseling interview A face-to-face discussion with an employee about a problem. It may be *directive* (the supervisor gives advice) or *nondirective* (the supervisor listens but offers no advice).

critical incident report A method of formal evaluation by which the supervisor details how an employee reacted in a particular situation.

decentralized authority See authority.

decentralized training Formal or informal training done by supervisors within their own departments for their subordinates.

decision making The process of making a conscious choice.

democratic leader A leader who consults subordinates before making a decision or giving an order.

demonstration A method of training in which the trainer shows the trainee exactly the way a task should be done and then asks the trainee to show his or her ability to perform the task correctly.

diagonal communication See channel of communication.

directing The management function of integrating various tasks by selecting, communicating with, training, and motivating employees.

direct interview A kind of second-stage interview in which relatively easy and nonthreatening questions are asked of the applicant, depending on his or her abilities, interests, and background.

directive counseling See counseling interview.

discharge Dismissal from employment. Also called *outplacement*.

discharging A supervisory aspect

of managing in which a supervisor ends a subordinate's employment.

discipline Restraints inflicted on a worker who does not perform according to rules or directives.

disciplining A supervisory aspect of managing in which a supervisor withholds rewards, threatens punishment, or actually penalizes subordinates for unacceptable work or behavior.

discussion A method of training in which people express opinions about the issue at hand and may or may not reach consensus.

downward communication See channel of communication.

electronic mail A communications system by which messages proceed from a word processor through telephone lines to a special center where they are coded and transmitted by cable or microwaves to a switching center near the destination and automatically typed.

employee requisition form A printed sheet used by an employer to show the need to employ a person. Indicates job title; grade; pay rate; whether work is full or part time, permanent or temporary; and hours.

employee stock ownership plan (ESOP) A financial reward by which employees may invest up to 15 percent of their pay in the organization's stock.

entry-level position A job that usually requires only modest skills and abilities and pays the minimum or near-minimum salary.

evaluating A supervisory aspect of managing in which a supervisor assesses the quality and quantity of work produced by subordinates.

evaluation The determination of an employee's or an activity's value to a firm. An evaluation may be *formal* (carefully planned and analyzed) or *informal* (not planned in detail and carried out casually).

exempt employee An employee who supervises two or more employees and who is not paid overtime or given compensatory time off for work beyond forty hours per week.

extrinsic reward *See* reward.

feedback In communication, the reinforcement the sender receives that indicates that the message was received and properly understood or not understood.

flextime A method of arranging work hours by which employees choose their arrival and departure times within limits.

forced-choice checklist A method of formal evaluation that presents brief, descriptive statements pertinent to employees and their jobs, and on which the supervisor is required (forced) to indicate whether each item is most or least descriptive of an employee.

formal evaluation *See* evaluation.

formal leader *See* leader.

formal organization The structure established by top management and observed by employees.

formal training Training that is planned and established.

fringe benefit A nondirect payment for services or protection for employees that is determined by management or obtained through union bargaining.

function One of the main activities of a firm. A function may be *line* (performed to achieve the firm's goals) or *staff* (performed to help achieve a line function).

functional authority The right of staff personnel to mandate changes be made or work be done by line personnel.

functional organization The division of work based on the major activities of an enterprise.

garnishment A legal process that requires that a firm withhold part of an employee's wages or salary to pay debts owed by the employee to an outside individual or firm.

goal A long-range target toward which an enterprise is directed.

grapevine The unofficial communications network that filters information based on rumor, gossip, or innuendo through an enterprise.

graphic rating scale A method of formal evaluation on which supervisors rate employees on a scale of sliding values for each trait assessed.

grievance An employee's official charge, usually evolving from an unresolved complaint, against another employee, a supervisor, or management.

grievance procedure A formal, step-by-step process that an aggrieved employee may follow to air and resolve a grievance.

group training Formal training in which various instructional methods are used to teach two or more people who have similar learning needs simultaneously.

halo effect The tendency to apply initial subjective impressions to all subsequent evaluations of a person.

Hawthorne effect The positive reaction of a worker in terms of motivation and productivity to being singled out and given special attention.

hierarchy The order of people in an enterprise from those with the most authority and responsibility to those with the least.

hierarchy-of-needs theory A theory of motivation developed by Maslow that views the needs of people as being built one upon the other, requiring that one need be satisfied before a higher one can emerge as a motivator.

horizontal communication   *See* channel of communication.

huddling   Unofficial, task-oriented discussions among employees.

hygiene-motivator factors   A theory of motivation developed by Herzberg that states that recognition, work itself, responsibility, and advancement (motivator factors) motivate people, while company policy and administration, supervision, salary, interpersonal relations, and working conditions (hygiene factors) prevent dissatisfaction but do not motivate.

in-basket exercise   A method of individual training in which a trainee is presented with various communications that might arrive at his or her desk and is asked to assess the importance of each, perform the work, and make decisions.

incident report   A record of the details of an employee's involvement in an event, good or bad.

individual training   Formal training in which various instructional methods are used to teach people singly, allowing them to progress at their own speed and learn only what they need to perform adequately on the job.

informal evaluation   *See* evaluation.

informal leader   *See* leader.

informal organization   A subgroup within an enterprise that is created by its own members, who choose their own leaders.

informal training   Training that is left to each supervisor to handle in any manner deemed desirable and occurs as a result of a felt need on the part of the supervisor or subordinate.

initial interview   A preliminary talk with a job applicant to determine whether he or she should be considered further for employment.

initial training   Formal training

given to new employees to prepare them to handle their job.

intelligence test   A test used to assess a person's ability to use acquired knowledge in novel ways.

intrinsic reward   *See* reward.

job analysis   The study of all the tasks involved in a person's work assignment.

job description   A written statement explaining specific tasks involved in a job, reporting relationships, results expected, relation of the amount of time spent on various tasks to the importance of them, salary range, skills needed, and physical demands.

job enlargement   A type of job redesign by which more tasks are added to a job.

job enrichment   A type of job redesign by which tasks are combined in a different way.

job protection   The right of workers to hold their job as long as the job exists and as long as they perform adequately.

job redesign   The process of structuring jobs so that tasks are more varied and employees have more responsibility.

job rotation   A type of job redesign by which employees are moved from one job to another.

job specification   A concise statement of the requirements of a job that may be used by an interviewer seeking to fill that job.

laissez-faire leader   A leader who allows subordinates to make decisions and take full responsibility for their own work.

leader   A person whose actions and attitudes others follow or copy. A leader may be *informal* (chosen by his or her peers) or *formal* (appointed by the firm).

leadership   The ability to influence or stimulate others' actions and attitudes toward a goal.

learner-controlled instruction (LCI) Any method of training by which an employee can determine the amount and/or speed of learning to be done.

lecture A method of training in which a trainer talks to a group about a given topic.

line function *See* function.

major policy *See* policy.

management The process of achieving an organization's goals through people who work in organized groups. Also, the top, middle, and lower echelon of bosses in an organization.

management by objectives (MBO) A system of managing by which the supervisor and the employee together set objectives to be achieved within a period of time and then evaluate the employee's progress at the end of the period. May be used as a motivator.

management-training program A special program of training within an enterprise to prepare people (usually with some college education) to do entry-level managerial or supervisory jobs.

manager An exempt employee who has assigned authority over other employees and who performs the functions of management.

managerial grid A chart developed by Blake and Mouton that allows a supervisor's concern about production and people to be analyzed.

matrix organization The division of work based on drawing employees from different units and assigning them to a special project for a limited period.

meeting An assemblage of people who are deliberately brought into person-to-person contact with one another to consider a topic of mutual concern.

minimum wage The lowest hourly amount employees may be paid.

minor policy *See* policy.

morale survey A method of formal evaluation by which employees indicate their degree of satisfaction with various aspects of their jobs.

motivating A supervisory aspect of managing in which a supervisor moves subordinates to want to do a good job.

motivation The process of moving a person toward action.

multidirectional communication Communication that involves sending and receiving messages among three or more people.

multiple-person assessment A method of formal evaluation by which an employee is rated by a group of fellow workers, including superiors and subordinates.

narrow span of control *See* span of control.

noise Any factor that prevents a receiver from understanding a message as the sender intended or that complicates the receipt of the message.

nondirect interview A kind of second-stage interview in which little or no guidance is given to the applicant and he or she is free to discuss any topic for any length of time.

nondirective counseling *See* counseling interview.

nonexempt employee An employee who is not a supervisor and who is paid overtime or given compensatory time off for work beyond forty hours per week.

nonfunctional authority The right of staff personnel only to advise, assist, or provide services for line personnel.

objective   A short-range target an enterprise seeks to attain in order to reach a long-range goal.

objectivity   The impersonal establishment of truth based on facts.

ombudsman   A person assigned to hear a grievance before it proceeds through the official grievance procedure.

one-directional   communication   Communication that involves a sender and a receiver but requires no response from the receiver.

open door   The policy by which supervisors encourage subordinates to approach them whenever subordinates have a problem or do not understand a communication.

open shop   A union agreement with an organization that allows management to hire any employees it wishes; these may or may not subsequently join the union and only union members pay dues.

organization   An enterprise, business, firm, library, school, doctor's office, law office, or other entity. Also may refer to the division of work into parts and the integration of those parts into the whole.

organization chart   A map that shows the divisions of work, lines of authority, and relationships of people within an enterprise.

organizing   The management function of analyzing and classifying a firm's goals, objectives, and plans by activities and tasks.

orientation training   A part of initial training that gives a new employee an overview of the firm.

outplacement   *See* discharge.

participative management   An approach to management that empha-

sizes workers' taking part in decisions about matters pertaining to their work.

patterned interview   A kind of second-stage interview in which preplanned questions are asked.

pension plan   A financial reward by which retired employees are paid money accrued from employer and/or their own payments made over years of work in a firm.

personality test   A test used to determine a person's traits, attitudes, interests, and habits.

personal stability   Emotional matureness, level-headedness, and dependability.

physical test   A test used to determine a person's fitness to fulfill the demands of a job.

plan   An outline or schedule that details the specific actions needed to reach the goals and objectives of an enterprise.

planned training   Formal training for which a need has been noted and a program established.

planning   The management function of setting overall goals and developing objectives and plans to teach them.

platoon system   A method of arranging work hours by which teams of workers are assigned to certain shifts to ensure coverage of those hours a firm on extended time is open.

policy   A statement of principles and standards that helps the enterprise achieve its goals and objectives. It can be *major* (applying to the firm as a whole and developed by top management) or *minor* (applying to various departments and derived from a major policy).

polygraph test   A test that tries to measure honesty by revealing if stress is present when a person answers certain questions.

procedure A guide to action that must be taken to observe a policy.

productivity chart A method of formal evaluation on which measurable output is recorded.

product organization The division of work based on the major products produced by an enterprise.

proficiency test A test used to measure an applicant's adeptness in a required job skill.

profit sharing A financial reward by which an employee is paid a percentage of the profits of the firm, based on his or her salary.

programmed learning A method of individual training that breaks material to be learned into tiny segments and gives immediate reinforcement.

project A method of individual training in which a trainee is presented with a problematic situation to resolve and must defend his or her solution.

promotion The giving of more responsibility, status, and/or money to an employee for a job well done.

promotion training Formal training given to prepare employees for advancement.

quality circle A method of participative management by which small groups of workers are specially trained and then meet regularly to identify and attempt to solve production problems.

question-and-answer session A method of group training that allows trainees to query the trainer about phases of training that were not clear or about which they would like additional information.

ranking A method of formal evaluation in which supervisors list subordinates' performances or the importance of tasks in order.

recruitment The process of finding people to apply for jobs.

reference A person or firm that a prospective employer may contact to find out about an applicant's ability, education, character, and potential for a job.

regulation A specific statement that governs employee's actions.

reliable A term used to describe a test or evaluation that yields the same results each time it is used for the same person or matter.

responsibility The obligation to perform assigned tasks in order to achieve desired results.

résumé A summary of a person's skills, knowledge, education, work experience, personal data, and job interests.

retirement The termination of employment at a given age and/or following a specified number of years of service.

retraining Formal training given to reinstruct employees in job skills because initial training was insufficient to enable them to perform their job successfully.

reward A pleasurable object or condition that employees receive for good work. It may be *intrinsic* (coming from within a person as a result of the job done) or *extrinsic* (resulting from a job and not part of it).

rewarding A supervisory aspect of managing in which a supervisor commends or grants some advantage to a subordinate for doing a job effectively.

role playing A method of training in which trainees act out a situation and then critique their own and others' actions.

rotating schedules A method of arranging work hours by which employees alternate working the early and late shift.

rule A statement of what may and

may not be done within the confines of a job.

scientific management A systematic approach to managing that emphasizes productivity of workers.

second-stage interview A more intensive talk with a job applicant who has successfully passed the initial interview.

selecting A supervisory aspect of managing in which a supervisor hires, transfers, promotes, or demotes employees.

seminar A method of training in which a series of meetings is held to discuss various aspects of a specific topic.

sensitivity training A method of training in which group members express thoughts, feelings, or impressions; learn to rely on others; and analyze others' reactions. Also called *T-group training* or *encounter training.*

sexual harassment Any unwelcome sexual attention on the job.

shop steward The union representative to whom a union member turns with a complaint or grievance.

simulator A training device that permits a person to practice the use of a machine under conditions that imitate real-life situations.

sociogram A method of formal evaluation by which the supervisor maps the interaction among subordinates.

span of control The number of employees who can be supervised effectively by one supervisor. A span may be *wide* (many subordinates report to one supervisor) or *narrow* (few subordinates report to one supervisor).

specialization organization The division of work based on the technology that serves many different segments of an enterprise.

staff function *See* function.

standard A model level of performance against which employees' work may be compared.

standing committee *See* committee.

status A nonfinancial reward by which an employee's standing in a firm is raised.

stress interview A kind of second-stage interview in which the applicant is purposely harassed in order to find out how he or she will respond to job pressure.

subjectivity The application of personal, internalized impressions, biases, thoughts, and feelings.

supervise To oversee for direction; to inspect with authority.

supervision The process of selecting, communicating with, assigning, training, motivating, evaluating, counseling, rewarding, and disciplining employees in order to achieve the goals of the enterprise.

supervisor A person who has the authority and responsibility to select, communicate with, assign, train, motivate, evaluate, counsel, reward, and discipline other employees in the interest of the employer, or to adjust their grievances or recommend such action. In some firms, this term is used to denote only the first-level overseer. However, any person who has responsibility for the work of others is a supervisor even though he or she may hold a position far above that of first-level overseer.

telecommunication The communication system of using satellites to convey messages to and from earth.

tenure Job protection usually given to teachers after a specified period of probation (usually three to seven years).

territorial organization The divi-

sion of work based on the geographical divisions of a firm.

theory x A theory of motivation
developed by McGregor that portrays
workers as lazy, unambitious, self-
centered, and resistant to change.

theory y A theory of motivation
developed by McGregor that portrays
workers as eager to accept responsibility, work toward organizational
goals, and adapt themselves to
needed change.

time and motion study An analysis of the movements workers make
and the speed with which they make
them in performing a task, conducted
to improve productivity.

time-management ability The capacity to schedule and perform mandated tasks within the allotted
periods of time.

time-shift organization The division of work based on the different
hours employees work.

training A supervisory aspect of
managing in which a supervisor develops people to enable them to perform specific tasks adequately and to
form the attitudes necessary to accomplish those tasks, work with others, and obey rules and regulations.

transactional analysis (TA) A
method of examining and changing
undesirable behavior by analyzing
three ego states—parent, adult, and
child.

transfer The moving of an employee into a job having equal status
and pay in the same or a different department.

two-directional communication
Communication that involves a
sender and a receiver and requires
feedback from the receiver to ensure that the message was correctly
received.

unclassified civil service See civil
service.

union An employee association

that is formed to maintain or further
employees' rights and interests within
their organization.

union shop A union agreement
with an organization that requires
that all nonexempt employees join
the union and pay dues after a grace
period, usually thirty days.

unity of command A situation in
which each employee reports to only
one boss.

unplanned training Informal
training that takes place constantly
as employees observe one another
and their supervisors during working
hours.

upward communication See channel of communication.

valid A term used to describe a
test or evaluation that measures what
it was meant to.

vestibule training A type of centralized training used to teach employees new techniques or how to
use machines away from the job site.

video-display terminal (VDT) A
machine with a typewriter keyboard
and a televisionlike screen that permits copy to be examined, changed,
and transferred to paper and stores
the original for later use.

white-collar worker A professional worker whose job does not involve manual labor and who usually
dresses in business attire.

wide span of control See span of
control.

word processing An automated
method of communicating in which
a person types copy and makes
changes on a special machine and directs it to type the copy perfectly.
The copy is stored in the machine for
later use.

written report A method of formal evaluation by which the supervisor writes an overview of a person's
performance on the job.

index